D1165580

THE PEOPLE OF DENENDEH

The People of

Denendeh

ETHNOHISTORY OF THE INDIANS OF CANADA'S NORTHWEST TERRITORIES

June Helm

with contributions by

Teresa S. Carterette and Nancy O. Lurie

University of Iowa Press IOWA CITY

University of Iowa Press, Iowa City 52242
Copyright © 2000 by the University of Iowa Press
All rights reserved
Printed in the United States of America

Design by Ellen McKie

http://www.uiowa.edu/~uipress

The publication of this book was generously supported by the University of Iowa Foundation.

Photographs without credit lines are by the author.

Printed on acid-free paper

LIBRARY OF CONGRESS CATALOGING-IN-PUBLICATION DATA
Helm, June, 1924–
    The people of Denendeh: ethnohistory of the Indians of
Canada's Northwest Territories / by June Helm; with contributions
by Teresa S. Carterette and Nancy O. Lurie.
        p.   cm.
    Includes bibliographical references and index.
    ISBN 0-87745-735-2 (cloth)
        1. Athapascan Indians—Northwest Territories—History.
    2. Athapascan Indians—Northwest Territories—Social life and
    customs.   3. Ethnohistory—Northwest Territories.   4. Northwest
    Territories—Social life and customs.   I. Carterette, Teresa S.
    II. Lurie, Nancy Oestreich.   III. Title.

E99.A86   H45   2000
971.9′2004972—dc21   00-034392

        00   01   02   03   04   C   5   4   3   2   1

To | TERESA S. CARTERETTE & NANCY O. LURIE
and the memory of
LOUIS NORWEGIAN & VITAL THOMAS

Teresa Carterette, Jean Marie River, 1952.

Nancy Lurie, Lac la Martre, 1959.

Louis Norwegian (1907–77), Jean Marie River, 1952.

Vital Thomas (1904–90), Rae, 1962.

CONTENTS

Welcome to Clearwater Library!
You have the following items:

1. Canoeing Canada's Northwest
   Territories : a paddler's guide
   Barcode: 101467467+ Due:
   2012-06-08 11:59 PM
2. The people of Denendeh :
   ethnohistory of the Indians of
   Canada's Northwest
   Territories
   Barcode: 1015524765 Due:
   2012-06-29 11:59 PM

BKCT-CLW 2012-06-01 14:47
You were helped by clwcirc

PREFACE

At an anthropological meeting some years ago, the point was made that general ethnographies of North American Indian peoples are not being written anymore. I inwardly acknowledged that I would not write one myself. But later the thought brought me to consider bringing together some of my writings about the Dene, "The People," the Indians of Canada's Northwest Territories. The land of these subarctic Athapaskan speakers, as designated by nineteenth-century linguistic classification, is known by the native term of Denendeh, "Land of the Dene."

In standard ethnological classifications these Canadian First Nations of Dene are grouped as Chipewyans, Slaveys, Dogribs, Mountain Indians, Bearlake Indians, Hares, and Kutchin, now Gwich'in. The Gwich'in's distinctive Athapaskan language and traditional social organization set them somewhat apart from the others. The other native peoples of the Northwest Territories are the Northern Metis, scattered throughout the area, and the coast-oriented Inuit.

From 1951 to the present, my anthropological career has drawn on broader or narrower aspects of Dene society, culture, history, and relationships with the impinging white world. Since a diligent researcher could retrieve most of my writings from their varied publication loci, why should I pull them together? More and more, however, I began to think of such a compilation not just as an offering to North American Indian studies, hunter-gatherer research, or subarctic ethnohistory but also as a historical resource for the people of all ethnicities who live in Denendeh, and especially a resource for the grandchildren and great-grandchildren of Dene whom I first came to know fifty years ago. My main aim is to offer a record of ways of life that, for all of us, grow dimmer as they recede year by year into the past. From this stance, except for chapter 1, I gladly ignore anthropological "theory."

Although my greatest attention has been on recording and reporting the ways and knowledge of Dene peoples whom I have known, I have at times turned to the reports of kw'etin or mola (whites, European-derived people) who preceded me in the Dene North: missionaries, fur traders, and, for the earlier stretches of interethnic contact, "explorers." Their records have served me as the reports of the district officers of the European colonial powers in the Middle East served ethnologist Robert A. Fernea (1995 : 1-2) as "an interesting source of information for an anthropologist. They had been there where I was, they knew fathers or grandfathers of some of the men I knew, they used the names of tribes and places with whom I had also become acquainted." Moreover, Fernea has come to realize that his own records and published writings are now sources of knowledge for present generations about their ancestors' lives and times. As Fernea says, "Handing a group of people a book about themselves may be presumptuous, but it is also a form of recognition, a token of esteem in most cases, a basis for cogitation even if it is wrong in particulars or in general according to local discussion." I hope that this volume may at the least serve these purposes.

Except for a visit to Rae in 1979 on an ethnohistorical inquiry (see the section on "Native Occupation and Status in Fur Trade, 1900-1925" in chapter 9), my research activities in the Northwest Territories ended in 1975, so the historical run in this book ends then. The increasing pace and dimensions of change since 1975 must be addressed by others, although in several chapters I have added short explanations, which appear in italics, and updates. My self-appointed task here is to offer what my research can speak to in the Dene experience from the time of earliest contact with the white world to the last quarter of the twentieth century.

The subtitle of this book is *Ethnohistory of the Indians of Canada's Northwest Territories*, not *An Ethnohistory* or *The Ethnohistory*. The omission of a defining article is deliberate. "The" or "An" suggests complete or comprehensive coverage. To this I do not pretend. The entries in this volume are drawn from several kinds of documentation: my published writings and unpublished field notes, unpublished essays and field notes of my field companions Nancy O. Lurie and Teresa S. Carterette, and some nineteenth-century records. At the beginning of each chapter and sometimes within a chapter, I have added short statements to provide context and connections among entries. There is order in this volume, but it may not be immediately discernible by the reader who expects a straightforward chronological narration on Dene history. The first chapter addresses long-lived theoretical preconceptions about human social evolution in the light of data from Denendeh and sets a framework of inquiry for the ethnohistory of the Dene through the span of Dene-white contact and beyond into deeper reaches of time. Part I introduces Dene life, work, and community as I encountered them in the middle of the twentieth century. After two historical overview chapters, the chapters of part II move progressively back in time from the early years of the twentieth century to the earliest contacts between Dene and whites; the last chapter then looks at the beginnings of the momentous changes in Dene-government relations in the 1970s. The chapters of part III consider embedded qualities of Dene traditional knowledge, meaning, and culture style.

I suggest that a reader approach this volume somewhat in the way I assembled it, piece by piece. Do some sampling, browsing through chapters and sections of chapters that seem most immediately interesting. Then at some later time read the book through. I have not in any way "dumbed down" the research papers that make up most of the chapters in this book. My only concession to simplification has been to clear up obscure or awkward wording and eliminate endnotes, most tables, and some page references of works cited. On the other hand, I have not "dressed up" the stripped-down transcriptions in my field notes of narratives in English or translations by interpreters. I hope these contrastive styles may provide a change of pace.

As I said, I had been wondering if I should again issue studies and essays that I had written through the years. Then something wonderfully fortuitous and inspiriting happened. Early in 1996 came a message from the North that I had not expected. Anglo-Canadian Thomas D. Andrews, subarctic archaeologist at the Prince of Wales Northern Heritage Centre in Yellowknife, asked me to read a paper that he and his Dene collaborator, John B. Zoe, chief negotiator for the Dogrib Treaty 11 Council, had written. This contact with Tom and John spurred me to think again about the people of the Northwest Territories and review material about them. The enthusiasm of Tom as an archaeologist and John as a Dogrib to build, through combined documentary and archaeological evidence and oral history, an enhanced history of the people fired me up as they themselves were fired up.

By happenstance I was able to do something for the Dogrib people, the Dene with whom I spent the greatest span of my field years. I have for many years been a professor of anthropology at the University of Iowa. When I came to Iowa in 1960 I already knew that a young alumnus of the university, Frank Russell, had been in the Northwest Territories in 1893 and 1894 collecting faunal and ethnological specimens for the university's Museum of Natural History. One item was a caribou-skin lodge purchased from the Dogrib K'aawidaa, the Bear Lake Chief. That tipi was stored over my head as I sat in my office in the museum building. Moved by my new at-a-distance friendships, I took the opportunity to arrange with the director of the museum that the lodge of the Bear Lake Chief be returned to the Dogribs. Within a year, Tom, John, and Elizabeth Mackenzie, a friend of many years and Dogrib elder, with her daughter Mary Siemens came as representatives of the people to reclaim the lodge as a palpable remembrance of life as lived a hundred years ago.

To set forth the names of all the people in the Northwest Territories who have helped me through five decades of research on the Dene of that land is impossible. For one thing, many Dene contributed to my field observations by just being there and being themselves. And then there are the nonnative residents who generously lent a hand when needed. (I think especially of Oblate fathers Jean Amourous, René Fumoleau, Louis Menez, and Jean Pochat-Catilloux, but there are many others.) In *Prophecy and Power among the Dogrib Indians* (1994), I thanked by name the many individual Dogribs from Rae and Lac la Martre (Wha Ti, today) who contributed to my understanding. For this volume, the range of grateful acknowledgment to all relevant individuals would be too vast. I think of the fifty-some members of the community of Jean Marie River in 1951 and 1952, the hundred or so people of Lac la Martre in 1959, and those whom I came to know in Rae in the 1960s and 1970s. Some of the Dene from other settlements who spent hours instructing or otherwise aiding me were Johnny and Annie McPherson of Fort Simpson, George and Christine Codzi of Colville Lake, whom I knew at Fort Good Hope, and Alexandre King of Fort Resolution. Many acquaintances and friends are now departed, but I remember and appreciate them.

Cindy Nagel, Carrie Schoenebaum, Miranda Church, and Drew Harrington did the fetching, copying, and other chores that brought this manuscript together. Through the years the University of Iowa has provided opportunity and funds for research, most recently through the F. Wendell Miller Distinguished Professorship in Anthropology. I have been fortunate.

Five persons have been my collaborators through the years. Beryl C. Gillespie shared her field notes and the fruits for her archival research; we co-authored the presentations in chapter 12. The other four are those with whom I worked in the field, and they are the two duos to whom I have dedicated this volume: Teresa S. Carterette and Louis Norwegian and Nancy O. Lurie and Vital Thomas. They made "doing fieldwork" not only rewarding but an enjoyment. The reader will meet Teresa and Louis and Nancy and Vital time and again in these pages.

Looking back over fifty years, my thanks go immediately to Tom Andrews and John B. Zoe for returning me to live interaction with the world of the

Dene. (They have also contributed passages that illuminate topics in this book.) In the final instance, my thanks go to all the people of the Northwest Territories I have known. I have had tremendous pleasure and gratification in recalling, re-encountering, and rethinking the people, places, and happenings that are embedded in the material in this book. To all I say, "Mahsi cho!"

ORTHOGRAPHY

The few Dene words in the text are usually rendered in the workaday orthography, not consistently phonemic or phonetic, of my ethnographic field
notes. The only symbols that do not have an approximately comparable
sound or usage in English are:

c   as in English *chip*.

gh   similar to *r* in French *rouge*.

n   indicates nasalization of the vowel(s) that immediately precede it,
      as in French *chanson*; *n* between vowels is sounded as a consonant,
      as in Dogrib *inin*, "spirit."

x   as in Spanish *jarro*.

z   as in French *azure*.

'   indicates glottalization of the preceding consonant or consonant
      cluster.

To avoid symbols not available in regular type, I have ignored the "barred *l*"
(breathy *l*). Tone and length are not usually indicated, nor is word-initial
glottal stop.

Today there is a very useful Dogrib-English dictionary prepared by the
Dogrib Divisional Board of Education (1996) that provides a basic lexicon,
some instruction in word morphology, and a consistent orthography and
guide to pronunciation in that language. The Dene Cultural Institute and
the Gwich'in Social and Cultural Institute have compiled language aids such
as lexicons and place-name lists. There were no such guides to the languages
when I did fieldwork, and I will not try today to second-guess my field
orthographies, inadequate as they might be.

One other minor linguistic transcription problem: The majority of
native-language names were first entered into Canadian records by French-
speaking Oblate missionaries. Since spoken French lacks the usual *h* sound
that most Dene languages have, *h* is converted to *fw* in the Oblate records.
The Dogrib chief Monhwi (as I phonetically recorded this name from Vital
Thomas's pronunciation) shows up in the written records as "Monfwi." Just

as the French speakers could not breathe *h*, the English speakers could not handle the nasalized vowels with which Dene words abound. English speakers simply fell back on "Murphy." I have acceded to the now-entrenched spelling of Monfwi. And I've also given up on the diphthong in "N*ai*dzo" (*ai* as in "ice"), the Bear Lake Prophet, as I heard his name from Vital. In Oblate French orthography and now in government records his name is Naedzo, so in this book I spell his name Naedzo.

NAMES OF COMMUNITIES
IN DENENDEH

Official Name *Previous Name in Italics*	Remarks
Aklavik	mainly an Inuit population
Arctic Red River	see Tsiigehtchic
Colville Lake	——
Déline	changed from *Fort Franklin* June 1, 1993
Dettah	often spelled Detah
Edzo	——
Enterprise	——
Fort Franklin	see Déline
Fort Good Hope	——
Fort Liard	——
Fort McPherson	——
Fort Norman	see Tulita
Fort Providence	——
Fort Simpson	——
Fort Smith	——
Hay River	——
Jean Marie River	——
Kakisa	——
Lac la Martre	see Wha Ti
Lutselk'e	changed from *Snowdrift* July 1, 1992
Nahanni Butte	——
Norman Wells	——
Rae	——
Rae Lakes	also known as Gamiti
Reliance	——
Snare Lake	see Wekweti
Snowdrift	see Lutselk'e
Trout Lake	——
Tsiigehtchic	changed from *Arctic Red River* April 1, 1994

Tulita	changed from Fort Norman January 1, 1996
Wekweti	changed from *Snare Lake* November 1, 1996
Wha Ti	changed from *Lac la Martre* January 1, 1996
Wrigley	——
Yellowknife	——

THE PEOPLE OF DENENDEH

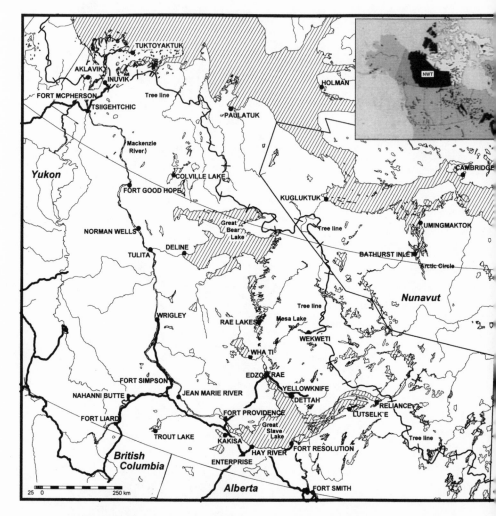

Northwest Territories, 1999. Courtesy of the Prince of Wales Northern Heritage Centre. On April 1, 1999, Nunavut was created as Canada's newest territory, leaving only the western-most sector of the former Northwest Territories to bear that name. Sachs Harbour (not on map), Holman, Tuktoyaktut, and Paulatuk are the only Inuit-based communities that remain in the new Northwest Territories. Inuvik was created in the mid-1950s as a government ad-ministration center. Norman Wells and Enterprise are Euro-Canadian settlements. All other settlements on the map are mainly or in part occupied by Dene. The names of the communities of Denendeh are listed on pages xix–xx. The heavy black line is "the highway."

HORDE, BAND, AND TRIBE

1 | SEEN FROM DENENDEH,
AN INTRODUCTION

In 1986 I opened a letter from the president of the University of Iowa inviting me to give the university's Presidential Lecture of 1987. My immediate reaction was a short expletive. I was then immersed in difficult documentary data on multigenerational fertility levels among the Hare Dene of the Northwest Territories. I was afraid that a break in that research would mean that I would not return to it. I was right. Then an aggravation came with the publication of the Presidential Lecture by the university in an elegantly produced booklet that allowed no works cited section. To me, this exclusion rendered the essay worthless as a scholarly guide and an embarrassment to boot. As a result, I sent out fewer than ten copies, only to closest anthropological friends. In this printing of the lecture, I have restored proper citations of references.

These plaints aside, I must admit that developing the lecture gave me the opportunity to review my field and library research on the Dene that bore on long-standing issues in anthropological theory about the structure of hunting societies.

In 1889 the young Franz Boas (1974 [1889]) attacked the notion that the evolutionary "primitiveness" of American Indian languages was revealed in their alleged phonological imprecisions, termed "alternating sounds." Rather, Boas demonstrated, the actuality lay in the "alternating apperceptions" of the European listener, "who apperceives unknown sounds [of an exotic tongue] by means of the sounds in his own language." In the struggle to comprehend whatever may be actuality, even more tyrannical than the culture-bound apperception has been, as Boas also recognized, the culture-bound *conception*. Such intellectual thralldom is well demonstrated in the history of anthropological thought and research on hunter-gatherer or foraging societies.

Both the variegated Boasian "school" that came to dominate American ethnology after the turn of the century and the "functionalism" of British social anthropology that was emerging in the 1920s abjured universalist formulations on the "origins" and evolution of human institutions and beliefs that had dominated nineteenth-century anthropological thought. Yet even

after research in the field on foraging peoples began to be undertaken by a few professional anthropologists in the decades before World War II, residues of nineteenth-century suppositions blocked comprehension of the nature and structure of the land-utilizing groups in these societies. Those residues tended to dominate theory building until a spate of ethnographic fieldwork in the 1950s and 1960s burst the confines of received knowledge and preconception.

In the history of anthropology, thinking about foraging societies has revolved around three term-concepts: the horde, the band, and the tribe. The concept of the horde was the first focus of formula making and theory building. Short of fantasy formulations, the horde was latterly incorporated into the problem of the band. Although collections of contiguous hordes or bands had long been lumped together under some sort of tribal rubric by investigators, the question of what a tribe of foragers might or might not be has been the last to be addressed critically by anthropologists. The concepts of horde and band, especially, tended to be reified as "things" that shared the defining characteristic of being fixed and solidary in personnel and in owned, circumscribed, and defended territory.

In the last third of the nineteenth century, in anthropological literature the horde was conceived not as a nomadic swarm, as in the Golden Horde, but as a small crew of foraging "savages." Theorizing about the horde took two avenues, both of them in the service of the schema of the universal cultural evolution of humankind from a primordial state. One approach we may term once-upon-a-time constructs of primal man. The other approach viewed extant foragers as exemplars or living fossils of the earliest stages of human society.

The once-upon-a-time constructs of the primordial horde served as the base for theories, in various combinations, of the origin of "group marriage," "wife capture," the incest taboo and exogamy, totemism and the Oedipus complex, and the patrilineal clan (Freud's "brother clan"). One theorist, the Edinburgh lawyer J. S. McLennan, emphasized a primordial state of chronic warfare and territorial defense among hordes.

In charting humanity's ascent from the brute, the nature of sexual relations within the horde was critical to these formulations. McLennan and the Rochester lawyer Lewis Henry Morgan postulated indiscriminate mating in the primordial horde. The alternative once-upon-a-time view was of the primordial horde as a patriarchal sexual group. "Looking far enough back into the stream of time," wrote Charles Darwin (1952 [1871]), "the most probable view is that [primeval man] aboriginally lived in small communities, each with a single wife or if more powerful with several, whom he jealously guarded against all other men." Alternatively, Darwin speculated, "he may not have been a social animal, and yet have lived with several wives, like the gorilla." Here Darwin was adverting to an account published thirty-five years earlier by an American missionary, Dr. Thomas Savage. According to Dr. Savage, his native informants of the Gabon region of West Africa "agreed that but one adult male is seen in the [gorilla] band; when the young male grows up, the contest takes place for mastery and the strongest, by killing and driving out the others, establishes himself as the head of the community" (quoted by Darwin). Dr. Savage's gorilla model as sexual despot informed Sigmund Freud's 1913 formulation in *Totem and Taboo* of the primal, parricidal horde, the last gasp of fanciful once-upon-a-time constructs (cf. Fox 1980).

Herbert Spencer was as thoroughgoing a nineteenth-century social evolutionist as one can find, but he made no recourse to hypothetical constructs of primeval society. He turned directly to the ethnographic record of his time. "Scattered over many regions," he wrote, "there are minute hordes— still extant samples of the primordial type of society" (Spencer 1916 [1876]). His "samples" included Australian Aborigines, Tasmanians, Andaman Islanders, South African Bushmen, Eskimos, Fuegians, and "Digger Indians" of the American Great Basin. Spencer's emphasis was on the absence of political integration, the "absolute independence of small hordes." He rightly saw that, at the hunting-gathering level of technology, environmental constraints kept foragers ordinarily in small mobile groups that might on occasion be able to congregate with like hordes. In his earlier writings, Franz Boas (1974 [1889]) accepted the reality of "a number of primitive hordes" in the ethnographic record, among whom the "solidarity of the horde" required the destruction of every stranger, seen as an enemy. Here apparently Boas fell victim to misemphases in the early literature on Australian Aborigines.

It was on the Aborigines of Australia that the term-concept *horde* became focused in the ethnographic literature. In an 1885 article, A. W. Howitt and Lorimer Fison, who had direct field contact with the few Aborigines still surviving in New South Wales, applied the term *horde* to what they also termed *geographical* or *local divisions* within the tribe. These local divisions they distinguished from *social divisions* predicated on principles of descent on which, in their interpretation, marriage regulations were based. Horde membership of males was fixed from generation to generation, and hordes were usually exogamous. In their words, "the daughter may go away when she marries but the son remains in the father's horde." A close reading of their writings (Howitt and Fison 1885 [1880]; Howitt 1967 [1880]) indicates that their *local divisions* or *hordes* were not coterminous with on-the-ground foraging camp groups, which might include men's sons-in-law, fathers-in-law, and other adult men not linked through male-to-male descent lines. But these camp groups they alluded to only in passing.

It remained for A. R. Radcliffe-Brown, an anthropologist trained at Cambridge, to extend Howitt and Fison's patrilineal *horde* as the model of aboriginal local organization throughout the Australian continent. Repeatedly, Radcliffe-Brown worked on his conception of the horde, from one of his earlier writings (Brown 1913) until the final one published after his death in 1955. That final statement was:

> The horde is a collection of parental families which regularly cooperate in the food quest [implication: as a camp group?], a parental family existing of a man and his wife or wives and their children. The unity of the horde and its connections with a certain territory result from the fact that all the married men of a given horde are members of one particular [patrilineal] clan. A woman belongs to her father's clan and to her husband's horde. The horde can be described as a "quasi-domestic" group. (Radcliffe-Brown 1956:365)

By 1918 Radcliffe-Brown had designated the horde as "the primary land-owning group . . . each horde owning and occupying a certain area of the country" (Brown 1918). Here he equated the male composition of the on-the-ground foraging camp group with the male members of the patrilineal clan, which collectively owns a religious "estate" of sacred sites within an associated territory as well as myths, rituals, and songs. Radcliffe-Brown's overriding message was that the horde as a local group was residentially solidary, bounded, and fixed through the male descent line and through "ownership," "possession," and "dominion" (Radcliffe-Brown 1952 [1935]:324) over a territory. Radcliffe-Brown's eminence as a theoretician of social anthropology surely worked to fix his model of the residentially solidary horde occupying its *own* territory so firmly in the minds of the world's anthropologists.

The work of the American anthropologist Julian Steward in the 1930s provided the foundation for modern approaches to socioterritorial units and their composition in societies of foragers. Steward (1955) sought to determine "cross-cultural regularities which arise from similar adaptive processes and similar environments." From this perspective of "cultural ecology," as he termed it, he analyzed the available literature on hunting-gathering peoples around the world. He identified three forms of socioterritorial organization among these foraging peoples.

One, the "family level of sociocultural integration," found its sole example in his own intensive field data on the Shoshonean-speaking Indian peoples of the Great Basin of the western United States. These included Spencer's "Digger Indians." Reconstructing from elderly informants the movements and social relationships among these peoples before the arrival of whites, in 1938 Steward pronounced them lacking in the "band level" of organization in that they lacked at a suprafamilial level *"permanent* groups of *fixed* membership" (Steward 1955:109, my emphasis).

As the second form of integration, Steward accepted Radcliffe-Brown's formulation of the exogamous patrilineal horde among the Australian Aborigines, though he abandoned the term *horde* for *band,* as I shall do henceforth. From the scanty evidence available to him, Steward attributed this form of organization not only to the Aborigines of Australia but to the Negritos of the Congo, the Bushmen of South Africa, and certain other hunting-gathering peoples. Steward assumed that there was an inherent strain toward the patrilineal band form of organization in foraging societies unless special environmental variables intervened.

The third type of organization he termed the *composite hunting band.* In Steward's interpretation of the evidence, the composite band consisted of many unrelated nuclear families integrated to form bands on the basis of constant association and cooperation rather than of actual or alleged kinship as in the patrilineal band. He attributed this form of organization to the hunting peoples throughout subarctic North America in "aboriginal times," including the Dene peoples with whom I was to work. The ecological basis of the composite band arose, he argued, from the opportunity or necessity for subarctic hunters to congregate regularly to hunt large game herds, such as caribou and muskox. These composite bands were, in Steward's formulation, "probably not only the political unit but also the land owning and subsistence social unit" among subarctic peoples (1955:143–47).

Steward's comparative work was a profound advance in ethnological thinking about structure and causality in the socioterritorial organization of foraging peoples. Yet his formulations suffered from a triple handicap. He remained constrained by presumptions of *boundedness* in the form of "owned" and delimited territories and in the form of fixed membership of the band and, as both cause and consequence of these presumptions, a third presumption: that the band was *the* singular significant concept for the comprehension of the socioterritorial organization of foraging peoples. Since his own meticulous reconstruction of social groupings and family movements among the Indians of the Great Basin showed these three presuppositions to be invalid for the Shoshoneans, he was forced to the conclusion of "no bands" among those peoples. By adhering to these presuppositions in assessing the data from other parts of the world, Steward went astray in regard to his constructs of both the so-called patrilineal band and the composite hunting band.

Steward's constructions were the state of the art when I first went to the subarctic in 1951 to carry out field research among the Indians of Canada's Northwest Territories. All but the southern edge of this vast land was then inaccessible by rail, road, or telephone. In 1951 there were only two published field reports by professional ethnologists on the Indians of the region. Their work, carried out in 1913 (Mason 1946) and 1928–29 (Osgood 1932), was in the old-fashioned ethnographic idiom that attended only to salvaging evidence of putative aboriginal culture traits. Trained at Chicago, where the Radcliffe-Brown school of "social anthropology" was emphasized, my goal was certainly not to inventory culture traits, aboriginal or otherwise. I aimed at a "functionalist" study of contemporary life. In any event, the received anthropological opinion was that the traditional social order of these Indians, along with their (quote) "culture," was now gone and unrecoverable, victims of the fur trade and its assumed consequences.

The total set of linguistically related, Athapaskan-speaking Indians of interior Alaska and the western two thirds of subarctic Canada may be collectively termed "Dene." Dene, in its linguistic variants, denotes "people," "the people," and the speaker's "own kind of people," as well as "person" and "male human being." The historical and ethnographic literature has parceled out the northern Dene under various "tribal" rubrics (see map). The site of my first fieldwork was in the Slavey hamlet of Jean Marie River, to which I assigned the pseudonym "Lynx Point." There, fifty-six Indians lived in log cabins on the banks of the great Mackenzie River, which drains into the Arctic Ocean.

In the course of my fieldwork among the "Lynx Point" Slavey, I learned how the community had grown through births and recruitment by marriage from a tiny mobile hunting and trapping group linked by parent-child and sibling ties that had localized at "Lynx Point" and built the first cabin there sometime around 1910 (Helm 1961). By the end of my stay, one of the number of questions that had been generated by the field data was, Was this kind of kin-community—whose nuclear families were linked by primary kin ties, parent-child and/or sibling-sibling, one to the other—a unique or recent development in northern Dene socioterritorial organization? If not, how

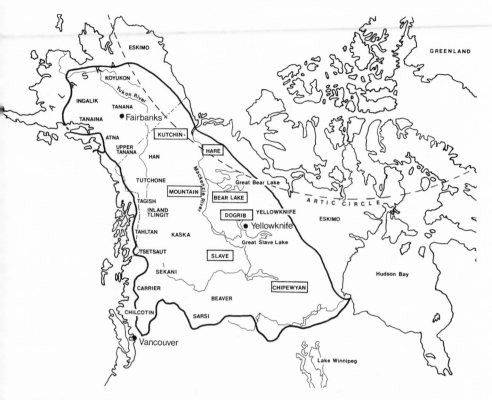

Major divisions of the northern Dene. The Mackenzie Dene are comprised of Chipewyan, Slavey (Slave), Dogrib, Mountain, Bearlake, Hare, and eastern Gwich'in (Kutchin) peoples. By the late eighteenth century, the Sarsi of northern Alberta had adopted the cultural attributes of the bison-hunting plains Indians.

was this structure to be reconciled with Steward's large "composite hunting band" composed of "unrelated families" to which he had assigned the aboriginal Dene? A search of the historical as well as the ethnographic literature, combined with fieldwork in subsequent years among neighboring Dene, the Hare Indians, and especially the Dogribs, began to clarify levels and patterns in northern Dene socioterritorial groups and organization. One thing that became clear was that there was no one singular entity that could be specified as *the* band in Dene society (Helm 1965a, 1968).

The spur to analyze rigorously my field data on socioterritorial groupings among the Dene came from the publication in 1962 of a book titled *Primitive Social Organization: An Evolutionary Perspective*. The author, Elman Service, rejected Steward's three forms of ecologically based socioterritorial organization among foraging peoples. Service argued, on formal structural grounds, that "the patrilocal band [Steward's patrilineal band] is early; it seems an almost inevitable kind of organization." Back to square one with Radcliffe-Brown's Australian horde as the prototypic model of socioterritorial organization for all foraging peoples. Wherever the patrilocal band is not in evidence among historical foragers, Service argued, it has disappeared in consequence of the catastrophic impact of expanding world systems.

I shall recur briefly to Service's formulation in light of both my research and that of other field ethnologists. At this point, however, we should take a short look at the long run of contact between the Dene of the Mackenzie region and the Western world.

Recorded history began on their home ground when the fur trader Alexander Mackenzie made first contact with these peoples in his voyage of exploration down the Mackenzie River [Dehcho] to the Arctic Ocean in 1789. In precontact times the ancestors of these Dene were probably as independent of alien economic, social, and cultural relations, pressures, or forces as it is possible to conceive. They relied on no other peoples for raw materials or items of technology. Their world contained no societal entities holding dominance or hegemony over any other. By this absolute standard of sociocultural autonomy, the Dene's voluntary involvement in the fur trade—as it developed after Mackenzie's voyage—marked the first time in their history when they entered into what came to be a needful relationship with another sociocultural system. Certainly, the Dene were in a disadvantaged relationship in that, to advance their material well-being, they needed the trade goods of the fur traders far more than the traders' world needed their furs. But the retreat from their former absolute sociocultural independence was partial and circumscribed. The Dene societal groups continued to manage their own affairs and feed and otherwise provide for the well-being of their members. No doubt the unquestioned worth of European technology, plus the traders' cultural arrogance, broke trail for the God-given authority assumed by the missionaries who entered the region in the 1860s.

Isolated and insulated by their subarctic domain, the Mackenzie Dene had, until World War II, little involvement with the Euro-Canadian world except through the narrow and selective channels offered by the fur trader and the missionary. When in 1959 I went to the Dogrib hamlet at Lac la Martre [today, Wha Ti], I found a community comparable to the "Lynx Point" Slavey community of 1951. True, by the late 1950s the Canadian government was initiating changes throughout the North (including day schools, effective medical services, and transfer payments) that were affecting even the most isolated groups. Still, in their isolation from most of the daily impact of the "modern" world (no roads, no television, little or no command of English, infrequent contacts with whites), these "bush" communities had retained much of a way of life that had endured for a hundred or more years. With the perspective gained from the historical literature, I realized that I was seeing the end of a sociocultural era that I came to term *contact-traditional* (Helm and Damas 1963).

To characterize the classic contact-traditional era: the only whites in the land are the personnel of the trading post and, in the course of time, the mission. Both are usually at the same site. In early times, Indians have no permanent dwellings at the trading fort or elsewhere. They live out in the land, taking moose and caribou, fish, and snowshoe hares. By 1905 or so, a few begin to build log cabins at the fort or at a major fishery or other site occupied for several weeks during the year. With ammunition and a few staples (flour, tea, tobacco) from the trader, Indians leave the fort in August before freezeup to prepare for winter in the bush. Subsistence hunting, fishing, and snaring are combined with taking of furs during the winter. Men come to the fort at New Year, and debts are paid with furs. With new supplies, they return to bush camps or hamlets. In March and April, furs are again traded and supplies obtained. Sometime after breakup in late May, they come to the fort with the beaver and muskrat pelts taken in the spring hunt. Ingatherings at the fort are occasions for festivities: feasts, dances, gambling games.

This way of life endured for over a hundred years, up to the 1950s, when events arising in the modern national purpose began to reshape the native scene. Certainly there was change, technological, social, and ideational. The sedentarization, growth, and stabilization of personnel at "Lynx Point" since 1910 of a former mobile hunting-trapping group is a case in point. But on the whole, the process of change was slow and untraumatic, even after the missionary joined the trader as the other agent of contact and acculturation.

My pursuit of social anthropological questions has gained much from taking a historical perspective. In my first foray into historical reconstruction (MacNeish 1956a), I surmised that early epidemics of European-derived diseases might have irreversibly altered Dene socioterritorial organization. But research on population levels within the historical era [Helm 1980a, chapter 11 in this volume] and continuing assessment of ecological imperatives and the historical record, interpreted in light of the specificities gained from contemporary field evidence and Dene oral history, have allowed me a substantial degree of confidence that my reconstruction of groups in the contact-traditional era holds in basic outline and principles for aboriginal socioterritorial organization as well.

In analyzing socioterritorial groups among the Mackenzie Dene, I addressed any form of human occupation lasting one night or more at a particular locale or over a range in respect to the nature of the social group constituted by the occupants of the locale or range. Setting aside for the moment the question of "tribe" or "society," I concluded that the traditional socioterritorial organization of the Mackenzie Dene took the form not of a single kind of "band" but of three analytically distinguishable kinds of groups that I designated task groups, local bands, and regional bands (Helm 1965a, 1968).

The task group is of brief duration and is explicitly created for exploitative activities. In size it may range from a hunting-trapping group of two or three families to perhaps a dozen families at a seasonal fishing camp. Sometimes the task group is composed only of men, such as a men's fast-traveling caribou-hunting party, with women and children left in camp or settlement.

Sometimes a small group of related nuclear families, usually focused around a core set of siblings, endures for a few or many years as a community body resident in one settlement or, formerly, as a mobile camp group. Thus duration jells a task group into a local group or local band, as in the case of the "Lynx Point" Slavey. The local band may comprise as few as two or three conjugal pairs and their children.

The regional band has tribelike characteristics. Its total range yields sufficient materials for the necessities of life (famine periods excepted) so that within its domain the regional band can endure as an identity for generations. (The regional band is the basis of Steward's construct of the northeastern Dene "composite hunting band" [1955:147n.].) Some of the constituent members of the regional band may be spatially and socially oriented as a local group. But the total constituency of the regional band is larger (one or two or so dozen nuclear families), and it lacks continual nucleation of camp or settlement. Its members are commonly scattered over its range in smaller groups. The dimensions of the regional band's range are defined in terms of its "roads," the main routes of movement for its constituent groups. The regional band's zone of exploitation thus has axes rather than boundaries or edges. Some roads lead from one regional group's range into its neighbors' ranges. We may speak of a regional band's traditional range as its territory, but it is territory without territoriality. Ties of amity and kinship bring people from one regional band to another, free to use its resources.

Traditionally, from the patterns of human ecology that the region imposed upon the Indians exploiting it, the region and its people are socially defined. At any moment in time, any individual—let us call him Joe Dogrib—can be placed in several socioterritorial identities. As a member of one of several Dogrib households currently hunting muskrats at the locale *kwekatelin*, Joe and that task group are Kwekatelinhot'in (Water-over-Rocks-Place people) on the basis of their temporary residence at that site. Since Joe has a cabin in a local group hamlet on Snare Lake, he will, in appropriate context, be identified as one of the House-Place-at-Ghost-Channel people. He is equally Detsinlahot'in, or Edge-of-the-Woods person, thereby specifying his regional band identity. Joe Dogrib's multiple territorial group identities demonstrate how misleading a simplistic definition of "the band" must be.

The documentary and field evidence laid to rest the idea of the Dene "band" being composed of "unrelated families." The Dene socioterritorial groupings that I have called bands, local or regional, as well as multiple-family task groups have a mode of alliance and recruitment based on principles of social linkage through bilateral primary kinship bonds from one conjugal pair to another (see the diagram of the kin bonds between pairs at "Lynx Point"). For the adult male, the kin connection is characteristically either his own primary consanguine tie or ties to one or more adults, male or female, of the group or his marriage bond to a woman who has one or more primary consanguine connections to the group. Thus for men, not only kin ties to father and brothers but affinal links through wife and married sisters serve as the mechanisms of potential affiliation with one group or another. By these modes of sponsorship, a couple may form a task group with others, join another camp group or local group, or move from one region to the next. (See Helm 1969a for a method of quantifying male versus female primary ties between marital pairs in socioterritorial groups.)

In the 1950s and early 1960s at least two dozen anthropologists were in the field working with those foraging peoples who still maintained at least some of their traditional subsistence pursuits. I had the opportunity for interaction and exchange with a number of these ethnologists in the course of three conferences that were held in 1966 and 1967. Beside the Slaveys, Hares, and Dogribs of the western Canadian subarctic with whom I had worked, foraging peoples studied by ethnologists explicitly concerned with socioterritorial organization included in the eastern Canadian subarctic the Montagnais and Mistassini Cree of Quebec and the Round Lake Ojibwa of northern Ontario; along the central Canadian arctic coast the Copper Inuit, Igloolik Inuit, and Netsilik Inuit; in Africa !Kung groups of the Kalihari desert, the Mbuti of the Ituri rain forest, and the savannah-dwelling Hadza of Tanzania; in India the Paliyans of the southern tip of India and the Birhor of

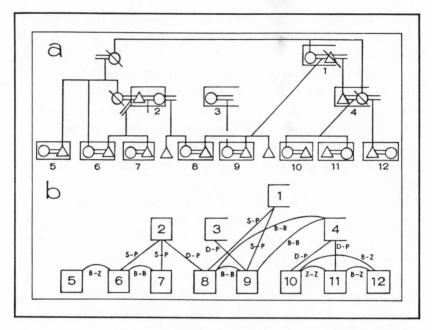

Primary kinship bonds between conjugal pairs in the "Lynx Point" (Jean Marie River) Slavey community, 1951. a: Closest genealogical relations between married and widowed persons. Men are indicated by triangles, women by circles. Marriage is indicated by the equal sign. An open-ended equal sign indicates that the deceased spouse was never resident. b: Primary consanguine relative relationships—parent (P), son (S), daughter (D), brother (B), and sister (Z)—between conjugal pairs as units.

northeastern India, both enclaved forest folk; and, in Australia the Walbiri of the central desert and the Gidjingali of northeastern Arnhem Land. Also shown on the accompanying world map are the locations of the Shoshoneans, Fuegians, Tasmanians, and Andamanese treated by Steward and Spencer. (I should remark, parenthetically, that more recent generations of ethnologists have carried out fieldwork among foragers in these areas and, in addition, in Southeast Asia, the Philippines, and lowland South America.)

Several major conclusions emerged from the field studies of these ethnologists. First, territoriality, in the sense of bounded, defended territory, is rare, if it exists. Regional groups do have territories in the sense of habitual ranges with which—indeed, *by* which—they are identified, but this is not territoriality in the animal ethologist's sense. Localized, restricted resource locales may be "owned" or controlled by the group but not be the group's or band's range as such. Second, among contiguous groups in their habitual ranges, membership is fluid. Individuals and families move from one group to another. This fluidity is even more pronounced in respect to residential camp groups or task groups. Finally, with the exception of the local bands of the Birhor of northeastern India, no field ethnologist encountered the patrilocal band, of whatever size, either as an actual on-the-ground coresidential camp group or as the exclusive region-occupying or region-exploiting group. Specifically, the Australian field-workers demonstrated that in actuality socioterritorial groups of any size are composed of men of *different* patriclans, whether in coassemblage as camp-task groups or as scattered residents of a range. Challenged by this conclusion, other field ethnologists have since refined and clarified the relationship between the variability of on-the-group composition in Australian Aborigine societies and those peoples' own cultural construct of the indissoluble bond between the patriclan and its sacred territorial estate (Yengoyan 1970; Peterson 1979; Blundell 1980).

Assessing adaptive strategies, both social and ecological, acted out by individuals, families, and larger units among the world's foraging peoples, field ethnologists rejected emphatically Service's formulation of the patrilocal band as "an almost inevitable kind of organization." What these ethnologists, embedded in context in the field, had done was to focus on *practice*—what people conceive, decide, and do while responding to the guidelines of a

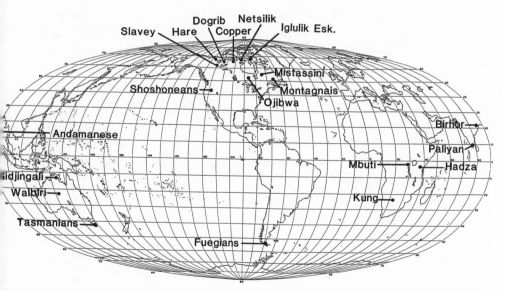

Hunter-gatherer or foraging peoples among whom ethnological research was carried out in the 1950s and 1960s. Also included on the map are the Shoshoneans, Fuegians, Andamanese, and Tasmanians who figured in earlier theoretical formulations on the structure of foraging societies.

given social and cultural structure. What none of us could counter, of course, were what Leaf (1979) calls the "theoretical presumptions of the necessary bases of order" that shaped the argument for the universality of the patrilocal band under pristine conditions. Neither contemporary field ethnologists nor prior observers were encountering peoples under pristine conditions, that is, before any form of contact with greater world systems. In the final analysis, the issue is whether one is willing to opt intellectually for a theoretical once-upon-a-time construct (cf. Martin and Stewart 1982).

In the years that have intervened since the excitement of the forager conferences of the late sixties, my research interests on the northern Dene turned to other questions. One recent project, however, led me by indirection to the question of maximal socioterritorial entities, tribal and supratribal, among the northern Dene. In developing a study [chapter 12 in this book] on the evidence of female infanticide among the Mackenzie Dene in the first half of the nineteenth century, my search of the literature on infanticide brought back the concept, refurbished, of the *bounded* band or population. The study in question presented computer simulations, modeled from population counts on several Inuit regional groups or "bands," of the maximal percent of female infanticide allowable if a small population was not to go extinct in 100, 200, or 300 years (Schrire and Steiger 1974). The population unit was posited as socially, genealogically, and biogenetically bounded and impermeable. The ethnographic invalidity of this assumption led me to return to questions I had addressed but superficially in my prior work on levels of socioterritorial organization among the Mackenzie Dene. Is there, at any level of inclusiveness, bounded socioterritorial entities among these peoples? If so, what is the quality or nature of that boundedness? What are these Dene that historically have been assigned names such as Slavey, Hare, Dogrib? Are these tribes? More precisely, is there any reality or usefulness to the concept of "the tribe" or some equivalent in respect to Mackenzie Dene peoples? Is "tribe" coterminous with "society"?

It is certain that the peoples that have come to be known as Hares or Slaveys or Dogribs aboriginally were not tribes in the sense usually employed by anthropologists. There were no tribalwide chiefs, councils, or other modes of political integration between constituent regional groups or even within those groups. At one conference I suggested that for these peoples the largest societal entity, the "tribe" or what-have-you, is to be defined structurally by "the greatest extension of population throughout which there is sufficient intermarriage to maintain many-sided social communication" (Helm 1968). At the same time, Joseph Birdsell (1968) set forth the idea of the "dialect tribe" among foragers, which, he argued, "both the natives and the anthropologists . . . have recognized as a reality." Within the dialect tribe, speech is homogeneous relative to other tribes. From, especially, the Australian data he established for the dialect tribe a modal value of about 500 persons. In Birdsell's analysis, "dialectical homogeneity at the simple level of hunters may profitably be viewed as a consequence of the pattern of density in face-to-face communications." Is it, then, in the dialect tribe that we find a meaningful dimension of socioterritorial boundedness among foragers under aboriginal conditions?

It is the charge and challenge of the ethnohistorian to contextualize a people through time in their matrix of interactive environing variables, inorganic, organic, intersocietal, and intercultural. Even for the documented past, environing variables are elusive of quantification, even specification. "Upstreaming" from the historical toward a reconstruction of the prehistoric allows substantial opportunity for missteps in judgment as to dimensions of change or continuity in sociodemographic manifestations and in the variables that govern them. Although chancy, the enterprise is legitimate as a historical method and may serve as a critical corrective to catastrophist assumptions about the obliterative consequences of contact between foragers and Europeans.

For the remainder of this presentation, I take the broader and longer view of the implications of evidence from the historical era for sociodemographic processes among the precontact Dene. The point at issue is that, unless historically known modes of Dene intergroup social alignment and communication can be demonstrated to have no bearing on prehistoric patterns, it is unjustifiable to posit hypothetical aboriginal Dene populations of some selected size and attributes as bounded populations that are the units of biogenetic or sociocultural survival or extinction.

Let me focus first on the Hare Dene. In 1862 the Oblate missionary Petitot identified 422 persons as Hare Indians (Peaux de Lièvre), most of them resorting to the trading post of Fort Good Hope on the Mackenzie River near the Arctic Circle. Among the Hares, the mutability of regional bands and the ranges with which they were identified within the historical era is attested "by the inconsistencies contained in the several band lists that have been published since the mid–nineteenth century" (Savishinsky and Hara 1981; also see Hara 1980).

One specific kind of mutability must here suffice to provide an example. In the 1860s Petitot (1865) identified two regional bands of Peaux de Lièvre who exploited the northern shores of Great Bear Lake. By the early decades of the twentieth century, these two regional groups were no longer identifiably Hare. They had become a part of a people self-identified as Sahtugot'ine or Sahtu Dene, Bearlake Dene. The Bearlake Dene are demonstrably a historical amalgamation of "Hare" and "Dogrib" peoples with some infusions of "Slavey" and "Mountain" Dene. Whether or not those particular Hare regional bands of the 1860s suffered population loss (an account by an elderly Dogrib migrant [Joseph Naedzo] to Great Bear Lake indicates that they did), they did not "die out" in the sense of extinction, either biogenetic or socio-cultural. Their descendants have been transmuted into new identities.

During the course of the historical era, the trading forts in the Mackenzie region became foci of social communication among the groups deployed over the land. That today "Hare is a well-defined dialect with little internal diversity," as attested by the linguists Krauss and Golla (1981), is almost surely the consequence of some 150 years of ingathering and interaction at Fort Good Hope. If Fort Franklin and Fort Norman at either end of the Great Bear River had never existed, the mélange genealogically identifiable as descendants of "Hares," "Dogribs," and other Dene would probably never have emerged as the "Bearlake Indians" now speaking a dialect "lingua franca," as Krauss and Golla characterize it. But the fact that trading forts became foci of linguistic, social, and marital interchange did not preclude a flow of visitors and of residence and marriage exchanges between groups "attached to" different forts and between groups identified on linguistic or historical grounds as different "tribal" entities. Native historical traditions recovered in my field research as well as documentary sources also testify to major territorial shifts and intertribal amalgamations within the historical era. These include, besides the emergence of the "Bearlake Indians" from the linguistically disparate groups who came to trade into Fort Franklin/Fort Norman, the "disappearance" of the Yellowknives into the Chipewyan population trading at Fort Resolution, the social and linguistic submersion of some of the easternmost Dogribs into the Chipewyans exploiting the south-eastern shore of Great Slave Lake, and the creation by joint land occupancy and intermarriage in the nineteenth century of the "Bâtard Loucheux" from Kutchin [Gwich'in] and Hare and their subsequent absorption into the Hare trading into Fort Good Hope (see map). The evidence is clear that among these Dene peoples neither the regional band nor the "dialect tribe" (when it can be distinguished) is, through *extended* time, genealogically or territorially encapsulated.

For the Lac la Martre regional band of Dogribs, a population averaging about 120 persons, I was able to establish the premarital "residence" of

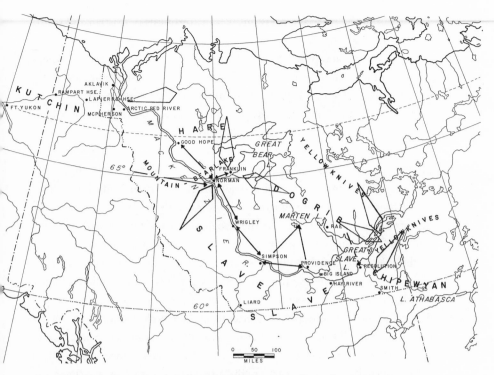

Great Slave Lake/Great Bear Lake area, 1860–1920. Major lines of communication, movement, and marriage between Dene groups trading into different posts are shown by arrows. Diamonds indicate intertribal territorial shifts and amalgamations.

74 persons who contracted mutual first marriages between 1911 and 1959 (Helm 1965a). Of these thirty-seven couples, in which either or both spouses were members of the Marten Lake group before marriage, 60 percent of the marriages were between men and women of the Marten Lake band; in 40 percent of the marriages either husband or wife came from another regional group. Outmarriage, or band exogamy, is underrepresented, since band members who married out or otherwise joined another regional group could not be included in the tally. In a priest's account of 1911, of the seventeen household heads of the Marten Lake band, five (29 percent) are recorded either as immigrants from Slavey country or sons of Slaveys. Overall rates of such intertribal, interlanguage marriages among the Mackenzie Dene are not known. Judging from a world sample of outmarriages in small populations (compiled by Adams and Kasakoff 1975), the rate would likely be on the order of 20 percent. At Fort Liard this level is confirmed for a Slavey group of about 120–130 adults (total population about 434), where

24 percent of the marriage decisions were exogamous (Christian and Gardner 1977).

In prehistoric and protohistoric times, before trading forts came into existence as foci of interaction, the web of social communication among regional nodes of Dene was probably more diffuse, less centripetal. But there seems no justification for arguing that in those times flows of personnel between regional and supraregional populations and, sometimes, shifts of exploitative ranges of groups did not obtain. No less than in contact-traditional times, major fisheries and passage routes of caribou would encourage seasonal congregations of regional and supraregional populations drawn from broad hinterlands. In the subarctic biome of the prehistoric as well as the historical era, the "constant" has been patchiness and flux, spatial and temporal discontinuities in food resources. Forest fires and successional aftermaths that alter faunal deployment, population crashes of species of food animals, shifts in range and migration routes of caribou due to climatological or other factors are some of the contingencies operating to promote realignments among Dene groups or impel shifts in their exploitative ranges. Short-term and more or less localized crises in food resources are apt to occur every several years, impelling groups to seek food and succorance beyond their usual range. (See Burch 1980 on the pre-1840 situation in northwestern Alaska.) At the other end of the scale there was almost surely the long-term resource crisis that every few generations would bring an extended period of hard times and major human movements over large areas. Amsden's study (1979) of the crash of the caribou population in northern Alaska between circa 1890 to 1920 and its drastic effect on the size, density, distribution, and inter-"tribal" alignments of the Nunamiut Eskimo is very apposite.

At any level of socioterritorial grouping, from one Dene group to another kin linkages by blood and by marriage were both the consequence and the conduit of population flow. Courtship and bride service removed a young man to the girl's camp group. A Dogrib legend begins: "There was a young man with great medicine who wanted to get married. He told his father and mother, 'I think I will go traveling so I can find some people.' When he said this, his father and mother knew he wanted to get married." Sometimes young men remained with their wife's group after completing bride service. Individual families left one camp group to visit or sometimes to relocate in another group where, usually, a primary relative of the husband or the wife served as sponsor (Helm 1965a). Any of these movements might occasion a shift in regional band or even "tribal" affiliation. One must envision interactional linkages from one regional node of Dene to surrounding nodes and from those to other groups yet more distant so that there existed an ever-radiating network—perhaps crochetwork is a more apt image—of sexual, social, cultural, and linguistic communication that transcended socio-territorial entities of the regional band or even "tribal" level. Periods or episodes of hostile relations between one regional or "tribal" population and a neighboring group would produce only a partial and temporary rupture in the network. The conclusion drawn by sociolinguistic research in the Fort Liard trading-post community of Slaveys speaks to the point.

> Ethnic . . . boundaries are not uniformly agreed upon by the people [under study]. We raise the question whether, in some cases, they even exist objectively, except as artificial constructs, like boundaries between colors; there are no marked discontinuities that would provide unproblematic . . . social or linguistic boundaries to be drawn. Perhaps we can operationalise the idea of dialect and other cultural variation as a steady continuum of discontinuity, interrupted occasionally by more marked discontinuity. (Christian and Gardner 1977:391)

The critical issue is the dimensions and modes of "communicative relationships among persons and groups" (Hymes 1968). To return to the Hare Indians of Fort Good Hope, throughout the historical era Fort Good Hope as point-of-trade has been a centripetal force that has served to intensify the "communicative relationships," including marriage, of those Indians trading into it. But those Dene and, perhaps more pronouncedly, their ancestors of the precontact era were embedded in a yet wider though more tenuous web of communication. Krauss and Golla's characterization of the structure of the linguistic relationships across the entire northern Dene domain treats of the same systematic feature expressed in the communicative mode of language:

> Athapaskan linguistic relationships . . . cannot be adequately described in terms of discrete family-tree branches. This is because intergroup communication has ordinarily been so constant, and no dialect or language was ever completely isolated from the other for long. The most important differences among Athapaskan languages are generally the result of areal diffusion of separate innovations from different points of origin, each language—each community—being a unique conglomerate. . . .
> Whatever the immediate, short-term language boundaries, the network of communication in the northern Dene linguistic complex is open-ended. (1981:68–69)

The open-ended structure of this network finds its homologue and its source in the network of Dene sociodemographic communication. Of the Edge-of-the-Woods Dogribs, whose traditional exploitative range fronts on the barrens and on the other sides is bracketed by the ranges of other Dogrib regional groups, a Dogrib commented, "They speak real Dogrib because they got nobody else [no other "tribe"] to marry."

The structure of the northern Dene social and linguistic network has its own distinctive order, but the principle is not unique. For, among others, Great Basin Shoshone and Australian foragers, Jane Hill (1978) rejects on the basis of linguistic evidence the model of "dialect tribes . . . predominantly endogamous and monolingual" in favor of the "area network," as she terms it. Phonological and lexical patterns in the manifestation of the area–network principle differ from one culture area of foragers to another. Another anthropologist (Kelly 1982) has built on Hill's general proposition to pursue evidence that "variability in these patterns is indicative of different forms of local and long-term adaptive strategies" among different collections of foraging peoples. Variabilities aside, the area network is seen as a "major level of structural significance" by Hill that is not a consequence of sociodemographic perturbation or breakdown due to historical contact crises. Rather, it is long-term and systemic. From particular culture-areal research perspectives, I and other forager ethnologists (e.g., Lee 1976) have come to the same conclusion on the grounds that, as Hill puts it, "in ecological terms it is only at the level of the area [a term for which she offers no precise operational definition] that we can see the systematic nature of the long-term mechanisms of homeostasis that allow the survival of human ways of life which involve very simple technologies." I would add the obvious: *and* the overall survival of those broad areal collections of human populations that are the creators and transmitters of those ways of life.

In conclusion: as genetic or societal congregations, regional bands and larger socioterritorial adhesions among the Mackenzie Dene have been potentially evanescent. Seen within the areal-network structure, that evanescence carries reduced import for the continuance of Dene population, society, and culture from far prehistoric times. The questions raised around Dene perdurance in the longer-run out of the past bear on the evolutionary processes, biogenetic and cultural, that acted on the foraging forebears of us all.

from "Horde, Band, and Tribe: Northern Approaches," 1987

Part I | COMMUNITY AND LIVELIHOOD
AT MIDCENTURY

Part I aims to provide a perspective on the life of the Dene in the Northwest Territories in the years around 1950. Chapter 2 briefly introduces the two kinds of settlements that were meaningful in Dene experience, the bush community and the trading fort. Day by day and season by season, the yearly round of people living out on the land is described in chapter 3, and chapter 4 follows up with some specifics of procurement and use of the land's food animals in the 1950s and in earlier times. Chapter 5 looks at the needs, pressures, and anxieties the people faced in maintaining themselves half a century ago.

THE BUSH COMMUNITY AND TRADING FORT AT MIDCENTURY

This sketch largely derived from my several months of residence during the 1950s in the bush communities at Jean Marie River (Slavey) and Lac la Martre (Dogrib). In the 1960s the Canadian government in part confounded my forecast about the demise of the bush community by buttressing bush communities with modern services and communication installations.

THE BUSH COMMUNITY

The bush Indian of the Canadian North—who comes to the fort only for trade and Treaty—is disappearing. Especially since World War II, increasing job opportunities and the lure of various Euro-Canadian comforts and services have accelerated the movement of the Indians of the Northwest Territories into the white-centered towns as permanent residents in permanent dwellings. For the anthropologist, many of the more traditional modes of social identity and social organization can be better seen in the small all-Indian settlements in the bush rather than in the larger communities created by and focused around Euro-Canadian institutions.

The bush hamlet of today represents a stabilization of the old fluid, mobile local band. The most visible feature of change is the log cabin dwellings that have replaced the tipi lodges. These permanent cabins and all the goods and gear from the Western world have made present-day Indians relatively less mobile than their ancestors. The bush communities of today are commonly situated along routes of travel navigable by canoe leading to the trading fort.

Within the Dene bush village, all members of the community are linked together by multiple ties of blood and marriage. All are kin. The bush community, once a mobile local band, characteristically is created when a man of unusual personality and ability settles at one site in the bush. Such a man holds the allegiance of his sons and brothers and recruits his sons-in-law and brothers-in-law. In the past, and to some extent today, the traditional custom of bride service serves as one mode of recruitment to the bush

band-community. When a young man marries, he is expected to remain with his bride's group, helping his in-laws, until the birth of the first child. If his father-in-law or one of his brothers-in-law is especially attractive as a good hunter, hard worker, or friend, the young man and his wife are apt to continue to remain in that community rather than to return to his group.

The smaller bush communities may be composed of only four to eight households. As death brings about the dissolution of the closer ties of kinship, such small local bands may fragment and, in some cases, disappear.

Life in the bush community reveals a prime characteristic of the social organization of the Northern Athapaskan peoples. It is a society by consensus. The diffuse, informal sanctions of gossip, exhortation, ridicule, and public disapproval operate to maintain social order in the absence of any formal or legal mechanisms. The role of the leader in the local band, as of all leaders in the past, is not to enforce physically the unwritten rules of Dene society but rather to reinforce by example of his own actions the basic moral obligations of community life. The principles of autonomy and equality—every man his own boss and every man as good as the next—are deep-seated themes in Dene social life. And in the bush community there still endures a third theme, that of the basic responsibility of each person toward all members of his localized group.

Many bush communities are small enough that any large game killed, bear, moose, or caribou, is shared with all households of the band. The family whose nets and snares have not yielded enough fish and rabbit for the day may expect to receive a share of a relative/neighbor's catch upon request. So, too, borrowing back and forth of tools and implements and of tea, sugar, and other store staples is continual. As in any small, closely woven, intimate community of human beings, frictions and factions are inevitable. But a sense of social solidarity mediated through kin ties is apparently sufficient to mute and dissolve conflicts before they reach a critical stage. And, if indeed they should, the dissident members can always move to another band or community where they have resident kin.

Two contrapuntal rhythms run through life in a bush band: the daily round of livelihood (fetching water and firewood, tending the nets and snares, all the tasks of maintaining the household), as well as the seasonal rhythms of the fall fishery, the winter trapline, the spring beaver hunt. For everyone, Sunday is a day of relaxation and, in some communities, of a group religious service.

In the simple division of labor in the bush, mainly, man provides and woman processes. From the meat, fish, and pelts brought by the husband

Teresa Carterette holding "school" at Marie River, 1951. Teresa and I gained entrée into the bush community of Jean Marie River by offering to "teach school." Louis Norwegian and other parents feared that sending children to yearlong residence at a mission school would make them "lose the head for Marie River."

into the household, the wife must cure moose and caribou hides for moccasins and mitts, stretch and scrape skins for the trader, and in summer prepare dryfish and drymeat. A man varies his trapping with hunting and his labor in the bush with trips to the trading fort. For the woman there are only small breaks in household routine: an expedition for berries in the summer with other women and their children, a short social visit on Sunday to the next house, or a few hours spent with a kinswoman while together they do the heavy work of wringing a moose hide. Perhaps at least once a year, at Treaty time, does the woman get a visit to the trading fort. But she shares the excitement of all on the return of the men from their trips.

The return of several men from the trapline or from an extended hunt is an occasion for partying and relaxation. Freed from the surveillance of white authority, the bush wife has had no problem in preparing a pot of brew for her husband's return. He and his cronies gather over the pot, each man to tell the tale of his fur take or of the excitement of a moose kill. Perhaps from time to time a cup is also dipped for the ladies present, and the children, enjoying the excitement of the occasion, tear about from cabin to cabin to miss nothing that is going on. Should too much brew release smoldering grudges, the women and near kinsmen are ready to lead potential combatants away to their own homes. The brew party serves to break the monotony of toil and isolation. The slow evolution of a brew party, as the alcohol in the cidery drink begins to take hold, allows a change of social and emotional pace that, in one way or another, all cultures of the world have institution-alized to accommodate the nature of the human animal. [Before 1959 it was illegal in the Northwest Territories for Indians to possess or consume alcohol in any form.]

The physical convenience and the economic and educational opportuni-ties of the white-centered community will surely in the future more and more dissolve the ties of the northern Dene to the bush environment. To the Indians of midcentury the rigors of bush living may be too great a price to pay for the more independent and self-sufficient life of their forebears. The bush village imposes isolation upon the Indians and economic bondage to the vagaries of the fur trade. [At the time I wrote this, the fur trade was sicker than I knew.] Yet by standards common to both Indian and white—the egalitarian relationships within the community and the almost complete ab-sence of crime, psychosis, broken homes, abandoned wives and children—the Dene bush community is a healthy social body. Many southern Canadian and U.S. tribes are not so fortunate.

from "Changes in Indian Communities," 1966

THE TRADING FORT

The ten "forts" established in the nineteenth century for pursuing the fur trade with the Athapaskan peoples of the Northwest Territories continue as major foci of congre-gation for Dene. As points-of-trade, in the early years several shifted locale, which in part accounts for "shifty" dates of year of founding. This is especially true for the establishments known under other names that in 1786 preceded Fort Resolution and Fort Simpson in 1803.

Peter Usher (1971) provides details and dates of the foundings of the ten forts. To the forts and the dates I attach the tribal designations of the Dene who frequented them through the nineteenth century: Fort Liard 1805, Slavey and Mountain Dene; Fort Resolution (1786) 1819, Chipewyan and Dogrib; Fort Simpson (ca. 1803) 1822, Slavey, Mountain Dene, and Dogrib; Fort Good Hope 1836, Hare and Gwich'in; Fort McPherson 1840, Gwich'in and also Inuit; Fort Norman, now Tulita, (1810) 1851, Slavey, Hare, Mountain Dene, Dogrib, and Bearlake Dene; (Old) Fort Rae 1852, Dogrib; Fort Providence 1869, Slavey; Fort Smith 1874, Chipewyan; and Fort Wrigley 1887, Slavey and Mountain Dene.

Three trading forts established in the lower Mackenzie Valley in the twentieth century that drew Dene trade and settlement were Arctic Red River, now Tsiigehtchic, in 1901 for Gwich'in; Aklavik in 1912 for Inuit as well as Gwich'in; and Fort Franklin, now Déline, in (1908–10) 1926 for Bearlake Dene, Dogrib, and Hare. These settlements continue as points of congregation of Dene populations. So do the following settlements of the upper Mackenzie region. Hay River (1868–75) in 1901 pulled in Slaveys from the year it reopened, as did Nahanni Butte in 1915. Snowdrift, now Lutselk'e, opened as a point-of-trade in 1926 for Chipewyans along the east arm of Great Slave Lake. Yellowknife 1937, formed as a mining town, drew Dogribs and Chipewyans but was never a native-focused settlement.

Most of these points-of-trade drew Dene of more than one linguistic/ "tribal" connection. Fort Rae, being off the transportation routes, was exclusively frequented by Dogribs.

FORT RAE IN 1962

The original Fort Rae (Ninhsin Kon) was established in 1852 by the Hudson's Bay Company at Mountain Island on the North Arm of Great Slave Lake. Ewaingho, the father of Chief Monfwi, who signed Treaty No. 11 in 1921, built the first cabin at the site of present-day Rae. According to Dogrib oral history, in 1902 he persuaded the "free trader" firm of Hislop and Nagle to set up a post at that site on Marian Lake. New Fort Rae emerged in 1906, and Old Fort died when the Catholic mission and the Hudson's Bay Company moved to the new site.

Rae is attractive with its rocky prominences, canal-like snies (the "Venice of the North"), and expanse of lake hemmed by the dark spruce bush, but the settlement is far from ideal for a concentration of population. Built mainly on bare Precambrian rock and surrounded by the shallow waters of Marian Lake, the village is [by 1962] beset by serious sanitation problems in the disposal of waste materials and consequent contamination of water. As the population increases, local resources of rabbits and fish are depleted, and the bush is cut back farther and farther to supply firewood. The general health problems at Rae are more acute than at the other Dogrib settlements, as are the stresses developing out of the shift away from a subsistence economy to an ever greater dependence on wage work, use of cash, and the market economy controlled by Euro-Canadian society.

The official Indian population for the Rae district in 1962 was 926, but substantially fewer than this number are regularly in residence at Rae. Some Indians reside year-round in several bush hamlets. Other families leave their cabins at Rae to go to fish in richer waters away from Rae in late summer

Rae in 1959. A bridge links Hudson's Bay Island, with the company's compound of white buildings, to Priests' Island, with its hospital–church–mission house complex. On the other side, a bridge links Priests' Island to Murphy's Point on the mainland.

and to go into the bush to hunt and trap in the winter. The present establishment of permanent homes at Rae, however, illustrates an increasing tendency of Indian people to settle around trading places and other sites of Euro-Canadian institutions. Previously, they made their regular homes at bush camps and came into the forts only for special purposes such as trade and Christian religious ceremonies.

In addition to the native people (Dogribs and a few Metis families), there are in Rae about fifty whites associated with the Hudson's Bay Company store, a Game and Wildlife station, the Royal Canadian Mounted Police station, a hospital run by nursing nuns with a resident government physician, a government primary school, and the Catholic mission staffed by two Oblate fathers and a brother. Besides the whites attached to the foregoing institutions, individual whites have recently settled at Rae, including a free trader (i.e., not of the Hudson's Bay Company) and a man who runs a taxi service between Rae and Yellowknife. Indian Affairs personnel stationed at Yellowknife make regular trips to Rae to oversee contract work such as the building of government housing for Indians, supervised by temporarily resident whites, as well as to administer other government activities relating to Indians. The Hay River–Yellowknife segment of the highway from Edmonton, Alberta, that connects Rae and Yellowknife was completed in 1961 and allows easy access for occasional visitors and tourists to the community. Although there has long been a winter road over the snow, the gravel road, which is open all year now, affords both Indians and resident whites more frequent contacts with Yellowknife than were previously possible with dependence on bush planes and water travel.

Although neither whites nor Indians would be at Rae except for the others' presence, the areas and means of social interactions are for the most part narrowly defined, and they operate as largely separate social worlds, with only occasionally individuals in the two groups entering into any kind of peer relationship. Discussions between white officials and Indians at Treaty time each summer make evident both the interdependence and the mutually unsatisfactory channels of communication on which such interdependence is based.

from Helm and Lurie, **The Dogrib Hand Game***, 1966*

Update 2000   Health problems arising from the pollution of Marian Lake, from which the residents of Rae drew their drinking water, resulted in a government plan to establish a substitute settlement, Edzo, which could be easily modernized. To push the Dogrib people of Rae to move to Edzo, the government imposed a freeze on the building of subsidized housing in Rae. Outside planners were called in to design the new modern facility, some twenty-four kilometers from Rae. The Dogribs of Rae, especially through the voice of Chief Bruneau, repeatedly explained why they did not want to move to the new site, and in fact they did not do so. (On the issues on both sides, see Gamble [1986].) At the end of the century, three decades after the Edzo project was conceived, Rae continues to be the focus of Dogrib settlement and congregation. The schizoid result of the opposing forces of government design and Dogrib commitment is now officially known as Rae-Edzo.

3

THE YEARLY ROUND OF THE PEOPLE OF "LYNX POINT," JEAN MARIE RIVER, 1951–1952

This chapter takes a closer look at a bush community at midcentury. Lynx Point is a pseudonym for the Slavey settlement of Jean Marie River, located above Fort Simpson on the Mackenzie River. In response to the anxiety of its members that the community might be gossiped about, I created pseudonyms for the hamlet and all its members and use them most times in this book.

THE HOUSEHOLD

Although the household activities of the day are not strictly scheduled, a certain routine is commonly followed. Adults usually rise between six and seven in the morning. One sleeps fully clothed, and there is little in the way of a morning toilet. The first concern is to build the fire; the first person to arise does this, often the husband. He may also start the tea or other food preparations. The three meals a day are commonly taken in the morning, around two in the afternoon, and about eight at night. Family eating is often a piecemeal process, especially if, for example, only a few fish are being broiled at a time.

In the summer, water is fetched daily in buckets from the Mackenzie. In winter, several days' supply may be brought up in an oil barrel from the family water hole in the ice, the community-owned horse pulling it on a sledge up the bank to the house. [Mac the horse was a unique possession in an Indian community.]

Several days' supply of firewood is brought to the household at one time, but there is the daily chore of sawing it into lengths with a crosscut saw and splitting it. Firewood is cut and stacked in the bush to season a year or so in advance of use. One man estimated that the smallest type of cabin (about twelve by twelve feet, with a low roof) requires fifteen cords of wood for the winter season. The horse is now used by each household for sledging the logs

into the village in winter. He can pull two to three times the amount that a dog team can. In summer, most of the wood used is driftwood, gathered by canoe or skiff.

Another chore, usually performed daily, is checking the rabbit snares. As many as fifty snares may be set in the bush by one household. Each family unit will also have one to four gill nets placed at eddies in the river. In summer, especially, some of these may be several miles distant, and they are ordinarily visited daily by canoe. They are set through holes chopped in the ice in winter. Snares and nets are usually visited in the afternoon.

Toward evening, the dogs are fed. Sometimes, when the supply is plentiful, each dog is merely thrown a fish or rabbit, but often they must be fed on "dog soup" (or "dog brew"), a gruel of "dog rice" or rolled oats, simmered for hours in a five-gallon gas tin over an outdoor fire. The gruel is then allowed to cool, afterward being poured into individual feeding cans placed beside the staked dogs. Dogs appear to be consistently underfed, but especially so in the summertime, because, it is explained, "they don't work" in that season.

There is no set bedtime; family members retire when they wish by simply lying down fully clothed and covering themselves with a blanket. The rest of the family and any visitors will continue their activities around them. Older children from the age of twelve on are usually free to stay up and out of the house as long as they wish. Younger ones are frequently called home by ten. By midnight the family is usually asleep.

Women's work, revolving as it does around the household and child care, varies much less with the seasons than that of the men. Scrubbing the floor in preparation for Sunday is a Saturday chore for most women. Washing of clothes and housecleaning are either performed by the adult women or delegated to female children. Cooking is primarily a woman's task, but men or children of either sex may also contribute. When the husband is absent or occupied, the wife or older children haul the water, saw the wood, and check the snares and nets. If the husband is free, he often performs these tasks.

Most women own a small hand-cranked sewing machine, and they often make from yard goods various items of their own or their children's apparel, such as shirts, undershirts, and dresses. A few items of men's clothing are commonly handmade also. These are the moosehide mitts, gloves, moccasins, duffel (blanket-cloth) wrappings for the feet, knitted socks, and the dark blue cotton gabardine parkas. Similar items are also made for the children.

Mitts, moccasins, and parkas are commonly decorated. Silk embroidery

Spring at Jean Marie River, 1952. The Mackenzie River in the background has not yet broken. The double house belongs to Johnny and Jimmy Sanguez. The fenced area in the foreground is a communal potato garden.

in flower motifs adorn the parka yokes and the mitts. Moccasin tongues (except for undecorated "work moccasins") may be decorated with silk embroidery on stroud or may be beaded or covered with an overall geometric design of dyed porcupine quills. Less commonly, the quill work may be executed in a floral motif. Parkas are also trimmed with fur (usually fox or wolverine) around the face and cuffs, with a double fringe of blue and red stroud around the embroidered yokes and with a rickrack edging along the hems. Gloves and mitts always have fur edgings and, if a gauntlet style, a fringe of moose hide along the outer seam of the cuff.

Footwear is a major and continual item of production for women. Only two or three individuals at Lynx Point own shoes of Euro-American manufacture, and they are purely for novelty. Several pairs of moccasins a year are required by each individual (they tear quickly if they become wet while worn). The common form is the ankle-wrap variety. The lowers are always

Celine Gargan scraping the hair from a moose hide, Jean Marie River, 1952.

of moose hide; the uppers, or ankle wrapping pieces, may be of moose hide, caribou hide, or canvas. Moccasin slippers, that is, without the ankle uppers, are occasionally made and are trimmed with beaver fur around the top. Mid-calf (for women) or knee-high (for men) mukluks are an occasional novelty. Though derived from the Eskimo boot (and called "Eskimo moccasin" in Slavey), the lower, or foot, part is of standard soft moccasin design. A woman will commonly have a pair of fancily embroidered moccasins in process, usually for her husband, which she will work on at odd moments.

Other items of female handiwork are rawhide (babiche) snowshoe webbing, braided moosehide dog whips, moosehide gun cases, usually fringed and beaded or embroidered, beaded ammunition pouches of black velvet or stroud, black cloth moss bags for infants, sometimes decorated, and fancily worked back-carrying straps for babies.

It will be noted that many of the foregoing items, especially the important moccasins and mitts, are made of tanned hide. The preparation of hides is a vital women's activity. As it is a time-consuming occupation requiring a fair degree of physical strength, girls do not actively begin to learn the techniques until they are in their teens. Moose are the primary source of hides at Lynx Point; the finished product is one-sixteenth to one-quarter inch thick. Caribou hide is thin and delicate in comparison to moose and is used only for moccasin ankle uppers or light gloves. (As babiche and rawhide, it serves for snowshoe webbing and drum heads.) The major steps in moosehide preparation are an overnight soaking; removal of the mesentery (to be cooked and eaten) and of the hair by cutting and scraping; two days of soaking in a solution made from boiled moose or bear bones and soap; another scraping (while wet) of both sides; wringing and drying over a fire; a further scraping (when dry); and four hours of smoking over a smoldering fire of rotten spruce wood for final softening and for preventing the hide from becoming permanently stiff should it become wet. Various forms of scrapers and fleshers are used in hide preparation. Stones or bevel-ended moose long bones may be used, or they may be made of various kinds of metal, perhaps from the lid of a tobacco tin, punched to make a graterlike object, or from a piece of broken trap.

Women share with men the ability to handle and shoot a .22 rifle (for rabbit hunting), to harness and drive dogs, to set traps for squirrel and weasel, and to set rabbit snares and weave gill nets. Some women know the techniques of trapping in general; widowhood often calls for the development of these abilities.

Any discussion of the harvesting of food or fur animals by the natives of the Mackenzie region is made awkward by the fact that many game and trapping regulations are in effect throughout the area. Furthermore, these regulations vary from one section of the region to another and change from time to time. During the period of fieldwork at Lynx Point (1951–52), some restrictions attached to all food animals except rabbits and caribou; for fish, the sole restriction is the forbidding of the use of fish weirs or traps. Moose hunting is legal only in winter, and only one moose a year for each hunter may be taken. Ducks, geese, and bears are "open" only for a brief period toward autumn. Porcupines are "closed" all year. Snaring any of the large animals is illegal. Caribou are "open" for hunting, but there are not reliable sources of supply in the area around Lynx Point. The animals just named comprise the types of meat foods commonly eaten, with the exception of certain trapped furbearing animals that are considered edible. Trapping regulations are addressed below.

For a people who, by inclination and economic necessity, derive much of their sustenance from the game of the bush, the restrictions are a source of continual resentment and give rise to such ironic jokes as "they are going to 'close' mice next." The common attitude toward the game laws among inhabitants of the region of all ethnicities is one of staunch laissez-faire. There is no moral problem involved in breaking a game law; the only question is whether or not one can get away with it.

LATE SPRING AND SUMMER

Breakup marks the end of the winter season. From early April the thaw is under way. Around the first of May, the jammed and heaped ice in Lynx Creek [Jean Marie River] starts to move. For a week or more, the little river displays fitful bursts of activity as its ice grinds out onto the still-frozen Mackenzie, jams, and then gives way before a further thrust of floes. The Mackenzie ice moves perhaps a week after Lynx Creek is clear. Its floes travel silently in great solid sheets. The initial flood of pent-up water often leaves the village beach hidden under massive slabs of ice. After the initial movement of Mackenzie ice, there are a few days of relatively clear water, and the community watches for the one final mass of floes that signifies the clearing of the mouth of Great Slave Lake. Beached ice continues to rim the Mackenzie shore into June. The interest surrounding breakup is intense. As the

Breakup on the Mackenzie, 1952. The ice in the foreground is from the breakup of the Jean Marie River. Twelve-year-old Minnie Norwegian is the figure at the extreme lower left.

Watching a diesel powerboat and barges go by, Jean Marie River, 1952.

men return from the spring hunt, paddling down the open Lynx Creek [Jean Marie River], they join the women and children in observing and commenting on each stage of the Mackenzie breakup. From mid-May through August the days are warm, and in July and August even the nights are mild.

Once the Mackenzie clears, the big diesel-engined riverboats appear, pushing barges of supplies north to the mining and oil camps and to the trading forts. The men of Lynx Point can identify each boat and its pilot, and throughout the summer as these vessels pass and repass the males of the community gather on the banks to watch their progress. Down the Mackenzie come fresh supplies to the trading establishments at Fort Simpson, and orders for "fresh stuff"—oranges, apples, eggs, vegetables—are sent from Lynx Point as some of the men make the first canoe trips of the season to the fort.

During the two summers (1951, 1952) of fieldwork, two sets of missionaries belonging to evangelist sects came down the Mackenzie by powerboat. In both cases, a loudspeaker played recorded hymns for a while as the men of Lynx Point squatted solemnly on the beach with some of the more forward children while the women and other youngsters looked on from a distance. Any visit will bring forth this same greeting pattern. The missionaries chatted, passed out tracts and booklets, and, in one case, held a short meeting. The Indians accept everything passively. As yet (1952), there has been no real effort on the part of the evangelist groups to proselytize Indians north of Hay River.

Even before breakup some families move into tents on the edge of the upper terrace overlooking the beach. As the ice melts from the shore, tents are pitched on the beach, and the houses stand empty. Commercial canvas tents are used. A prepared platform of boards, large strips of spruce bark, or springy spruce boughs (changed every few days) are laid as flooring. Canvas sun shelters are rigged at the doors of the tents, and various pole racks and sometimes tables are erected nearby.

All hunting and traveling expeditions in the summer are primarily by water transport, as the muskeg, thickets, tree windfall, and especially insects in the bush make overland travel extremely arduous. By June it is only near the water that one can escape the mosquitoes, and even there they grow vigorous at night, and net mosquito bars are necessary for sleeping. The "bulldogs," large biting flies, are present throughout July, and in the bush the mosquitoes and black flies are vicious. By August only the black flies are left in any number, and they do not frequent the open camp area.

Summer is a time of travel and visiting for recreation. Throughout the

People, dogs, and the horse Mac going to Fort Simpson on the Jean Marie River barge, 1952. Fred Norwegian is in the foreground.

In the hold of the Jean Marie River powerboat, 1952. The little girl to the right is Margaret Norwegian.

spring, canvas canoes are patched and painted, outboard motors are over-hauled, and plank scows are caulked in preparation for summer travel. The sound of a "kicker" on the river is frequently heard—families going into Simpson or en route to a visit with relatives, or men out on a hunting or fishing jaunt. Some Indians, but not Lynx Point band members, spend pro-tracted periods in summer at the fort, simply visiting and vacationing. Some-times the travelers stop to visit a friend or relative at Lynx Point. Only in summer are the Lynx Point women likely to get a nonemergency trip to Simpson. The men, as in the winter, make several trips for supplies. The process of traveling is in itself a recreation. But at all times in traveling the men remain alert, with guns close at hand, for any game, from ducks to moose. Frequently, the canoe will stop at good bluefishing spots along the shore. There are always peeled poplar fishing poles in readiness in the canoe, and everyone joins in angling for bluefish, the most succulent of the river fish. Perhaps thirty minutes will be spent fishing—one individual may catch a score or more in that time. A fire is made, and some of the catch is con-sumed on the spot. This is the common practice when any amount of fish or game is taken.

A visit to Fort Simpson may provide several recreational delights not avail-able at Lynx Point. For the women and children especially, the novelty of new faces and of the goods at the trading posts is enjoyable. The men and boys often attend the once-a-week movie, women and girls rarely. On Sun-day there are church services. In former years the payment of "treaty money" was an important event that drew most of the surrounding population to Simpson. According to the Indian agent, interest in the event has declined somewhat; recent government orders restrict the donation by the agent of flour, lard, rice, tea, and other comestibles for the preparation of the post-Treaty feasts and dancing, and the agent predicts that this will further lessen the interest in Treaty. Certainly for a decade or more the five-dollar treaty payment has been of financial interest to only the children and perhaps some women. A week's stay in Simpson will consume, in foodstuffs alone, a fam-ily's treaty money.

The social highlights of the time around Treaty are the "tea dances." The chief usually sponsors at least one tea dance. Tea and comestibles are served in a nearby dwelling in the course of the dance. Subchiefs may give dances also, and unsponsored dances may occur as well. "Fiddle dances," with vio-lins and guitars providing jigs, reels, and "cowboy music," are sometimes held in the fort, but they are not a summer or Treaty feature.

The aboriginal hand gambling game, traditionally played when large groups gathered, had not been played at Fort Simpson since 1928. In that year a terrible influenza epidemic wiped out most of the elderly people. In mourning for the "old people" the game was not played in the years following and was never reinstated. Many of the younger adult generation of Fort Simpson saw the game for the first time in 1955 when visiting "Liard men" reintroduced it.

[Festivities at the forts during Treaty time, as exemplified by those of the Dogribs at Rae, are described in chapter 16 and chapter 17.]

Since the Indian agent is present in Simpson for Treaty, it is a time when grievances may be aired or requests made by the Indians. (The resident doctor serves as government representative to the Indians for the rest of the year.) Also, new government regulations or expectations are explained at this time, and the Indians attending the meeting may be asked to present their opinions on certain issues, such as projected changes in game regulations, for example. In the last few years, a mobile X-ray unit has accompanied the Treaty party. Apparently the majority of Indians who are in Simpson at that time do take advantage of the antituberculosis service. [The TB X-ray program ceased in the 1970s.]

Various men from Lynx Point have worked at summer jobs in Simpson, digging house foundations for new buildings at the now defunct sawmill or for the agricultural agent, for example. Three Lynx Point men and their families moved from the village to the fort to work for part of the summer of 1952.

At most Indian settlements along the Mackenzie River there are one or more gardens under cultivation, producing potatoes and sometimes turnips and occasionally other vegetables. There are three gardens currently (1952) being planted at Lynx Point, and during the last half of May they are plowed, hoed, mattocked, and seeded. Occasional weeding may be done throughout the summer. Summer is also the time for house repairs and building of any new structures.

In this season, as in others, much of the food for the people is provided by the natural products of the region, and most of the man-hours of labor are directed toward these ends. In the first few weeks after the Mackenzie breaks, bluefish and suckers are running up the smaller streams. (There is later, in August, a good period for bluefish angling.) Forty or fifty fish a day may be snared in gill nets. Some families may move to the mouths

Weaving a gill net, Jean Marie River, 1952. Widow Irene Sabourin, mother-in-law of Jimmy Sanguez, with her granddaughter Nora.

of streams rich in fish during this season to make dryfish: any fish not immediately consumed are gutted and slashed open, then hung over poles to be dried by the sun. This preserves them for a period of several months. Dryfish are intended primarily as dog food and are used for human consumption only when more desirable foods are lacking. Fish weirs were formerly constructed in the streams, but game laws now forbid them. Since they may be easily seen from the game warden's airplane, there is no attempt to operate illicit weirs. Fish commonly taken in gill nets are jackfish (pike), dory (pickerel), suckers (varieties of carp), bluefish (Arctic grayling), connies (*poisson inconnu*), and, rarely, whitefish. Jackfish are the major catch. Only bluefish and whitefish are valued for human food, though the other kinds will on occasion be eaten.

Rabbits (varying hares), snared or shot, may on occasion be sun dried. Once in awhile in the summer a bear may discover a rabbit snare line and will visit it regularly, stealing the catch. The snare owner may attempt to snare or shoot him.

Migratory waterfowl such as ducks, geese, and cranes are available in summer and are prized as delicacies. Moose and black bears are the only big game in the summer. The flesh of edible mammals is preserved during hot weather,

Checking the nets for the fall fishery on Great Slave Lake, 1952. Left to right: John Nahanni, Johnny Sanguez, Louis Norwegian.

as are fish, by sun drying. Large chunks of meat are transformed into thin sheets by the women, who cut the thick pieces of flesh in an accordion-pleated fashion, slicing almost through the chunk, first on one side, then on the other, so that it stretches out into one thin piece. Usually the meat is hung over a smoldering fire for the first two days; green poplar leaves may be thrown on the flames from time to time. The resulting smoke is not considered necessary for the drying process but is employed to drive away the flies that would infest the meat with their eggs. When there is "nothing else to do," or when meat supplies run short, or when a fresh large game "sign" has been noted in the bush or on the riverbanks, the men will go out for a day or two of hunting, usually in twos.

There is little reliance on wild plant foods. Among these are ten or so varieties of edible berries, including cranberries, raspberries, strawberries, blueberries, bearberries, and rose hips, but they are no more than a delicacy in the diet. The women and children do the berry picking; the main purpose of the expeditions is recreational—an outing. In the same way, children may be taken into the bush in early summer to scrape and chew the fresh bark of young poplar trees. Throughout the year, children gather spruce gum for chewing. Wild onions are likewise an occasional novelty, and certain mushrooms are known to be edible if they are picked before they become infested with insects and larvae. Also, during the summer the women must gather and heap for drying enough moss to serve the babies' diaper needs throughout the coming winter.

In August the first preparations for winter begin at Lynx Point as three or four expeditions are made to grassy areas a few miles down the Mackenzie to cut hay with scythes for the winter food supply of the community-owned horse. Throughout the summer some of the men and women mend and wash the forty or more large nets to be used for the autumn fishing in Great Slave Lake.

Around the middle of August, with the insects abating, families start dismantling their tents and moving back into the houses.

AUTUMN

The major event of the season for the Lynx Point men is the fishing expedition to Great Slave Lake. Those Indians of the Great Slave and Upper Mackenzie region who possess scows of adequate size may go to the "fall fishery" as do the Lynx Point men. Using a sixty-foot barge pushed by a powerboat, the Lynx Point band has the biggest vessel—their record catch was 27,000 fish in 1949. [The barge and powerboat are part of the group acquisitions and enterprises of the Lynx Point "Venture": see Helm 1961 and the section in chapter 18 on Louis Norwegian.]

Departure for Great Slave Lake is usually between September 15 and 25, with the return in early October. First, however, a trip to Simpson is made for supplies—oil, gas, and food. Two or three of the men remain at Lynx Point to hunt and provide for the women and children. One or two Indians or Metis from Simpson accompany the powerboat to the fishery. There are usually several petitioners for these positions, since men who do not own a vessel of some size would ordinarily be unable to go, and the ones selected are chosen by virtue of being "good workers." In return for their labor, the non–Lynx Point men receive the same number of fish that each Lynx Point family gets, the actual amount depending upon the size of the catch.

The major catch in Great Slave Lake is whitefish, with some jackfish. At spots in the lake known to be rich in fish, several rows of nets, ten nets in each row, are set out. Wooden floats and rock weights, with a large rock at each end of a net, control the position of the nets. Each set of nets is visited twice a day, at daybreak and about six in the evening, by two men in a skiff. The resulting catch of fish is then transferred from the skiffs to the barge. The fish are skewered in groups of ten on peeled willow sticks, each set being a "stick of fish." Freezing weather is common at this time of year (a coating of ice

Gabriel Sanguez mending a net for the fall fishery on Great Slave Lake, 1952.

once threatened to sink the barge), and the discomfort of working amid wind and water at these temperatures is often extreme. Great Slave Lake is usually rough, and sometimes the boat must sit out a two- or three-day blow in a sheltering cove. The time is spent in mending nets and in aimless recreation.

The amount of catch is variable, fluctuating in a three-year period from 2,700 sticks (27,000 fish) in 1949 to 920 sticks in 1951. In the latter year, each worker received 60 sticks, most of which were consumed by Christmas. One man estimated that 125 sticks is the amount sufficient to last a household and its dogs throughout the winter. If there is a sufficient supply, these fish serve as dog food all winter, thus circumventing a not inconsiderable expenditure on commercial feed; they also serve for human consumption. As the fish have frozen, no further preparation of them is necessary, and they are simply piled on one's roof or in the cache house for storage. A compromise must be struck between the number of sticks desired for consumption and the number that must be sold to pay debts for the operation of the powerboat at the fishery. Fish are sold in Simpson either to the Catholic mission hospital for food for the patients or to the Hudson's Bay Company, where they are resold to local natives at an advanced price.

Upon the return from the trip to Simpson to deliver the fish, the power-boat and barge are beached for the winter, for by this time ice is forming in the rivers. Besides the usual subsistence activities, the other autumn duties are the potato harvest and the readying of traps and other equipment for the coming trapping season.

A LETTER FROM JEAN MARIE RIVER, 1952

This letter, received about three months after Carterette and I left Jean Marie River, picks up on the importance of the fall fishery and other economic activities of the season. Sadder and more stressful events are recounted as well.

From Jean Marie River
Dec. 5, 1952
To Mrs. June McNeish
Was very pleased to recieve your letter but we are sorry we did not have a chance to write you soon. Now I have a good chance I am writting my boy Douglas [Norwegian] is going to town tomorrow.

We sure had a lucky fishery this year. Gab. [Gabriel Sanguez] went with them now as a boss [Louis Norwegian was usually the "boss"], and they catch 19 hundred sticks fish [double the catch of the prior year], that's 10 fish on a stick as we hope [you] know. They stayed at the fish camp about 1 week. It took them only 16 days from Marie River, going and back. They came back on Oct. 11, 1952.

We unloaded our fish here and went down to Simpson to sell 300 sticks with both our boats, we sold all our fish for $2.00 a stick, we used to sell for $1.50 but now as time are hard for us, so we put the price up, but Old J Crege [Craig, Hudson's Bay Company manager] won't take them for that price, so we sold all to R.C. mission. We came back here on the 18th of Oct. We started to pull up our boats and finish before the 20th of October and still no ice on Mackenzie.

We were happy we had a lucky fishery and had our boats on shore, but a messenger from simpson sent to us from Dr. E. Baker, that Gabriel Sanguis mother that was a patient at the hospital passed away on the 27 October. So myself [Louis Norwegian] and Gab, Johnny Sanguis all went down with kikker and canoe for her funeral. We were very sorry to loose her. She was the old mother for us all.

Cecile Sanguez: "She was the old mother for us all." Jean Marie River, 1952.

And still no ice on Mackenzie River, we came back from town on the 21th of October. And now its time for trapping season, but we could not set any traps because there was no snow too, because we had to go by dog team and there was about half an inch of snow was to bad no snow and no ice.

So we could not stay around and not trapping any longer so William Hardisty and Charles E. Gargan [brothers-in-law and trapping partners] went up to the fish lake to set nets and a few traps. They went on Monday Nov. 10 and stayed up there a week came back on Saturday night. When they came back, there was William H. latest baby Pat E. Hardisty in a coffin, passed away. The morning of Saturday Nov. 15th.

William H. is very sorry he did not even see his baby go. we buried him here at Marie River.

As for our school house [the first school in the Northwest Territories to be installed in an all-Indian settlement], its all finish on the outside, roof, doors, windows. But the inside is not even started yet. They said there was lots of work yet and could not finish this year so the[y] all pack up and went down to Simpson when we passed down on our fishery to town. Said they will start on it again next June. And the boss down in town said no use working anyway. They could not find a teacher. Sorry Teresa went out she would have stayed in a beautiful school sur look good. [Teresa Carterette had stayed through the winter of 1951–52 and taught school in return for firewood and other help from the community.] Next time we write hope to send you a picture of the school sure is a nice building we build.

Since you left us we had that wooping cough and now there are all kind of sickness around with us. There was a sickness going around town all summer last. they call it yellow fever. sure is a bad sickness, and right now we have it here but none is very sick with it yet. some are over and some just starting. But so far we are all well some are a little sick but they get over. As for the children they are all well. They shure tauok a lot about Teresa, mostly Laura [Gargan] and Minnie [Norwegian]. Right now the [Mackenzie] river is still running meaning ice is still floating down, first ice we saw floating was on Nov 4 on election day in U.S.A. So dear friend write us soon we sure like to hear from you and Teresa. Charles G. wrote a letter

On the portage trail, March, 1952.

when we came back from fishery so Douglas might bring back a letter from her when he come back. From Louis Norwegian for M.R. [Marie River] boys

Excuse me for my mistake on some words. [The scribe is Charles Gargan.]

WINTER AND EARLY SPRING

Ecologically, winter begins when the small lakes and streams have frozen and enough snow has fallen to permit overland dogsled travel. For a few weeks before, there is a period when travel at any great distance is out of the question. Travel and thus trapping are usually possible by the first to the middle of November. The Mackenzie River may not become solidly frozen until into December. During the winter trips to Simpson are made by dogsled over the "portage trail," a direct route which runs overland and traverses several small lakes. It is a distance of about thirty-five miles, ten miles shorter than the Mackenzie River route. A man makes the trip perhaps once a month, usually in the company of several others, to sell some of his furs in order to purchase supplies for his family. As a rule the travelers stop several times to rest the dogs and "make tea," which usually means having a meal. Often they will camp out one night on the trail. Total travel time may vary from seven to fourteen hours. Occasionally, a sled from a settlement upstream on the Mackenzie will stop the night at Lynx Point before taking the portage trail to the fort.

THE TRAPPING PARTNERSHIP

The only standardized socioeconomic relationship between two or more individuals (except for the husband-wife team) is the trapping partnership. The partners, usually a pair, are commonly related by blood or marriage. Partnerships of real brothers are frequent. The partnership is the only institutionalized relationship that may obtain between men outside the ties of kin. The term "partner" in the Indian's vocabulary may be extended to designate a close, good friend outside the kindred. This usage suggests the closeness and intimacy which real partners customarily feel.

There is no division of labor within the partnership except insofar as one man's special capacities may consistently be called into play. If there is a great disparity in age, for example, the younger and stronger of the team will probably always assume most of the task of breaking trail. The primary practical advantages of working with a partner rather than alone are the simple mutual aids that are possible, such as setting up camp together, helping one another's sleighs over steep terrain, spelling one another in trail breaking, and so forth. Each man has his own set of equipment from dogs, sleigh, and traps down to eating utensils. Any decisions, such as when to depart for the line, are reached by mutual discussion and agreement.

A man may have a short, separate trapline or one branching off from the main line which he ordinarily tends alone. But he travels the major line with his partner. Along this line, the partners commonly alternate their traps—first one man's trap, then the other's. Occasionally, one member of a partnership will tend the joint line alone. In these instances, only the furs caught in his own traps are his; those collected from his partner's traps belong to the partner. He will reset his partner's traps also. A fur animal always belongs to the owner of the trap that caught it unless a man is poaching on another's trapping area, in which case the abused party, if he discovers the traps, will confiscate the furs.

Each man in the Lynx Point area has one or more traplines. The long lines are usually worked by two or three partners, while one running but a few miles may ordinarily be visited alone. Different lines may yield somewhat different catches. The Yukon brothers' line, extending into a set of hills, is good for marten. Another line may yield a relatively high proportion of

William and Sarah Hardisty preparing beaver pelts for scraping, Jean Marie River, 1952.

mink. The fur animals present in the region are marten, fisher, mink, otter, red fox, weasel (ermine), lynx, wolverine, skunk, squirrel, beaver, and muskrat (called "rats" locally). Wolf is present but of no commercial value; wolves are trapped or poisoned only when they are raiding the fur traps too frequently. Marten, mink, fox, lynx, weasel, squirrel, beaver, and muskrat are the major catches; fisher and otter ordinarily command high prices but are almost nonexistent in the region. Traps are placed along the line at a short distance from the trail. As part of his technical lore, the trapper must know the habits and be able to recognize the "sign" of various animals; he must know the different kinds of bait attractive to each species and the correct size of trap for each. Native deadfalls as well as traps may be set for mink, marten, and weasel. One man had been "told about" a type of deadfall set for beaver "in the old days." These are no longer made.

Currently (1951–52), limits are imposed by the game laws on marten (five to a trapper) and beaver (two hundred for the Lynx Point area). Also, open season for marten and beaver was, at the time of fieldwork, limited to April and May.

Women and older children (from nine or ten years on) may set weasel and squirrel traps near the village. A boy may accompany adult males in the spring to shoot muskrats. The carcasses of the fur animals are brought home, where husband and wife skin them, stretch the pelts, and, in the case of beaver, scrape them.

The tempo of visits to traplines is variable. One or two nights out may suffice for the shorter lines; men tending the longest lines may be gone well over a week. Usually, a bed of spruce boughs and a large fire suffice for nights on the trail. On longer lines, the partners may erect semipermanent tipi-shaped shelters of split logs at one or two spots along the trail, or they may set up a tent for the winter out on the line, or, if enough sleds are going, they may carry a tent and even a stove for just the one trip.

One older Lynx Point man and his young wife who have no children established a small winter camp in the bush at a lake some twenty miles from the village. Here they may remain for a couple of months at a time. This practice has several economic advantages: the trapping area is close by, the meat game such as rabbits and moose is more plentiful, and small inland "fish lakes" such as this are incomparably richer in fish than are the rivers. As regards food, one can "live off the land" completely. The disadvantages lie primarily in the social isolation, the lack of comforts of house living, especially once one has children to tend, and the increased inaccessibility of store food.

Several items of aboriginal technology remain all-important in the pursuit of livelihood in the winter. Of these, the moccasin and the snowshoe have remained unchanged in use and design; each family manufactures its own. Actually, there are two types of snowshoe, the smaller snowshoe for traveling on packed snow and the "big snowshoe" for breaking trail and for travel through deep snow, as in pursuit of moose through the bush. In shape, both types are the same, long in relation to width, with pointed, upturned tips. The mitt, another aboriginal item, is still typically home-manufactured from moose hide, though it could be replaced by commercial items (horsehide mittens are stocked by the traders). Two other items of aboriginal culture are vital to winter living, but they have undergone modification in use in response to the trapping economy. These are the toboggan and the domesticated dog. Actually, an amalgam has occurred, dog power having replaced human power in drawing the toboggan. The dog is also used for packing in the spring, but its important role is in toboggan traction. From four to seven dogs are hitched in tandem to draw the toboggan or "sleigh," as it is called in the North. Marcel, now forty-five years old, recalls that when he was a youth, people were "poor" and could afford to maintain only two or three dogs. The toboggan, with canvas cariole, is now commonly purchased. At present, a "sleigh" costs about forty dollars. For travel over the wet snow of spring, two strips of steel, about three inches wide, are attached lengthwise along the bottom of the toboggan.

Hunting in the winter is most commonly carried out in conjunction with trapping trips. The trapper is alert for signs of moose and other game. If necessary, he will tie his dogs on the trail and set out through the bush in pursuit of the game. Moose is the major and most highly valued food item. Stalking so as not to alert the animal is a skilled and often fatiguing process, and it is recognized that men may differ in their abilities as moose hunters. Caribou are encountered less often, but, since they travel in groups, several may be killed at one time. One variety is the barren-ground caribou, which, during their forestward winter movements, usually swing into the Horn Mountain region, touching the northeasternmost extension of the Lynx Point area. The two men whose trapline runs into the Horn Mountain region survey the area from an eminence during their trapline visits and, if they locate a herd, may make a considerable kill. Caribou of a different sort, apparently woodland caribou, are found in the western section of the Lynx Point area, according to the men.

The only other large game taken in the winter is an occasional hibernating black bear, dragged from his hole and dispatched. Rabbits are the major small game. A couple of kinds of grouse are shot in some number, and ptarmigan are occasionally taken. Of the fur animals, lynx, beaver, and "rats" are commonly eaten, if freshly killed. Fish are taken in two fashions during the winter: by setting nets through holes in the ice and by placing hooks through ice holes. The latter technique is used for loche and for jackfish. Like the nets, the hooks are inspected every few days.

Because the amount of weight carried in the sleigh is a vital consideration and because the family at home must be left well supplied, men commonly do not carry with them on long trapline trips sufficient food for themselves and their dogs. A man may carry no food but only tea and bannock makings; he counts on his rifle, snares, and gill nets to feed himself and his dogs. Extra fish or meat accumulated during one trip may be cached for the next visit.

Sometimes, if the trip is of some duration, the trapper may undergo considerable hardship. Marcel recounted such an incident: "Sometime, hell of a time. Damn near starve last winter" (of 1950–51). Marcel and his partner, Karl, with Marcel's seventeen-year-old son, crossed the Mackenzie by canoe in the late autumn before the river froze solidly, threading their way among the ice floes. This was their first trip of the season to their line running into the Horn Mountains. When they reached the fish lake toward the end of the line, they set gill nets and remained there for "three nights." (Units of time on the trail are reckoned in terms of nights rather than days.) They caught very few fish, however, barely enough for the dogs only. They hunted during this time, but "no tracks at all." At one place they finally found fresh caribou sign, and Marcel trailed and killed one by "workin' all night." They made camp in the mountains and attempted to shoot and snare sufficient rabbits there for the dogs, but there were no rabbits. There were lots of fresh marten tracks, but since there was nothing to feed the dogs with, they could not stay, and they made a hurried return trip to the Mackenzie. They feared that the river might have too much ice for crossing by canoe and yet not be so solidly frozen that they could cross by sled, thus leaving them stranded for an indeterminate period on the opposite side of the river from the village, where food awaited them. Fortunately, however, the river had frozen. "Pretty lucky. Come right across. . . . Altogether eighteen days that trip."

The waning months of cold, March and April, are devoted to the procurement of beaver and muskrat, a major fur crop. Traps for other fur animals are taken up. Gaffing of beaver is illegal, and as the beaver houses destroyed in the process are easily visible to the game warden from the air, it is no longer practiced. At the time of fieldwork the shooting of beaver was also illegal. Shooting is much preferred by the men, since they must chop

Two sprucebark canoes and a handmade canvas canoe returning from the spring beaver hunt.

through thick ice at each visit when using traps. However, shooting can occur only after the ice has broken and the beaver can emerge.

Visiting of traps set under the ice is carried on by dogsled until the final period of fur procurement, the spring hunt, on which the men of the village may be absent for two or three weeks. By this time in April the snow is rapidly melting. Partners start out with dogsleds if snow conditions permit or with pack dogs and backpack. They carry a minimum of food, clothing, and blankets, as the conditions of travel are arduous. Hip boots are worn, since the hunters are traveling over flooded ground much of the time. They visit various lakes and streams, usually ones draining into Lynx Creek, and in the final stages they reach the shores of Lynx Creek, far upstream from the village. By this time this small river has broken, and most of the ice has moved out. Canoes are made, usually from canvas carried by each set of partners. If canvas is lacking, the partners construct a sprucebark canoe. The dogs are turned loose to find their way home; if a man has a surplus of dogs, he will probably take this opportunity to shoot one or two. Pelts are loaded into the canoe, and the men return downstream to the village, picking up a few extra beaver along the way.

Dog team on the melting snow of the Mackenzie River, 1952. Jimmy Sanguez is bringing his wife Mary Louise and their newborn home from the hospital in Fort Simpson. Mary Louise experienced trouble late in her pregnancy, and Jimmy made a hurried dog team trip to Simpson (no radio contact in those days) to the resident doctor, who called in a ski plane to bring Mary Louise to the hospital.

In April the first ducks and geese of the season are sighted, an event which is quickly communicated to all the village. Bears emerge from hibernation. Some men speak of the pleasures of the bush at this time of year, of how "pretty" the birds sing and of the play of beaver kits. In their spare time, men have been whittling net floats and canoe paddles. Last-minute trips to Simpson before breakup must now be made on the Mackenzie ice, as the snow and the lake ice of the portage trail are gone. The ever-growing patches of water at the creek mouths that enter the Mackenzie foreshadow the great movement of the Mackenzie ice and, once again, the advent of summer.

from **The Lynx Point People,** *1961*

FISH CONSUMPTION, RABBIT USES, AND CARIBOU HUNTING AMONG THE DOGRIBS

4

This chapter first expands on the uses of two Northern Dene resources, fish and rabbits, that were touched on in the preceding chapter on the yearly round at the Slavey community of Jean Marie River. The setting here is the Dogrib bush community of Wha Ti, then Lac la Martre, as Nancy Lurie and I documented fish and rabbit use in 1959. The last part of the chapter presents depictions of caribou hunting from the early 1960s back to the 1820s with a fast forward to 1999.

FISH CONSUMPTION

With the introduction of netting twine, fish became a staple in human and dog diet. In fact, in the twentieth century the dog teams of trappers' households could only be sustained by intensive fish production.

At Lac la Martre, as elsewhere in Dene country, the gill net is the prime device for taking fish. Whitefish and trout are the primary food fish, with jackfish, sucker, and loche caught in fewer numbers and less prized. The fishing season begins roughly from the beginning of breakup, variously designated by locals as March, April, or May, and lasts until just after Christmas. It is generally agreed that hardly any fishing is done during January, February, and March because the ice is too thick and "the fish leave the lake." Lac la Martre village is not ideally situated for year-round fishing as it is on a shallow bay of the lake proper, and even where the ice may not freeze to the bottom the fish seek deeper water for more oxygen. According to one person, whitefish leave first, and even at the entrance to the river, where nets can be placed late in the season, only trout are caught. For periods in December and in June only suckers are caught in abundance.

The people at Lac la Martre make close to 100 percent utilization of fish caught as possible. Only rarely and for very short periods are fish excluded from the daily diet. A minimum estimate of human consumption is two fish

daily for a family of two adults and four children, or a total of 730 fish a year. Dogs consume more fish than do people during the year. An average household has a team of five dogs. During the winter season when the dogs are working, each dog is fed one fish per day. Thus, a five-dog team requires some 1,050 fish during the period of about 210 winter days, that is, from October through April. They are fed far less during the 155 nonworking days of summer, the entire team being fed only two or three fish per day—at two per day, a total of 310 fish for the team. Over the course of a year, then, a five dog team may consume about 1,360 fish. The dogs actually eat more fish than this since they are given all entrails, heads, tails, and bones not consumed by human beings. [Unlike at Jean Marie River, the households at Lac la Martre do not have to buy "dog rice" or other supplemental food to keep their teams from starving.]

Observations during several months at Lac la Martre in 1959 indicated that the fish in high frequency averaged eighteen inches and two and a half pounds. (Occasionally, huge trout weighing upward of twenty pounds are caught.) Calculating the 730 fish consumed by human beings and the 1,360 fish consumed by dogs at two and a half pounds each, the grand total for a household as described comes to at least 5,225 pounds of fish consumed per year, or over two and a half tons. The eighteen households at Lac la Martre therefore consume over forty-seven tons of fish per year. This estimate probably errs on the conservative side, since some households possess more than a single team of dogs. However, for periods of a week to a month some families are occasionally able to live on caribou or moose, which reduces fish consumption. Despite this fact, the estimate may still be somewhat too low.

from Helm and Lurie, **The Subsistence Economy of the Dogrib Indians of Lac la Martre,** *1961*

RABBITS

Throughout the subarctic, Indians say, "You can starve on rabbits." Yet "rabbits" had a role in keeping Dene fed and warm, as shown in these passages. Nancy Lurie especially pursued the question of rabbit-skin cordage and clothing, as presented here.

Gah in Dogrib, "rabbit" is the English term applied to the varying hare. Rabbits are obtainable throughout the year and provide a minor semistaple in the diet of the more bush oriented members of the community at Lac la Martre. The usual method of taking rabbits is with snares, but after the snow falls unbaited small animal traps such as are used for peltry animals may also

Mrs. Louis Beaulieu taking fish from her under-the-ice gill net, Lac la Martre, 1959.

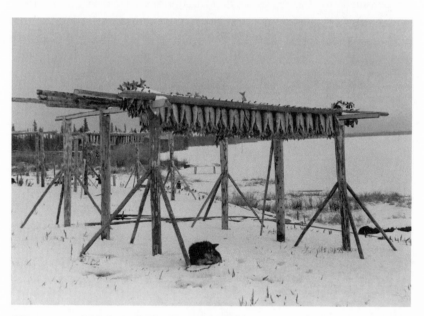

Winter storage of fish for dog food at Marten Lake (Wha Ti), 1959.

be set under the snow in the rabbit runs. One man in the village reportedly set ten such traps besides his twenty snares. Men also hunt rabbit, ptarmigan, and grouse with .22 rifles, while women often take a rifle with them when going out to gather wood in the hope of encountering rabbits en route. Northern Indians comment that the time of the first snowfall is good for hunting rabbits as the pelage of the still-brown rabbits stands out against the white background.

Of the eighteen households at Lac la Martre, four were reported as never setting snares; certainly, five regularly set snares. Both men and women set snares, but it appears to be primarily a task for elderly and middle-aged women. The snares are usually set in the bush close to the settlement, but in August one elderly man paddled across the bay from the village to set out his snare line. The snares are set along the regular runs or trails which the rabbits make through the bush and which can be easily seen summer or winter. The same area may be exploited indefinitely, as the rabbits do not change the course of their runs. The Lac la Martre people reported rabbits as plentiful during the period of study [1959] and said they recalled no complete failure of this game, as has been reported for several years at Good Hope and elsewhere.

In a later year, however, Vital Thomas of Rae said that Dogribs are aware that the hare disappear and then "come back." As Vital told it, "When there are no rabbits, the people say, 'No rabbits, funny!' And then a man from Hislop Lake comes in and a man from Rae Lakes and another from Marten Lake, and they all start to say the same thing: 'The rabbits are coming back.' So we hear the news from all over. And that's the truth. When the rabbits come back, it is like thunder hits the ground, there is a big noise. And when you tell the old people, 'I heard the sound of the rabbits drop,' they say, 'Mahsi, Mahsi, Mahsi, the rabbits are coming back!' "

At Lac la Martre, the reports of snares set by a given person ranged from twelve to thirty, and the daily take ranged from two to five rabbits. The snares are visited every day unless the weather is bad or it is Sunday. Snares are reset if a rabbit is caught. One man complained on one occasion that ravens had raided his snares. Among the Slaveys the black bear was mentioned as a culprit in this regard.

Rabbits are skinned by cutting around the pelt at the head and peeling the pelt off like a sweater. Incisions are made at the feet so that the paws with claws are pulled off with the pelt. Sometimes the heads are severed from the bodies and left attached to the pelt along the back of the neck, but usually the head is left on the animal. The ears are trimmed down when the head pelt is removed. The animal is slit and stripped of viscera except for the heart, lungs, liver, and kidney, which are eaten. Heads with eyes and brains are also eaten. Apparently, the usual method of cooking rabbits is to boil them complete with the edible organs. Little of the animal is wasted, as the entrails are fed to the dogs.

It is impossible to estimate the quantities of rabbits consumed on the basis of available data. As noted, those families which regularly set snares might obtain from two to five rabbits daily, but no count could be kept of the occasional rabbits shot in the course of other activities and added to the larder. A cleaned rabbit, including the weight of bones, does not usually weigh over a pound. It is obvious that these animals are considered a supplementary food that adds variety to the diet but that is inadequate to maintain a family. (Rabbits are ordinarily so lacking in fat that they probably are not a nutritionally adequate flesh food.) Even those households most active in the almost daily snaring of rabbits also set fish nets with the same regularity as those households that did not set rabbit snares.

As far as could be observed, the brown summer pelts are simply discarded, but the white winter pelts may yield a number of by-products, although their use is rapidly diminishing. The skins are left inside out as they are peeled off the rabbits and hung up to dry. They may then be simply pulled over the feet, fur side inside, as a moccasin pac or may be made into rough socks. For the most part, home-knit socks or purchased socks and stockings as well as pacs of duffle cloth have just about completely replaced the rabbit-fur pacs. One infant in the community small enough still to be carried in a moss bag was wrapped about the lower limbs with white rabbit fur which had been placed between the moss packing and the fabric cover of the bag.

Formerly, blankets and underclothing were netted of rabbit-fur yarn or cord. Allegedly, this craft is no longer practiced, but two small blankets were produced by Annie Pig (Mrs. Firmin Pomi) simply to oblige us.

To make rabbit-fur cordage a women holds the pelt, turned fur side in, in her teeth at the head end and with a sharp knife cuts a continuous strip, spiraling the length of the pelt. Leg and paw portions are simply allowed to remain attached to the strip as the spiral is cut around. The strip is twisted as this work is done, and it continues to twist as a result of the drying of the pelt, which is worked on when it is freshly peeled or is dampened to be cut. The strip thus forms a completely furred, twisted cord. If the strip is cut about an inch wide, a single rabbit pelt will yield about four feet of completed rabbit-fur cordage. The final twisting of the strip is accomplished by

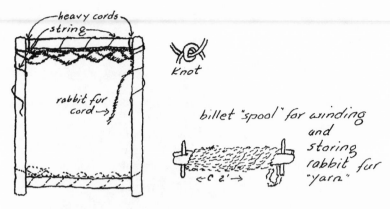

Rabbit-fur netting technique. Drawing by Nancy O. Lurie.

either twisting it around a piece of commercial cord and pulling the cord out later or simply twisting it tightly by hand. One strip is spliced to the next by cutting a slit in the end of one strip, drawing the end of the next strip through it, folding it back, and twisting the splice tightly.

To carry out netting, heavy cords are tied to the upper corners of a rectangular pole frame which is set up in a vertical position against any handy support. A string is attached to one of the corner cords and wound around the top pole of the frame with spaces of about two inches between each successive spiral of the string and about half an inch of clearance between the bottom of each successive twist of the string and the bottom side of the pole. (See illustration.) The string is then secured to the heavy cord at the other upper corner. Strings are attached to the heavy corner cords and allowed to hang free for use as work progresses. Ordinary commercial string and cord are used. The rabbit-fur cordage, dampened for work if not still wet, is tied to the heavy cord at one corner and passed through the spiral of the string around the top pole. Working from left to right, when the rabbit-fur cordage has been drawn to the far right, the dependent string there is looped around it to hold it to the side of the frame in the same manner by which it is secured by loops along the top. The twisted fur strip is then carried to the left: at about two-inch intervals the furred cord is taken around the above line of furred cord and secured at each interval by a double looping or knot pulled as tight as possible. When this second row is completed it is secured to the left side by being looped through with the dependent string, which is then wrapped about the left pole of the frame by one turn. The process continues back and forth, producing a diamond-shaped mesh. The shape of the mesh, however, is obscured by the thick fur. The blanket is finished off at the

"Rabbit-skin [Hare] Indian boy" in netted rabbit-skin outfit, Fort Good Hope, 1921. Mary Saich Collection, Northwest Territories Archives.

bottom by looping string at intervals, as it is wound about the poles, through the final row of fur cordage. The bottom corners are automatically secured to the bottom of the frames by looping of string along the sides of the bottom. The netting is allowed to dry on the frame for a day or so until its shape is set and the strips of twisted rabbit-skin cordage have shrunk taut and hard.

Annie Pig's specimen blankets were each made of fifteen rabbit pelts and were about two by four feet in size. Blankets were formerly made of sixty or seventy pelts, it was said, and were the size of a double bed blanket. The netting technique was used to make underwear, jackets, and pants or leggings. Presumably, these garments were fashioned of a number of separately made rectangular sections of netting which were sewn together rather than netted to the shape of the garments in one piece. The jackets were open down the front and held together with ties. Although such garments have been replaced by commercially made underclothing, persons in their late forties and early fifties in 1959 recalled wearing them when young.

fom Helm and Lurie, **The Subsistence Economy of the Dogrib Indians of Lac la Martre,** *1961*

CARIBOU

The two large animals on which the Canadian Dene have always relied for food and clothing are the moose and the barren-ground caribou. (The woodland caribou are only thinly distributed.) The people along the Mackenzie River, such as the Jean Marie River ("Lynx Point") people, are preeminently moose hunters. Moose are to be found in all the forested areas exploited by all the northern Dene. In contrast, the barren-ground caribou have a more restricted range in Dene lands. In winter they forage in the forest lands (taiga) rimming the barren grounds (tundra) that extend from the northwestern quadrant of the shores of Hudson Bay to the Arctic Ocean. The summer pasturage and the calfing grounds of the caribou are in the full tundra, which is beyond the Dene exploitive zone. As fall approaches, the caribou move toward the tree line. Usually they are in their general wintering areas in the open subarctic forest by early December. The winter range of the caribou extends, from northwest to southeast, from the Anderson River and the lakes that feed its headwaters, through the lands between Great Bear Lake and the east arm of Great Slave Lake, and then on to the lands bracketed by Lake Athabaska and Wholdaia Lake and beyond, still trending southeastward (Kelsall 1968: map 1). This broad range corresponds to that part of open subarctic forest that is designated the Northwest Transitional section of the Canadian boreal forest region (Rowe 1972). Throughout their winter habitat the barren-ground caribou were the main major prey of the Hare, the bygone Yellowknife, the Chipewyan, and the Dogrib Dene.

The contrastive habits of the solitary moose and migratory herds of barren-ground caribou not only encourage but require distinctive organization of the hunters and groups relying on these two members of the deer family, thus the single or paired moose hunters of Jean Marie River and the multiple crews of Dogrib hunters from Rae pursuing the caribou.

THE DOGRIB FALL CARIBOU HUNT, EARLY 1960S

Among the Dogribs, "in August, we eat mostly fish"; a two-week run of fish allows the people once again to rely on fish for their daily food. The prime excitement in August, however, is the fall caribou hunt.

In August the barren-ground caribou approach the tree line, coming in small bands from their summer pasturage in the tundra. Dogrib hunters head for the edge of the woods to arrive by the end of August. They are eager to meet the caribou as soon as possible, because only on the August skins is the hair right, "not too thick and not too light," for making furred caribou parkas. Hunters travel in several "crews." A crew may consist of ten or twelve men in two or three canoes or five or six men in a single canoe. From Rae, where crews assemble, there are two alternate water routes leading to Snare Lake and another that follows the Emile River. These routes take the hunters northeast from Rae to the edge of the trees along the lakes feeding the Coppermine River. (A route following the Yellowknife River was once common for the Yellowknife Dogribs, but apparently [as of 1962] they are likely to join mixed Chipewyan-Dogrib populations along the east arm of Great Slave Lake on yet another route, more southerly, to the barren grounds. Sometimes a crew or two from the Rae join them.) Crews going the same route travel together until they approach the hunting grounds.

The journey to the hunting grounds involves many portages, which the men cross at a fast dogtrot, carrying canoes, outboard motors, gas, and other supplies. Each portage usually requires a couple of trips by most of the men to get all the gear across. Dogribs take pride in being good travelers, starting early, traveling long and fast, sleeping little. The Snare River–Snare Lake route to the hunting grounds has forty-seven portages and is over one hundred air miles from Rae, probably almost two hundred overland. It is sometimes covered in five days, all upstream.

Each crew has a *k'awo*, or "boss." While a set of crews are together, one *k'awo* is in charge of all. A *k'awo* decides when to camp and travel and, once caribou are encountered, determines the directions in which small parties of two or three hunters fan out. As Jimmy Fish described it: "When a bunch goes on a caribou hunt, they work just like they are own brothers. If one

Portaging at the edge of the barrens on the fall caribou hunt, out of Rae, 1959. Photo by Jean Amourous.

man is short [of supplies], they help one another until they get back. They don't charge nothing. And if some poor man is too loaded [on the portages], the *k'awo* is going to tell them, 'He's pitiful. He's a poor man to work, so you might as well give him a hand.'" A successful hunter may be directed by the *k'awo* to hunt with a man who has killed little. If one group of hunters encounters many caribou, word is carried to the *k'awo*, who in turn sends word to the other scattered groups.

Once enough caribou have been killed or the season has advanced, the *k'awo* directs the groups of men to spread out in various small bays and creeks where there are sufficient stands of willow to make drymeat. With the water content reduced, much more meat can be transported home. Drymeat is made by slicing chunks of flesh into thin slabs. The slabs are then hung over poles and turned every hour. A smoldering fire of willows and moss under the meat hastens the drying process and drives off flies. From a successful hunt each man takes home a "bale" of drymeat as heavy as he can carry, a "bale" of skins, and perhaps some marrow encased in a sewn birchbark box.

The fall caribou hunt lasts only three or four weeks. The Dogrib hunters hurry back to their families, who await them at the fort or in fishing camps.

It is now September, and if the men delay at the edge of the woods they may get caught in the early freezeup there. The drymeat brought home by

Fish camp of women and children on Marian River awaiting the return of the caribou hunters, out of Rae, 1959.

the hunter lasts only a few days, for custom calls for the hunter to serve cooked meat in his home to those who come and to give away portions.

from "The Dogrib Indians," 1972

HUNTING RESTRICTIONS

During the Dogrib Treaty parley at Rae on July 2, 1962, Game Warden Gene Earl speaks through an interpreter and a discussion, verging on a hassle, follows. The gist of Earl's speech is: "The population of the caribou is still on the downgrade. Don't kill fawns and cows. Report any caribou you see with ear tags—tell us the day and where you saw them. If you kill a caribou, save the lower jaw and bring it in."

Johnny Simpson, a middle-aged, first-rate hunter: "I am going to the barrens soon. What am I supposed to do about cows?"

Earl: "Cows are off-limits the year round."

Johnny Simpson: "I'm going out anyway. I am my own boss." [The apparent implication is that he will kill what he pleases.] "If there are lots of caribou, then I won't kill cows."

A general babble ensues; the men seem very pleased with Johnny's response. In response to this expression of attitude, Earl explains (what he has no doubt said dozens of times before): "If you don't kill the cows and calves, that will allow the herds to increase again."

Alexis Charlot, councillor for the town-dwelling Dogribs of Rae: [We can't hear all of the interpreter's translation, but part of Alexis's speech goes:] "In winter there is not much point in shooting calves; there is not much meat in them anyway. In summer their coats aren't good enough."

Chief Bruneau: "I never agreed not to shoot cows and calves." (A few cheers, "Hey, hey," from men in the audience.) "We depend on caribou in winter. Caribou are ours."

Earl: "What about future generations? Maybe they will want caribou, and there won't be any."

Chief Bruneau: "In the old days, everyone thought of caribou. Now, the young ones hang out in bars—that's all they ever think about." ("Hey, hey" of approval from Indians throughout) . . . [We can't hear parts of the interpreter's translation.] . . . "You fellows don't give us anything. . . . We are all living on the caribou. . . . We haven't got any money. We get out in the bush, get a little meat, that's what we eat. You guys all got jobs. You walk in a restaurant and buy food with your money. Out there, the caribou is our money."

Chief Bruneau then changes the topic, asking a question about the dates for Treaty at other forts. *from the 1962 field notes*

A CARIBOU KILL IN 1864

Almost one hundred years before the Dogrib hunters' "discussion" with the game warden, in late May 1864 the missionary Emile Petitot found himself in the midst of a caribou slaughter. In his words:

The cry, "Caribou! Caribou!" goes up. [Petitot emerged from his tent in a Dogrib encampment to see at the western extremity of the lake he calls Eau-glacée] a long file of caribou moving toward the mountains. They are returning to their [summer pastures in the] high and barren lands.

Twenty hunters spread around the frozen lake and attacked the antlered mass from several points, firing into the pack. At the sound of the firing, the caribou broke apart and scampered like young colts. They did not go far. The stupid beasts stopped again and looked around curiously with the great eyes of gazelles. They appeared to regret their cowardice. The hunters cried, "Hou! Hou!" cupping their hands to make their voices carry. The caribou retraced their steps, coming straight at the hunters, who fired directly, the fire crossing at several points. Several caribou fell; the others dispersed only to form up again farther on. Meanwhile, the Dogribs decimated them. The larger the herd, the more the caribou seemed to have confidence in themselves and to ignore danger.

Then the hunters are on the lake. Only then do the caribou comprehend. They have seen their enemy, they have been dazzled by the flash of guns, they have smelled the powder and have scented blood. Bewildered, terror-stricken, they fled in all directions, dashing into the woods, scaling the rocks. Some of them run through the camp, mouths open, showing a foot of black tongue. They passed before my eyes faster than the arrows that the children shot at them. One was struck down amid the bursts of laughter and the transports of the women.

The Dogribs call the caribou *nonteli*, the travelers, the nomads. But the generic name for caribou is *ekfwen*, flesh. Are they not the daily food, the very subsistence of these eastern Dene?

from Petitot, **Autour du Grand Lac des Esclaves,** *1891, abridged, my translation*

HUNTING TECHNIQUES OF THE 1820S

Capt. John Franklin was one of those excess British naval officers who took to exploration after Napoleon's defeat rendered them superfluous for the defense of the realm. Franklin's account of his first expedition, Narrative of a Journey to the Shores of the Polar Sea in the Years 1819–20–21–22, *from which the following excerpt is taken, provides the kind of description seldom found in the records of the on-the-ground fur traders on whom explorers relied and from whom they got much of their information. Chapter 12 presents Akaitcho, the Copper Indian leader on whom Franklin equally relied.*

The Copper Indians [Yellowknives] kill the rein-deer [caribou] in the summer with a gun, or taking advantage of a favourable disposition of the ground, they enclose a herd upon a neck of land, and drive them into a lake, where they fall an easy prey; but in the rutting season and in the spring, when they are numerous on the skirts of the woods, they catch them in snares. The snares are simple nooses, formed in a rope made of twisted sinew [not sinew, babiche], which are placed in the aperture of a slight hedge, constructed of the branches of trees. The hedge is disposed so as to form several winding compartments, and although it is by no means strong, yet the deer seldom attempt to break through it. The herd is led into the labyrinth by two converging rows of poles, and one is generally caught at each end of the openings

Dogrib caribou snare of three-ply twisted babiche (rawhide line), coil diameter six inches. Of his stay with the Dogribs in 1893–94, Frank Russell (1898: 179) writes, "These [caribou snares] are now used as a last resort when ammunition cannot be obtained. I saw but two in the country." Frank Russell Collection, University of Iowa Natural History Museum.

by the noose placed there. The hunter, too, lying in ambush, stabs some of them with his bayonet as they pass by, and the whole herd frequently becomes his prey. [See "The Copper Woman" legend in chapter 15.] Where wood is scarce, a piece of turf turned up answers the purpose of a pole to conduct them towards the snares.

The Copper Indians find by experience that a white dress attracts [the caribou] most readily, and they often succeed in bringing them within shot, by kneeling and vibrating the gun from side to side, in imitation of the motion of a deer's horns when he is in the act of rubbing his head against a stone.

The Dogrib Indians have a mode of killing these animals, which though simple, is very successful. It was thus described by Mr. Wentzel [a trader of the North West Company], who resided long amongst that people. The hunters go in pairs, the foremost man carrying in one hand the horns and part of the skin of the head of a deer, and in the other a small bundle of twigs, against which he, from time to time, rubs the horns, imitating the gestures peculiar to the animal. His comrade follows treading exactly in his footsteps and holding the guns of both in a horizontal position, so that the muzzles project under the arms of him who carries the head. Both hunters have a fillet of white skin round their foreheads, and the foremost has a strip of the same kind round his wrists. They approach the herd by degrees raising the legs very slowly, but setting them down somewhat suddenly, after the manner of a deer, and always taking care to lift their right or left feet simultaneously. If any of the herd leave off feeding to gaze upon this extraordinary phenomenon, it instantly stops, and the head begins to play its part by licking its shoulder, and performing other necessary movements. In this way, the hunters attain the very centre of the herd without exciting suspicion, and have leisure to single out the fattest. The hindmost man then pushes forward his comrade's gun, the head is dropped, and they both fire nearly at the same instant. The herd scampers off, the hunters trot after them; in a short time the poor animals halt to ascertain the cause of the terror, their foes stop at the same instant, and having loaded as they ran, greet the grazers with a second fatal discharge. The consternation of the deer increases, they run to and fro in the utmost confusion, and sometimes a great part of the herd is destroyed within the space of a few hundred yards.

from Franklin, **Narrative of a Journey,** *1824, 2: 8–11, abridged*

Update: The Hunt of 1999   For two days in mid-September of 1999, Tom Andrews (subarctic archaeologist of the Northern Heritage Centre in Yellowknife) "had the pleasure of joining one of the Dogrib fall caribou hunts in the barrenlands." From his detailed account I have here excerpted passages that point up the striking play between change and continuity in the hunt through time.

Hunts organized by the band councils of the four Dogrib communities [Rae-Edzo, Wha Ti, Gamiti, and Wekweti] were taking place at the same time and in the same general area. The camp locations had been chosen carefully the week before. Hunters first referred to satellite maps distributed weekly to the communities by the Department of Resources, Wildlife, and Economic Development (RWED), which show the locations of 14 collared caribou cows. These are usually posted on a bulletin board near the band office and always attract lots of attention. The RWED study is designed to examine the impacts of recent diamond mine exploration and development on the Bathurst Caribou herd, which numbers nearly 350,000 animals. The satellite transmitters on the collars send signals once every five days for six hours. The location data are downloaded by biologists in Yellowknife and maps are prepared and sent to the communities. Once a general location was chosen, the bands then chartered a small plane to scout for caribou and, ultimately, specific locations for the camps. The caribou are widely distributed in small groups ranging in size from a few animals to thousands, over an area of many thousands of square miles. The preparation in locating suitable sites is necessary because the bands use expensive aircraft charters to move hunters and camp supplies to the caribou. In contrast, just a generation ago hunters traveled to the barrenlands by canoe and were consequently much more mobile and able to cover large distances in pursuit of caribou. With the use of aircraft, the camps are set up at locations where caribou are fairly numerous and hunters range from camp on foot. Consequently it is important to choose areas where sufficient numbers of caribou are moving through to make a successful hunt.

Though the satellite maps provide current data regarding the distribution of the herd, it really only parallels Dogrib traditional knowledge of caribou movements and behaviour. Indeed the camp we visited had been used over many generations and the lakes and features in the area all have Dogrib place names. [For example,] Grizzly Bear Lake (known as Diga Ti, or "wolf lake" in Dogrib) is located on a traditional canoe route used to access the summer/fall hunting areas. Consequently it was no surprise that we located two archaeological sites during our visit. One . . . consisted of an old stone ring measuring 4 metres in diameter (used perhaps to anchor the covering of a caribou skin lodge), a grave (surrounded by a picket fence, and consequently dating to the twentieth century), and the remains of three birchbark canoes. Based on the state of preservation, the canoes are likely less than 100 years old. There were also a small number of stone flakes scattered throughout the site indicating a potentially much older use. A second site was located on a high bedrock hill . . . where we found a large surface scatter of stone flakes. The hunters we were traveling with had stopped there to rest and look for caribou. In discussing the site, the hunters felt confident that the flakes were the result of an ancestor from long ago sitting on the top of the hill passing his time by working on a stone tool while looking for caribou. It was interesting to reflect on these two episodes, separated by time and vast differences in technology, yet linked by the knowledge of the area passed down through the generations.

from a letter from Thomas D. Andrews of September 23, 1999

THE SECURITY QUEST AT "LYNX POINT," JEAN MARIE RIVER, 1951–1952

5

A return to Lynx Point offers a view of the level of living of the fur-trapping families of the Mackenzie region, their needs, and the economic pressures on them at mid-century.

MODE AND STANDARD OF LIVING

Today [1951–52] a blend of a subsistence and a money economy exists at Lynx Point. The single area of need most nearly provided for from the natural environment is that of nutriment. If the flesh foods that are obtained by the hunting, fishing, and snaring activities were removed from the present diet, the remaining items of consumption would not suffice to maintain life. Impressionistic observations of eating habits suggest that at least half of the total food intake by volume is wild flesh or fish. Most of the remaining intake is of starches in the form of commercial flour, rolled oats, and homegrown potatoes. At Lynx Point potatoes are the only nonpurchased vegetable food of any significance in the diet; in volume of consumption they rank well below flour products. Commercial lard consumption accounts for a substantial portion of the intake of fats.

Items of material use are derived as secondary products from the game animals. Moose and caribou hides are one of the most important of the by-products, primarily for the manufacture of mitts and moccasins and for the babiche netting of snowshoes. Occasionally, babiche is still used for lines, lashings, and snares. Sinew is employed in sewing hides. Bones of large animals have a minor use in the preparation of tanning solution and in manufacturing fleshers or scrapers. Rabbit skins are occasionally fashioned into children's vests and foot wrappings. Duck feathers may be saved to serve as filler for outdoor sleeping bags. As a substitute for babiche, the skin of the loche may be used in the manufacture of temporary snowshoes. Porcupine quills, aniline dyed, serve for moccasin decoration.

Fur animals, procured primarily for the market, provide some subsistence as well. The flesh of the lynx, beaver, and muskrat is often eaten if the animal is freshly dead. Sometimes carcasses of furbearers may be fed to the dogs. Of minor importance is the use of furs for trimming on parkas, mitts, and moccasins and the employment of beaver and rat castor as bait for those and other fur animals.

Of the flora of the region, only the trees are of major importance in the subsistence economy. Other plants provide only such relative minor products as diaper padding and cabin chinking (moss) and food treats (berries and wild onions). Certainly, the most vital of all the uses to which the trees of the surrounding forest are put is that of fuel for warmth and cooking. With the exception of one or two gasoline camp stoves, used but rarely, the people are completely dependent upon the forest for fuel. Logs for the cabins and cache-houses are another major product of the forests; however, if need be, people are able to live quite comfortably year-round in canvas tents. Twenty years ago [about 1930], lumber for roofs, floors, plank scows, and suchlike was whip-sawed from logs by hand, but today it is purchased ready-made.

Other objects handmade from wood include snowshoe frames, axe handles, paddles, net floats, net-weaving needles, sawhorses, ladders, and fur-stretching boards. Poles are put to myriad uses, as frames for hide preparation, hoops for stretching beaver skins, cooking tripods over outdoor fires, tent poles and stakes, and drying and cache racks and in the construction of snares and deadfalls. Large logs are employed as rollers for beaching and launching the group-owned powerboat and barge, and two capstans are made of short logs of massive girth. Occasionally, the men make spruce-bark canoes to return from the spring hunt. Wood ribs, thwarts, and gunwales are made, and the sheathing bark for the canoe is peeled in one large piece from the spruce tree and sewed up at each end with spruce roots. Moss and spruce gum plug branch holes in the bark.

The bush provides fuel and a substantial portion of nutriment, but in other areas of consumption the trading post and the mail-order house today contribute much more heavily than does the natural environment. The Lynx Point people are thoroughly enmeshed in the market economy. They are never at a loss to know what to do with money, but their desires are often checked by a lack of sufficient income.

As the men do the family shopping, they are the most cognizant of prices and their fluctuations. They are avid bargain hunters insofar as the limited trading facilities allow. The fact that a particular brand of sunglasses was for sale at three different prices in the four trading establishments of the area was

Chinking a new cabin with moss. Madelaine Romi at Wha Ti, Lac la Martre, 1959.

an item of comment, and each price could be quoted. Any drop or rise in the prices of commercial foods or other goods is one of the major items of news after a return from town. A new purchase by an individual will be discussed thoroughly: the price is quoted by the purchaser; others often volunteer the amount paid for similar articles in their possession; prices of former years may be recalled; and so on.

Sprucebark canoe. Louis Norwegian (in picture) and Jimmy Sanguez made the canoe to return from the spring beaver hunt, Jean Marie River, 1952.

Interior of sprucebark canoe, Jean Marie River, 1952. A coiled withe is in the nose and in the stern. Nails hold the thwarts to the gunwales. Loose sheets of bark lie in the bottom. See also the photos of Dogrib birchbark canoes in chapter 9.

Flour, lard, tea, and sugar are the basic food purchases; they provide the bannock and tea that, with fish and the flesh of country game, are the dietary staples. Rolled oats or package macaroni-and-cheese dinners serve as occasional substitutes. Yeast is usually kept on hand, primarily for making home brew, but some women employ it in baking bread at fairly frequent intervals. Households with small children usually purchase powdered milk for the younger ones. Molasses and currants are bought in small, steady quantities, for, along with sugar and yeast, they are the standard brew makings.

Consumption of other commercial foods, such as canned butter, meat, fruit, and vegetables, is scant. For most families this is due to a disinclination to spend scarce money for what are considered luxury foods. In the winter the problem of transporting any large amount of these foods from the fort is a subsidiary deterrent. In the spring there is a limited consumption of "fresh stuff" from the newly supplied traders. A man usually brings a pound or two of candy for his children when returning from the trading post. There is a steady purchase of fine-cut tobacco for cigarettes and pipes. Two or three packs of "tailor-mades" are often purchased as a treat from town. Only the men smoke regularly.

All households possess axes and hatchets, files, knives, and saws. For the pursuit of his livelihood, each man has a set of traps, a rifle or preferably two (.22 and .30-30) and perhaps a shotgun, and a "sleigh" (toboggan) and dog harness. Today toboggans are purchased, though knowledge of their manufacture (such as the steaming and bending process) still exists among the older men and would probably be reverted to in a time of extreme penury. Other necessary expenditures are for ammunition and for twine for fish nets. To save money, nets are usually handwoven rather than purchased ready-made.

Most adult men own a commercial canvas canoe or perhaps a plank skiff, usually homemade from purchased lumber. The latter can be propelled only by an outboard motor; the larger canoe with a flat stern is also designed for use with a kicker. At present, out of the nine households, only four outboard motors are owned at Lynx Point. Most men have owned several in the past; outboard motors usually have a life of only a few years. Upon the demise of one kicker it may be several years, dependent upon fur prices and other needs, before an individual can afford the investment of $250 to $400 for a new one. Gas and oil for the kicker are further items of expenditure, and occasionally spare parts must be ordered from "outside." A few mattocks, shovels, and hoes for gardening are individually owned in the community.

In the construction of the house itself, purchased items include nails, milled lumber for roofs and floors, window sashes and glass, doors, tar paper

Interior furnishings of a log cabin, Jean Marie River, 1952. David Gargan is in the hammock. His sister Laura sits near the door.

roofing, and rolls of heavy paper for indoor wind proofing. Every house has one or more cast-iron stoves for heating and cooking, one or two gas lanterns, a chair or two, one or more tables and cupboards (often homemade from purchased planks), beds of wood slats, with perhaps one iron bedstead and springs, perhaps a mattress, one or more small trunks for clothing and storage, blankets and comforters, and curtains made from yard goods. All cooking, eating, and drinking utensils are purchased. Galvanized pails and forty-five-gallon oil drums serve for water portage and storage. Women have ember-heated flatirons or, in one case, a gas-run iron, scrub boards, and tubs, and several own small hand-cranked sewing machines. For summer, every family owns a canvas tent and mosquito bars (curtains of cheesecloth sewn into an open-bottomed box form under which one sleeps).

For home sewing, cloth, thread, needles, rickrack, and embroidery silk are purchased. For wet weather, everyone must have rubbers or rubber boots to protect moccasins, and in the spring the men require waders (hip boots) of canvas, rubber, or (a recently discovered substitute) plastic. Most men have owned one or more "good" wristwatches ($30 to $60) and wear rings

Johnny Sanguez with violin, Jean Marie River, 1952. His brother Gabriel is behind him in the pilot house of the powerboat.

(usually costing from $10 to $30). Various small items of adornment are purchased: cosmetics, barrettes, and ribbons for girls, for boys and men, barrettes and brooches for their caps, silk scarves, studded belts, and the like. Observations indicated that in most households more money is spent on the man's clothes than on the wife's or child's. A man's rigorous outdoor life, of course, demands a greater supply of clothing, but the men are the "snappy dressers" of the society, and they buy clothing for dash, style, and novelty as well as for utility.

A number of expenditures contribute primarily to enjoyment and recreation. Into this category fall such purchases as guitars, violins, concertinas, and harmonicas, phonographs and records, inexpensive cameras, and radios, the latter requiring [in the early 1950s] further expenditures on large batteries, tubes, and licenses. Young men and boys buy boxing gloves, soccer balls, Flexible Flyer sleds, ice skates, and "cowboy" cap pistol sets. In Fort Simpson, the Saturday night movie is a minor recreation expense. Once or twice a year, the men usually have opportunities to indulge in bootlegged liquor or beer sprees (perhaps spending $50 or more) or in high-stake poker games, in which upward of $75 may change hands. One other expenditure that should be classed as primarily recreational is that for brew makings. One to three pots a month are made in each household.

ECONOMIC PROBLEMS

The Lynx Point people are eager to maintain their present standard of living and, if possible, to better it. But their present mode of economic life is such that they can see few guarantees of stability at the present level or of advancement in the future. The several factors that make for this insecurity are of two sorts: those stemming from the ecology of the natural environment and those springing from the money and market economy of the greater world. These security problems find frequent voice among the men of the community, and their responses range from impotent railing at the game laws and "the government" to attempts at long-term planning that have led to the joint purchase and building and operation of a powerboat and barge.

FOOD

Since the Lynx Point community relies heavily on fish and game of the bush for sustenance, a decrease in supply means that there must be an increased expenditure of ever-scarce money for store foods if consumption standards are to be maintained. This leaves less money to fulfill other wants. Also, the isolation of the community prevents a quick and easy supplementing of the larder from the store, even if money is at hand. In point of fact, a shortage of flesh foods usually means a decrease in food consumption, although the intake of bannock may be stepped up in partial compensation (in volume, at least, if not in terms of nutrition). Besides these objective considerations, the likes and dislikes of the people lead them to reject most canned foods in favor of wild flesh. Although considered tasty by most, canned fruits and vegetables in their eyes are not real food. They do not fill one as meat and bannock do, and canned meat "tastes terrible." Certainly, no one who has attempted to eat only canned meats for several months will argue this point.

What are the present-day ecological conditions affecting the food supply? Fish and rabbits are normally the backbone of the meat diet—they assure a daily supply of flesh food. But the rabbits are subject to a rising and falling in population. In some years they may be almost unobtainable. There appears to be a major population cycle of ten years peak to peak. During 1952 a marked fluctuation occurred. On my rearrival at the community in March I was repeatedly informed that rabbits were very abundant, yet by our departure in August the people were commenting on their scarcity. Letters informed me that they were scarce all the following winter. The summer of 1955 was another period of scarcity. The only conjecture obtained regarding this marked decrease was that the rabbits had "moved" to an area many miles downstream, where they were reported to be plentiful.

Fish are subject to seasonal and yearly fluctuation, and we have at least one report of their actual failure. Spring, with its bluefish and sucker runs, is the most bountiful season for taking fish from the river; winter is the least. In establishing a permanent village on the main transportation route—the Mackenzie—the people of Lynx Point, like many present-day bush bands, have relinquished the benefits of living at an inland lake, for these lakes are much richer in fish than are the rivers. Knowledge of "the old days" suggests that the aboriginal pattern was to winter at a "fish lake," thus assuring a food supply. At the fish lakes there is almost always enough fish for human beings and their dogs. It is to supplement the insufficient supply of river fish that the Lynx Point men go to the "fall fishery" on Great Slave Lake, but even there the yield is in some years insufficient for the winter's needs.

Other small game, including those trapped furbearers considered edible, are obtained only sporadically or seasonally and cannot, except for beaver, be counted as an important article of diet.

Of the three kinds of big game, two are available only in certain seasons. Bear is rarely taken during the winter months of hibernation. Woodland caribou may be encountered in the winter when some traplines take men into the area frequented by these animals, but the riverine hunting required in summer months does not bring the hunter into contact with the caribou. The barren-ground caribou are likewise available only in the winter if their migration brings them into the Horn Mountains. The pair of partners whose trapline runs out to the Horn Mountain region watch for this advent. Some years, and 1952 was such a year, the barren-ground caribou do not come at all. In other years the discovery of a large herd may provide twenty or thirty animals, enough meat for rich eating for the whole community for a month or more.

The moose is the major big game animal of the region. Of all the flesh foods, it is the most highly valued. The delight and excitement, manifested in random running and crying of the news, with which the women and children greet the advent of fresh moose meat reflect the value placed upon it. Its indispensable hide contributes to its value as well. The years of 1951 and 1952 were not considered to have been adequate in moose. Summer tends to be a poor time for taking moose, as they can be hunted only along the Mackenzie and tributary streams.

Marcel, recalling earlier years, stated that moose are markedly fewer in the area than they were about twenty years ago. At that time, one would hear men firing at moose "two or three times a day." They were so plentiful that the dogs were fed on their flesh, a thing never done today. The nadir in the supply of moose was reached about five years ago; the present-day take is considered a substantial improvement. There are probably a number of eco- logical factors within the bush, the wolf-moose relationship, for example, that may have played a part in the decline of the moose population. Two elements in the human ecology, however, may also have contributed to the situation. First, the community has been established for over forty years—it seems likely that over this period the moose of the surrounding area are being progressively hunted out. Aggravating this, the population has quadrupled from the time of establishment of the permanent village. Over the years, more and more moose must be slain if a given standard of consumption per individual is to be maintained. It appears to be a vicious circle. The game laws, limiting the take in the region to one moose to one licensed hunter each year, are, of course, an attempt on the part of the government to regu- late the harvesting of moose in accord with the moose population. This law has no effect upon the human population, however, except occasionally during the summer, when a visit from the game warden is likely. There was no evidence that the hunters ever spared a moose when it could be taken safely. The quota on moose is bitterly resented and seen as another cruel blight visited by the government upon the helpless Indian. In justice, it must be recognized that strict observance of this regulation would work a severe hardship.

In some men, pride and enjoyment in hunting and appreciation of wild meat are doubtlessly so strong that they would by preference always take much of their sustenance from the bush. Other men appear to find little interest and challenge in bush life and, given an ample supply of money, would probably cease most of their hunting activities. They, along with some of the women and especially the children, would welcome an increased va- riety and consumption of store-bought food, if it could be attained without sacrificing their desires for other types of commercial products.

In sum, we may say that the Lynx Point people do not always obtain as much food from the environment as they need or desire and that they have no assurance that their needs will in the future be met. The food supply for next month and next year is always unpredictable.

THE SUPPLY AND CONSERVATION OF FURBEARERS

Over the past years, the most important furbearers in the Lynx Point area, on the basis of market value and abundance, have been beaver, mink, marten, lynx, and red and cross fox. In rating the Greater Simpson region (including the posts of Liard and Wrigley) against seven other major fur areas of the Mackenzie district, M. J. and J. L. Robinson (1946) designate Simpson as a fine fur area; "this section . . . ranks first in the production of beaver, marten, and lynx, the more valuable furs [at midcentury]."

Several of the furbearers of the Mackenzie region are subject to cyclical fluctuations in population. Beaver is apparently an exception; marten has been too much reduced through overtrapping to permit analysis of possible population cycles. Lynx evidently has a ten-year cycle of abundance which is correlated with the cyclic abundance of rabbits. Mink appears to have a seven- to nine-year cycle. Fox apparently has a ten-year cycle. The regional totals for ermine fluctuate, with slight peaks occurring every two or three years. It is likely that at least some types of furbearers are affected by certain climatic variations as well. No cycle for muskrat is given by the Robinsons. The 1952 spring muskrat catch at Lynx Point was very low and had been predicted by the Indians, for they had seen few muskrats the previous summer. Marcel attributed the muskrat decline to high water during freezeup the previous autumn, caused by the ice forming so high on the riverbanks that the muskrats, trapped under the ice, perished in their holes.

These population cycles, of course, in themselves may affect the earnings of the trappers. The current fur price trends, however, must always be considered in conjunction with amount of fur production. The very high prices during the war years coincided with what was apparently a peak (culminating in 1944−45) in the lynx population. This was an important factor in the high income of the Indian trapper in these years. Lynx were plentiful in the 1951−52 season (probably again approaching the peak in the cycle), but prices were so low that Lynx Point men did not consider it worthwhile to take advantage of the situation; they set few traps for lynx. In instances of this sort, the market has altered the tempo of the fur catch in the Mackenzie region, either accelerating or decelerating it in accord with good or poor fur prices. In other words, the amount of a particular fur taken in any year is not necessarily in direct ratio to the abundance of that fur.

Charles Sanguez's fur take, Jean Marie River, 1952. Jimmy Sanguez, left, has a lynx pelt over his shoulder and holds two mink skins. Charles, center, and Louis Norwegian, right, display marten pelts.

An additional factor affecting the catch of beaver and marten has been the imposition of quotas on these furs by game authorities to combat the decline in population through overtrapping. Fur quotas on beaver were first instituted in the Mackenzie region in 1928 and on marten in 1936. Toward the end of World War II, beaver and marten were "closed" for several years in some of the region, including the Lynx Point area. A steep drop in income hit Lynx Point in consequence of this, for the trappers had been profiting greatly from the high fur prices of wartime. In 1952 the Lynx Point community was allotted a beaver catch of two hundred per year, predicated on the number of beaver lodges in the area. Marten is limited seasonally to five or ten per trapper, depending on the location of his lines. Seals for the allotted beaver and marten are distributed by the game wardens, and one must be affixed to each pelt before it can be accepted by a trader.

The limitations imposed on these two furs are evaded to some extent by the practice of "buying seals." A trapper who has taken beaver or marten in excess agrees to give a cut of the fur sale to a less successful trapper, who sells the fur using his extra seals. The usual cut ratio for beaver is at present about one fifth of the sale. As it was explained, if the pelt sells for $15, the owner of the seal receives $3; if the pelt sells for $25, the seal owner's cut is $5.

As with restrictions on food animals, the efforts of the conservation authorities are little appreciated. There is unpredictability and instability in the supply of furbearers, but the major source of insecurity for the Lynx Point trapper springs not from the realm of supply but from the operation of the fur market.

SOURCES OF INCOME

For the Lynx Point people, as for practically all Indians in Canada's northland, the trapping and selling of furs is the major source of income. There are few other means of making a living in this region.

For many Indian households the "family allowance" provides an income second in amount only to the fur trade. Since 1944 the Canadian government has paid a monthly bonus for every Canadian child at the rate (in 1951–52) of $5 a month for children under six, $6 for children from six to nine years, $7 from ten to twelve, and $8 from thirteen through fifteen years. Thus a family with four children, one in each age group, would receive a yearly income of $312 from the government. The bonus is paid by check, and the traders who cash the checks and sell the goods must see that only food and other items of direct benefit to children are purchased with the money. Coffee or cigarettes, for example, may not be bought with family allowance money. The family allowance is the only dependable and predictable income for most Slavey families, with the exception of the yearly "Treaty money" ($5), which most Indians consider not worth bothering about. The old age security program (inaugurated in 1951), which brings $40 per month to individuals over seventy, aids a few families.

There are perhaps six or eight permanent year-round jobs held by male Indians or Metis in Fort Simpson: a clerk in each of the three trading posts and a few handyman jobs with the government agricultural agent and the doctor and hospital. There is some female employment, full- or part-time, in housework for the few whites or at the Catholic mission hospital (the latter paying $1 a day and meals).

During the summer, a few seasonal jobs or other money-making possibilities are open. In Simpson there are mainly a few wage-labor jobs, such as gardening for the agricultural agent or some carpentering or repair work for other local whites. When a riverboat arrives, a few hours' wages can be made at unloading. Occasionally, an Indian has the opportunity to rent his canoe and kicker, plus himself as operator, to government officials or other individuals who need water transportation.

In response to these opportunities to earn some cash during the summer, some Indian trappers whose permanent homes are in the bush move their tents and families to Simpson and take employment. Several of the Lynx Point men have done this. Top wages in Simpson at present (1952) are those paid by the government offices. The minimum wage for government employment is $1 per hour (up to $8.50 per day). But family living in Simpson is expensive, and most of the cash must be spent immediately. Zachary of Lynx Point, with his wife and four children, attempted during the summer of 1952 to save (for his autumn stake) $4 out of his $8 a day. This was considered a stringent regimen by other Lynx Point men and accounted, one of them speculated, for Zachary's apparent loss of weight. Food prices are high, 50 to 85 cents for one tin of meat, for example. Most expenditure is for food for the human beings and for their dogs. The area around Simpson is very poor in fish and rabbit, and only if a man has a kicker for his canoe can he set snares and nets outside the depleted Simpson environs. And then there is the cost of gasoline, plus the fact that a man putting in a full work day seldom has the time or energy to make a two- or three-hour trip nightly to snares and nets. Furthermore, the presence of the game warden prevents supplementing the larder with illicit bear and moose meat or with such smaller items of game as ducks and porcupines.

A few Indians may make a little money cutting logs for firewood and towing them behind a canoe to town, where today (1951) they receive about $10 a cord. The family or families involved in such projects move their tents and possessions to the wood-cutting sites. Members of the Lynx Point band cut and sold some eighty cords of wood in August 1951, using their horse, powerboat, and barge in a joint operation. However, burned-over areas near the riverbank, which are the only practicable sources of dried (seasoned) wood, have been almost used up for over fifty miles out of Simpson, so that this money-making activity is becoming, in the opinion of the Lynx Point men, too difficult to be worthwhile.

The Lynx Point situation is unique in that in recent years most of the community has been able to obtain some additional income from the joint enterprises that employ the cooperatively owned barge and powerboat. Four different kinds of activities of this sort have been undertaken: cutting and hauling firewood for sale in Fort Simpson; renting the boat and barge, plus the labor of two to four Lynx Point men on hauling jobs for whites; setting channel buoys in the spring under government contract and beaching them in the autumn, for which they receive per diem payment for the use of the powerboat and for the labor of the three-man (Lynx Point) crew; and, lastly, autumn fishing in Great Slave Lake, part of the catch ordinarily being sold

Loading cordwood on the Jean Marie River barge for sale in Fort Simpson, 1952.

[see "Letter" in chapter 3]. Income from the barge and powerboat has fallen short of the original hopes and expectations, but even the poorest seasons have, so far as could be determined, produced sufficient cash to pay for supplies and upkeep on the equipment. In those instances such as the buoy-setting job, where crewmen receive individual pay in addition to a direct payment for the use of the vessel, the emolument of the crewmen is not pooled but is directly pocketed by the individuals.

Let us return now to the core of the money economy of Lynx Point—the fur trade. Most of the Lynx Point fur catch is sold either to the Hudson's Bay Company or to the two free traders in Fort Simpson. Each man during the winter goes to the fort about once a month, taking most, if not all, of the furs he has caught in the interim. Part of the proceeds from the sale of these furs is used immediately to purchase flour and other staples and perhaps some other needed or desired items as well. There are a few other outlets for furs, however, besides Fort Simpson. A white trader [an American named Browning] some thirty miles upstream from Lynx Point draws some of their business. In the spring of 1952 most of their beaver catch was sold at Hay River. Furthermore, fur-trading firms "outside," at Winnipeg, Edmonton, and Vancouver, occasionally send circulars to the trappers, advertising their prices for the better-paying fine furs such as marten, mink, and beaver. Some of the trappers have sent out two or three of their best pelts per year to these "outside companies" and, in these instances, have generally received higher prices than those current locally. The need for immediate cash for provisions, however, is a major deterrent to this practice.

In Fort Simpson the Lynx Point men usually shop for the best price for their more valuable furs; a one- to five-dollar difference may sometimes obtain. Furthermore, they are alert to rumors or information from travelers regarding the prices being paid by the upstream trader and the three Hay River free traders. (The Hudson's Bay Company post at Hay River is correctly assumed to be paying the same as the post at Simpson.) In response to such reports, most of the Lynx Point men took part of their 1952 spring beaver catch to the upstream trader and did indeed receive somewhat higher payments for their furs than the going rates in Simpson. During their buoy-setting trip to Hay River the previous spring, they had established that beaver was getting higher prices there than in the Simpson area. It was with this knowledge that most of the men held all their beaver that did not have to be used to purchase immediate necessities (food, primarily) until they could send it to Hay River with the men making the buoy-setting trip. The prices offered by each Hay River trader were investigated, and the furs were sold to the one offering the most money. Unfortunately, in that year there was but a slight gain over Simpson prices.

In Fort Simpson the Lynx Point men are known as "Hudson's Bay Indians," meaning that they sell to and trade with the Bay. As the above accounts show, however, the Lynx Point men are usually ready to take advantage of higher prices offered elsewhere for fine furs. The men do the family purchasing, and for such consumer items as clothing and equipment comparative shopping is common. Often, indeed, the decision is that one of the mail-order houses offers the best bargain and is accordingly patronized. However, the men usually make their headquarters when in town on a fur-selling trip at the Bay's "Indian house" (a lodging provided by the company) rather than at that of a rival trader. If for various reasons it is not thought worthwhile to shop for fur prices, it is to the Bay that they sell. Most of the immediate staples they require are purchased from the Bay. (Food prices appeared to be uniform among the three trading posts.) Also, it is with the Bay that most of the men contract "debt," supplies and equipment advanced in the autumn to tide the trapper over from the impoverished summer season until he can start producing furs. The amount of debt allowed to a trapper by the trader is predicated in part on the man's reliability and estimated producing power, but it is primarily decided pro rata on the basis of the estimated market value of the various furs in the coming season.

The most disturbing factor in the Indians' economic life is the fluctuating prices of the fur market. This phenomenon is, of course, completely beyond the control of the Indians. The causes are little comprehended by them, although they are cognizant of the role that the domestic fur supply from mink and fox fur farms may play in price determination, and some Indians give voice to suspicions about the integrity of the fur traders. Thus Zachary surmised, apparently with some seriousness, that the Hudson's Bay manager was paying low fur prices because he needed greater profits to support his children than did the previous manager, a bachelor. On the whole, however, the price fluctuation problem is accepted as inevitable and inexplicable, with no personal imputations being advanced.

There was a pronounced boom in furs during World War II, with a ragged decline in values between 1944 and 1950, and beaver, marten, and lynx took several drops between 1950–51 and 1951–52. The severe decline in the value of lynx (from $20 to $4, top price) is a heavy blow, for it is an abundant fur in the Lynx Point area. Even further cuts appeared to be in the offing for the 1952–53 season; top price for marten, for example, was predicted at $8 compared with $48 of two seasons before.

For the 1951–52 season the range of from $700 to $1,200 probably covers the income from furs of each Lynx Point household. Incomes approaching the higher end of the range appeared to have been achieved in large part by the taking of beaver and especially marten in excess of the legal allotment. If extra seals were not available, only the best pelts were selected for sale.

SUMMARY

The living standard of the Lynx Point people is heavily dependent upon a capricious and fluctuating fur market. Outside of trapping, the financial opportunities to be found in the white settlements are few and far from golden. Most men must trap for a living whether they like it or not. In their trapping, the population cycles of the furbearers and the limits on the catch that the authorities impose in consequence of population decline of furbearers provide another element of insecurity.

The Lynx Point people are a receptive market for commercial products of many kinds. They desire more and better clothing and household equipment, new radios, outboard motors, rifles, tents, boats, watches, jewelry, and a myriad of other tempting items that blossom in the pages of the mail-order catalog. They seek more ease and comfort (a better sleeping bag for subzero nights on the trail, a kicker to replace muscle power) and more attractiveness and variety (a new dress or shirt for the tea dance) in their lives. But there have been few years when it has been financially easy to fill these needs and desires. Most of the time, the Lynx Point people are, in Marcel's phrase, "just gettin' by."

The desire for an easier, more abundant, and secure life finds verbal expression, often in the form of anxiety and resentment, as these passages from the field notes indicate:

May 17, 1952. Henri has just heard from a passing Indian that "blanket [large-size] beaver" is selling for only $16 at Simpson. Henri comments that prices paid for fur are pretty low, while food stays high and gets higher.

March 10, 1952. While drinking, Karl is looking at a magazine containing pictures of the royal funeral. Daniel starts to talk about how much money was spent on the funeral, and this reminds him, as it usually does, of how low fur prices have become and how high the price of store goods is. Later, we talk about how hard up things are here, a topic raised by Daniel. He says that the last time the men were in Simpson, Marcel and Henri were talking about how something would have to be done—a revolution. "Know who to shoot, anyway," says Daniel. "Who?" "The game warden." Daniel tells how all the lynx were stacked up on the floor of the Bay store and the big stack did not come to $100. The stuff on the shelves was "up," and Marcel complained to the manager about the prices.

February 26, 1952. Marcel, high but not drunk, starts to talk about how the Indian has to support the game warden to make trouble for him, to pay taxes to support him just like one's own family. [Marcel pays no taxes.] He goes on to talk of how bad the plight of the Indian is—how he has only one way of making a living whereas the white man has many ways and should show them to the Indian. Marcel repeats several times that the Indian is human, just like the white man, and should be entitled to earn his living just like the white man.

May 8, 1952. Zachary, somewhat high, discusses the poor fish catch last autumn by "the Lynx Point fishery outfit." Goes on to say that "this bunch" is the only one with an outfit with which to fish Great Slave Lake on a large scale. "The people at Fort Simpson [where the surplus is sold] need that fish." If it is not a good year for rabbits, then that fish is all they have that is cheap to buy. They can buy a stick of ten big whitefish for $1.75. I comment that that is a lot better than paying fifty cents for a can of meat. "Fifty cents?" says Zachary, outraged at my ignorance, "eighty-five cents!" and then says canned meats are all salt.

Zachary says that the government should give food to the Indian if it restricts hunting. "A man loves his family; he can't just sit around, not do anything." Zachary got five beaver in traps this spring. "That's not enough." That is why he shoots beaver (which is illegal).

Zachary complains that "the old people" think you can live without money. They think you can get along like in the old days. They don't realize everything costs money—clothes, shells, canoes, etc. He enumerates everything one needs that costs money. Zachary says there is no future in trapping, got to think of the children's future. Trapping is going to get worse. The government should do something. "We've got to have equipment."

from **The Lynx Point People,** *1961*

Part II | LOOKING BACK IN TIME

On the day I arrived at Rae in 1971, I encountered two Slavey friends from Jean Marie River ("Lynx Point") of twenty years before. Their very presence at Rae brought home to me the extent of the changes in communications and perspectives in the two decades since I first came to the Northwest Territories. Louis Norwegian and Jimmy Sanguez were in Rae as representatives from the Fort Simpson Band (with Chief Cazon) to the meeting of the newly formed (1969) Indian Brotherhood of the Northwest Territories (IB-NWT). Within the first two days at Rae, I was so taken with the changes in everyday life that I sat down to record immediate impressions and observations. Preceded by a reflective essay by Nancy Lurie, my notes made on these two days make up chapter 6, which initiates this section.

By 1970 I knew I was to be the editor of the Subarctic *volume of the* Handbook of North American Indians *that was being planned as a twenty-volume publication of the Smithsonian Institution. (*Subarctic, *volume 6 of the* Handbook, *was published in 1981.) That prospect and the Athapaskan Conference in Ottawa in 1971 (Clark 1975) led to a graduate seminar at the University of Iowa in which several students joined with me to work on a survey of the contact history of the subarctic Athapaskans (chapter 7). That broad historical overview buttressed comprehensions I had developed in the field and library over twenty years. I was thus preadapted to respond to the request of the IB-NWT to serve as an expert*

witness in the efforts of the Brotherhood to establish a caveat on land development in the Territories.

In August 1973 I testified before the Territorial Supreme Court regarding the nature of Dene land use throughout the historical era to the present day, as well as my understanding of the natives' comprehension—or, rather, lack of comprehension—of the implications for land alienation in the treaties signed in 1900 and 1921. As I was being the "expert" in the witness's dock in Justice William Morrow's court, Joe Tobie, multilingual Dogrib, leaned over to Beryl Gillespie (also an "expert witness") sitting with him in the audience and observed, "We could have told him that!" Of course Joe Tobie and other Dene could have testified to the same points I was making. It brought home to me how strange are the criteria of the whites' courts: for summarizing what the people know, the courts accept me as an "expert" because I have a Ph.D.

Within a year, Beryl Gillespie and I were working for the Brotherhood in land claims research. I developed a field project in which young members of the Brotherhood, as they interviewed Dene of the Northwest Territories, plotted on maps the routes and resources (e.g., good furbearer locations) that men and their families used across the land. The project's aim was to establish the facts of native land use and deployment as part of the Brotherhood's effort to maximize Indian control over land use and development through negotiation and/or judicial process. (See Nahanni [1977] and Asch, Andrews, and Smith [1986] in which, curiously, no acknowledgment of Helm as the project designer is made.)

In 1975 I was called on to provide an ethnohistorical overview at another government hearing, the Mackenzie Valley Pipeline Inquiry. As oral testimony recorded by the court stenographer, it had redundancy and a few confusions. I have worked over the transcript to present it as chapter 9 in this book.

The first three chapters of this part, arising from encounters and events in the first five years of the 1970s, provide a staging position from which to move back through the first fifty years of the twentieth century, thence into the 1800s, and then into the furthest reaches of documentary and oral history of the Dene of the Mackenzie region (chapters 9, 10, 11, 12, and 13). Chapter 14, the last chapter of this part, returns to events of the "Berger hearings" of 1975: the views presented by the IB-NWT and the views by "ordinary" Dene citizens in the community hearings held by Mr. Justice Thomas Berger in the Mackenzie Valley Pipeline Inquiry.

The tremendous changes in years since 1975 I do not address. Now the Dene people have generated their own scholars of and active participants in the events of the last twenty-five years, to which I can make no contribution.

6 | CHANGING TIMES

In 1951, the year I first came to the Northwest Territories, "the highway" from the south reached only as far as Hay River. In 1961 the extension to Yellowknife was opened. Another ten years later the extension of "the highway" to Fort Simpson was being constructed. "The highway" is emblematic of the quickened pace of change for the Dene recorded in the selections in this chapter.

The year after our joint 1967 season with the Dogribs, Nancy Lurie brought her perspective on the cultures and history of the Indians of the western Great Lakes (especially the Ho-Chunk or Winnebago people of her native state, Wisconsin) to bear on the changes coming to the Rae Dogribs in the wake of the highway that linked them to the "outside" world. Nancy's account follows.

In 1967 we saw the effects on the Dogribs of the new highway which connects Yellowknife to Edmonton, Rae being joined to the highway by a seven-mile spur. I was struck by the fact that developments which took place over a century, roughly 1820–1920, in the western Great Lakes region of the United States were compressed into half a decade for the Dogribs at Rae. Despite accelerated pace and newer technological innovations, there are strong parallels of sequence between the two areas and eras in regard to Indian reactions to crises posed as a community becomes less isolated from the larger society.

Easier access to Yellowknife was already becoming important for the Rae Dene in 1962 when the road between the two towns was less than a year old, but at that time cars were few in Rae, and the major effect we observed was the thriving taxi/bootleg business of a frontier-type entrepreneurial white man. In that year a great deal of charter air traffic (by pontoon or ski) still reflected Rae's isolation in regard to delivery of goods and visits by government personnel. There were virtually no tourists or casual white visitors to

the settlement. By 1967 plane landings at Rae were rare; visitors now arrived by car or on the thrice-weekly bus.

The economic aspect of the road for the Rae Dogribs is underscored by the introduction of a number of government services employing natives. The services include a new sanitary plan whereby chemically treated water is delivered by truck to the Indians' homes; plastic liner bags for toilets are delivered daily, and the bags of waste are removed and trucked to a dump; firewood cut in the bush is hauled to the road and trucked into town and from there delivered by truck to native homes; and trash is collected from trash barrels on a regular schedule. Arrangements for the services have varied. A series of private white operators and a cooperative that operated briefly at Rae in 1967 have done the work under government contracts; one overall result has meant employment for those natives who can drive.

Employed native people, such as the game warden's assistant, store clerks, and others, have quickly acquired trucks and cars. These vehicles have begun to break down, and derelict automobiles begin to give Rae an appearance approaching that of many Indian communities farther south. Cars are really an unnecessary luxury and expense for most at this point, but there is potential utility in terms of increased employment opportunities available in Yellowknife and elsewhere as more members of the community learn English and learn new marketable skills. This is a parallel development to that farther south where Indians travel great distances by car to places of employment. Adaptable travelers who took to kickers for canoes and availed themselves quickly of air travel when it was introduced, Dogribs will likely see automobiles and the road as a means of commuting to and from new sources of support. Mechanical ability acquired early to keep kickers in repair is being transferred to automobiles.

There is widespread interest in cars, and driver training was one of the most popular projects promoted by the cooperative. The students included many women. Because of the new community services using trucks, some fairly passable roads now lace the town, and many youngsters have bicycles, an item virtually unknown at Rae in 1962.

The road and the use of motor vehicles have become important even to those Indians who will not learn to drive or ever be able to afford cars. A bus running three times a week between Edmonton and Yellowknife stops at Rae, allowing an increased amount of casual visiting between the Dogrib people at Rae and those in Yellowknife and the adjacent native village of Dettah. There is a good deal of hitchhiking to and from Yellowknife by arrangements between Indians and friendly whites (RCMP, hospital and school personnel, etc.) who own cars. Furthermore, there is casual hitchhiking on the road itself, usually between the Stagg Lake and Trout Rock settlements and Rae or Yellowknife. If paid passengers are agreeable, taxi drivers will pick up hitchhikers, as will truckers and other drivers. In the wintertime Indians using dog teams appreciate having the highway department "break trail" along the road with snowplows, as they go along the highway to spur trails to snare and hunt. This is also true of the freight road to Great Bear Lake, open only during the winter. If men have killed a number of caribou, they bring them by sled to the road in hope that a friendly trucker will take the load into town. As one Dogrib described Indian hunters' enthusiasm for the convenience of trucks, "They follow with empty sleigh as they ride with the dog team all the way along with a big smile."

The highway from Rae to Edmonton is also becoming important to Dogribs, although more for social than economic purposes at this time. However, one hunter, Jim Drybones, has put the highway to good use. His son-in-law is steadily employed by the game warden and has now bought his second pickup truck. The son-in-law takes Jim with his gear to a particularly rich moose area about halfway to Fort Providence and lets him off. The hunter heads into the bush, usually manages to kill one or more moose, and returns to the road for his son-in-law to pick him up on an agreed-upon day.

There is increasing dependence on a cash economy for a greater variety of consumer goods. The people are hard put to provide for their wants. Wage work in Rae is limited. There are more opportunities in Yellowknife for those with skills and the ability to get there, and there will be increased opportunities farther south. The series of events parallel to those in the South is particularly impressive in regard to Indian reaction to mounting pressures on their lands, resources, and traditional way of life of the fur-trade era. The highway has certainly contributed to the influx of whites and was built in anticipation of greater development of the North.

At the same time, the road has also contributed to the acceleration of reactive behavior by the native people which took a century to form in the Great Lakes region, because in that region industrialization and rapid means of transportation were only beginning to develop in the nineteenth and early twentieth centuries. Among the Dogribs, between 1962 and 1967 we saw the genesis of a systematized antiwhite sentiment, the introduction of a reactive nativistic (or revitalization) movement, and the involvement of the Dogribs in pan-Indianism and the tourist trade.

Antiwhite feeling seems to follow a predictable pattern for Indian people. It is not directed as a rule to all whites or very many specific white persons but to those white institutions believed to be responsible for the breakdown of parental control of children such as the schools or believed to hold back help from the Indians such as the welfare office, game laws, and Indian "agency." The competition among white institutions (e.g., the Roman Catholic mission, competing missionaries, and the cooperative; Hudson's Bay store and private trader; welfare office and Indian office) have resulted in the same kind of negotiating and playing-off of white interests to gain ends for Indian interests that is now an old and familiar story in the Canadian provinces and the United States.

The celebration of the centennial of the arrival of the Grey Nuns at Fort Providence occurred during our summer stay at Rae in July 1967. Available space in a friendly linguist's station wagon was commandeered to transport Chief Bruneau and as many prominent Dogrib men as possible along with us. The Roman Catholic mission helped with arrangements to charter a bus to take other Dogribs to Providence where they could stay with the local Slavey people. Ostensibly, the Indians from Rae went to attend the Catholic religious and secular program in honor of the occasion, but apart from the midnight mass, procession to the graveyard, and feast provided by the mission, the Dogribs and Slaveys were clearly bored by a taped orchestra concert and ballet performance. The Dogribs got a tea dance and a hand game going. The Slaveys had not played the hand game in many years and were eager to play, but the Dogribs became exasperated with their ineptness and lack of seriousness in clumsy and joking efforts to cheat. The dancing was a great success, however, and when the celebration was over a number of Slaveys climbed on the bus and went back to Rae with Dogrib friends. There, more dancing and hand games took place to honor the visitors, who eventually drifted back home by bus. The highway to Alberta had already carried Dogribs (with the sponsorship of the Catholic church) to a shrine near Edmonton and thus facilitated contacts with other Dene and Crees as well as with a Slavey prophet movement in northern Alberta. Continuing highway contacts brought the major Alberta prophet to Rae and fostered the development of Dogrib prophet activities. [For an account of the Dogrib prophet movement, see Helm 1994.]

In 1967 we soon became aware of interest in pan-Indian activities, in contrast to the parochialism of outlook in 1962. The knowledge of such intertribal efforts reached the Dogribs largely through white sources. One Dogrib had been receiving the U.S. publication *Indian Voices* as a gift over the last several years. The celebration of Canada's centennial year in 1967 also had an influence insofar as the various caravans and other activities stressed revival of old-style costumes. This too has parallels in the influence of white-inspired Wild West and Indian medicine shows in the development of pan-Indianism in the United States. However, the lasting appeal of nativism and pan-Indianism to the Indians stems from felt needs of their own. The Dogribs today, like Indians farther south in the 1880s, are beginning to see themselves as part of an Indian world contrasted to a white world. They are no longer simply Dogribs dealing as best they can with local whites. Likewise, we noted among those few older people who had gone away to school an interest in intertribal gatherings to revive friendships with Indians of other tribes and even Inuit they had known as children in school—echoes of old Carlisle Indian School graduates in the States who became the early leaders in the more political aspects of pan-Indianism.

On the basis of past experience, the Canadian government has brought leaders from different northern tribes together for conferences much earlier in the crisis period than was done farther south and in the United States. This doubtless will contribute to a more rapid development of political aspects of pan-Indianism. The Indian-Eskimo Association, established in 1961, parallels the National Congress of American Indians founded in 1944 and earlier organizations with more white leadership in the United States. The association's representative in Yellowknife is able to drive up to Rae at a moment's notice, thanks to the road.

Other parallels expedited by the rapid breakdown of Dogrib isolation are seen in factions of "progressives" and "conservatives" and division of function between their organizations, the former concerned with economic development and relations to the larger society and the latter concerned with morals and order within the community. Finally, the tourist trade begins to loom as a new source of income as more people from the provinces travel the road on holiday outings and Yellowknife whites visit Rae on weekends. Changes in crafts reflect catering to this market. Beadwork, for example, has almost completely replaced silk embroidery, and new "junk jewelry" and bone carvings are being produced purely for sale to whites. The Dene like beadwork for decorating their own clothing as well, but the for-sale change was instigated and encouraged by a local Grey Nun who thought tourists would consider beads more typically Indian than Dene silk embroidery, which she believed "all" white women do. The nun began a handcraft shop. The shop passed into the hands of the cooperative sponsored by the Cooperative Union of Canada (CUC). By the time we left, the shop remained the only important institutionalized legacy of the CUC's brief involvement in the community.

History does not really repeat itself, but recurrent social processes develop out of similar conditions. Noteworthy is the fact that despite massive technological acculturation and pressure to assimilate, Indian identity, values, and attitudes among the Indians of southern Canada and the United States endure, and the long-expected "disappearance" of the Indians seems less likely than ever to occur at any predictable future time. Herein lies the major implication of the parallels between Rae from 1962 to 1967 and the western Great Lakes from 1820 to 1920.

from an unpublished manuscript by Nancy O. Lurie, 1968

NEWS OF JEAN MARIE RIVER AFTER TWENTY YEARS, 1951–1971

I [Helm] have had several short conversations with Louis Norwegian and Jimmy Sanguez of Jean Marie River who are serving as representatives from the Fort Simpson Band at the Indian Brotherhood meeting at Rae. New features at Marie River ["Lynx Point"] include a store for goods such as flour, lard, etc., which Louis says is run by him under the managership of his son Douglas. Douglas has four children now and Louis's daughter Minnie has five. Louis's son William is planning to get married. His son Fred is employed by the government. At Marie River they have a new motor in the powerboat (and possibly a new hull too?) and also have a barge, a sawmill, a DC-6 Cat, and a speedboat with a forty-horsepower Johnson outboard to take them to Fort Simpson. [Q.] Yes, the latter is owned by the group as a whole as is the sawmill, etc. [See the reference to the Venture in the section titled "Louis Norwegian" in chapter 18.]

Jimmy tells me that his oldest son Maurice is now in Fort Smith and owns a pickup truck. Louis says he owns a pickup truck at Marie River. They can drive to Fort Simpson on a winter road. The highway going through to Simpson will pass within ten miles of Marie River. The government has allotted $2,000 to build a ten-mile spur between Marie River and the highway. Louis says that $10,000 would be more like it. [Louis's skepticism was certainly justified. "The grand opening of the year-round access road" to Jean Marie River occurred twenty-six years later (*News/North*, October 20, 1997). DOT records give the final cost at $2,045,000.] Apparently, the Jean Marie River men will have a contract to build the road if the price is right.

The Nahannis have moved to Simpson. Phoebe Nahanni is here at Rae for the Indian Brotherhood meeting; I spoke to her briefly. Her father is right

Louis Norwegian and Jimmy Sanguez at the IB-NWT meeting at Rae, 1971.

now at Kakisa Lake. Louis's (half) sisters Celine Gargan and widowed Sarah Hardisty are well. But Louis tells me Charles Gargan, Celine's husband, "got lost in Simpson." [Did he get a ride on the winter road to Edmonton and thus disappear?] F. J. Browning [an expatriate American who had a "farm" on the banks of the Mackenzie River some miles above Jean Marie River] died a couple years ago while hauling logs with his tractor. The tractor slipped and went down a bank and rolled over on him. All of Browning's equipment remains sitting on the riverbank at the site where he was working. His sons have not picked it up. It is rusting. Louis estimates $6,000 worth of equipment.

Jimmy Sanguez and his wife, Mary Louise, have had fifteen children. I think Jimmy said Nora and Florence, their two oldest, are both married and have a baby or two. Louis says he is now sixty-two. Both he and Jimmy, who is about ten years younger than Louis, look their usual dapper selves and not any older than they did twenty years ago.

Yesterday one of the Rae priests told me that there was recently trouble at Jean Marie River. There was a drinking party, and the schoolteacher went to break it up. He got beaten up.

Today I took a picture of Jimmy and Louis and said I would send a copy to Teresa [my field companion at Jean Marie River in 1951 and 1952]. Jimmy asks with pleased surprise, "Is she still alive?" Since he has already told me that Johnny, his younger brother, has never married, I said "yes" and for him to tell Johnny that Teresa is waiting for him to marry her.

from field notes of July 4, 1971, Rae

CURRENT STYLES AND MATERIAL POSSESSIONS, RAE, 1971

There is an extremely sharp distinction between the attire of the teenagers and persons in their early twenties and the rest of the community. I have seen a couple of young women, probably still in their early twenties, wearing the standard apparel for all women only ten years ago: moccasins and moccasin rubbers, lisle hose, and shapeless dresses and cardigans, with a baby lashed on their back with a blanket. But the schoolgirls of the "younger generation," as my friend Vital calls them, are almost all in pants, never wearing moccasins, many going in for the southern-type Indian craft of beaded necklace, and the boys have their hair hanging to their shoulders and below, a few wearing headbands. In other words, the usual so-called hippie dress styles.

Looking at the older persons attending the Indian Brotherhood meetings this week, I find that I am unable to gauge whether they will be wearing moccasins or not by the rest of their attire or by their age. Twenty years ago, everyone would have been in moccasins. Today, several women in their fifties and sixties are wearing low-heeled oxfords. So are men of comparable age. There are a number of men in their forties and fifties, however, who are wearing moccasins and rubbers. Often the moccasins are of the slipper type, although there was at least one pair of ankle-wrap moccasins with beautiful solid beadwork on the collar.

Generally, all men, young and old, who are not of the "schoolkid" generation have their hair closely clipped and barbered in the older generation whiteman style. The contrast between them and the school generation is just as one would see outside.

The "younger generation" today is wearing granny specs, while the older generation is in standard horn rims, often with silver trim, that one finds outside. This attention to eye care is a notable change in the last ten years. As I recall, I was struck by the proliferation of eyeglasses first in 1962 when the schoolchildren returned from boarding school that summer. Suddenly the town was full of eyeglasses. The older generation had not yet been fitted at that time. [Jim Drybones, the moose hunter described by Nancy in the preceding account, now has, as the cliché has it, glasses as thick as Coke-bottle bottoms. How did he see *anything* through the years, even a moose?] The

Yellowknife newspaper notes that Dr. Elizabeth Cass is pressing for eye clinics to be established at various communities of the North so that better eye service can be given, rather than it coming all from a touring eye doctor based in Yellowknife, as Dr. Cass is.

The town is now full of transistor casette tape recorders. Vital Thomas also has a casette recorder. I have given him the tape of Naedzo, the Bear Lake Prophet, that Beryl Gillespie recorded at Fort Franklin. [All my tape recordings are deposited in the Northwest Territories Archives.] Vital has borrowed another tape from me so that it can be played while his cronies are having a card game in his house. Casettes of rock and other contemporary art forms are now available both here and in Yellowknife. Many of the houses at Rae ring with noise, giving an indication as to how widespread casette recorder and boom box ownership is. Also, kids are now walking along with tapes blaring.

Vital estimates there must be at least a dozen skidoos (snowmobiles) now in town. Ten years ago, no Indian owned one. There must be about fifteen to two dozen automobiles or trucks owned in town, by my estimate. It is hard to be sure, as some of those touring the streets may be from Yellowknife. Most of them are driven by teenagers or men in their early twenties. There is one bright green Pinto that tears around town repeatedly, full of kids. One of the government-built houses has the classic scene of beat-up automobile stripped of tires and resting on its axles, its seats pulled out and lying on the rocks exposed to weather. I have not yet inquired about automobile accidents, but there apparently have been some, as reflected in the concern of councillor Alex Charlot in his speech to the Indian Brotherhood yesterday.

Ten years ago no Indian house had electricity. Now I see an electric portable zigzag sewing machine for sale in the Bay. I do not know if many or any Indian families now have these. Mrs. Vital Thomas is still sewing on her ancient hand-cranked Singer. One of these is available for sale in Arnie's store. Mrs. Thomas has been sewing up lengths of canvas for a new canoe cover on the machine, using a double seam.

from field notes of July 6, 1971, Rae

THE CONTACT HISTORY
7 | OF THE SUBARCTIC ATHAPASKANS:
AN OVERVIEW

The "we" in this chapter refers to the seven persons, six graduate students and myself, who assembled the data that shaped this chapter. Since the chapter deals with populations in both Alaska and Canada, I only rarely employ any particular language usage such as "Dene"; "Athapaskan" encompasses all divisions, and a group/tribe/society/ nation is usually referred to in the singular. The specification of "Northern" or "subarctic" Athapaskans reflects the fact of the existence of Athapaskan-speaking peoples in southwestern Oregon and northwestern California and the Athapaskan-speaking Navajo and Apache peoples in the U.S. Southwest.

As Athapaskan speakers, the linguistic unity of the aboriginal peoples of the interior of northwestern North America was recognized by 1850. It took another eighty years for an ethnologist explicitly to attend to the total Northern Athapaskan domain, when Cornelius Osgood (1936) surveyed the available evidence on the blending and overlapping Athapaskan-speaking populations of Alaska and Canada to provide identifications of maximal societal-dialectic "groups." [See the map on the inception of the contact-traditional stage that accompanies this chapter for the "names" that designate these maximal units in modern ethnological classification (per Helm 1981b).]

Fieldwork and the earliest documents available as ethnological resources make each ethnographer working with Northern Athapaskan peoples aware that, apart from archaeological recovery, our only evidence of Athapaskan cultural forms comes from within the contact era. Yet as of this writing [late 1960s], no student of the Athapaskan North has attempted a general summary of the social and cultural trends and transformations in those years since 1700 to the present. Personal scholarly experience has made it evident why this is so. Both in terms of precontact culture and habitat and in terms of the events and conditions of the contact era, I find that, from the vantage point of the Mackenzie basin, my broader ethnohistorical view turns "naturally" to the east to the cultures and contact experiences of the subarctic Algonkian

speakers of Canada's prairie provinces, Ontario, and Quebec (Helm and Lea-cock 1971) rather than west into and across the cordillera to the rest of the subarctic Athapaskans. In spite of the linguistic break between Algonkian and Athapaskan speakers in the subarctic culture area, the contact events of the last 250 years, as well as the precontact conditions of the physical and inter-cultural environment, provide a more immediate comparability of subarctic Indian adaptations and experiences from the eastern slopes of the Rockies to the Labrador Peninsula than obtains across the Northern Athapaskan do-main per se. Thus Athapaskanists have from the arctic drainage looked to the east and south for impinging influences, protocontact and postcontact, while those working on the western side of the cordilleran watershed have faced toward the Pacific littoral, whether the "outside" influences are those of coastal native cultures or of European goods and actions approaching from that direction.

To the ethnohistorian attending to Indian-white contact, the ultimate goal is to comprehend the cultural and societal consequences for the native peoples. Toward that end we here take the first step, to identify through time and across space in the Athapaskan subarctic the main features of the chang-ing intercultural environment, that is, those experiences and conditions in-troduced directly by Europeans (whites of any nationality) or through inter-mediary native groups. To flesh out the specific entries we offer a provisional sketch of the major trends and transformations—stages, if you will—in the contact experience of the subarctic Athapaskans.

[The original study (Helm et al. 1975) was geared to a "Synoptic Chart of Culture Contact Events" that recorded in five-year intervals each class of significant events that affected each major "tribal"-linguistic group of the subarctic Athapaskans. The chart is too large to be included in this volume.]

The salient classes of external factors seem to be these:

1. *First direct contact* by an entering European with a native group in the lat-ter's own territory. This contact may be of no great immediate significance in native life, but it serves as a convenient marker and reminder of dates and routes of penetration into Athapaskan country.

2. *Trade activities* resulting from the European presence, either internative trade, in which furs are exchanged for European goods, or the Indian-white trade relationship itself.

3. *Hostilities* between Indian groups exacerbated, if not created, by the Eu-ropean presence. Hostile action visited by Indians upon a white establish-

ment was rare. Hostile actions initiated by Europeans were limited to the area of Russian occupation.

4. *Epidemic diseases.*

5. *Missionization* and ensuing Christianization.

6. *"Shock" intrusions* of whites and their activities or the growth of relatively large scale white-dominant settlements and neighborhoods. These include large-scale gold rushes through areas as well as gold strikes in them, influxes of homesteaders, and, since the Second World War, the growth of administrative, commercial, or industrial urban centers.

7. *Governmental enactments* or activities, especially in the twentieth century.

8. *Transportation facilities.* In the nineteenth century the water-transport systems that were developed on the two great rivers, the Mackenzie and the Yukon, provided opportunity for travel and interethnic contact for those native men who worked as trackers, deckhands, and so on. Air service in recent decades has affected movement of goods, persons, and ideas, but overland transportation, especially highways, has provided even greater opportunity for new experiences and change, at least for those populations residing along or near the facility.

It must be remembered that for different regional subgroups there may be considerable variation in exposure to any type of contact condition. This is especially so when the maximal unit (e.g., "Slave" or "Chipewyan" nation) is made up of a number of widely spaced regional groups. "Shock" intrusions, for example, may expose only a portion of a "tribe" or "nation" to critical and transforming pressures.

STAGES IN NORTHERN ATHAPASKAN CONTACT HISTORY

The term "contact" in adjectival form (e.g., "contact history," "contact-traditional," "early contact phase") is ethnographic shorthand to encompass a condition in historical time when Indians, as populations and as culture-bearers, were reacting, adapting, borrowing, and innovating in the face of exposure to elements of European (white) culture and/or its human agents. We refer to white and Indian in the physical presence of one another as "direct contact."

As in all historical process, events and alterations cumulate in the western subarctic so that the reader of the records can say, "These people are in a different economic, social, political, or cultural condition than they were one hundred, or fifty, or twenty years ago." Yet, as in drawing lines on the map between culture areas, the analyst is pulled between the usefulness of bounded zones or intervals and the intransigence of ongoing variation, trend, change, and process. Furthermore, from group to group the course of contact experience has not been unitary, and the record is very uneven. In an effort to produce a generalized picture of manageable proportions, we offer demarcation and description of three successive stages in Northern Athapaskan contact relations: (1) the incipient-early contact stage; (2) the contact-traditional stage; and (3) the modern or government-commercial stage.

Other ethnologists of the subarctic have wrestled with the problem of delineating and labeling major eras. The term "government-commercial" is suggested by a phrase of E. S. Rogers, reporting on contemporary life among the subarctic Algonkians. Other efforts to capture the dominant tenor of present trends are encapsulated in the phrases "government-industrial" (Helm and Leacock), "micro-urban" (J. G. E. Smith), and "period of planned change" (John Honigmann). They indicate that since World War II the subarctic Indians have become continually more subject to pressures that issue from big government, large-scale commerce and industry, aggregation into white-dominant settlements, and the accelerated communication of aspects of white lifestyle.

I coined the term "contact-traditional" in a joint paper with David Damas. For our purposes at the time, we (Helm and Damas 1963) used contact-traditional narrowly and in reference to a specific community type. Here contact-traditional is employed to comprehend a way of life that developed as a historical era in northern native culture. In that era, contact with the Western world was channeled preeminently through the few agents of the fur trade and the church, and contact with these figures was infrequent. More indirect factors of change were nineteenth-century technological developments, increasing biological and cultural interpenetration between European and Indian peoples, and alterations in the formal political and legal relations between Indians and government. These generalities would seem to hold for subarctic Athapaskans as a whole, Canadian and Alaskan, despite pronounced regional variations in time of inception and in duration and stability of the era. These points will be considered below.

The hyphenated phrase "incipient-early contact" emphasizes the beginnings of knowledge, experience, and response by an Indian group to the European cultural presence rather than face-to-face contact of Indian and white. "Incipient contact" denotes specifically the condition of access to

European goods by an Indian population only through Native American intermediaries. The Tagish, for example, had come to rely on items of European material culture such as guns in advance of seeing the first European (McClellan 1953). "Early contact" refers to direct but initial or irregular contact by at least a portion of a "tribal" population with agents of European culture. In both cases, the emphasis is that the Indian group is not yet fully committed to the dual economy of the contact-traditional stage, when items of European manufacture—guns, implements, utensils, clothing, tea, and tobacco—have become "necessities," and to obtain those necessities the Indian group is committed to regular procurement of fur (or post provisioning), which significantly reorders the group's relationship with the natural and sociocultural environment.

THE INCIPIENT-EARLY CONTACT STAGE

The beginnings of contact in the western subarctic followed the pattern general to woodland North America. The European contact agent was preeminently the fur trader, but commonly his goods and diseases preceded him. Native groups in direct contact with European traders became the geographic and economic middlemen for tribes farther into the interior, imposing substantial markups on the implements and utensils and items of adornment that they exchanged for furs.

European penetration into the Athapaskan subarctic was shaped by three main features of physiography: the seas, the inland waterways, and the mountains. The first two provided routes of contact; the third constituted a barrier.

Points-of-trade on the west side of Hudson Bay and along the North Pacific rim were the sources of the earliest trade goods reaching Athapaskan populations. Of the specifics of percolation of early trade objects from one group to another farther afield from the point-of-trade there is, by and large, no record. Some Chipewyans adjacent to the Cree of the Hudson Bay region had probably received English trade items out of York Fort by 1700. By 1714 a few Chipewyans had themselves ventured to the fort on the coast. "Copper Indians" (Yellowknives) and a few of the "Dog-ribbed Indians" were probably obtaining some items within the second quarter of the eighteenth century (Hearne 1958 [1795]).

Russian coastal exploration and trade was under way among the islands and along the southern coast of Alaska after 1741. By 1800 enduring points-of-trade were established at Kodiak and Sitka, and Eyak had visited the post at Nuchek. The propensity of Russian traders, like those of the Hudson's Bay

Company in the east, to hold to the coast placed those native peoples nearest the Alaska coast in the position of middlemen. In part at least, the internative trade was an extension of already established Chuckchi-Eskimo-Indian connections into the Yukon and Kuskokwim drainages and of "grease trails" between Northwest Coast groups and interior Athapaskans. The continuing coastal ship trade further enhanced the trading positions of Tlingit and Bella Coola vis-à-vis the adjacent Athapaskans dwelling in the western flanks and basins of the cordillera (McClellan 1953; Goldman 1940).

Relations between Indian groups and between Indians and Europeans had a different cast at either end of the Athapaskan domain during this era. East of the Rockies, the first contacted tribes—Cree, Chipewyan, then Beaver and Yellowknife—obtained firearms and turned to raiding and general bullying of their defenseless Athapaskan neighbors and, when possible, each other. The "Slave Indians," as a notable example, emerge in the literature as a contemptuous designation by the armed Cree of defenseless Athapaskan groups in the lands abutting the southwestern side of Great Slave Lake and along the Upper Mackenzie. Groups of Sekani and Dogribs were also harried and forced to flee customary territories by Beavers and Yellowknives, respectively (Jenness 1937; Franklin 1824). Since inter-Indian hostilities interfered with trade, the white traders worked to achieve peace among the Dene peoples of the East. There was no initial hostility of Indians toward whites, and later instances were, for each "tribe," usually one-time events. In the eastern Dene zone, Indians apparently made no attempt to block traders from establishing trading forts in the lands of "clients" or enemies.

Early interethnic relations along the archipelago and southeastern coast of Alaska were markedly distinct from those in the eastern zone. The coastal ship trade as such posed no threat of an overt foothold on Indian land. But where Russians established landholds they introduced a style of violent subjugation of native populations unknown in British–Athapaskan relations in the East, where the purely commercial goals of the traders were achieved by catering to the nomadic natives as much as possible. (Whereas in the early Russian trade, for example, firearms were prohibited to Eskimos and Indians, British and Canadian traders traded them freely to better the Indians' livelihood so that they might devote more time to fur taking.) By and large, the Alaskan Indian populations contacted were resistant to Russian settlement. Sites of direct contact drew hostile actions from Tlingit and the Athapaskan Tanaina, Koyukon, and Upper Atna.

There was inter-Indian aggression in the West (e.g., Gitksan against Sekani and the Tlingit destruction of the Tsetsaut). The first-contacted tribes of the North Pacific coast, however, showed no propensity to move into the territories of the inland mountain peoples. The contrastive environments of the two zones is indubitably the key. Where penetration and "take-over" occurred, they took the form of trading dominance by the coast-oriented group, sometimes in combination with quasi-social absorption through marriage with the "hillbillies" of the interior (McClellan 1953). Generally, a distinctive feature of the western edge of the Northern Athapaskan domain is the trading hegemony that non-Athapaskan middlemen groups near or on the coast were able to sustain for many decades.

Excepting the hostile stance of noncordilleran Alaskan groups (e.g., Tanaina and Atna), Northern Athapaskans from the cordillera to Hudson Bay usually welcomed the establishment of points-of-trade within their territory. Wentzel (1821:6) provides a vivid example from the Mackenzie River region:

Notwithstanding that no promise had been made of returning at a future period to trade with them I was sent . . . [in 1816] with six Canadians in a large canoe and a small supply of goods to renew the intercourse. In the course of my passage down the river as far as Fort Good Hope, I fell in with several parties of all the different tribes, and was welcomed by them with extravagant demonstrations of joy. They danced and cryed by turns, rushing up to their knees into the water to pull my canoe ashore, begging at the same time that the whites would return to their lands and promising their utmost endeavours to render our situation with them as comfortable as possible.

THE INCEPTION OF THE CONTACT-TRADITIONAL STAGE: TEMPORAL INTERVALS AND REGIONAL ZONES

With an enduring point-of-trade in its own country, an Indian group had direct, regular, and unmolested access to white trade goods. Even if the regularity of direct contact was for some but once or twice a year, the source was dependable if furs or other tradable commodities such as dryfish and drymeat were produced. Especially in times of trading monopoly, it led to credit relationships and in the lands of the British traders, at least, enhanced the authority of "chiefs." The Athapaskans were free on the land, and it was in the interests of the fur trade that they remain so, but they became increasingly

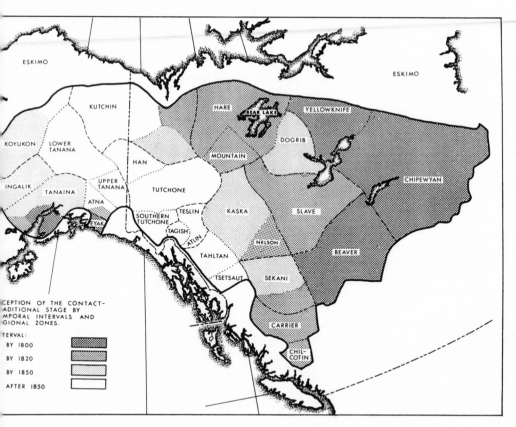

Map showing the inception of contact-traditional stages by temporal intervals and regional zones.

dependent on the post as the source of a new level of living. Subsistence on wild game and fish remained, and some items of clothing, shelter, and transportation continued for many decades to be fashioned of materials from the land. But the tools and implements to process natural materials derived more and more from the trader. We take, therefore, as the shorthand marker of transition from the incipient-early contact stage to the contact-traditional the establishment of an enduring trading fort within or close to a particular group's regular range or territory. In certain cases we include easy access, with no danger of hostile neighbors or interruption of contact, to a point-of-trade outside of the traditional zone of the group. It follows that the contact-traditional era sees the establishment of permanently peaceable relations between Indian and white.

Although crude, this simplified indicator of transition allows a grasp of successive intervals of contact experience across the Northern Athapaskan expanse. Four intervals emerge. When mapped, they demarcate rather well the major physiographic zones of the western subarctic as they allowed or inhibited penetration by European agents and the transportation of goods to supply a point-of-trade.

Interval A: By 1800 East of the cordillera, the year 1800 found Chipewyan, Beaver, and Yellowknife Indians with one or more points-of-trade established in their own territory by the "Montreal pedlars" or the recently formed North West Company. From Montreal, along the chain of inland waterways linked by the Grand Portage and Methy Portage, these traders had by then established posts as far west as the Peace River country of the Beaver and north to the North Arm of Great Slave Lake where Old Fort Providence provided the locus of Yellowknife ("Copper Indians") contact.

On the North Pacific coast, the (non-Athapaskan) Tlingit had been involved for a number of decades in the ship trade. The process of Tlingit expansion into Eyak country was largely completed by the end of the eighteenth century. Russian posts at Yakutat (formerly Eyak country) and Sitka were founded just before 1800, but both were destroyed within ten years. Yakutat was not rebuilt.

Russian trading interests were able to establish permanent posts in the Tanaina area following forceful subjugation of the hostile Indians; "successful" operations, however, were only in the coastal region of Cook Inlet. Chugach Eskimo and some Tanaina operated as middlemen between Russians and Atna and Eyak groups. The first direct contacts between the Russians and these latter peoples were hostile: Russians had taken Eyak hostages by 1800, and Russian efforts to ascend the Copper River met with attacks by natives.

Interval B: By 1820 The inception of contact-traditional relations between 1800 and 1820 occurred mainly in the area marked physiographically by the Mackenzie River and Upper Peace/Fraser River routes of European advance from the east. This is the era of full expansion of the North West Company. In terms of present-day identifications, the Mackenzie River groups involved are Slavey, Mountain Dene, Bearlake Dene, Hare, and Kutchin [Gwich'in] of the Mackenzie Flats (Mackenzie's "Quarrelers" or "Squint-Eyes"). In addition, those Kaska known as the Nelson People (or Tselona) who crossed the mountains to trade into Fort Nelson are to be

included (Honigmann 1954). In the Fraser River drainage, Carrier, Chilcotin, and southerly Sekani are included (Jenness 1937).

South of the Alaska Range, Russian trading relations were extended into
the Iliamna region of the Tanaina (Townsend 1970), and Copper Fort was
established in the Taral area of the Atna (de Laguna, personal communication). Copper Fort did not remain continuously open, however. The Upper
Atna and Inland Tanaina are apparently still not in regular, peaceable trading
relations with Russians in this period.

Interval C: By 1850   The year 1821 saw the incorporation of the North
West Company into the Hudson's Bay Company and the establishment of
points-of-trade in all "tribal" areas east of the continental Height of Land,
notably the Peel River Kutchin (Slobodin 1962) and the remaining Sekani
and Kaska. In the latter's area, the sites of trading points shifted about in this
period and later, bringing about a kind of scrambling of regional groups
(Honigmann 1954).

Assignment of the Dogribs poses a problem. Apparently, they were displaced by Yellowknife aggression from part of their traditional lands, those
on the northeastern side of Great Slave Lake, up to 1823 (Franklin 1824;
Simpson 1843). They did not have a point-of-trade central to their own territory until the establishment of old Fort Rae in 1852. They did have early
access to a North West Company post and then Fort Simpson in Slavey territory, and they were also trading at the posts on Great Bear River in the first
decades of the nineteenth century (Keith 1890). Sometime after 1823 Fort
Resolution on the south side of Great Slave Lake became a point-of-trade for
the southernmost Dogribs. But on the whole, the Dogribs stand out as an
isolate in the generally easy trade contact afforded the neighboring peoples
of the Upper Mackenzie drainage by 1820.

In westernmost Alaska, direct, regular contact was possible for the Ingalik
with the establishment of St. Michael's Redoubt in 1833 and for the Koyukon
by 1839 with Russian traders' presence at Nulato. The scene is complicated,
however, by evidence of extensive trading relationships prior to the presence
of Russian posts, particularly the Koyukon position as middlemen trading
into Kotzebue Sound, initially with Chuckchi and later with independent
European traders (Zagoskin 1967).

Trade agreements with the Russians first brought American traders to
the shores of the Alaskan archipelago in the 1820s, followed in a decade
by Hudson's Bay Company posts, which remained until the Alaska Purchase.

Hudson's Bay posts were also established on the British Columbia coast after 1821. Trade goods from coastal posts, however, reached the Athapaskans in the interior only through Indian middlemen.

Interval D: After 1850   The peoples inhabiting the terrain between the Continental Divide and the Pacific coastal ranges finally come into view.

The northwesternmost post in the British/Canadian trading domain was Fort Yukon, established in 1847. Since this date is so near our 1850 dateline, we place in Interval IV those peoples who had regular or intermittent trade contracts into Fort Yukon. These are the Kutchin [Gwich'in] within the Pacific drainage as well as Han and probably sectors of the Tanana. Probably the northeasternmost Koyukon also fall in this interval.

From the Pacific side, Tlingit and those Atna and Tanaina nearer the coast continued to block direct contact between European traders and adjacent interior Athapaskans, which included Upper Tanana, Tutchone, Inland Tlingit, and Tahltan. The interior groups' direct contact in their own territory occurred only after successive gold crazes and other mineral strikes smashed the barriers of terrain and the opposition of coastal natives, in some cases not until the twentieth century (McClellan 1964).

THE TRADING POST AND THE MISSION

Hiatt (1968) has characterized the Australian mission stations from the Aborigines' point of view as "super-waterholes." For the subarctic Indians, the trading posts were equally prodigious new resources placed upon the land. The existence of a permanent trading post tended to reorient spatially Indian populations who, though living out in and off of the land, accommodated ingathering at the post into their yearly cycle. Orientation to the point-of-trade sometimes may have created "new" native groups who came to be defined and to regard themselves as a distinctive people. In Canadian lands some Indian groups obtained an especially advantageous economic position by producing large amounts of native foods to provision the chain of trading establishments of the Hudson's Bay Company, for example, Dogrib procurement of caribou drymeat (Russell 1898) and Carrier salmon production (Harmon 1911 [1778–1845]).

In the Great Slave Lake and Mackenzie River region the period of commitment to the traditional fur trade was longest and had the fewest extraneous complications. As such, it provides a simple, "classic" model for the contact-traditional stage. Whether "contact-traditional" serves as a useful or adequate concept in reference to the Athapaskans on the Pacific side of the cordillera remains to be tested. From the beginning, elaborated internative trading patterns and resistance to European penetration had set the white-contact relations of Tanaina, Ingalik, and Koyukon groups apart from the rest of the Athapaskans. Also, for Athapaskan groups in the cordillera and along the southern edge of the subarctic the "simple" Indian-white relations of the fur trade were complicated or truncated by gold booms and home-steading. To this point we shall soon return.

Throughout the subarctic, disease and epidemic shook populational sta-bility and, we may surmise, cultural continuity until well into the twentieth century. Even simply to assemble the piecemeal record of the incidence and severity of disease in this era is difficult. This subject, therefore, is also with-held for separate consideration.

The missionization of Athapaskan populations was a signal and general feature of the contact-traditional era. Rather in the Spanish style in Meso-america, Russian Orthodox missionaries as an arm of the state were on the scene early in southern and coastal Alaska. In terms of the total Indian peoples of Alaska, however, their proselytizing activities were limited. By the latter half of the nineteenth century they had converted the McGrath Ingalik (or Kolchan [Hosley 1968]), perhaps their farthest inland extension. After the Alaska Purchase in 1867 Catholic and various Protestant denominations completed the conversions of the natives of Alaska.

In British/Canadian territory, the policy of the Hudson's Bay Company had been to keep the Indian as free as possible from exposure to any aspect of Western culture that did not contribute to his efficiency as a fur procurer. Only after 1850 did the Dene peoples in Canadian territory experience mis-sionary activity, Roman Catholic and Anglican.

Generally, the groups in the Mackenzie drainage (except for the Beaver [Faraud 1866]), the northern cordillera, and interior Alaska did not resist proselytizing and were quickly converted after missionary contact. In the southern cordillera conversion was more difficult. Although missionaries did not meet with overt hostility, they found the Carrier, for example, resistant to commands condemning potlatching (Morice 1905).

By 1900, all except the most isolated Athapaskan groups in the subarctic were nominally Christian. By this time, a few residence schools were oper-ating in conjunction with the missions in Canadian lands. In Alaska the U.S. government had by then taken over direct responsibility for native education from the missions. In most areas the impact of the mission schools upon the native population at large was slight. Only a small number of children were exposed to mission education, and a small number as adults altered their lifeways significantly in consequence.

BOOM FRONTIER AND SETTLED FRONTIER

In our "classic" model of contact-traditional intercultural relations, the trading post and the mission are the only two significant white installations in native lands. Both are there because of the Indian. But, beginning about 1860, portions of Athapaskan territory in central Alberta and British Columbia, the Yukon, and montane Alaska witnessed intermittent intrusions of substantial numbers of whites. As gold seekers or homesteaders, these whites, unlike the trader and the missionary, entered the land for purposes which did not include the Indian. In both homesteading and mineral strike situations, local native populations tended to become fringe groups around a frontier variety of white-dominant settlements that usually included stores, schools, saloons, and churches to serve whites. Although Indians might provide goods (country food and items of clothing and footgear) and services (guiding, packing, casual labor, prostitution) to whites, they were not integral or necessary figures in the scene.

At the risk of proliferating terminology, these intrusions may be distinguished as "boom frontiers" in the case of the flood and ebb of whites in gold rushes or other mineral strikes and as "settled frontiers" where, as in the valleys of the Peace, Fraser, Tanana, and (in the 1930s) Matanuska Rivers, a stable white population has taken over tracts of land for farming and ranching.

In most gold strikes the initially large white population quickly diminished, in some cases in a matter of months, leaving only a handful of people. To those Indians who could respond selectively, the boom frontier offered economic opportunity and the glamour of travel and new-found sophistication, for example, the "Dawson boys" of the Peel River Kutchin (Slobodin 1963).

Once introduced from the East, Indian-white fur trade relations had stabilized quickly in the southern (British Columbia) sector of the cordillera, facilitated by the practice of building trading posts close to the fishing villages of the semisedentary Chilcotin, Carrier, and Tahltan. The series of gold rushes between 1860 and 1900 opened sections of Carrier and Chilcotin country to railways, roads, and homesteaders whose numbers increased greatly after 1900. The Indians responded with a partial involvement in wage labor and farming and ranching activities. Homesteading in the Peace River area of Alberta since 1890 has promoted similar diversification among the Beaver Indians there. The continued commercial and population growth of Anchorage and Fairbanks, sites important in the Alaska gold rushes, has resulted in urban complexes within the traditional regions of the Tanaina and Tanana. Tanaina began working in commercial canneries on the coast by 1915 (Townsend 1970). In the Upper Yukon drainage of Alaska no large white-dominant settlements followed the bust after the gold booms.

Where the settled frontier appeared in the lands of the Northern Athapaskans, it initiated the kind of contact relationship known throughout southern Canada and the United States. Indians found themselves in a self-conscious minority position vis-à-vis a dominant white population immediately present upon the land. In terms of the economic, social, and cultural submersion of the Indian within the white man's greater society, "modern" conditions arrived for some of the Athapaskans of the North fifty or more years in advance of their more isolated brethren.

THE GOVERNMENT–COMMERCIAL ERA

Due to the limits on research and documentation in this survey, we must reduce to a generalized sketch the variations and complexities of contact experience that have brought the Northern Athapaskans into the present day [to 1975]. The designation "government-commercial era" encapsulates two of the ever more dominating features in contemporary native life. The native peoples of the North have entered, albeit on the lower monetary rung, into the "consumer society" of North America, and government is inextricably the major mover in the commercial phase of the modern era.

As inculcator and enforcer of whiteman values, morals, and standards, government in its multiple aspects as lawmaker, educator, and welfare dispenser has come to usurp and enlarge the role once filled by the mission as the self-appointed caretaker of the Indian. In legal terms, the details of the government's relationship with Indians have of course varied according to national and subnational political divisions and have altered through time. But from the Indian perspective, "Government" has been a monolithic, if inscrutable and uncontrollable, entity.

Generally, the federal level of government has been more prominent in affecting Indian life. Inception of formal relations between both U.S. and Canadian governments and Northern Athapaskan groups began after 1867. In the ground rules laid out by treaties (in Alberta, Saskatchewan, and the Northwest Territories) and/or simply introduced as "Indian policy" (in

Alaska, most of British Columbia, and the Yukon Territory) the Indian was constrained to observe the laws as encoded, and in return the federal government assumed, at least on paper, certain responsibilities toward the social, economic, and physical welfare of the Indian. In Canada (in contrast to Alaska) almost all responsibility for direct action remained vested in the missions for many decades. The Yukon and the Northwest Territories present an extreme case of "governmental lag"; almost no direct governmental involvement in Indian health or education was taken until after the Second World War.

The effort in the 1960s of the Athapaskan peoples of Alaska and northwestern Canada to enunciate and establish land claims based on aboriginal territories is one of the most politically significant developments. It remains, however, a specific feature within more encompassing trends in Indian-government relations. In both Canada and the United States there came a shift in perspective regarding the responsibilities and relationship of the nation-state toward all its citizens that has brought accelerated changes in Indian life in the North that [were] still emerging in the 1970s. Whether under bills relating specifically to Indians or to the public at large, both Canada and the United States enunciated the goals of elimination of social, economic, and legal inequities and of the attainment of an "acceptable" level of living for all persons. These are manifest in new or expanded welfare measures for children, the poor, and the aged, in public housing, in school building and expansion, and in the elimination of discriminatory legal provisions against Indians (e.g., invidious alcohol consumption laws and denial of the vote at the subfederal level). Canada has gone further in general social welfare measures by providing to all Canadians the family allowance and the old age security programs.

It can be demonstrated that under these provisions Indian education, health, and level of living have improved by the criteria ordinarily applied (more children in school for more years, lowered death rate, new housing, etc.). But attentive observers, Indian and white, recognize that these factors introduced into Indian life have had substantial consequences that are less easy to "statistify" and evaluate. We can only suggest some of the dimensions [again, as of 1975]:

Item: The tangle of legal requirements and definitions and the bureaucratic chains of command in the dispensing of welfare subsidies and public housing baffle the applicant and place him in a supplicatory position under the discipline of omnipresent and omnipotent Government. Not granted effective powers to deal with Government, the "government chief" bears the brunt of disaffection and factionalism that the system engenders.

Item: School requirements, routines, and performance standards aim at providing the Indian child with "advantages" in coping with the white world. But School, as experienced, seems often to place the child early in life in the same baffled, defeated, and impotent posture in which Government places his parent (see King 1967).

Item: Day schools, public housing, the post office that brings government subsidy checks of one sort or another combine to hold the Indian family in the settlement or town, where, commonly, opportunities for wage employment do not begin to accommodate the resident Indian population. Perhaps an even greater lure to town living are the attractions of a micro-urban lifestyle offered by the store, the bar and beer parlor, the movie house, the Saturday-night dance.

The accelerated growth of the Indian population will, it would seem, increase the pressures building at present.

To reiterate, exposure to whiteman standards of living through broader individual experiences, through mass media, and through the educational system has brought new levels of aspiration in consumer standards. These aspirations go beyond what fur production could provide (and, indeed, deflect the Indian from bush life) and beyond what is available to most natives in most parts of the North through wage employment. As government services and the diversions and attractions of mass culture have increased, Indians have increasingly retreated from the land as the source of subsistence and as the site of a relatively autonomous community life to take up an urban or micro-urban existence.

With the loss of native language and the attrition of knowledge and commitment to traditional culture, the "Indian" identity of the generations to come seems at present to be lodged in the growing pan-Indian movements in Alaska and northwestern Canada. These have taken political form [as of 1975] in the Alaska Federation of Natives, the Union of British Columbia Chiefs, and the Indian Brotherhoods of the prairie provinces and Territories of Canada. These organizations aim at creating economic and, especially, political leverage (e.g., "land claims") for Indians as a depressed minority within the greater society.

EPIDEMICS AND POPULATION PATTERNS DURING
THE CONTACT-TRADITIONAL STAGE

Terry Alliband researched this section.

A significant, too often catastrophic, feature in North American Indian-European contact history has been the introduction of new diseases and disease-producing conditions among the native peoples. In most cases, the effects on population levels and the social and cultural consequences have yet to be adequately assessed. [Krech (1983) addresses disease and possible effects on Mackenzie drainage populations of 1800–1850.] In this section of our essay we again attempt only an initial inquiry. We present available data on disease (which takes almost exclusively the form of evidence on epidemics) and on population patterns during the contact-traditional stage of Indian-white relations in the Athapaskan North. Epidemics may have brought havoc and depopulation to Northern Athapaskan groups in earliest contact times or even prior to the physical advent of the European (e.g., did the smallpox epidemic of 1775 among the Tlingit of the Alaskan coast spread inland?), but documentation is largely lacking. Recent population figures in those areas where the specifically Athapaskan component of the population can be identified are considered later. It is apparent that the native population take-off that began in Alaska about 1925 and in the Northwest Territories about 1959 is directly the consequence of the introduction and expansion of medical services.

Data concerning both disease incidence and population fluctuation during contact-traditional times must be viewed with caution on a number of grounds. Deaths due to nonepidemic diseases, notably tuberculosis, are usually not so identified, even as estimates. With respect to the data on epidemics, the problem of the hit-and-miss nature of the information is difficult to overcome. [By exploring several archival collections, McCarthy (1995) has recently provided an enhanced record of epidemics in the Mackenzie region from 1857 to 1928.] We encounter records of apparently discrete outbreaks of smallpox or scarlet fever, for example, occurring in separated geographical locations within a year or two of one another. Are we then dealing with scattered, unrelated outbreaks, or do they in fact represent an epidemic wave which affected larger numbers than the available literature records?

Documentation on epidemics largely takes the form of occasional comments by persons untutored in medical diagnostic techniques who happened to be in a given region during an outbreak of some sort. Often the information is fairly reliable and reasonably detailed, although many writers provide only gross mortality estimates or are content to note that the rate among a disease-stricken people was "severe."

In regard to population sizes in general, an often unresolvable question is the possibility of inaccurate enumeration or grossly skewed estimates. An allied question is whether successive population figures based on Indians of a particular region or those frequenting a particular point-of-trade represent the same group or groups each time. [This problem has been controlled for the Mackenzie Dene forts; see chapter 11.] In this respect, government censuses and other forms of data, usually based on administrative units, are often inaccurate and misleading or they ignore linguistic/tribal identities. Given these considerations, our notations of epidemic conditions and assessments of population patterns during the contact-traditional era are tentative.

Based on the available evidence on contagious epidemics, scarlet fever and smallpox produced the heaviest mortality among Northern Athapaskans prior to about 1900. After that date, outbreaks of influenza and measles are recorded as causing severe epidemics.

The first recorded widespread epidemic among the Athapaskans was a smallpox epidemic among eastern Chipewyans (and western Cree) about 1781 (Hearne 1958 [1795]). It is not known whether or not this outbreak spread into the Mackenzie River region. Smallpox broke out among the Tlingit, Tanaina, Ingalik, and possibly other Athapaskan groups about 1835– 39 (Krause 1956; Townsend 1970; Zagoskin 1967; Bancroft 1886; McKennan 1969). Although the Russians attempted to administer smallpox vaccinations for the amelioration of this epidemic, the natives were reluctant to be vaccinated; an estimated 25 to 50 percent of the people in the affected group died during this siege (Stearn and Stearn 1943; Elliott 1887). Outbreaks of smallpox occurred around 1862 and 1865 among the southern Carrier (Jenness 1943; Morice 1905) and among the Tahltan in 1864 and 1868 (Emmons 1911).

Petitot (1891) states that the "Mal du Fort Rae" in 1859 took over four hundred lives from a population of about twelve hundred. Petitot was unable to establish the epidemic's nature. One of the first reported instances of a scarlet fever epidemic occurred among the southern Tutchone about 1851 (Dawson 1888). A number of scarlet fever epidemics were reported in the years between 1862 and 1867. This period saw the extermination of the Birch Creek Kutchin and Lower Yukon Kutchin, heavy mortality among the Chilcotin, and the abandonment of Fort Anderson because of scarlet fever mortality among the Kutchin and Hare (Osgood 1934; Voorhis 1930; McKennan

1969). Influenza is recorded to have killed one thousand Indians from Fort Simpson to Peel's River (Slave, Bearlake, Hare, and Eastern Kutchin populations) in 1865 (Stewart 1955).

A widespread eruption of measles occurred about 1902 among the Hare, Bearlake, Dogrib, eastern Kutchin, and possibly other Athapaskans in the Mackenzie River region (Thomas 1970; Constantine 1903). At approximately the same time, measles epidemics struck the Ingalik, Koyukon, Lower Tanana, and possibly other Alaskan Athapaskans as well (Stuck 1917). As is so often the case, the extent of mortality is not known, although Constantine (1903) tells us that seventy out of a band of eighty Kutchin died, and sixty Dogribs are recorded as dead from this cause at Fort Rae alone (Helm 1969b).

Influenza outbreaks ravaged the Alaskan Athapaskans in 1917–18, killing an estimated 10 percent of the native population in that region (Anderson and Eells 1935). The Tagish, Tutchone, and Inland Tlingit of the Yukon were also "devastated" (McClellan, personal communication). Influenza struck the Mackenzie River region in 1928, taking a toll of at least six hundred lives (Godsell 1934) from Fort Resolution to Fort Good Hope [see chapter 9]. No large-scale epidemics are reported from the subarctic Athapaskans after this date, although further searches may reveal statistics on epidemics of local severity (e.g., measles at Ross River in 1951 [McClellan, personal communication]).

Population changes caused by venereal disease and chronic diseases such as tuberculosis are difficult to assess because of lack of data for this period. These diseases lack the dramatic nature of epidemics and hence may not have been recorded because of their commonplace quality.

There can be little doubt but that tuberculosis in particular has been a factor in determining the population level among Canadian and Alaskan Athapaskans, although documentation is scarce prior to recent times. When it exists (e.g., Garrioch's [1929] account of apparently tubercular "scrofula" destroying the Fort Vermilion Beaver in the 1870s), it is unaccompanied by statistics. In the 1940s tuberculosis was described as the major mortal disease among the Indians in both Canada and Alaska; in Alaska it accounted for 43 percent of the deaths among the Eskimos, Aleuts, and Indians (Haldeman 1951; Wherrett 1947). During the five-year period 1937–41, tuberculosis took the lives of Northwest Territories Indians at a rate of 761.4 per 100,000, compared to a rate of 43.7 per 100,000 for whites and 314.6 per 100,000 for Eskimos for the same period (Wherrett 1947). This rate of mortality due to tuberculosis among subarctic Athapaskans closely approximates that existing in urban U.S. cities during the early nineteenth century when up to

30 percent of all deaths were caused by tuberculosis, and the death rate in Philadelphia due to pulmonary tuberculosis was 618 per 100,000 (Lowell et al. 1969). Hence, while the importance of this disease as a population factor in late contact-traditional times cannot be detailed, it can reasonably be inferred. With respect to syphilis, Haldeman (1951) notes that its incidence in Alaska among the Indians and Eskimos is low in recent times but once introduced into a region can reach epidemic proportions.

One might predict that the combination of the effects of widespread disease epidemics such as smallpox, measles, scarlet fever, and influenza with those of introduced attritional diseases such as tuberculosis would result in severe and continuing population decline among the Northern Athapaskans during the contact-traditional period. However, generally reliable data from the Mackenzie River area falsify this prediction, for that region at least. In roughly the last two thirds of the contact-traditional era (from 1858 to 1941), the population level of these subarctic Athapaskans evinces only a slightly declining, almost static quality, despite known short-term population losses due to epidemics. The "recuperation" factors that produced this relative homeostasis over time are puzzling and not adducible from present knowledge. [I addressed this "puzzle" in a later study and, I believe, "solved" it. See chapter 11.] Over a span of 112 years, the overall Athapaskan population associated with ten forts in the Mackenzie River region declined by 9 percent [2,966 to 2,691] during the period 1858–1941 and increased by 56 percent [2,691 to 4,214] from 1941 to 1970. The post–1941 increase coincides with government medical services begun in the 1940s. [See Gibson (1988) for illuminating testimonies by three medical practitioners about medical care and native health in the North in the 1950s and later.]

In respect to Alaskan Athapaskan population, data by "tribal" or dialect groups at any time period are generally unobtainable. (From 1930 up to this writing, U.S. census figures do not make any linguistic differentiation between Alaskan Indians.) From 4,059 persons recorded for 1880, the Alaskan Athapaskan population hit a nadir of 3,520 in 1890 and rose to 4,935 by 1930, an overall gain in fifty years of 18 percent (U.S. Census Bureau reports). Reliable data on the post–1930 population of Alaskan Athapaskans would probably show a continuing sharp increase if the Canadian case can be taken as an analogy.

from Helm, Alliband, Birk, Lawson, Reisner, Sturdevant, and Witkowski,
"The Contact History of the Subarctic Athapaskans: An Overview," 1975

OVERVIEW HEARING AT THE
8 | MACKENZIE VALLEY PIPELINE
INQUIRY, 1975

At the start of the Mackenzie Valley Pipeline Inquiry (MVPI) hearings in 1975, J. K. Stager, a geographer from the University of British Columbia, and I shared the task of surveying the human populations of the Mackenzie region, along with overview presentations by specialists on the flora, fauna, and geology of the region. This chapter comes from the transcription of my oral testimony at the overview hearing. Dr. Stager's portion of our joint presentation mainly addressed Inuit contact history and white economic interests and enterprises and is omitted. For Mr. Justice Thomas R. Berger's encapsulation of the conclusions from the full MVPI, see Berger (1977).

Commissioner Berger:

Well, Dr. Helm, Dr. Stager, you have prepared your presentation, your evidence for the Commission in a form that is suitable to yourselves, and I would ask you to introduce it and carry on, please.

Dr. Helm:

Thank you. Dr. Stager and I did have the opportunity to meet a few weeks ago and discuss what we felt were the most critical points to bring up in a very limited time period relating to what we may call the contact history of native and nonnative persons in the Northwest Territories. Our areal research concentrations indicated that I should attend mainly to the area upstream of the Mackenzie River delta and to the Dene Indian groups there, although I will occasionally refer to Inuit as well. Dr. Stager's activities have been concentrated in the delta and coast, so he will give his perspective on those areas. Indeed, the contact histories of the two areas have been somewhat different, so our division of labor corresponds to historical circumstance itself.

I might add that we are going to try to cover about half a million square miles and 250 years in three hours.

The first topic which I am taking is a survey of native peoples and linguistic geography of the Northwest Territories. We must recognize that the aboriginal inhabitants belong to two great language families: the Eskimoan, represented by the Inuit or Eskimo peoples, and the Athapaskan, represented by the Indian peoples or Dene (or variants of that term as they express it in their own languages).

I cannot take time to go into the archaeological evidence from the present into the past, but we have evidence of aboriginal occupation in this land as soon as the great continental ice sheet began to retreat and it was possible for man and animal to subsist. Indeed, in several areas we now have archaeological connections by what we call the direct historical method—from known sites of historic contact times back into the past—where we can pretty well pinpoint that the ancestors of Dene people were at least two thousand years ago living in areas in which we find them today. [See Noble (1981) on the Taltheilei Shale Tradition.] In other words, I am establishing the credentials of both Inuit and Dene as peoples who have been essentially in their respective areas since, as we say, "time immemorial."

The distribution of these two sets of peoples in Canada corresponds to the great major environmental-ecological zones of the North. The Inuit are coastal peoples; they are sea mammal oriented. They lived on the margins of the polar sea or on the sea ice for much of the year. The Dene peoples, and these include not only the Indian peoples of the Northwest Territories but also those of the Yukon Territory, are subarctic, interior forest–oriented peoples. The Dene are large land mammal oriented. The barren grounds, or tundra, is a zone of seasonal exploitation for both of these great native American groups. In Canada we find one Inuit group, the Caribou Eskimo of Keewatin, who live inland year-round. But the emphasis for most Inuit had been to exploit the sea, to move inland to caribou and fishing sites in the summer and then retreat to the coast, whereas the Dene traditionally stayed within the woods or at least within the forest-tundra ecotone. Only in early fall did Dene go beyond the edge of the woods in pursuit of caribou. Then might Dene and Inuit on occasion encounter one another at such places as Contwoyto Lake.

I should speak briefly to bilingualism and the problem of language loss. I'll speak just of Indians. At present [1975] the Kutchin [Gwich'in] people are the Indians of the Northwest Territories who are most concerned with loss of the native language in the younger generation. Many more Kutchin have been bilingual in Kutchin and English much longer than the Dene up-stream in the Mackenzie drainage. There is a concern on the part of the people now that the younger generation may be losing its command of or ability to speak Kutchin. Of the other Athapaskan Indian groups, in most settlements the native language is spoken in almost all the homes. Most over-forty persons are illiterate, and many of them are monolingual in the native language. [Reader, please remember that I speak here as of 1975.] In these Dene populations native language retention has been very good so far, but we know from the United States that in one generation a language may be overthrown. [Krauss (1997) provides a quantified update on Northern Atha-paskan language retention.]

There is another native group of the Northwest Territories. These are the Metis people, who are, by one kind of definition, of mixed Indian and Eu-ropean bloodlines. But that's not really a critical issue. There are many per-sons who have some white ancestry who are considered to be Indians by other Indians. The important point is that the Metis derive from a dual cul-tural heritage. And in terms of that dual cultural heritage we can make the distinction between two kinds of Metis in the Northwest Territories. One kind are those who are descendants of the Red River Metis, the people of Louis Riel, who were created by the marriages à la façon du pays of Cree and Ojibwa women with French (and some British) fur-trade transport workers. These Metis moved west and north with the fur trade. The second kind of Metis in the Northwest Territories is a more recent emergence. For them, Professor Slobodin (1966, see also 1981) has suggested the term "Northern Metis." These are persons of Athapaskan (or Inuit) plus Scotch/English, English-speaking backgrounds. I should point out, of course, that the Red River Metis' descendants—identified by such names as Beaulieu, Bouvier, Mercredi, and Lafferty—have intermarried with Dene peoples of the North, so their Indian ancestry is not simply Cree-Ojibwa (Algonkian-speaking) heritage.

Metis are people who have a footing, either in the first generation or later generations, in two cultures, Indian and European. It is most immediately manifested in bilingualism. As a result, Metis have historically served as in-termediaries in communication between the incoming European or Euro-Canadian and the Indian who is monolingual.

Then there are the nonstatus Indians. These are persons of native descent who for one reason or another have "gone off treaty" or whose father did, or are Dene women who married whites and those women's children. Non-status Indians disappear from the government band rolls and census counts of

"Indian." And, of course, the nonstatus Indians have a different legal position vis-à-vis the government than do their "treaty Indian" relatives.

CONTACT HISTORY TO WORLD WAR II

I'm going to move into the historic dimension, to cover the major historical events and developments from the beginning of contact to World War II. It has been useful to me in trying to think about this through the years and using the documentary sources to divide this span into two periods: the period of early contact between Indians and Europeans and the period of stabilized contact. This latter period I have sometimes called the contact-traditional era. The early contact period represents the beginnings or the formation of relationships between native peoples and incoming outsiders. The contact-traditional era represents a stabilization and development of contact relationships, with change going on, certainly, in this long period, but not an overthrow or destruction of a native way of life.

PERIOD OF EARLY CONTACT

I'll approach the period of early contact in terms of a few significant dates and associated events.

In 1717 the Hudson's Bay Company began building Prince of Wales Fort, near the present site of Churchill, to attract the Chipewyan Dene of what is today northern Manitoba and the southern edge of the Northwest Territories. Chipewyans were hesitant to visit the established bayside forts because of the threat of Cree aggression. The new fort farther north allowed Chipewyans safely to bring furs to trade for European goods. Some began to operate as middlemen, taking trade goods far into the interior to barter for furs with Dene groups who might not see a white man for another half-century.

The next important date is the winter of 1778–79, when Peter Pond wintered on the Athabasca River. Pond was one of those entrepreneurs pushing west, circumventing the Hudson's Bay Company's legal monopoly of the fur trade in the Hudson Bay drainage. By crossing the height of land at Methye Portage into the Mackenzie River drainage, Pond brought trade directly into this remarkably rich fur country of the Dene.

By 1789 Peter Pond and other "free traders" were forming the North West Company, rival to the Hudson's Bay Company. In that same year Alexander Mackenzie, aided by information from Pond (who apparently had been as far as Great Slave Lake), went down the "Grand River" to the tidewaters of the Arctic Ocean. In the course of his journey he contacted Hares,

Slaves, Dogribs, and Loucheux [Gwich'in], and as he passed Point Separation he found abandoned Eskimo camps. [The Grand River became the Mackenzie River. This river is Dehcho, the Big River, to Dene.]

From 1790 to 1821, several trading posts of the North West Company were set up from Great Slave Lake to the Lower Mackenzie. The date that marks the close of this early contact period is 1821. In that year the Hudson's Bay Company merged with the North West Company. In most of the land the Hudson's Bay Company maintained an effective monopoly almost to the turn of the twentieth century, although its legal monopoly lapsed earlier.

During the early period of contact, the Indians were only very lightly committed to the fur trade. A few moved into richer fur regions, such as those Chipewyans who moved from the edge of the woods into the lowland area between Lake Athabasca and Great Slave Lake where fur was better [see chapter 13]. Generally, however, the traders complained (and in some areas they continued to complain for many decades) that the Indians brought in fewer furs than the traders sought.

Since European trading posts were often short-lived, for many Indian groups contact with the trader was irregular and to a fair degree unpredictable. They didn't know whether a post was going to be there next year, and some populations such as the eastern Dogribs and the Mountain Indians hardly experienced direct trade contact until well after 1821. In this period there were perturbations in intertribal relations caused by the greed that could be excited in some Indians who had muzzle-loaders to attack Indians farther off who did not yet have firearms. There was a relatively short period of—"warfare" is too emphatic a word—raiding and killing. Before 1800 there were Cree incursions in the Great Slave Lake and Upper Mackenzie River area, and in the early 1800s came the aggressions of Akaitcho's "Copper Indians" against Dogrib and Bear Lake peoples [see chapter 12].

With the exception of the Fort Nelson (British Columbia) massacre in 1812, Dene-trader relationships were without deaths on either side. If relations were not always enthusiastic, they were peaceable, because the two sides had a mutual interest in each other. The Indian wanted trade goods and the trader wanted furs. The trader couldn't get furs without the Indian, and he was in no position to coerce the Indian. Of the trade goods, iron implements were critical. Dene immediately recognized the difference between going through a foot of ice using a piece of caribou or muskox horn as a chisel and using one of iron. Ice chisels, files, axes, and a few firearms were perhaps the most important new tools. There were also some luxury items, such as beads, received in exchange for furs. The Dene continued to take all their food from the land.

THE CONTACT–TRADITIONAL ERA

Insofar as one can ever put a beginning and ending date on an "era," the contact-traditional era starts in 1821, when the North West Company and the Hudson's Bay Company merged, and lasts up to the Second World War. In this era the Indians' major contacts with European-derived persons and culture were channeled through the few agents of the fur trade and the church. For the first forty years, the only significant "alien" was the fur trader. Then in the 1860s the missionaries arrived, Anglicans and the Oblate order of Roman Catholics. Within a couple of decades the missionaries had at least nominally converted most of the Dene inhabitants of the Territories. Throughout the era native society and culture underwent adjustments, responses, and innovations to emanations from the European world but apparently, except for the traumas of epidemics, without severely disruptive factors.

Reliance on wild game and fish for subsistence remained, and some items of clothing, shelter, and transportation continued to be taken from the land until into the twentieth century—moose and caribou hide for mitts and footgear, birchbark for canoes, for example. But through time more and more implements with which to garner and process natural materials came to derive more and more from the fur trade. Indians became more dependent on the goods at the trading post as a source of a new level of living. Items of European manufacture such as guns, various kinds of implements, pots and utensils, cloth and clothing, and tea and tobacco became necessities. With modifications, the Indians' yearly round that developed and was sustained through this era could until recently still be seen, especially in bush communities such as Rae Lakes [Gamiti] where there was not yet a white installation such as a settlement manager, or school, or store.

The fur trade dominated the scene in this era. Through the decades the native fur procurers had to submit to the ups and downs of the fur market. It's worth emphasizing that 1939 was the first year in the Northwest Territories in which the value of production of all other resources of the Territories exceeded that of fur production. In other words, in the Canadian economy fur remained the predominant resource of the Territories up to the start of the war.

Direct contact was infrequent between the Indian trapper-hunter living in the bush and the trader at the fort, but the relationship was enduring. The trader kept records of each man's productivity and reliability through the year, and that would determine the amount of the man's credit issued in the form of ammunition and other supplies for the coming season. That which the Canadian government now calls a "band" was being defined in this era. It wasn't a band in the sense of how native people organized themselves out on the land. It was the list of Indian trappers carried on the books of each trading post. These trappers and their families were not necessarily in interaction with one another before that post was established. The existence of the post did tend to reorient Indian populations, especially to accommodate ingathering into the fort into their yearly cycle, and this aggregate associated with a specific trading post became what one may call the Trading Post Band. From this aggregate derived the government's idea of an Indian band—the "Yellowknife 'B' Band," the "Dogrib Rae Band," the "Fort Simpson Band," the "Fort Good Hope Band," the "Fort McPherson Band," and so on. With the "taking of treaty," government imbued these Trading Post Bands with formal membership recorded on the government's band lists.

There were some native occupations in white enterprises during this era. One was the dog team driver carrying mail between posts. Another was the fort hunter. He was responsible for recruiting and directing a small crew of men to take caribou or moose in quantity for provisioning the post personnel. He was paid in goods and supplies, much of which was distributed to his men. Also there were fishing crews. (Fort Resolution was a great fishery.) These men were employed in season to stockpile fish for the permanent trading personnel at the post. Sometimes native "trippers" worked for the trader, going to Indian camps with goods to trade for furs. Probably more Metis than Indians were in these jobs. At the trading establishment itself there was the native interpreter-clerk, usually a Metis because he had to be bilingual. A similar intermediary status that was created at the beginning of the twentieth century was the special constable ("Mountie special"), who enabled the policeman to travel and communicate to native persons. Earlier in the era, Indians and Metis were employed by the score for the summer-long tracking and rowing of York boats. A York boat came from each trading post, carrying the year's furs from each fort out, bringing the year's supplies in. Beginning with the steamboat *Wrigley*, which ran the length of the Mackenzie River for the first time in 1887, paddlewheel steamboats replaced York boats on the Mackenzie. Metis usually filled the newer transport jobs available, and the jobs were much fewer. Scores of men for brute human labor were no longer needed. The Metis worked as deck hands and pilots. They have continued to follow these occupations with the introduction of the gas tugboats (about 1920), followed by diesel tugboats and steel barges.

In the last decade of the nineteenth century "free traders," some allied with larger organizations and some operating as individuals, appeared between Lake Athabasca and the southern shore of Great Slave Lake, bringing competition to the Hudson's Bay Company and pushing up the payment for furs. White trappers were increasing also. In the first decade of the twentieth century free traders entered the other areas of the Territories. This had a significant effect on Indian access to trade goods. A much greater variety of goods was offered the trapper at lower prices. This is the period when steel traps came into common use. Prior to the free traders, the Bay was not pushed to offer modern steel traps. The Indians were using deadfalls and snares to take fur. The free traders also introduced a money economy. Before then, the price of trade goods and furs of all kinds was reckoned in terms of beaver pelts, the famous Hudson's Bay Company's Made Beaver, as the standard unit of value. Many of these small-scale free traders survived only a few years, but their advent broke the Hudson's Bay Company's monopoly.

In 1901 the nonnative population of the Northwest Territories was 137 persons. Most significant for the natives were probably the several free traders, Hudson's Bay Company traders, missionaries, the white school personnel of the three church residential schools. (I should add that only a small minority of Indian children were exposed to schooling.) By 1911 the white population of the Northwest Territories had expanded to 519 persons, many being white trappers and free traders (Zaslow 1971:238).

The North-West Mounted Police began patrols in the Northwest Territories in 1903. The subsequent Royal Canadian Mounted Police established all of their present-day posts only after 1921, when Treaty No. 11 was signed with the Indians north of Great Slave Lake. Between 1900 and World War II other government occupational groups included two or three men perhaps serving doubly as Indian agent and doctor, a few nursing sisters, a few game officers. A few white wives were by this time also in the land. Spates of white trappers and prospectors came and went. For the Indian people, the most portentous event in this era was treaty making. The Inuit were never asked to sign a treaty, so I'm speaking now of the Dene. In 1899, with some additions in 1900, Treaty No. 8 was established with those Indians of the Northwest Territories living in the area south of or trading at Fort Resolution on the south side of Great Slave Lake. Treaty No. 8 was modeled on the treaties that had been negotiated with Indians throughout the prairie provinces since Confederation. The immediate impact on Indian life was slight. No reserves were established. The gold strikes in the Yukon Territory and Alaska in the last decade of the nineteenth century presaged a possible flood of whites heading down the Slave River and the Mackenzie, thence over the mountains to the gold fields. The treaty was perceived by the Indians as an acknowledgment that they would not obstruct the entry of whites into the land. The Indians were guaranteed a yearly allotment of ammunition and twine for nets and a few other items. Metis were not included in Treaty No. 8. They were issued scrip, as had been the Metis of the prairie provinces.

Treaty No. 11 was signed in 1921 (and in 1922 by the Liard Slaveys). This treaty was negotiated with the Indians north of Great Slave Lake and the 60th parallel, all those Dene north of the Treaty No. 8 lands. Treaty No. 11 guaranteed goods and the opportunity for reserves at some future time, very similar in substance to the earlier Treaty No. 8. This time, however, Metis were given the opportunity to take treaty because, as the Indian agent at Resolution had emphasized, most of the Metis of the Treaty No. 8 area were living as bush Indians and yet were denied the yearly issue of fish-net twine and ammunition. They were denied—well, I was going to say health services, but health services were nonexistent except for that box of medicine that was to be issued each year.

What the Indian leaders could not have grasped—as they "signed" with crosses Treaty No. 8 and Treaty No. 11—was the implications of the words "the said Indians do hereby cede, release, surrender, and yield up to the Government of the Dominion of Canada . . . forever, all their rights, titles, and privileges whatsoever to the lands."

To both trader and missionary the native was an indispensable resource. The trader had to have the natives on the land to bring in furs. To the missionary the natives were the essential wellspring of souls for the church. With the coming of Treaty came the Indian agent and the Mountie. To these officials the native was not a resource but a charge.

At this point, Professor Stager addressed "Contact History to World War II in the Delta and on the Coast," followed by "Major Economic Stimuli in the Mackenzie Corridor Region in the Postwar Period."

FROM WORLD WAR II TO THE PRESENT

Professor Stager has just dealt with developments during and after World War II in the transportation-communication industry and some of the con-

TABLE 8.1. *Ethnic Sectors, 1941 and 1971*

	Population Total	Treaty Indians	Inuit	Other
1941	12,028	4,334 = 36.0%	5,404 = 45.0%	2,290 = 19.0%
1971	34,805	7,108 = 26.6%	11,400 = 32.7%	16,225 = 46.7%

Intra-ethnic rates of increase from 1941 to 1971: Treaty Indians, 64%; Inuit, 107%; Other, 608%.

sequences in terms of wage labor. Since he has emphasized the technological and economic aspects of the last thirty to thirty-five years, I'd like to look at some significant kinds of social changes less immediately apparent in terms of gross territorial product. One thing to look at is the growth of population and the components of population over a thirty-year interval (see table 8.1). The category "Other" includes all persons who are not identified as Inuit or Treaty Indian, so the native Metis population is included with whites under "Other."

In these figures we see almost a threefold growth in total population and absolute growth in all ethnic sectors, but the proportional figures are the more interesting. In 1941 both Treaty Indian and Inuit as population units far exceeded the Other sector. By 1971, however, instead of 36 percent of the total population being persons registered on the Treaty rolls as in 1941, Treaty Indians make up about 27 percent. For the Inuit people, their percent in the total population has declined from 45 percent to about 33 percent. On the other hand, the Other category swells from 19 percent in 1941 to over 46 percent in 1971: essentially, this is the white or southern Canadian–derived category. Within each ethnic group, and I use the word "ethnic" only in terms of the categories that the census provides us ([Treaty] Indian, Inuit, and Other), in thirty years the absolute increase of Treaty Indians has been 64 percent; the Inuit population has doubled in size; but then look at Other, a 600 percent increase. Native population growth has been due to a lowered death rate as well as a birth rate above the national average. But the white growth is due mainly to in-migration.

It is important to note that the native population is a young population. About half of the total population of the Northwest Territories is under the age of twenty-five. Of the Inuit population, 70 percent are under twenty-five; and of the Dene population, 60 percent are under twenty-five. And these figures are from before 1971. Most of the native people have their reproductive years still ahead of them. Nonetheless, the conclusion that must be drawn from the figures given above is that a numerical swamping of the native population by southern-derived whites is under way. [*News/North*'s "Opportunities North" of May 27, 1996, records a population for 1991 of about 66,000, divided into approximately 19 percent Dene, 7 percent Metis, 37 percent Inuit, and 37 percent Other.]

Another way to look at population is in terms of sociologically significant components: who is interacting with whom, both within a group and in terms of a power structure hierarchy. In the early 1960s Professor Jacob Fried (1963) surveyed the various settlements of the Northwest Territories. He set forth what he called "the three vital populational components of the larger northern settlements." One component he identifies as "transient southern Canadians," represented by government civil servants and other private agency–sponsored, southern Canadians. The second component is "non-government northern whites," those whites who for some reason or other have settled in the North. These are trappers and prospectors who have stayed on, along with former employees of the Hudson's Bay Company and of the mines and transportation companies, and "a few hardy business men trickling into the north." The third sociologically significant component is the native population of Dene, Inuit, and Metis.

In Fried's analysis, the coming together of these three components has created what he calls a "dual social structure" in the larger settlements. The two parts of that dual social structure he calls "communities," although they are within the single settlement. First, there is a "modern, highly organized occupational community made up of discrete autonomous agencies in which the population consists of jobholders," not settlers. The second part of the dual social structure is "a more traditional frontier society" of natives and independent whites. This is an evolved echo of the populace of the late contact-traditional era.

In the white sector of the population of the Northwest Territories, what impresses an observer of twenty or more years is the growth in the numbers and significance of the transient southern Canadian jobholders, those who create what Fried terms the "occupational community." Their presence is coupled with the emergence of urban centers of a magnitude that, compared to twenty years ago, is impressive. Yellowknife, now [1975] a population of 8,000 or 9,000, Hay River, Fort Smith, and Inuvik are the major settlements one thinks of. Although small compared to Edmonton or Winnipeg, they nonetheless represent and in many ways replicate an urban way of life and are the focal points of urban services, even as those services spread out far-ther into the land. These urban centers, of course, are strongly geared to the interests of and in some part are financially buttressed by the "occupa-tional community": the government jobholders, the jobholders in the banks, the jobholders in mining. Certainly a number of the northern white settlers are dependent for their livelihood on providing, either at first or second hand, goods and services to these members of the transient occupational community.

The increase in transient government jobholders has been striking. The ranks of the job categories have greatly expanded, as in, for example, the military installation at Inuvik and the education and health and welfare di-visions. I was able to pull one set of figures: in 1953, there were about 225 personnel of the Northern Administration branch of the federal government working in the Yukon Territory and the Northwest Territories; in 1967, there were about 1,275 (Phillips 1967: 169, 176). So in fourteen years, gov-ernment personnel working for Northern Administration in the North in-creased almost sixfold. I would not hazard a guess what the figure would be today, in 1975.

Again I emphasize that my own area of interest is in native life and expe-rience rather than the white sector of the North, and I would like to char-acterize major trends of what we might call the "modern" era in native life, beginning at about World War II and accelerating in the most recent decade [the 1970s].

Within the last few decades the natives of the Northwest Territories have become continually more subject to the pressures that issue from big govern-ment, large-scale commerce and industry, the aggregation into settlements and especially into white-dominant urban centers, and the accelerated com-munication of aspects of southern Canadian lifestyle. The trading post has given way to the commercial store. The present-day Hudson's Bay Company outlet or any other erstwhile trading establishment [as of 1975] may still buy fur, but the year's profits are from the sale of thousands of kinds of commer-cial goods, including the fads, fashions, and gimmicks that we are familiar with in southern Canadian living.

Many of the greatly increased number of employees in the North are in jobs directly or indirectly affecting native life. Game and forest management personnel, welfare workers, health officers, schoolteachers, to name just a few, and the intensity of their instructional and their regulatory roles in bringing the native to accommodation and submission to the national Euro-

Canadian system far exceeds the regulatory or controlling roles that the trader and the missionary were able to achieve in the past. [For Dene views, see chapter 14.]

The government programs affecting native life in these last few years have been very important, and I shall remind you of a few of them. The development of transfer payments and social assistance has had great impact. The first thing that hit the North was the family allowance, instituted in 1944. Of course, that was an all-Canadian benefit, as was the old age security program that followed in the early 1950s. For the natives of the North, these were the first subsidies to augment income from trapping. They were very important to families whose cash income might be only $200 or $300 per year from trapping. Other, more limited programs soon followed: welfare relief payments, TB allowance, the blind person's allowance.

Health care is another area that has had profound ramifications in native life. One result of generations of absolute neglect of native health across the North is evidenced in the fact that in 1956 one seventh of the entire Canadian Inuit population were in TB sanitoria in the South (Phillips 1967). The establishment of Camsell Indian Hospital in Edmonton in the 1940s plus the introduction of the yearly TB X-ray program marked the beginning of minimally adequate and responsible health care offered to the Dene peoples. [By the mid–1970s the TB X-ray program was no longer needed.] From 1941 to 1970 for the ten Mackenzie River region forts the population went from 2,691 to 4,214, an increase of 56 percent. Population figures are one of the best indicators of what increased attention to the health of the people has meant. Some of the statistics from one report to the next seem to vary. One report gives rather sharp drops in the Dene and Inuit death rates between 1962 and 1971, but they are still above the national average. The national average of 7.3 deaths per 1,000 in 1970 compares to the Indian average in the Territories of 8.7 and the Inuit figures of 11.3. So there still is catch-up to be achieved if native health is to be at parity with that of the public at large. But still, the long-term figures are a significant reflection of improved health care.

Government-subsidized housing for Dene and Inuit began in the 1950s and took off in the 1960s. (One analyst has pointed out that the government scheme turns home owners into renters.) The sixties also saw electric lighting coming into the Indian homes in such settlements as Rae. Also in the sixties, oil heating became available for many native homes in place of firewood logs rafted or brought by dogsled by the householder.

Of all government-induced changes that have occurred, education will in the future have the greatest impact on native society. Again a few figures, derived from one of the annual reports of the commissioner of the Northwest Territories: in 1955, less than 15 percent of the school-age children of the Northwest Territories had achieved any appreciable amount of formal education, and that 15 percent largely represented the white sector. That was the year that the authorities developed a program for education in a *public* school system. By 1967 approximately 90 percent of school-age children were enrolled in school (if not always attending). And by the end of the 1960s young men and women with secondary school or college-level education were returning to their home communities fluent in English and sophisticated in the ways of southern Canadian society.

Some of the consequences: the expansions in the services and conveniences of an urbanized setting, including subsidized housing in many cases and day-school attendance by children, are pulls that have combined to encourage the native family and the hunter-trapper husband to remain in the settlement or town rather than living in and off of the produce of the bush. Town living of course requires substantially greater cash outlay for food, fuel, and so forth. The exposure to southern Canadian standards of living, through broader individual experience, through the mass media, and through the educational system, has brought new levels of aspiration in consumer standards. These developments, combined with the growth of the native population, will surely increase the social and economic pressures that are building at present to a degree that I could not have identified twenty-five years ago.

The question touched on by Professor Stager to which perhaps I should also briefly speak is: "Well, if there is an expanding Indian population and the economy of the Territories is not keeping up with it, why don't the natives go 'out'? Go 'out' permanently?" That is certainly not happening so far—

The Commissioner:
To the South, you mean?
Dr. Helm:
Yes, "out"—in the sense of the old northern term "outside"—the urbanized world beyond the North.
If I may impose my interpretation of what I understand to be the temper and the spirit of the people, a long-term, permanent, "outside" southern life is apt to mean abandonment of one's sense of ingrained identity. The importance of the sense of being one of a people and of keeping social connections

with kinsmen, friends, and a shared way of life intact is a commitment long noted in southern Canadian and American Indian groups who have undergone much more severe pressure than the people here have yet experienced in terms of the press of the "outside" world. I would be surprised to see very soon any substantial retreat on the part of the native people from this land to southern areas where, the "objective" analyst might argue, much greater economic opportunity awaits.

Here Professor Stager discussed "Modern Social and Economic Trends."

CONCLUDING OVERVIEW

With the advent of the fur trade, the aboriginal way of life accommodated to include a degree of fur procurement in order to obtain some tools of Western technology. Through the decades the native peoples of the Territories came into sustained economic involvement with Western society. That involvement, however, induced accommodation and adjustment of aboriginal, pre-contact patterns of man-to-man and man-to-nature relationships, rather than the overthrow of those patterns. Native cultures have continued to emphasize on-the-land skills and the social ethics of aboriginal times.

In the last few years a kind of nature dual economy is emerging. It is one that still puts individuals and families on the land but in a somewhat different way. Instead of trapping plus hunting, it now is wage work plus trapping-hunting. Persons may work for a period at a full-time job, then will retreat. Or alternatively, as Professor Stager points out, family members may be in full-time or part-time work for cash income and still take country produce in their free hours. What sustains commitment to this sort of "dual economy" is the strong traditional value of living in intimate relation to the land and its sustenance, as well as the sense of accomplishment and prestige that derives from effective bushcraft, and for the Inuit I should say "coastcraft" as well. Combined with these values and tied to them is a more subtle but no less important one, in that reaping the harvest of the land places one within the traditional mode of cooperation and aid between kinsmen and among members of the small communities. The value of the traditional mode of community interaction lies both in one's image of being an Inuk or a Dene, a man or a woman of the land, and being in the setting of one's community and kinsmen.

Any economic opportunity as seen by the economist as opportunity has to be weighed and I think *is* being weighed against the possible losses that an individual may experience in terms of the commitment to remain an Inuk or a Dene in the full meaning of those words to the people who apply them to themselves. Thank you.

The Commissioner:

Thank you very much, Dr. Helm and Dr. Stager.

from MVPI Overview Hearing of March 6, 1975,
in Yellowknife, Northwest Territories

MOVING BACK THROUGH THE FULL FUR AND MISSION PERIOD

Earlier chapters have reviewed the contact history of the Dene from early contact through the stabilized fur trade. In native historical memory, the stabilized fur trade is the traditional past. To emphasize the native perspective on the past, I have termed this long period the contact-traditional era. Once the Christian missionaries arrived in the 1860s, the final ingredient was in place to set a way of life, the full fur and mission period, that spanned almost a century.

"Epidemic," "mission," and "treaty" label the great surges of change that punctuated the years between 1860 and the end of the Second World War. Chapter 7 has cited major epidemics among the Mackenzie Dene and those across the entire Northern Athapaskan domain that repeatedly shook social stability and, when elders' generations were struck down, cultural transmission. In the Northwest Territories, the advent of the missionaries in the 1860s and of the federal commissioners in 1900 and in 1921 to "negotiate treaties" with the Dene groups imposed ever more lasting impacts upon the people. But these impositions of Euro-Canadian purpose did not as such shake the stabilized adaptation to the fur trade.

Moving back in time, this chapter first looks at the last great pandemic among the Mackenzie Dene, the influenza epidemic of 1928; at special native occupation and status in the fur trade in the years between 1900 and 1925; at an Indian's memory of the first treaty in 1900; and then at the start of the missions. The chapter concludes with a nostalgic look back into the past by Joseph Naedzo, the Bear Lake Prophet.

THE INFLUENZA EPIDEMIC OF 1928

In the summer of 1928, the Hudson's Bay paddlewheeler Distributor *carried influenza from Fort Smith to Fort Resolution and thence the length of the Mackenzie River. Fumoleau (1975:254–66, 357–80) has assembled white observers' harrowing accounts of the suffering and deaths endured by the Dene as the flu swept fort after fort. One estimate puts the death toll at almost six hundred. I first learned of the 1928 epidemic from Louis Norwegian of Jean Marie River ("Lynx Point"). "That time,*

all the old people die," Louis told me, among them the leader and founder, Old Sanguez, of the Jean Marie River community.

Vital Thomas and I had touched on the flu epidemic of 1928 among the Dogribs in a conversation on July 4, 1969. By his recall, about seventy-four Dogribs trading into Rae died. (The Rae mission books record sixty-eight deaths in 1928 up to November 12. Between July 17 and August 24 there were forty-three deaths entered, many noted to be in the bush.) The next day, Vital and I continued in more detail.

Vital Thomas:
Mostly, it was all of the old-timers who died. Like medicine guys. Not many young persons. The first person to die was Old Lamouelle, Susie's father. [Q: Who took care of the dead?] In those days, the Mounties were [already] here. They hired Antoine Liske and Pierre Quitte and me, there were three of us for digging about two days. The first day altogether nine died, old people. The second day, five or six. A coffin comes and while we were burying that one, another comes, and another. The poor relatives, they all cried.

The flu came in August, after Treaty payment, just before when the Indians leave to go back to the bush. [Were all the families in town as well as the men?] Like the people at Marten Lake [Wha Ti], some men had brought their families, some didn't. [After leaving the fort] some people died before they could get to the end of the lake [Marian Lake, heading for Lac la Martre]. There are graves all along the shore. And when they came to Marian River Village [at the end of Marian Lake], about half a dozen died there, they said. And going to Marten Lake, about half a dozen or so died before they got to the portage [probably the long portage at the falls Naìnliin]. At the same time, they didn't have much to eat so they kept on going. The sick caught cold traveling. If they had stayed in one place they might not have died. As soon as they got sick, they wanted to move, to get away from the others.

From here at Rae to Trout Rock [down the North Arm] and right to Yellowknife, quite a number died. Because some of them had come from Indian Village [near the later site of the town of Yellowknife] to Rae, to the [Rae] traders to get supplies. And some went to Resolution. Those that had big boats [in which to cross Great Slave Lake] went to Resolution. Those with only small canoes came here.

If one person died they wouldn't spend a day at the place of the death. As soon as they buried him, they moved on to the next island. It didn't matter if

Distributor at Resolution

The Distributor *at Fort Resolution. This photograph was taken in the same decade, 1920–29, in which the* Distributor *carried the influenza epidemic down the Mackenzie River. Besides the steamboat, three other kinds of watercraft in use on Great Slave Lake can be seen: schooners (boats with mast and sail), a modern canoe with kicker, and a beached family canoe (Algonkin-Ojibwa type), apparently made of birchbark. See the section on watercraft in this chapter. Northwest Territories Archives.*

they are sick or not. Then another one dies, so we keep moving. That is why there are all kinds of graves between here and Yellowknife. [Why do they keep moving?] Moving is the Indians' own way. In the olden days, when there is a death they were not supposed to camp there. They had to move to the next island or point.

During the flu, some people had really bad luck. Like Francis Blackduck. He was married to his first wife that summer, Madeline Nitli. His mother-in-law was a widow. He'd just got married and in three or four days the flu came. And as soon as some died here, he wanted to move to the west channel, where the bridge is now. His mother-in-law and his father and mother and brothers and sisters were there. He moved there, and in about two days later his father died. So he paddled here, he had no kicker then. He came to get boards for the coffin and he went to see my mother and asked if I would take some lumber back with my kicker. My mother said all right. The mission handled the lumber. Francis tells them that his mother and mother-in-law and brothers are sick and he doesn't know if they will all live, so he thinks he should need lots of lumber. The priest gave him enough lumber for two or three coffins. So we go back there and his father is dying. While we are working on the coffin for his father, his mother died. So we build another and by the time we finish his brother Alexis is pretty low. There are three dead now. We made three coffins. Two or three guys went to dig the graves. We take the coffins to the graves and when we get back his mother-in-law has died. So we got to make another coffin. We got to bury her but we have no more lumber. His brother-in-law—they called him Wew'aule, "He Doesn't Speak Much"—is dying. We can't stay at that place, so we move amongst the islands toward Old Fort. We went as far as the mouth of Stagg River, and there his brother-in-law died.

The bunch at Gros Cap, that was the worse. Some guys had just landed, coming from Resolution [their point-of-trade, across Great Slave Lake]. It was a big camp, there were maybe twelve or fifteen families at Gros Cap. Charles Goulet was like a *donek'awi* [trading leader] for the Gros Cap people, so lots of people followed him, he's got a big camp. Most of the people had log houses. They said that they found out about the sickness while at Resolution. But some bugger made a story about how home brew was the only medicine for the sickness. The Gros Cap people had it in the canoes, and they landed at home and started to drink, singing all night. The next day they all dropped dead, caught cold. They sent for the police [from Resolution], and an old priest came with him. There were guys lying on the floor and in between the houses, drunk, dead. When the priest saw all of that, he was crying. That cleans the whole village, in one group, the Lake people, like. [According to a trader's wife, twenty-six persons died at Gros Cap, "the seven survivors having fled in panic" (Fumoleau 1975:265).] The police shot all the dead people's dogs.

from the field notes of July 5, 1969, Rae

NATIVE OCCUPATION AND STATUS
IN THE FUR TRADE, 1900–1925

On July 1, 1913, the young anthropologist John Alden Mason arrived at Fort Resolution on the south shore of Great Slave Lake. On July 22 he left by boat for Fort Rae and remained there from July 28 until September 7.

As was the norm for that era of American ethnology, Mason's concern was

"Indian (Yellowknife?) lodges, Yellowknife, Fort Resolution, 1913." J. A. Mason Collection, National Museums of Canada.

"Slavey informant [Tinite] singing into phonograph, Slave, Fort Rae, 1913." J. A. Mason Collection, National Museums of Canada.

to record surviving aspects of "aboriginal" culture. Although at Fort Rae he was at the trading center of the Dogrib Indians, most of his ethnographic data came from an elderly Slavey resident who spoke some English. According to Mason, his name was Tinite, although Elizabeth Mackenzie of Rae knows of him by the epithet "Boss for the Nets," referring to his medicine power over fish. Due to his heavy reliance on Tinite, a large proportion of the data accumulated by Mason was on Slavey traditional culture. In his full report (1946) he carefully specified when Dogrib or Chipewyan or Yellowknife data were being presented.

In a brief summary report, Mason (1914:376) said, "The social and religious life seems to be quite as bare as heretofore supposed. No evidences appear of any ceremonies or ritualism, totemism, clan organization, civil organization of any kind, theology, or even demonology. The social organization appears to be very weak with little or no recognized authority. . . . To sum up in a single phrase," Mason concluded ruefully, "the impression received is that the culture of these peoples is on a strictly individual basis."

Mason's short summer in the field resulted in a very limited number of topics in the photos he took. There is a heavy representation of the watercraft that he saw that summer at Fort Rae and during his transit of Great Slave Lake from Fort Resolution to Fort Rae in the Northern Traders company York boat. He also made a few portrait photos.

In the summer of 1979 I took forty-one selected 8-by-10-inch mounted photos (and a large magnifying glass) to Rae to see what memories they might elicit from elderly Dogrib Indians. Here too there were major limitations. Most elderly Dogribs have spent their lives as bush Indians and have had little experience with the water transport scenes that Mason photographed in his crossing of Great Slave Lake. Furthermore, the photographs were too early; that is, they had been taken sixty-six years before. Even men in their midseventies were children in 1913. Therefore, most of the persons in the photographs were not recognized, although there were a few unexpected exceptions. Had they been able to see them twenty years before, the portraits or scenes of identifiable persons would no doubt have been more evocative. In consequence, I went through the photographs in detail with only one person, seventy-five-year-old Vital Thomas, who is knowledgeable about fort life and Great Slave Lake travel. In the captions of the photographs here illustrated, Mason's brief identifications are enclosed in quotation marks. For some photos, they are followed by identifications or other remarks that the photographs elicited from Vital.

From Vital and the few others who viewed them, these photos evoked some information that had escaped my previous field inquiries. But primarily they served to illustrate or to reinforce data gained from consultants' accounts in past years. The significance of the photos is that they illustrate ethnographic and historical data of the period *not* covered in the published field materials of Mason. In pursuit of this point I here address two topics seemingly unrelated: first, kinds of watercraft in operation on Great Slave Lake in 1913, and second, kinds of prestige, rank, and special occupation among the natives of that period. Actually, the first topic leads comfortably into the second.

WATERCRAFT

Mason's photos show the two kinds of native watercraft, both sheathed in birchbark *(k'i)*: the decked hunting or portaging canoe and the larger, so-called family canoe. Being of native manufacture, these are the only craft used by Indians on which Mason reports. That the family canoe, which Mason designates as "large" or "woodland" type and Adney and Chapelle (1964) label "Algonkin-Ojibwa type," is not an old form among the Dogribs is attested by Vital's term for it, *(k'i) ts'i*. *Ts'i* is the Chipewyan word for "canoe" (Li 1933). Assuredly, this Algonkin-Ojibwa-type canoe is not an "aboriginal" Chipewyan form but an introduction of the early fur trade. Size apart, the rounded fore-and-aft profile of the family canoe contrasts markedly with the pointed, angled (roughly fifty-degree) profile of *(k'i) elà*, the Dogrib birchbark hunting canoe, Adney and Chapelle's "kayak form canoe." *Elà* is the Dogrib word for canoe. Today's canvas canoes are now simply *elà*, although their sheathing can be specified as *nombalà elà*. With the puzzling exception of the scow, *detsinkà elà* (board boat), the Dogrib terms for European-derived craft carry the Chipewyan term. As Vital Thomas explained in the case of the schooner, "We can use some Chip words. They saw the schooner before we did, so we call the schooner *ts'imbà ts'i*, 'sail boat.' The York boat is *detsin ts'i*, 'wood boat,' and steamboat is *kon ts'i*, 'fire boat.' "

In addition to canoes, Mason photographed York boats. York boats had replaced bark freight canoes of the Algonkin-Ojibwa type on most of the waterways of the Northern Department of the Hudson's Bay Company after its coalition with the North West Company in 1821. Each summer York boat brigades manned by Indians and Metis took furs "out" and returned with the year's supplies for each trading fort the length of the Mackenzie River. In regional parlance on the Upper Mackenzie, "head of the line" still refers to

"Dogrib Indian women in canoes, near Fort Rae, 1913." J. A. Mason Collection, National Museums of Canada.

"Natives, large type canoes, Dogrib, Fort Rae, 1913." According to Vital Thomas, "That man [major figure at far right] is Henri Lafferty. He came to the Old Fort [Old Fort Rae, abandoned in 1906] when the first mission came [1859], when he was a little boy. He's the one that spread all these Laffertys!" The Laffertys are an extensive Metis "clan" in Rae and Resolution. J. A. Mason Collection, National Museums of Canada.

"Dogrib Indians in York boat, near Fort Resolution, 1913." J. A. Mason Collection, National Museums of Canada.

the place on the river where, the current slackening, "tracking" (towing by manpower) of the York boats ceased, and the fur-laden vessels were rowed or sailed to Fort Resolution on the south shore of Great Slave Lake, thence tracked and rowed farther south up the Slave River.

On the Mackenzie River, the Hudson's Bay Company's steamboat *Wrigley* replaced the York boat brigades after 1886. But the company continued to operate a York boat between Fort Rae (at both its "old" and present location) and Resolution. That boat took Vital as a seven or eight year old (probably in 1912 or 1913) to seven years' residence at the Roman Catholic mission school at Resolution and then returned him to his mother at Rae. By this evidence, it appears that the Hudson's Bay Company's York boat was in use until about 1920. At least through 1913 Northern Traders Ltd. (NT) also had a York boat, the one in which Mason traveled to Rae. In Vital's recall, by about 1920 NT had only a scow at Rae. The employment of Indian crewmen on the York boats was, of course, strictly seasonal.

In the transit of Great Slave Lake between Resolution and Rae, no tracking was required. The York boats proceeded by sail or, in complete calm or rough weather, by the efforts of the oarsman. After the open water traverse

"Wilia, Dogrib Indian Steersman, Great Slave Lake, 1913." J. A. Mason Collection, National Museums of Canada.

from the south shore to the North Arm of Great Slave Lake, the route to Rae along the North Arm of the lake was rocky and sometimes shallow. As men grew fatigued on the oars, one spelled another at the prow as "watcher" for rocks. The special position in the crew was that of pilot or steersman (*ts'i k'endi*). The steersman had to know the channel. As in the case of Wilia, the NT steersman in Mason's photograph, this occupational specialty could provide a guaranteed income each summer on top of the winter's fur catch.

It is said that before arriving at the fort the York boat pulled into shore to allow the men to change into their best clothes. Vital's first comment on the photograph of Wilia was, "He must be a gentleman, because he's got a necktie on."

"GENTLEMEN"

Indians not only worked seasonally as crew on the trader-owned scows and York boats plying Great Slave Lake, but in the early twentieth century a few Indians owned York boats or schooners. Rae is situated on Marian Lake, separated by Frank Channel from the North Arm of Great Slave Lake. The extreme shallowness of Marian Lake is the reason, Vital said, why Rae Dogribs "don't care for [did not own] York boat or scow here." It was a few important men whose bases were farther down the North Arm toward the main lake who owned York boats. These were of the southern sector of Dogribs who had long traded into Fort Resolution across Great Slave Lake and whose headmen had "signed" Treaty No. 8 at Fort Resolution in 1900. (Most of the Dogribs, those trading into Rae, did not "take treaty" until 1921.) Two men who owned York boats in the early years of the century were Old Drygeese, the headman at Weledeh at the mouth of the Yellowknife River, and Charles Goulet, *naindidon* (see below) at Gros Cap across from Fort Resolution on Great Slave Lake. Also, a few Dogribs of that area are remembered as owning schooners. Apparently, the ownership of scows in this period was limited to a few Metis of the Fort Resolution area who, according to Vital, built the craft themselves. The schooners and York boats were sold to natives by the Hudson's Bay Company. In 1969 Susie Abel (1888–1979) of the Weledeh Dogribs, a man then in his eighties, recalled that York boats were "big boats, eight rowers, that cost too much for one person," so partners or a father and son would combine to buy one. In his recollection a York boat cost $1,000 in "skins," that is, Made Beaver, the unit of exchange value of the traditional fur trade.

Possession of a schooner or York boat was a clear demonstration that the owner was a man of consequence. All men who enjoyed the elevated prestige

*Moosehide boat, Fort Norman, 1920s. The Mountain Dene trading into Fort Norman con-
structed large moosehide boats, apparently modeled on the York boats of the contact-traditional
era, to bring an entire camp down the Keele River in the spring. The last moosehide boat was
made in 1981 and is in the Prince of Wales Northern Heritage Centre in Yellowknife. Mary
Saich Collection, Northwest Territories Archives.*

accruing to a man of consequence had attained it by their own abilities and
efforts. (Of course, being the son of such a man gave a would-be achiever a
leg up.) Such a man was referred to as *donahxe*, "gentleman" or "bigshot,"
as the term may be translated, or as *donets'et'in*, "man whom we respect."
The man deserving of these epithets was "the best hunter [this includes fur
trapping], the one that's got lots of money. If he's got good equipment for
hunting and trapping, he's a bigshot." At the other end of the prestige scale
there was "a man that's always bumming, a good-for-nothing. . . . If a man's
a poor hunter [and trapper] and got no equipment, we say, 'We don't listen
to him.'"

In Mason's photos, the black Stetsons served immediately to identify men
as "bigshots" to Dogrib viewers. "Good hunters!" an elderly Dogrib exclaimed. He recalled that the black Stetsons cost $50 and gray ones $25.
Watch and watch chain and ring were other accoutrements of men of consequence. Vital conceded, however, that even without these appurtenances
of achievement the superior hunter-trapper who owned fine equipment
would be regarded as a "gentleman" or "man whom we respect."

Besides the generalized prestige category of "gentlemen" or "men whom
we respect," special role-statuses were recognized. [Here I set aside the role-
status of band headman and others not directly pertinent to the fur trade;

"Dogrib Indians encamped on Stony Island, Great Slave Lake, 1913." According to Vital Thomas, "This guy has an eagle feather in his hat; that means he's a medicine man. [Mason records the same symbol in his report.] They've got one York boat and two family boats. See that pole [attached to the fore canoe]? If the water is too deep to beach a canoe, you have to put one end of a pole on the shore and the other end tied to the canoe so the canoe won't hit the rock. A birchbark canoe like this, if it hits the rock it breaks the gum and the canoe starts to leak. You've always got to carry spruce gum in a birchbark basket. In case the canoe starts to leak, you've got to head for shore." J. A. Mason Collection, National Museums of Canada.

these are treated in chapter 10.] With the advent of the Hudson's Bay Company into the Dogrib world, there arose *donek'awi*, "people's trader," the opposite number of the Hudson's Bay Company trader, who was also termed *ek'awi*. *Donek'awi* was a band leader who operated as a trading chief by receiving supplies on credit from the company with which he aided his followers and by bringing his band in as a group for trade, which, by Indian and company tradition, he parlayed into a feast for the group on company supplies. When, at about the turn of the century, free traders appeared in Dogrib country in competition with the Hudson's Bay Company, the role of *donek'awi* collapsed. The free trader was designated *naindidon*, "buy-and-sell man." Very shortly, in place of *donek'awi* emerged the counterpart of the white free trader, the Indian *naindidon*, who operated as a kind of exchange conduit between a trader at the fort, either of the Hudson's Bay Company or a free trader, and the Indian trappers in the bush. By this means the traders carried their competition with one another into the bush in the form of their *naindidon*. The Indian *naindidon* received supplies on credit from the trader with whom he was affiliated. He visited the bush camps (sometimes with a helper or two), trading those supplies in return for fur, which went to the trader. Also, trappers needing supplies might seek the *naindidon* at his home base, as at Weledeh or Gros Cap. For a period (probably about 1915–20) Susie Abel was a *naindidon* for the Hudson's Bay Company, which at that time apparently had a *naindidon*/"representative" at almost every hamlet. Apparently a *naindidon* did not (usually at least) mark up the price of the goods above that of white traders. The trader gave the *naindidon* without charge free goods "on top of" the goods he took to trade with. This constituted his profit or commission. These men also trapped for themselves. Unlike *donek'awi*, the role of *naindidon* did not per se involve band leadership. Of the six Indians whose names I have recorded as owner of York boats or schooners, in two cases the man, and two cases his son, was a *naindidon*.

At Rae, by about 1925 the traders had abandoned the commissioning of *naindidon*. But other avenues—such as effective band leadership, superior hunting-trapping enterprise, one-man fur-trading entrepreneurism—to the status of *donets'et'in* remained.

CONCLUSION

Dogrib oral history tells us that at the time of Mason's field trip three broad levels of social ranking and prestige obtained for the men in Dogrib society: the majority of ordinary Dogrib "citizenry"; those (probably very few) individuals denigrated as good-for-nothing, worthless in their lack of productivity and self-reliance; and, at the other extreme, men of consequence, known generically as *donets'et'in* or *donahxe*. A band leader was ipso facto in this last category. Within that class of men of substance, in consequence of the coming of the free traders there emerged for twenty-five or thirty years the special role-status of *naindidon*. Considering the esteem and recognition accorded these achievers in Dogrib historical memory, it seems clear that for the Dogribs of 1913, if not for the ethnologists of that era, social life was *not*, in Mason's words, "quite as bare as heretofore supposed."

from "Dogrib Folk History and the Photographs of John Alden Mason," 1981a

THE SIGNING OF TREATY NO. 8
AT FORT RESOLUTION IN 1900

By 1971 it was apparent that the IB-NWT needed evidentiary ammunition for the upcoming confrontation with the government on aboriginal rights. So I took the oppor-

Susie Abel, Dettah, 1972. Beryl Gillespie Collection, Northwest Territories Archives.

tunity to interview elderly Susie (Joseph) Abel (1888–1979) about the first treaty,
Treaty No. 8, signed by Dene in the Northwest Territories. We met Susie Abel in
the preceding section on occupation and status in the fur trade. In 1900 he was in his
early teens (he may have been baptized rather than born in 1888) when the southern
Dogribs who traded into Fort Resolution along with three other "tribal" groups "took
treaty." Susie Abel's lively memory must have been reinforced through the decades on
each Treaty day as old-timers recollected the events of the first occasion. The rest of the
Dene people of the Northwest Territories entered into treaty relations with the govern-
ment of Canada upon the signings of Treaty No. 11 in 1921–22. (René Fumoleau's
book, As Long As This Land Shall Last *[1975], is the preeminent source on the*
documentary and oral histories of Treaties No. 8 and No. 11 in all their implications.)

Vital Thomas to Susie:

Tell us the story about First Treaty. (Susie knows what is expected, as Vital had talked with him yesterday about making this tape, and Susie had already in Vital's house recalled the events of the signing of Treaty No. 8 at Resolution in 1900.)

Susie Abel:

Before Treaty, we used to come [to Resolution] every summer to sell our furs, so that's the place everybody joins together. That's the time when I was young. My dad and mother were still alive, but my mother was very sick. After we got into Resolution, after we sold our fur, there were lots of people. There wasn't much to eat—no fish or game—so some people left to go back where they could find something to eat. We stayed at the fort. We couldn't move back to the bush because my mother was really sick. Finally she died. After she died, we heard that they were going to pass treaty, that the agent would come. Dad says, "We may as well eat." So we started to hunt for ducks, moose, something to eat.

A man came in paddling a birchbark canoe. He had happened to see the agent coming with a boat. [The reference is to the person termed "Commissioner," J. A. Macrae, in the Treaty records.] The man says, "He will be here any time now. Maybe in one or two nights." Then another guy came in. He said that the agent's boat was coming closer, but traveling awful slow. They had no engines, just rowing. Across from Resolution Fort is the Mission Island, and there is a little sny between the island and the mainland. The man says, "They are in the channel right now."

Finally, the agent shows up. They came up the sny, crossing the bay. We had never seen a scow before. It was just like a little rocky island, it was so big. And when he gets closer, we see a red cloth. We know now that it was a flag. They are getting closer, closer. Now we see the big oars, splashing water once in awhile, one oar for one man. The boat's got no head [that is, the boat is not pointed in the bow]. We had never seen a boat before with no head. The sun was just about setting. After sundown they landed.

We all went to meet the boat. We had never seen a scow before. It hit the shore with its flat head. It was just like a wharf. We all looked at how it was made.

The agent walked up to meet us. He says, "I'm pleased to see all this bunch. It is late in the season. I was afraid everyone had left for the bush. On the Queen's [Queen Victoria] word, I have come with money. I'm going to issue the money to all the Indians. I am pleased that lots of people are still here." And one of the Indian leaders (*denerak'awo*) told the agent: "You are glad to meet us. But everyone is pretty near starving. We were supposed to leave the fort. But we heard you were coming, so we've been waiting without food." The agent said, "I haven't got much food, but I brought some flour and bacon. I can give you some flour and bacon for the kids and old people. It is late now, so we won't talk more. But I will give you 700 pounds of flour and 300 pounds of bacon. You can divide it among yourselves."

So the Indians took the flour. One of the leaders gave it out to all the people. They opened the sack and gave a cup to every person. In those days we didn't have much dishes. So some guys take their shirt out and they took the flour in their shirts. But some, even in their camp, had nothing to put the flour in. Some women, in those days they wore aprons, they picked up their aprons to put the flour in. Someone cut the bacon. They threw it in the apron on top of the flour. When they had given out all of the flour and bacon, everyone was so happy, they were frying bacon and cooking bannock. You could hardly see all night from the smoke of the frying bacon.

The agent said, "Tomorrow I am going to put up a tent. We will have a meeting before I give money. Everyone, old and young, has got to come and hear what is said." So the Indians went home [i.e., back to their tents], and the agent went back to the scow. In the scow there was a place to sleep. We saw all the mosquito bars rigged inside the scow. In those days there were no white men [at Fort Resolution] except the trader, the mission, and the [Metis] interpreter. So there was no place for a [white] stranger to sleep.

In the morning the agent put up a tent. We had never seen a one-pole tent before. It was a great big one. Everyone went over to listen. When we got to the tent, there was a table and chairs for the agent and interpreter. We sat on the ground on one side.

Agent said, "We don't come to make trouble. We come for peace and to talk about money. We come for peace. From now on, there will be lots of white men. So if the white men come, you will treat them just like your own brothers. And the white men, if they see a poor Indian in trouble, they'll help, just like he was their own brother. That is why we came here. There will be lots of mix [of whites and Indians] later on. From now on white men and Indians are going to be like one family. That is why I tell you this. We have never talked about this before, and you will remember it. That is why I brought this money."

An Indian by the name of N'doah. [VT: He was a leader from Resolution (a Chipewyan).] Some kind of a *denets'et'in* or something. He says, "Funny, this is the first time we have gotten free money." Nobody [none of the Dogrib Indians] liked the way N'doah sounded [the implication is that they were afraid he would make trouble]. So they [probably "they" here means the Dogribs] said that they were going to take another man [a Dogrib] to speak. So they took Old Drygeese [Susie refers to him as Andare Weta, "Henry's Father"] for the [Dogrib] Indians. The old people said, "Andare Weta is the man to talk for us." And Andare Weta says, "All right, I will talk for you." [From this point on, Andare Weta will be referred to as Drygeese or Old Drygeese.]

Drygeese says, "This money never happened before, so we'd like to know if something will be changed later. If it is going to change, if you want to change our lives, then it is no use taking treaty, because without treaty we are making a living for ourselves and our families."

The agent says, "We are not looking for trouble. It won't change your life. We are just making peace between whites and Indians—for them to treat each other good. And we don't change your hunting. If whites should prospect, stake claims, that won't do any harm to anyone. I come here to issue this money, that's all."

So Drygeese says, "All right, if you're going to give us money. But before you issue money, I want you to sign [write down] what you said. Let me have one sheet [copy] of what you sign."

Drygeese says, "We won't stop you to give us treaty, but we are going to have a meeting amongst ourselves, especially the old people, today. So if you want to give treaty, it will have to be tomorrow."

So everyone went home. The old people were talking amongst themselves. I [Susie Abel] didn't follow the old people because I was just a young man, so I don't know what they talked about.

The next day they came back to the tent for treaty. When they had all gathered, Drygeese spoke to the agent: "Don't hide anything that I don't hear. Maybe later on you are going to stop us from hunting or trapping or chopping trees down or something. So tell me the truth. I want to know before we take treaty." The agent says, "I do what I'm told—to give you fellows money. There will be no trouble for nobody. We won't stop anything."

Drygeese: "If that's the way it is, I want to tell you something. [As you, the agent, have said:] As long as the world don't change, the sun don't change, the river don't change, we will like to have peace—if it is that way, we will take the money and I want you [agent] to sign that that's the way it's going to be."

The agent says, "OK." So he signs the paper. They gave us the money now. [At this point, a discussion between JH and VT brings out that Susie told Vital the day before this tape was made that the "agent" gave Drygeese one sheet, and there was a sheet for the agent, and one for the Hudson's Bay man to keep. The agent signed four sheets. Probably L. Dupirer O.M.I., who was there, got the fourth sheet.]

That was the first time we saw money. Every person got twelve dollars, even the kids. I was young. [Vital explains: Susie Abel was a young fellow then and in those days, if your dad was alive, you were not the boss and your dad did all the trading—that is, in this case, collected the money.]

In those days, we had never seen cash before, we just traded. We don't know how to use money. So the trader tells the Indians, "If you want to spend money in here, the money you got for your whole family, if you spend it here in my store, I'm going to give you extra goods, maybe ten or fifteen dollars extra."

There were two stores, Northern Traders and the Hudson's Bay Company. The Indians don't know how to handle the money. They just take one dollar and buy this, another dollar and buy that. So that's why the trader offered us maybe twenty-five dollars or so in extra goods if we spent it all in his store. [The base money would have comprised of twelve dollars times the number of persons in the family for the head of the family to spend.]

So they gave us treaty. And they picked up all the chiefs' and councillors' names from all over. [Besides the leaders of the Dogribs who traded into Fort Resolution, Treaty signatories represented "Yellowknives" and "Chipewyans" and also "Slaves of Hay River."] For the Dogribs they put [as signatories] Drygeese as head chief, and next is Benaiyah, and the next is Sek'eglinan. These were the three chiefs for Weledeh. [Susie Abel uses the terms *gwatindeh*, "big chief," to refer to Drygeese and *gwati* to refer to the other two men.]

After my mother died and Treaty was over, we bought some stuff and we left with my grandfather and my aunt. Dad says, "We'll follow these old people as far as Reliance. Everybody is going for caribou." Everyone went for caribou every summer in those days, for clothing and everything.

from the account in Dogrib by Joseph (Susie) Abel of Dettah, taped on July 5, 1971, Rae; translated by Vital Thomas and entered into field notes of July 6, 1971

THE MACKENZIE SOUL RUSH OF THE 1860S

In 1858 the Roman Catholic order of Oblats de Marie Immaculée established at Fort Resolution the first permanent Christian mission in the Northwest Territories. Within a month in that summer there began a slow-motion race between the Roman Catholic Church and the Church of England for the souls of the Dene of the Mackenzie River area. An Anglican missionary leap-frogged Fort Resolution heading for Fort Simpson, and the Catholic missionary from Fort Resolution took after him. This created an awkward situation for the Hudson's Bay Company, for the only transport for the two of them down the Mackenzie River was the company's barge (Phillips 1967).

The contest for souls continued throughout the 1860s. Besides establishing a mission for the Slaveys trading into Fort Simpson, the Anglicans soon established a mission at Fort McPherson for the Gwich'in. The Catholic Church vied with the Church of England at the same trading posts when Oblates became yearly "visitors" to Fort Simpson and worked for a foothold among the Gwich'in trading into Fort McPherson. (Eventually, after 1895, the Catholic Gwich'in had their own locus and establishment at Arctic Red River.) At Fort Good Hope (1859) and Fort Providence (1862) the Oblates almost immediately founded missions. Fort Norman, Fort Rae, and Fort Liard were repeatedly "visited," and permanent Oblate "residents" occupied new missions within a few years (Duchaussois 1928). (McCarthy [1995] provides a fuller account of the sectarian struggle in the 1860s.)

Throughout the 1860s the Oblate Emile Petitot traveled from one post to another and into the bush to proselytize and reinforce conversions of Dene attached to Forts Resolution, Rae, Providence, Norman, Good Hope, and McPherson. (Good Hope became his major residency.) The first Catholic missionary to contact the Dogribs arrived at Fort Rae in 1859. A permanent mission was not established at Fort Rae until 1872, but the Dogribs were visited by several Oblate missionaries in intervening years, including the peripatetic and prolific writer Father Petitot. Traveling through Dogrib territory, "planting crosses everywhere," he achieved 319 baptisms. Petitot described a set of potential Dogrib converts on the move in 1864:

Like an anthill at which someone has hurled a stick, the horde starts moving from all sides, assembling the dogs and harnessing them to the sleds. The babies were stowed—this one in a sack, that one in a big kettle—and solidly attached to the sleighs. Each person put his snowshoes on, and the tribe went off in Indian file.

It was a spectacle worthy of Gustave Doré. One saw on the ice a long file of sleds and dogs of a spectral thinness, women bent under their heavy loads, and men stepping lightly with a gun and a tambourine [drum] for their entire burden. On the flanks the children frisked. Then there were the cries, a confused sound of voices, the grave ones of the men, the sonorous and musical ones of the women, of imprecations against the dogs, of joyous shouts thrown to the wind, mixed with the monotonous refrain of shamans or of the *oudzi* [hand game] players. [See chapter 16 on the hand game.]

In the midst of this movement, I was aware that everybody, large and small, young and old, men and women, were bedecked with the cross—on the chest, on the arms, on caps, on the hunting equipment. It was on the moccasins and on the knife sheaths, on the sack filled with white lichens that served as the swaddling clothes of the babies, seen on the sleds and the harnesses of the dogs. These crosses were generally white and embroidered in glass beads, in silk, or in porcupine quills. But there were even those of lead, of copper, and of iron. One young man named Ettsouzé carried around his neck a cross of wood 20 centimeters long. There was nothing in all of this religious and Christian display that had to do with my presence in the tribe. These emblems were old. [Petitot goes on to say that, even though they might be attached to some superstition, they are in the last analysis connected with the worship of the true God. He does not point out that Red River Metis of Catholic heritage had been in interaction with Dene around Great Slave Lake and beyond since the 1790s, through employment first by the North West Company and then the Hudson's Bay Company. "Le Patriarche" Beaulieu is one likely early transmitter of Christian ideas and symbols to Chipewyans and Dogribs long before the priests arrived (see Duchaussois 1928:138–41).] However [Petitot continues], I saw with pain some representations of phalluses intermingled with these Christian emblems. This did not surprise me in light of these people's complete ignorance. (1891:213–14, abridged, my translation)

*Fort Providence on the Mackenzie River, Catholic church and "convent," 1906. On July 15,
1906, "The church bells were ringing out a call to the Sunday morning service. The convent
hard by was decorated with flags betokening some joyful occasion, while the Indian pupils in
their pretty costumes accompanied by their teachers, the sisters of the mission, lined the bank to
welcome the founder of the school, Sister Ward of Montreal" (Stewart 1908: 81–82).*

Within the decade of entrance into the present Northwest Territories, the
Roman Catholic Church brought to Fort Providence a complement of Grey
Nuns. They were the first teachers. "The churches provided almost of the
education the North knew until the 1950s. . . . Children were taught in large
residential schools of which there were three Anglican and three Roman
Catholic, all in the Mackenzie District" (Phillips 1967: 126). (See Rea [1968:
287–92] for a succinct and precise account of schools in the Northwest Territories up to the early 1960s.)

In 1887 the Anglican bishop "estimated the whole population of the dio-
cese [of the Mackenzie] at 10,000, of whom one half were under Romanist
influence, while the other half the Church of England had won 3,000, and
2,000 were still unreached" (Phillips 1967: 122). As recorded in the 1973
Treaty Indian band rolls, the proportion of Roman Catholic to Church of
England adherents shows that the Church of England never gained on the
Roman Catholic Church. At 6,709, the total population count in 1973 was
well below the estimated 10,000 of 1887. The 1973 records show 80 percent
of the population of Treaty Indians to be Roman Catholic, 16 percent to be
Church of England, and 4 percent not assigned to either group. Of the six-
teen government "bands" on the 1973 treaty rolls, only two, McPherson

The "personnel" of the Catholic mission school at Fort Resolution, ca. 1912–17. Duchaussois, 1928.

and Aklavik, were heavily Anglican. Hay River and the small populations of Norman and Wrigley were divided but leaning to Roman Catholic. All others—Arctic Red River, Good Hope, Liard, Hay River, Providence, Fitz/ Smith, Resolution, Snowdrift, Dogrib Yellowknife "B," and Dogrib Rae— were predominantly or overwhelmingly Catholic. Fort Simpson was the only major population divided between both faiths, although the Catholics predominated at three to one.

By the late 1990s, only two Catholic priests remained in Dene parishes. About his own people, John B. Zoe writes:

> *As you may or not know, the Catholic clergies are hard to come by in the North. . . . There has been a push in recent years to devolve responsibility of spirituality upon the Dogrib by the Church. More and more people are taking on roles that the clergy has done in the past. Eventually the Diocese will turn over their building. People have decided to remove the traditional bench pews in favour of chairs in a wide circle with the altar moved from its original position to the centre, etc. There are plans to expand the buildings [at Rae] in the near future, with funds being raised. They no longer use the old Chipewyan hymn books, and they are being replaced with hymns*

translated into Dogrib to strengthen the use of the language. I think people are looking more toward one another as a source of strength.

from a letter of May 2, 1998

NAEDZO LOOKS BACK AT THE OLD DAYS

Joseph Naedzo, born in 1887 or at least baptized in that year, became in his last years a major figure for the Dogrib and Bear Lake Dene as he emerged as a prophet at the end of the 1960s (Helm 1994). Moralist, preacher, and raconteur, Naedzo was for elderly Dene and ethnologist alike an impressive source of memory of the old days. In the following taped narrative, translated by Vital Thomas, Naedzo presents an idealized view of the great days of the fur trade, when the Hudson's Bay Company trader and the missionary were the only white men in the land, and three great donek'awi, *"people's trader," represented the Indians trading into Fort Rae.*

Naedzo was one of the Sahtigot'in, Bear Lake people, who followed the Bear Lake Chief. The Bear Lake Chief has several names in white men's records and in Dogrib memory—Naohmby, Yambi, K'aawidaa, Toby Kochilea's Father, and Ek'awidare are some. Naedzo calls him Gots'ia Weta (Gots'ia's Father).

The three men whom Naedzo names as donek'awi *are found in the account by Frank Russell (1898:165) of the early 1890s: "The principal Dog Rib leaders at [Old Fort] Rae were Jimmie, Rabesca, and Naohmby, while Beniah, Little Crapeau, Dry Geese, and Castor traded at Resolution." Matching Russell's account with that of Naedzo: Jimmie is Dzemi, leader of the Edge-of-the-Woods Dogribs; Rabesca is Ewainghon, leader of the Rae Lakes regional group; and Russell's third leader, Naohmby, is Naedzo's Gots'ia Weta, the Bear Lake Chief. "The gratuities [given to* donek'awi] *from the traders are liberally shared with their followers, and the most eloquent begging is kept up as long as they remain at the post," writes Russell (1898: 164). Russell's "gratuities" are the "side pay" in Vital's translation of Naedzo's narrative.*

Naedzo also speaks of k'awo, *a man whose status in relation to* donek'awi *Vital usually translated as "foreman." More generally,* k'awo *simply means "boss" or "leader." I have condensed and realigned the content of Naedzo's account, but generally I have stayed close to Vital's phrasings (e.g., "groceries," "lots of fun").*

When the whitemen came, they made *donek'awi* ["people's trader," i.e., trading chief]. They made three *donek'awi.* Trading into Fort Rae, Dzemi [Ekawi Dzimi] was the headman, the head *donek'awi,* and the next was Ewainghon, and the third was Gots'ia Weta. Each *donek'awi* had a *k'awo.*

After the trapping season closed, after the spring hunt, before we leave for the fort, we would say, "We better send someone to get some groceries." So each leader would send one man to get groceries, tobacco, tea to leave with the families [while the men went to the fort]. And when the *k'awo* returns, *donek'awi* puts the stuff in one pile and puts a feast up before the men go to the fort.

Everything was going fine. We had three *donek'awi*. They were just like the Mounties, we respected them. These were three gentleman, *donek'awi*. When the *donek'awi* met at the fort, the Hudson's Bay manager gave some side pay to each *donek'awi*, gave them groceries. The trader gave *donek'awi* clothing too, a suit of clothes. He was sure treating the *donek'awi* good. And a big feast was put up for all the people. When the feast is over, the people started to dance. Once they started to dance, they went all day, all night, all day, and all night again. And on the third day you would see some of them lying on the ground, sleeping. That's the way we used to play! Not just for three or four hours. Sure lots of fun!

We had a good time in the old days, because there was just the post manager and his [Metis] interpreter and the mission [the priest]. They were the only three whites. Later [about 1900] a few free traders came and some other whites. That's the first time we saw any other whites.

Everybody follows *donek'awi* in those days. Whatever *donek'awi* says, we do. Which way you're going to go to trap, to hunt, *donek'awi* knows the country. He knows where there are marten, fox, where you can find muskox. Groups of five or six trappers and their families would go different directions for fur. We used to get all kinds of fur in those days. *Donek'awi* used to bring all kinds of fur, many bales, to the trader. The more fur they bring, the more side pay *donek'awi* gets. In those days, it couldn't be better, everyone was so happy, everything was going fine. And then almost all the old people died and all the *donek'awi* also died.

I told you that we had a good time and lots of fun, because there was just straight Indians, no whites. We didn't have to worry about anything. That was good. Now it's just like something is broken. We remember way back, and now something is broken, because more and more white men come. There are more whites than Indians now. And they brought stuff we knew nothing about before. The poor people! Some drowned, some got killed. All the kinds of foolish things the whites brought in! Lots of people have died just on account of liquor. It would be better if they had left the Indians alone. Let the Indians continue to live the way they were raised. It's the white man's fault. Everything is like it's upside down. Lots of poor Indians didn't know anything. They knew just religion, about God. And now that too is getting less and less.

In old days, you couldn't beat it, because *donek'awi* was preaching to us just like the priest does in church. And everyone was very happy in those days. It's just like we're lost now. We don't know which way to go. We are like in a fog, especially the old people who remember way back. Now we're just worrying, worrying. We're very hard up right now, because we don't eat what we want and we don't hunt for what we want, because those who *could* hunt, drink instead. In old days, in the morning, at daybreak, *donek'awi* goes outside and yells to the band about which way we are going to hunt, which way to go to get furs. If we are short of meat, every man has got to hunt. Everybody goes like we are one. You don't talk back to the headman. But now who's going to talk to us? That's the way it was even before *donek'awi* [was created by the fur trade]. Everyone obeyed one another. Nowadays, it is not as good as before, because no one listens or cares for one another. Old people like myself who remember the way we had a good time way back, I bet they feel sorry. It's not their own way now. Now just a few people talk good about religion, about God. The priest talks nice to us. But most people don't know which way to turn. And we feel sorry for them. The only thing is to listen to one another like in olden times. Then everything was fine. Now it's terrible, it's just like we're lost. It's not only in one place, I think it's pretty near all over. The whites are getting more and more populous. Their way, it's not our way. It's going to be terrible.

From now on, I don't think anyone will give you good advice, because the old fellows will be dead. But in the old days, *donek'awi* was with you. If you get a few caribou, in the evening *donek'awi* comes out from his tent and yells, "I want to see all the old people. Come on!" So everyone runs over and we all have a great feast of caribou meat. And then *donek'awi* tells a story about how to make a living, which way the fish are running this time of year, where you go to find moose, all the things like that. He was teaching young and old. But who's going to talk like that now?

Another thing, too. I don't know how it happened that at New Year we started shooting in the air. It's like saying "Happy New Year." It went on until everyone goes to bed. Then New Year morning we would start to shoot again. And all the band in the camp would start to cook whatever they got. In one big tent they put everything that was cooked for the whole band. *Donek'awi* is in his own tent and the men start to shoot until *donek'awi* comes out of his tent. Everybody goes into one tent and have great feast. We sure had a good time. Nowadays, that's dead too. Now, New Year day is just like any other day. [See the account in chapter 17 of the New Year observances at "Lynx Point," Jean Marie River.]

I'm telling you the true story about the old-time way. I'm talking in this tape recorder so anyone can hear my speech. I'll be glad of that. I don't think that from now on anyone will be talking about the Indian way. Pretty near everyone is starting to talk about the whiteman's way. I think the Indian way was better. We didn't have much trouble, not like now, because we listened to one another and treated one another just like brothers.

If the old people are able to hear my speech on this tape recorder, I'll be glad. The only thing is to behave yourself and to listen to others. Then you won't be sorry, here or in the next world. I'll be glad if everyone hears my speech. It's just like it's no use talking about it. Young fellows, or anyone who hears my speech, I am not making up the story. It's what I know and what was going on. But these stories of what is past, they are dying down. From now on, not many will sit and talk like this. Not many will listen.

As long as you hear my story, that's good.

Joseph Naedzo, recorded by Beryl Gillespie at Fort Franklin, May 1971;
translation by Vital Thomas, July 8, 1971, at Rae [abridged]

THE HISTORICAL RECORD

Here I explore the historical literature for evidence on the sociopolitical organization of the northeastern Dene through the contact-traditional era, as manifested in patterns of leadership. I was spurred to this search of the writings of, mainly, early explorers and fur traders by the leader role of Louis Norwegian ("Marcel Renard") and the group decisions of the men of Jean Marie River ("Lynx Point") as I came to know and record them in 1951–52.

SOCIOPOLITICAL UNITS

"The Athabascans do not consider themselves as composing neat political or cultural units," Osgood (1936) observed. Osgood refused to use the word "tribe" for the peoples he classified as Hares, Satudene [Bearlake Indians], Mountain Indians, Slaves, Dogribs, Yellowknives, and Chipewyans. He employed the correspondingly vague term "groups." For convenience sake, I here use "tribe" to designate the major divisions just cited. [I exclude the Gwich'in, whose main cultural connections lie to the west in Alaska.] For the Slaves trading into Fort Nelson, British Columbia, Honigmann (1946) distinguished regional groups within the tribe which are almost equally nebulous in outline. These he called "macrocosmic bands." Except for the degree of inclusiveness and of internal linguistic variation, the macrocosmic group [which I later came to term "regional band"] has the same characteristics or, more properly, lack of distinctive characteristics as the greater category, "tribe."

[Up to the 1950s, when this essay was written,] the following set of conditions were all that ethnologists had to work with when staking out a "tribe" or other major division of the northeastern Dene: a set of people living in physical contiguity (but not necessarily together), speaking a mutually intelligible tongue (though often with regional dialectal variations),

sharing a common culture (though not necessarily one distinct in essentials from neighboring tribes), and having at least a vague sense of common identity which might be based in whole or part on the foregoing conditions. Regarding the last point, we know that in earlier days its obverse aspect, namely, the lack of sense of affiliation with or, more emphatically, the sense of being in opposition to certain other groups was sometimes actively manifested in hostilities against others. This negative expression is the nearest thing to political behavior to be found at the tribal level. And when there is evidence of it, as in the case of the Yellowknives (Copper Indians) versus their neighbors, we feel justified in drawing tribal boundaries.

There is evidence that some recruitment and coordination between segments of a tribe might occur for purposes of warfare (see below). A statement by Back (1836:162) in the 1830s, however, indicates that in some of the retaliatory warfare between tribal groups a kindred was the social unit involved in the aggression: "[Two Indian acquaintances] informed us that, in a dispute between a Chipewyan and their countrymen, the Yellowknives, the former had been killed; but as he was an orphan, no one would avenge his death." In any event, it is plain that consistent or all-inclusive tribal-wide coordination or integration in regard to external relations was not the case. This condition has its parallel in the lack of any sort of structured action, coordination, and role and power differentiation regarding intratribal matters.

In the nineteenth-century literature, John Franklin, around 1820, presents the richest material that we have on the relations between parts of a whole "tribe," namely, the Copper Indians or Yellowknives, who were only 190 persons by his estimate. Imbedded in Franklin's narrative is a picture of friendly and occasionally cooperative relations between "chiefs" and between bands (of fluctuating personnel) but adventitious and without structure. Even the Copper Indian leader Akaitcho, unique in the literature for his outstanding authority and prestige, was not the tribal leader in any overtly recognized sense; his "adherents" or acknowledged followers represented about half of the small "tribe" (Franklin 1824).

The broad interpretation here given to the term "political" allows us to consider kinship units to be capable of having a political facet. In northeastern Dene society, however, the main significance of kin affiliations, politically speaking, is that they serve as the "in," the entrée to band units. Bilateral descent is the rule in northeastern Dene society, the kindred being the resultant kinship unit. The role of the kindred is seldom brought out in the earlier literature. But the importance of kinship, bilateral and both consanguineal and affinal, in determining association and ties between individuals and the personnel within communities, as evidenced, for example, in the local groups of Slaveys along the Mackenzie, must represent a tradition of long standing. More or less recent investigators recognized this condition in neighboring areas (Honigmann 1954; Mason 1946). [I later pursued this question among the Hare and Dogrib Dene (Helm 1965a).] Probably there is so little information on the functions of the kindred because it is, in a sense, invisible. A kindred has no "shape" or boundaries and, as a correlate, no well-defined political manifestations such as a leader or collective interests, activities, and goals. We do have some record of the practice of blood revenge in earlier times (Back 1836; Field n.d.; Richardson 1851) and adjudication of wergild (Field n.d.; Keith 1890), but apparently only sets of primary relatives or band-kin segments are involved, not total kin groups, that is, kindreds per se. Indeed, the latter situation would usually be socially impossible. As Murdock (1949:60–61) points out, "Since kindreds interlace and overlap, they do not and cannot form discrete or separate segments of the entire society. Neither a tribe nor a community can be subdivided into constituent kindreds. . . . One result of this peculiarity is that the kindred . . . can rarely act as a collectivity. One kindred cannot, for example, take blood vengeance against another if the two happen to have members in common."

All available data lead to the conclusion that neither the kindred per se nor, except in the segmental exercise of hostilities against other tribes, the regional groups or the tribe had a political component. To all ethnographic knowledge (Honigmann 1946; Jenness 1937; Osgood 1932), even the government invention of regional "chiefs" and councils, appointed or elected, has [up to 1955] effected no significant change or innovation in the political orientation of these Athapaskans at the regional or tribal levels.

It remains to look at those territorial segments that are actual physical groupings-together of persons. It is difficult to gain from the historical literature any clear picture of the norm, the variations, and the ranges in size and stability of the groupings of the northeastern Dene, especially through time.

First, there was definitely the basic unit, the coresidential hunt band—a group of people who traveled and camped together, sharing the take of game in common. A single nuclear family might sustain itself as a discrete territorial and economic unit apart from others for an indefinite period of time (Franklin 1828; Great Mackenzie Basin 1888). This condition may be taken as the extreme of minimality of the local group. More commonly, several nuclear families grouped together to pursue their livelihood. The number of families involved might range from two or three (e.g., Richardson 1851) to perhaps a dozen (e.g., Petitot 1891). An upper limit is difficult to determine. There were no formal ties or commitments to bind the component families to the band. Any family might part from the coresidential group, either to go it alone or to join another band as economic circumstances and/or personal inclinations directed (Richardson 1851; Mason 1946; Osgood 1932). The group was therefore potentially unstable: personnel altered, a band fragmented and coalesced. As pointed out above, these bands were composed of kindred, in all likelihood with a linkage of primary relations extending between all the families composing the small bands. [See Helm (1965a) for fuller documentation from field data.]

Despite the chronic vaguity of the data, it seems justifiable to see certain sorts of groupings as distinct from the coresidential band, although in some cases the line of demarcation may blur. The other groupings were intermittent and brief in nature; they were also characteristically larger than the coresidential band, drawing as personnel either selected members from several bands or several band complements in their entirety.

From early contact times, one sort of large assemblage was what Hearne called the "trading gang," a number of men assembled under a "chief" for the purpose of trading their furs through him as intermediary. All those Indians, often under several "chiefs," who traded into a particular fort were another sort of aggregation. Besides coming in to trade, they gathered at the fort in large numbers for special events such as the New Year celebration and, in more recent times, for Treaty.

Other kinds of large assemblages continued from aboriginal times. Large-scale caribou hunts drew together people from several coresidential bands into a camp prior to breaking up into smaller hunt groups (Russell 1898). As in the case of trading gangs, the aggregation might be limited to older boys and men. Some of the peoples in the wooded Mackenzie area drew together seasonally in large groups to exploit fish runs. A generation and more ago in the Simpson-Providence region families traveled to Great Slave Lake for fall fishing, gathering for a time in a great camp above Providence, enlivening their stay with gambling games, song, and dancing. According to a young Slavey, the "old people" told him that there used to be great gatherings in the summer on the island in the Redknife River, a tributary of the Mackenzie below Providence. The number of people was so great that when they held a "tea dance" the ring of dancers extended out to the edges of the island. At this time people might shift from one coresidential band to another. Probably some of the assemblages were gatherings of those regional populations [regional bands] referred to earlier.

War parties (extinct since the earlier 1800s) are a final and variant type of temporary group. The scant evidence available indicates that they were often composed of members of more than one band (Honigmann 1954; Hearne 1911).

THE SOCIOPOLITICAL MILIEU

"As to forms of government, police and regulations, they have none," wrote Wentzel in 1807 of the Slaves of the Fort Simpson area. As for the Dogribs who frequented Fort Franklin and Fort Confidence at Great Bear Lake during Richardson's sojourn in 1847–48,

> order is maintained in the tribe solely by public opinion. It is no one's duty to repress immorality or a breach of the laws of society which custom has established among them, but each opposes violence as he best may by his own arm or the assistance of his relations. A man's conduct must be bad indeed, and threaten the general peace, before he would be expelled from the society; no amount of idleness or selfishness entails such a punishment. (1851, 2:26)

Similarly, with the Dogrib bands trading into Fort Rae in 1913, "There is evidently little or no effective authority beyond the coercive sentiment of the band, which may be ignored or avoided by leaving the band or by changing allegiance" (Mason 1946:34).

It is plain that the ultimate locus of power and decision in Dene society was in the largely unorganized sentiments and opinions, coupled with not always effective diffuse sanctions, of the social body as a whole. These probably found their most effective expression at those times when the adult men of a group informally came together to exchange news and views of current events and problems, even as they do today. There is an early account (circa 1800) of such a gathering among the Chipewyans. The social "manners" described are still observed today.

> Their government resembles that of the patriarchs of old, each family making a distinct community and their elders have only the right of advising but not of dictating—however in affairs of consequence the old men of the whole camp assemble and deliberate on the subjects which have caused their meeting. . . . The women and children having been previously turned out, at last often a few groans and pious ejaculations from the old men which are answered by the young with great readiness, all this ceremony being done,

Quaker-like the spirit moves one of the elders who gets up and makes a long harangue. The young men are permitted to be of the Council and even frequently interfere in their debates which they do with great asperity, particularly when they regard the Europeans or the neighboring nations of whom they entertain an implacable hatred—however the sage councils of these old Patriarchs act as a counterpoise to the great impetuosity of youth. . . . Some of them are great orators and are said to deliver themselves with great perspicuity and address but particularly they apply their speeches more to the passions than to the understanding; the greatest silence prevails and they make it a fixed point of never interrupting one another while speaking; in general they are grave but not serious and will either join in solemn or gay subjects of discourse. (Macdonell n.d.)

The "Council" here referred to is obviously not a political organ of special and explicit function but the totality of the politically responsible members of the community—the men.

From Keith in 1810 comes a rare report of deliberate and formal assembly of interested parties, two sets of kinsmen, to deal with a "legal" problem.

The Natives of this establishment [the Fort Liard Slaves] entertain very just ideas betwixt right and wrong, and decide matters of this nature as coolly and impartially as could be expected from a set of people who are much attached to their most distant relations and who have no determined principles or principal persons for settling such matters. We have had two instances lately of their conciliating disposition. Two Indians, not of the same family, were, at different times, wounded by their companions upon a hunting excursion; one died soon after of his wounds and the other recovered. The latter accident was soon settled by the aggressor giving his gun to the other, but in the former case was debated by a full convention of both parties evidently segments of the kindred of the two men, and at last, the affair being proved to be accidental and not willful murder, the criminal was acquitted on giving up all his property. (1890:88)

The "full convention of both parties" was not a regular occurrence; it was evolved by an uncommon, crisis situation. There is no regularity of assembly or personnel.

In this unstructured milieu of group governance by consensus and custom the only differential in role and power to be discerned is in the figure of the leader.

Three kinds of at least putative leadership may be distinguished: the leader of the basic coresidential band, the trading chief, and the war leader. Also, those men who by virtue of their powers of prediction and manipulation of the supernatural exercised influence over group behavior might be considered a fourth variety. The documentation brings out that two or all of these roles were often or commonly enacted by a single individual.

The trading chief was a creation of the fur trade. Hearne describes the position of this chief at the beginning (1770s) of the historic era:

> It is a universal practice with the Indian leaders, both Northern [i.e., Chipewyan Dene] and Southern [Cree], when going to the [Hudson's Bay] Company's Factory, to use their influence and interest in canvassing for companions; as they find by experience that a large gang gains them much respect. Indeed, the generality of Europeans who reside in those parts, being utterly unacquainted with the manners and customs of the Indians, have conceived so high an opinion of those leaders, and their authority, as to imagine that all who accompany them on those occasions are entirely devoted to their service and command all the year; but this is so far from being the case, that the authority of those great men, when absent from the Company's Factory, never extends beyond their own family; and the trifling respect shown them by their countrymen, during their residence at the factory, proceeds from motives of interest.

Hearne goes on to give a good account of the behavior and motives of the trading chief in enacting his role:

> The leaders have a very disagreeable task to perform on those occasions; for they are not only obliged to be the mouthpiece, but the beggars for all their friends and relations for whom they have a regard, as well as for those whom at other times they have a reason to fear. Those unwelcome commissions, which are imposed on them by their followers, joined to their own desire of being thought men of great consequence and interest with the English, make them very troublesome. (1911:284)

By stimulating greed or arrogance, the European-made institution of trading chief on occasion encouraged high-handed behavior by that chief. Concerning the Dogribs of Fort Franklin–Fort Confidence, Richardson tells us:

The power of a chief varies with his personal character. Some have acquired an almost absolute rule, by attaching themselves in the first instance an active band of robust young men, and using them to keep in order any refractory person by claiming his wife after the custom of the tribe. [A man may take another man's wife by besting him in a wrestling match.] It is in vain in such cases that the poor husband, dreading to be deprived of his most valuable property, retires to a remote hunting group; for he is sure to receive a message, from some passing Indian, expressive of the chief's intentions; and he generally comes to the conclusion that submission is the best policy. He is certain to fall in with the chief and his band sooner or later, either as he goes to the fort for supplies or ammunition or elsewhere. (1851, 2:27–28)

The fact that a trading chief might use the white man's evaluation of his status as an argument for the imposition of his desires is illustrated in a first-hand account by Petitot of a clash between a Slavey chief and his band. While visiting a Slavey "village" in 1878, Petitot spoke to the assembled people on the need to render respect and obedience to the chief, "whose authority is derived from God."

Young Hunter [the chief] was pleased with my speech. Without knowing it, I had put my finger on a sore spot. The chief enjoyed only slight respect. His orders were openly scorned, his authority was challenged, and his own sons themselves were not free from insubordination. The reason? This man wished to impose his wishes instead of making them accepted through his kindness. Father, he had obeyed. Tyrant, he furnished a pretext for insubordination. [Later that day,] building on [Petitot's] discourse, the chief commenced a harangue in which he signified to his people that he was ready to lay down his charge if he was not better obeyed. Then one of his peers, Old Sabourin, rose and spoke in the name of the village. He charged the chief, as one of his main faults, with forcing young people to marry against their will. "This is why there is trouble among us."

At this moment an indescribable uproar was made in the lodge of Young Hunter. Twenty girls, twenty married women raised themselves all at once against their poor chief, to reproach him to his face for the same wrong. Seeing himself condemned by the public voice, he remained silent. (1891: 326–27, abridged, my translation)

Further vehement attacks convinced Petitot that the chief had been imposing upon his group for a long time, no doubt presenting himself as master through God "but especially through the English commercial agent [Hudson's Bay Company manager] of Fort Providence, who, I know, opposes us [the Oblate missionaries] in secret."

The fur traders attempted to enhance the authority of trading chiefs by giving them clothing and medals and according them gun salutes. And, in line with this concern in having as trading chiefs men of authority, they endeavored to recognize as "chiefs" those men who already enjoyed special influence and respect among their countrymen (Mackenzie 1960 [1889–90]). Accordingly, McLean (1932) says, the "best hunters" were those selected to be trading chiefs. Several other sources indicate more or less directly that being a superior hunter was a usual precondition to the achievement of superior status and influence.

Richardson's summation on leadership in Dene society in the mid–nineteenth century is the richest.

> Superior powers of mind, combined with skill in hunting, raise a few into chiefs, under whose guidance a greater or smaller number of families place themselves, and a chief is great or small according to the length of his tail [the number of his followers]. His clients and he are bound together only by mutual advantage, and may and do separate as inclination prompts. The chief does not assume the power of punishing crimes, but regulates the movements of his band, chooses the hunting-ground [Richardson is writing of caribou-hunting Dene groups], collects provisions for the purchase of ammunition, becomes the medium of communication with the traders, and extends his sway by a liberal distribution of tobacco and ammunition among his dependents. At present, the rank of a chief is not fully established among his own people until it is recognized at the fort to which he resorts. A free expenditure by the chief of the presents he receives from the traders, and even of the produce of his furs, is a main bulwark of his authority, in addition to the skill which he must possess in the management of the various tempers with which he has to do. (1851, 2:26–28)

We see that to attain leadership three sorts of attributes were necessary. In fur-trade times the final validation was the recognition as "chief" by the Euro-Canadian trader. But to establish preeminence, the individual had first to be successful in the vital activity of hunting. With the further attribute of certain favorable aspects of character, he met the requirements for leadership.

[The historical literature yielded only scraps of observations or generalizations about leadership in hunting. Here I have dropped the shreds of "evidence" provided by the early writers that I had cobbled together in a single paragraph. When writing this article in 1955 I had not yet moved from moose hunters (Mackenzie River Slaveys) to caribou hunters (Dogribs) in my fieldwork. Dogrib oral history and their contemporary caribou hunting allowed me to grasp the meanings of hunt leadership among hunters of the caribou herds. Hunting organization and leadership among those Dene are presented in a following section.]

War leaders existed into the first three or four decades of the historical era. The last recorded incident of warfare between northeastern Dene tribes occurred in the 1830s (Simpson 1843); Athapaskan-Cree warfare had evidently ceased by that time. Possibly a few hostile encounters between Chipewyan-Yellowknives and Inuit occurred in later times, but I have found no record of it. [I have excepted the Gwich'in from this survey.]

Writing in 1807, Wentzel describes the status of the war chief among the Slaveys of the Fort Simpson area:

When war is declared upon them, they elect a chief from among the old men; to him they submit for advice and commandment; so soon as peace is obtained, this chief is no more obeyed or attended to any further than to support him and his family when old, and ask his opinions in time of trouble. These chiefs [and apparently Wentzel is still speaking of war chiefs here] hardly merit the title they enjoy. Na-kan-au-Bettau or Great Chief is the only one who is a little respected and obeyed; he is a middling sized corpulent fellow, not without a competent share of common sense, at least enough to procure skins and provisions without hunting for them. (1889:89)

In 1821 Franklin said:

The chiefs among the Chipewyans are now totally without power. . . . This is to be attributed mainly to [the Chipewyans] living at peace with their neighbors, and to the facility which the young men find in getting their wants supplied independent of the recommendation of the chiefs which was formerly required. In war excursions boldness and intrepidity would still command respect and procure authority, but the influence thus acquired would, probably, cease with the occasion that called it forth. (1824:142)

Is the implication here that one or more of those men currently acting as trading chiefs would be the ones to assume war leadership should hostilities commence? We know from Richardson (1851) that the Yellowknife chief Akaitcho combined the three roles of band headman, trading chief, and war leader. [The publication (Davis 1995) of Franklin's journal and correspondence regarding his first expedition provides at times an almost quotidian account of Akaitcho's activities.] Apparently, the same was true for the "northern," or Chipewyan, chief Matonabbee with whom Hearne traveled to the Coppermine River.

From Hearne we have the only eyewitness description of a war party in action, at the massacre of the Eskimos by the Chipewyans at Bloody Falls. In this case, a traveling group [escorts for Hearne] turned into an adventitious war party. As far as Hearne's description goes, there was no recruitment or other special activities on the part of any leader. One passage describing the preparation for the assault is suggestive, however:

> Soon after our arrival at the river-side three Indians were sent off as spies, in order to see if any Esquimaux were inhabiting the river-side between us and the sea. [Two days later the spies and the main party joined up, the spies bringing news of five tents of Eskimos, now about twelve miles away.] When the Indians received this intelligence, no further attendance or attention was paid to my survey, but their whole thoughts were immediately engaged in planning the best method of attack.

> [Just before describing the actual attack Hearne says:] It is perhaps worth remarking, that my crew, though an undisciplined rabble, and by no means accustomed to war or command, seemingly acted on this horrid occasion with the utmost uniformity of sentiment. There was not among them the least altercation or separate opinion; all were united in the general cause, and as ready to follow where Matonabbee led, as he appeared to be ready to lead, according to the advice of an old Copper [Yellowknife] Indian, who had joined us on our first arrival at the river where this bloody business was first proposed. (Hearne 1911 : 174–77)

The tenor of this passage and the remainder of the account is that there is no real leadership involved in the attack except, perhaps, for the old Yellowknife (who with three companions had joined the party only two days before) serving as tactician prior to the assault. As for Matonabbee, Hearne (1911 : 330) states that "when we went to war with the Esquimaux at the Coppermine River in July 1771, it was by no means his proposal: on the contrary, he was forced into it by his countrymen."

It seems likely that successful leaders in secular ventures such as hunting were commonly attributed with exceptional powers in the supernatural realm. [See the Dogrib *wedzitxa* later in this chapter.] The only clear affirmation in the earlier literature of this supposition, however, is Mason's (1946: 34) statement regarding the Dogribs of Fort Rae in 1913: "These leaders are elderly men as a rule, often the paternal patriarchs of the band, and being generally good hunters, experienced woodsmen, and more efficient than the majority of their fellows, their judgment is respected by the members of the gang. . . . The chiefs or leaders were either elected or appointed but were those whose powerful 'medicine' caused them to be feared and respected and whose authority, knowledge, and competency were admitted to be superior."

An early manuscript by Roderic Mackenzie (1795) speaks of a "great Chief [of the Chipewyans] who is also their High Priest." Hearne presents the man with medicine power operating as an equivocal agent of social control. Speaking of the custom of one man forcing another to yield over his wife by besting him in a wrestling match, Hearne (1911:143–44) says, "Some of the old men who are famous on account of their supposed skill in conjuration have great influence in persuading the rabble from committing those outrages." But he then goes on to say that they seldom interfered in cases where one of their own relatives was the aggressor but rose to the defense when the challenged husband was a kinsman. Fear of the one with medicine power stifled protest from others. Concerning "doctors" of a generation ago in the Liard-Simpson area, Angus Sherwood (a long-time resident of the Northwest Territories) said that they were, by their prestige and exertion of moral pressure, in a sense agents of social control.

Osgood describes an apparently unique situation in regard to leadership. According to Osgood's consultant, "formerly" the "Oldest Man" was the primary "chief" among the Hare Indians; second to him with less authority was the "Best Hunter" (1932:74). This is the only unequivocal statement we have making leadership an ascription due solely to age. And we have at least one case, in the 1820s, where the major leader, Akaitcho, was not even the eldest of a set of brothers.

The varieties of leadership discussed have of course undergone changes along with the rest of the Dene way of life in the course of many decades of contact with the Western world. Christian missionary teachings after 1860 and whites' attitudes in general undermined the possession of powerful medicine as a source of prestige and opening for dominant status. War and war leaders, though perhaps stimulated at the beginning of the fur-trade era, died out in the early decades of the nineteenth century. The trading chief flourished in the heyday of the Hudson's Bay Company (which governed the Territory until 1870) in the nineteenth century. Today, his function as "mouthpiece" for his followers has been partially filled by the "government" chief, who is supposed to mediate between his constituents and government officials.

PATTERNS OF LEADER–FOLLOWER RELATIONS

Closely following the words of the early observers, we have so far considered the areas of activity in and through which a man might achieve leadership. At the risk of some reiteration, it is now possible to block out the generalized pattern of sociopolitical relations between the northeastern Dene leader and his followers. Then there are the related questions of the universality of the leader figure and the personal variables that came into play.

The domineering and exploitative behavior of those Dogrib Indian leaders described by Richardson who were actually able to exercise physical coercion over their constituents by using strong-arm men stands out in the literature because, except for a rather vague statement by Keith suggesting an oppressive quality in Dogrib leadership, it is so at variance with the picture gained by other observers. Petitot's detailed description exemplifies the more common condition of leader-group interaction. The case of Young Hunter—the Slavey chief whose authority was challenged because "this man wished to impose his wishes"—will be recalled. Young Hunter found that his "authority" existed only so long as his aims were deemed right and desirable by the group. Cued by a responsible male (who was perhaps in turn cued by the presence of a prestigious alien), even the women and girls felt free to express open insubordination. Besides certain unspecified demands upon his sons being rejected by them, the chief found that the group refused to accord him demand-right regarding marriage unions. Indeed, the general tenor of the literature indicates that the Dene leader or chief had no firmly established demand-right in any area of activity.

Along this line, another incident from Petitot (1891:349–51) may be cited. It took place in a Slavey "village" on what is now the Petitot River (east-southeast of Fort Liard). Nadi, the younger brother of the chief, asks Petitot, "Who is master, a woman or her husband?" He goes on to explain, "We have a chief, you see, who lets himself be guided and ruled by his wife. *He listens to our advice*, but his wife is of a contrary sentiment, and he gives way to her. 'I agree with you' he says [to us], 'but my wife does not wish it.' What do you say to that? Is he a chief?" (emphasis and translation mine). Petitot informs the reader, "Less than two years later, a letter from Providence apprised me that the old chief had been removed and that Nadi had been chosen [*èlu*] in his place." Nadi's complaint is not that the chief is acting independently, only that he is yielding to the wrong influence, that of his wife instead of his male peers.

The view that the power and control of the chief and/or leader over his group was ordinarily trifling is to be found in most reports. Hearne's generalizations on the lack of authority of Chipewyan chiefs have already been cited. Another observer at the beginning of the contact period, Alexander Mackenzie (1970 [1889]), wrote that "none of the principal men" of the "Redknives" [Yellowknives, Copper Indians] living around the Slave Lake fort had "sufficient authority" to be appointed a trading chief. And Hearne (1911:223) recorded that more than once the Chipewyan chief Matonabbee was so enraged by the pilfering of his property "and other insults" by his followers that he threatened to leave and go "reside with the Athapuscow [Cree] Indians." In the early decades of the nineteenth century, we find that "[the Liard Dene] are ungovernable in some respects by their chiefs, whom they obey only in hopes of being recompensed. . . . They pay no external marks of respect to their leaders, and indeed the latter are little regarded. A boy will often refuse to run an errand for them unless he happens to be a nigh relation." And the "Long Arrowed Indians" of the Bear Lake area "have no leaders of any authority or note amongst them" (Keith 1890).

Regarding Dogrib chiefs, Russell (1898) said 120 years later that Hearne's remarks were "equally true today," and Franklin, McLean, Mason, and Petitot passed similar judgments in different decades on the chiefs of generalized "Chipewyans" (including Dogribs and Yellowknives), the "Mackenzie River Indians," the Dene of the Great Slave Lake area, and the Northeastern Athapaskan tribes generally.

In sum, the leader characteristically had a very tenuous position in northeastern Dene society. He might serve as advisor, coordinator, director, and perhaps initiator of specific military actions and/or of occasional and particular economic activities beyond the day-to-day hunting and snaring routine. Also, by virtue of prestige gained from superior abilities and awe-inspiring powers he might act as the prime opinion giver in social matters within the band. His "authority" lay in putting his stamp of approval upon decisions or viewpoints arrived at by the group as a whole or, more specifically, his male peers. The wise chief or leader had his finger upon the pulse of individual and group opinions. He had to woo others to his way of thinking or, that failing, to alter his course accordingly. His position might be buttressed by the attribution of powerful medicine and by the Europeans' evaluation and use as "trading chief" of his already dominant role. But the power of a strong or "great" leader lay in his influence rather than his "legal" authority. Ordinarily, he had neither the moral nor the physical resources to impose his will. Birket-Smith's (1930) characterization of the Chipewyan chief as primus inter pares keynotes the position of the northern Dene leader.

There is little reason to suppose that all or most local groups had a headman or leader by even the feeble criteria given above. The fluidity and lack of structure of all groupings argue against the likelihood of leader as a characteristic figure in every group. The intermittent nature of the macroassemblages did not allow for continual exercise of the leader role, and apparently only in the trading gang and the war party was it ever enacted at all. [In the literature, the consensual task-group "boss," or k'awo, as I encountered him in field research, was not evident; see below.]

In the coresidential hunt band there is no firm evidence that a "leader" had any really vital function in economic or other matters. The gaining of superior prestige-cum-status was an outcome of individual skills and endeavor. In a society where communal distribution of large game is a cardinal rule, a superior hunter was a good man to fall in with. If he was also a man of sound social judgments and techniques, his influence and following were so much the greater. But it is quite likely that in many hunt bands no adult male could be singled out as consistently exercising more influence and being accorded more deference than any other.

Certain situational factors did encourage the establishment of headmen. A superior hunter and/or quasi leader who was recognized by the Hudson's Bay Company trader as a trading chief would find his position stabilized, and some recognition of his status would be called forth from all individuals who used him as an intermediary in their dealings with whites. Such exigencies as war or white exploration parties needing Indian helpers (as in Akaitcho's case) might call a man of superior endowment to the fore. The authority gained in this role might color his relations with other men after the end of the immediate event.

There were two immediate and basic conditions, suggested in earlier passages, operative in the establishment of leader-follower relations: kin relationships and personal qualities. Such bits of documentation as do exist, plus an extrapolation from my observations, indicate that the sentiments of kinship have been the base upon which the leader builds his influence and his following. "To become a general leader requires numerous relations," says Keith (1890). Primary relationships, that is, sibling-sibling or parent-child, probably characteristically formed the core of the leader-follower syndrome. [See Helm (1965a, 1969a) on analysis of modern groups.] In Franklin's (1824) account of the Yellowknives, we find Humpy, the older brother of the leader Akaitcho, mentioned several times in a way that suggests he served as a close associate and lieutenant of his younger sibling. In a small family band, the father would be the usual source of any leader behavior (e.g., Keith 1890). In a larger assemblage [e.g., a regional band] of several fully mature (related) men, a specific kin status would not be a necessary condition of leadership.

As to those personal qualities that enabled a man to attain and maintain the position of leader, the early literature gives us few details. Success in hunting, in manipulating the supernatural, and in war as paths to dominant status have already been emphasized.

A leader of any real accomplishment had to possess, in Richardson's words, "skill . . . in the management of the various tempers with which he has to do." But, except for Keith's (1890) vague phrase that a leader needs "some address and ability," Richardson is the only observer to speak of good social technique—the ability to attract, influence, and manipulate others—as a quality of leadership. The only specific social technique cited is that of generosity. Generosity may also be considered an ingrained aspect of character, but for a chief, at least, the distribution of gifts obtained from the trader was a social requirement, whether it was a natural impulse or not. We may well suppose that the exercise of the opposite trait, that of niggardliness, much contemned today, would be a serious handicap in commanding prestige.

Courage as an attractive aspect of character is mentioned, and "superior understanding and conduct" (Keith), "superior powers of mind" (Richardson), and "superior knowledge and competency" (Mason), unhappily vague phrases, are cited as attributes of the successful leader. In King's description of Akaitcho's behavior are exemplified further qualities necessary to a leader of real stature—the willingness to give most fully of his energies and persistence and endurance in the face of difficulty or crisis, promoting the morale of his group.

Akaitcho, during this appalling season of calamity [a winter famine], proved himself well worth the rank of chief of the Yellowknives. . . . He set the example of hunting early and late every day, and, by continued exertion, made every attempt to alleviate the distress which was pressing heavily upon his tribe. The bold manner with which he encountered every difficulty, mitigated in a great measure the growing evil and dispelled the gloom which had seized both the old and the young. (King 1836, 1 : 173)

From Keith's (1890) comments on Dogrib leaders of the early nineteenth century comes an uncomplimentary phrase, "ferocity tinctured with an inclination to dominate," recalling Richardson's Dogrib bullies. The urge or will, suggested in these two characterizations, within the individual toward exceptional influence or control over events and people must, we may surmise, always be a factor in the attainment of effective nonascribed leadership. But for a Dene this trait of character is highly idiosyncratic in a way that the preceding ones are not. The attributes previously mentioned fulfill certain Athapaskan cultural ideals—the hard worker and good provider, the supernaturally endowed, the wise man, the generous man, and so on. But in the Dene view the will to power per se is not conceived to be admirable or socially desirable. The reaction to this will when encountered nakedly is not just indifferent, it is negative.

This distaste for subjugation to the authority of another or, phrased in positive terms, the motivation toward personal autonomy is a dominant aspect of the ethos of the northeastern Dene. The existence of what may be called the cultural theme of autonomy might be suspected from the very fact of the unstructured nature of the social groups that this documentary survey has yielded. Explicit reference to this emotional quality may occasionally be found in the early writers: "The whole of the Chippewayan [northeastern Dene] tribes seem averse to superior rule" (McLean 1932:341). The ingrained dislike of the authoritarian figure has remained over the decades an intangible but enduring barrier with which that individual who is impelled toward a dominant, let alone dominating, role must cope.

from June Helm MacNeish, "Leadership
among the Northeastern Athabascans," 1956a

BOSSES, LEADERS, AND TRADING CHIEFS
AMONG THE DOGRIBS

The preceding section drew on European and Euro-Canadian descriptions of Dene leadership in, mainly, the nineteenth century. This section moves from outsiders' views to an insider's comprehensions, especially as articulated by Dogrib Vital Thomas, of the history and the qualities of Dogrib leaders and trading chiefs.

In the fall caribou hunt [of the early 1960s] of the Dogribs an old exploitative pattern may still be seen. From Rae, perhaps fifty or sixty hunters depart in several "crews" of several canoes each toward the barrens to meet the caribou on their first swing toward the wooded country in August or September. Families are left at the fort or at fish camps. Each crew has its "boss," or *k'awo*. Should a crew find it necessary to divide into two groups going different ways, a second boss is selected (by the group or the first *k'awo*) for the second group. As described by Jean Amourous, O.M.I., who accompanied the fall hunt of the Dogrib in 1959, "It was the hunt leader's role to make decisions as to when the group should stop in its journey because of bad weather, when to make camp for the night, who was to go out and look for 'sign,' etc. When a question arose, everybody said what he thought, then the leader made a decision, taking the discussion into account. Once the leader had stated his decision, no one argued, even if not in agreement initially."

Once in the hunting grounds, the crew splits up daily or overnight into parties of two or three hunters each, each party going a different direction upon the advice of the leader and consensus of the group. The boss of each crew, as part of his role, oversees the even distribution of each day's kill to all members of the crew, after the food for the day has been set aside. The hides are taken by the slayer of each animal.

K'awo may be applied to any man who is the recognized initiator and adjudicator of action and allocation of any sort. In this sense, any man in the role of boss over a group may be termed *k'awo*. Assignment to the status may be by (male) group consensus, but the designation is equally applied to a "foreman," that is, to a lieutenant designated by one in higher authority to oversee a particular group venture, such as a hunt or the moving of an advance camp.

In his reconstruction of vanished days, Vital Thomas distinguished a quasi-temporal progression of Dogrib leaders of greater stature than *k'awo*. First comes the mythical prime hunter, the *wedzitxa*, whose supernatural power over caribou [*wedzii*, male caribou] bound a large band following to him. The *wedzitxa* often hunted alone to supply the whole band, dividing up the meat so that everyone got an equal share; "he saved nothing for himself." Any prime leader among the Dogribs, including the mythical *wedzitxa*, might be titled *wek'axots'edeh*, "great man whom we all follow." Upon the taking of treaty in 1921, the status of *wek'axots'edeh* was obliterated by the creation, by government fiat, of the head chief, *gwatinde* [*kw'ahtinde*], and councillors. Lesser headmen, each serving as the locus of decision and judgment within a band group but deferring in prestige and judgment to the greatest group leader (when, indeed, such a man was so recognized), were the *denerak'awo*, "boss for a people," as the *wek'axots'edeh* could also be called. The *wek'axots'edeh* was a great hunter; "he fed everybody and was the headman of all." Furthermore, because the *wek'axots'edeh* was a "good hunter and trapper, he got all kinds of supplies from the Hudson's Bay Company. And what we asked for he gave us." In this aspect, the *wek'axots'edeh*'s role as responsible provider merges with that of the *donek'awi*, the "people's trader." Within the classic fur-trade period, there was no status of *wek'axots'edeh* apart from *donek'awi*.

No specific kin status vis-à-vis followers was prerequisite to becoming a recognized leader. The men performing as *wedzitxa*, *wek'axots'edeh*, and *donek'awi* shared the prime attribute of controlling access to the most vital resources of the people's environment—not only the large game upon which life depended but, in the case of the *donek'awi*, or trading chief, access to the commercial fur trader, upon whose goods life came equally to depend.

The era of the trading chief in Dene history endured in the Mackenzie River region close to a century, from about 1820 to after 1900. In midcentury Richardson (1851, 2:27) summed up the trading chief: "A free expenditure by the chief of the presents that he receives from the traders, and even of his produce of furs, is the main bulwark of his authority, in addition to the skill which he must possess in the management of the various tempers with which he had to do."

This characterization agrees with the Dogrib's-eye view. With a strong sense of the golden past, in 1962 Vital Thomas presented an archetypal version of the role of trading chief, or *donek'awi*. [This was nine years before Naedzo's similar outlook (chapter 9) was recorded.] Here is Vital's picture, edited and condensed:

> *Donek'awi* [or *ek'awi*, also *k'awi*] is "people's trader"; it means something like "Hudson's Bay Company man" or "trader." There couldn't be any higher man; he was a great man. If strangers came, they asked for *donek'awi*'s tent. They shook hands with him before anyone else, and he had to feed them all. The Hudson's Bay Company used to give all kinds of supplies, clothing, and ammunition to *donek'awi*. If his bunch ran short of supplies, *donek'awi* could send two of his men to Resolution or wherever. Those two men would say, "*Ek'awi* sent us for grub," and the [company] trader had to send what he was asked for back to *ek'awi*. In the springtime or Christmas [traditional times for trading at the fort] *ek'awi* paid back the trader with fur.

Donek'awi had five or six helpers, hunters and fishermen. For a helper, *donek'awi* picked a good man. A man had to be a hard worker because some of *ek'awi*'s helpers had to hunt and some had to stay and help *ek'awi* keep the camp going.

Donek'awi and his helpers had to feed the whole band, so pretty near all of the Indians had to follow him to whatever place was a good hunting place, a good trapping place. Maybe there would be a hundred people following him and everybody got the same amount. He didn't charge anything. It did not matter if a man was poor, lazy, or lame. *Ek'awi* had to help everyone.

Only a man asked by *ek'awi* would be a *k'awiceke*, his special helper. *Ek'awi*'s helpers gave all their furs to *ek'awi* who, when they got to the fort, sold all the fur for all his helpers. Married or single, each of his men got the same amount of goods in trade. Just like one family.

Anyone that wanted to go with an *ek'awi* as a member of his bunch could go with any *ek'awi* they chose. [For example,] a Marten Lake man could go with the Edge-of-the-Woods *ek'awi*'s bunch, it was up to him.

Some men worked for themselves, [that is,] they had no *ek'awi*. Men that dealt [directly] with the Hudson's Bay Company trader [not going through an *ek'awi*] were the ones that kept themselves out of *ek'awi*'s bunch. But if such a man was in the bush and short of something, he would ask *ek'awi* and *ek'awi* would help him. If *ek'awi* knew that man was honest he would give him anything he wanted. And then that person had to pay it back later to the *ek'awi*.

When Old Hislop [the first free trader] came, then there were two traders [the Hudson's Bay Company and Hislop]. Everybody could [and did] go anyplace, wherever they wanted to. And that's how they cut out *donek'awi*.

"The Bay stopped giving stuff to *donek'awi*." Monfwi, whom the last great Dogrib *donek'awi*, Ek'awi Dzimi, was grooming as his successor, therefore never became *donek'awi*. With the taking of treaty in 1921, band leaders of the order of *donerak'awo* were in effect made into elected councillors (*gwati* [*kw'ahti*]), and the "biggest" man among them, Monfwi, became government head chief (*gwatinde* [*kw'ahtideè*]).

Among the northern Dene, a set of prized attributes—outstanding hunting success, force of character, and open-handed responsibility—drew followers. In the leader the social ethic of generosity was institutionalized. In building one's position as prime adjudicator and disburser in matters of group welfare, one must have more than others in order to give more away. But although hunt-band leaders and trading chiefs exercised something of a directive and redistributive role, this leadership was in no way crucial to production and distribution within the society. No "boss" was needed to enforce the rule of communal distribution of large game. Small groups of two or three related families and even single nuclear families were able to go it alone, attached to no larger group or important leader, much of the time. But the best survival insurance was group insurance. Among the Dene, the basic economic nexus lay not between categories of kinsmen but within the group banded together at the moment (granted, a group threaded through with consanguine and affinal ties). The leader's prime function was not physically to enforce the basic obligation to share one's fortune with the group but morally to reinforce it.

from "Patterns of Allocation among the Arctic Drainage Dene," 1965b

CHIEFLY SUCCESSION AMONG THE RAE DOGRIBS, 1867–1971

Dogrib oral history about their leaders combined with several returns to Rae through the years allowed me to grasp the run of a hundred years of polity commitment.

Jimmy Bruneau succeeded to the office of head chief of the Rae Band of Dogribs in 1934 as the choice of the dying Dogrib chief Monfwi. The latter had been the successor in 1902 chosen by Jimmy Bruneau's father, the trading chief Ek'awi Dzimi, who for thirty-five years had been the prime leader of the Dogribs trading into Rae. The "passing of the mantle" by a sort of paramount Dogrib leader—a role established at least two long generations before it was transformed into "government chief" by Treaty No. 11 of 1921—had, by all evidence, simply reinforced, rather than replaced or conflicted with, the essential process of consensual male decision by which leaders of any level or duration had traditionally been selected. Would the consensus tradition be maintained, or would the Rae Dogribs at last resort to the elective method that most Canadian Indian groups now practiced?

In 1962 I heard comments that the chief was getting old (he was eighty) but that he had not yet said what he "had in his mind" concerning his successor. When I returned in 1967 the comment was, "We've been talking about a new chief for two years now." The old chief was now extremely deaf; although he had expressed the desire to step down, he had not designated a successor. One man prominent in community discussion for successor (but not by the chief) was a man from another regional band, the Et'at'in. In 1968 the old chief was still in office, and the issue of land rights and Indian

Dogrib Chief Monfwi (d. 1934). Rae, 19??.
Provided by John B. Zoe.

Dogrib Chief Jimmy Bruneau (d. 1975).
Rae, 1962.

reserves, introduced by government officials at the annual treaty payment
that summer [see chapter 14], seemed to have flooded out other concerns
from the people's minds. In 1969, I again arrived at Rae in time for Treaty.
This would be the occasion when a new chief would formally take office. If
there were to be a change, the decision would be made shortly before Treaty.

After a meeting on other issues with a territorial official a few days prior
to Treaty, a group of men formed outside the old chief's house. Discussion
ranged widely as to who should be the new chief. Some expressed the opinion that it should be someone who could speak English and who could read
and write. Some younger men's names were mentioned, as well as illiterate
but well-regarded older men. There appeared still to be a push on the part of
members of the Et'at'in regional band to place one of their important men
in the office.

Sunday, the following day, word went out to the older men of Rae to
gather at the house of a respected band leader who had been a central participant in the previous day's discussion. Although there had been some talk
of a formal election, the parley and mode of decision making followed traditional lines. ("Not very democratic," commented a young Indian activist
whose generation had not figured in the decision making.) As an accom-

modation to the old chief, who was manifesting reluctance to retire, some men of consequence approached him with the proposition that he step down in favor of his son, a sixty-year-old monolingual. Also, in an effort to induce him to relinquish his office voluntarily, they pointed out that one of the most respected band councillors had stated his intention to retire. Old Chief Bruneau accepted the proposal.

No one, except the new chief, seemed happy with the compromise. Although respected as a hard worker in the bush, he was not seen to have other attributes, either traditional or modern, desired in a leader. Within two years a movement to select another chief climaxed. In order to avoid outright rejection of the incumbent, the strategy was to hold for the first time a formal election, with the incumbent running against three other men (one the Et'at'in candidate), but there seemed to be a general understanding as to which one was likely to emerge the winner: Alexis Arrowmaker, a respected monolingual of the Edge-of-the-Woods people (Decinlahot'in), the regional band of Chief Bruneau, Chief Monfwi, and Ek'awi Dzimi. His pride wounded, the incumbent chief refused to run. The election brought Alexis Arrowmaker to office by a two-thirds majority.

Their polity defined and redefined by government fiat for fifty years, the Dogribs had at last retreated from their principle of the consensual political community. Subsequent events demonstrated that this step instituted an irreversible alteration of their political processes.

from "Long-Term Research among the Dogrib and Other Dene," 1979

EPILOGUE

Alexis Arrowmaker (b. 1920) was the first chief of the Rae Dogribs to be selected by formal vote rather than consensus. Although other men succeeded him as elected chief in the years that followed, Alexis Arrowmaker continued to be an important actor in Dogrib affairs. John B. Zoe offers a telling anecdote.

In 1995 we [representatives of the Dogrib Treaty 11 Council] were meeting with some federal bureaucrats in Rae. They were responding to pressure from the Dogribs to clean up the old Rayrock uranium mine site. They had a proposal of several options for cleaning up the mine site, using funds earmarked from a federal program. As required, they were consulting with us and wanted us to select the option we would prefer. They also mentioned some potential contractors for the job. We recommended very strongly that they put dollars aside to get the people's story, their view of how they were impacted by the development and eventual abandonment of the site [see Legat et al. 1997].

Dogrib Chief Alexis Arrowmaker. Rae, 199?. Courtesy of Dogrib Treaty 11 Council.

Alexis Arrowmaker was with us at that meeting. He was frustrated when he realized that the bureaucrats already had a plan laid out and that it was not going far enough to clean the site properly. He was trying to express to them his thoughts on the issue. It was a rough day for the translator. After every translation, Alexis would make it known that it wasn't translated the way he said it. When a break was called, I sat next to Alexis, and that's when he told me the story of how it would have been different if . . . As told by Alexis Arrowmaker to John B. Zoe on February 22, 1995:

When I was a young boy, I did not have a family so I was living under the roof of Chief Monfwi. It was during the summer and boats had come in. The nuns were walking around Rae asking who would go to Fort Resolution for schooling. In those days, when you went you were gone for five or six years. Even though I was living with Monfwi, I didn't tell them who my guardian was. I just agreed to go.

Without telling Monfwi, I went home and rolled up my sleeping blankets and got on the boat. Monfwi must of been told that I was on the boat. He came down to the shore and ordered me off because he needed me to work for him and to keep his fire going. I still had my bedroll tucked under my arm. I got off the boat and followed him home.

I sometimes wonder, in terms of being able to understand and speak the English language, what the results might have been on matters like those we are discussing today.

from a letter to June Helm from John B. Zoe,
January 26, 1998, with later emendations by John Zoe
Alexis Arrowmaker has agreed to this recounting of his story.

FEMALE INFANTICIDE,
EUROPEAN DISEASES,
11 | AND POPULATION LEVELS
AMONG THE MACKENZIE DENE

This chapter moves further back in time, beyond living Dene experience, to assess the significance of population figures from the first half of the nineteenth century.

This is a dense, tightly argued research paper. The "light" reader may want to skip it. A researcher should use the full article that was published in the American Ethnologist *in 1980; its notes, which are intense, are here omitted, and they are necessary for full documentation and assessment of data. I felt that it was impossible to present this article, however, without including the tables that support the presentation, tables that themselves are heavily burdened with explanatory notes. Nor is it possible to drop the final section on population models that demonstrate the thesis underlying the conclusions. (Line misalignments and undue complications in table 2 of the original publication have been corrected in table 2 in this chapter. An erratum in Population Model II of figure 2 has also been corrected.)*

In this essay I do not ask, Why infanticide? The necessary first step is to determine whether the population data support the attribution of female infanticide. The two statements at the beginning of the essay are drawn from native recollection of times past.

Years, years ago when a woman was ready to have a baby, she would take off into the woods and have her baby under a tree. People had such hard times surviving in the old days that if a woman had a baby girl she would kill the baby by putting the afterbirth against its mouth to suffocate it. If she had a boy, she would save him as men were the ones that would hunt and do other things to keep the people alive.

—POLDINE CARLO (1978:25), *Alaskan Dene woman*

My mother's mother used to tell of this. It was hard then, hard for clothing. If it is a big family especially, the girls they don't keep, the boys they need for hunters. So when a girl is born they throw her away. What can you do to clothe them? To clothe the whole family is hard.

TADZI, 1872–1971, *Mountain Dene woman*
(Gillespie 1971; Laura Yakaleya, interpreter)

Infanticide—rates, functions, and consequences, as well as societal and familial reasons—has been featured in a number of anthropological studies in recent years [citations omitted]. In the comparative studies especially, inquiry has focused on the significance of female infanticide as a damper on population growth. Calculations or estimates, inferred from skewed sex ratios, of rates of selective female infanticide among historic or contemporary hunter-gatherer populations have served as a basis for conceptualizations of demographic "equilibrium systems" of Pleistocene and other prehistoric populations [citations omitted].

The database on rates of female infanticide among hunter-gatherers and other low-energy societies on which comparative or generalist studies rely is generally weak. Population data covering entire sociocultural collectivities or connubia (not just portions thereof), adequately comprehended in their ethnographic and historical matrix and spanning progressive slices of time, are in short supply. Nineteenth- and twentieth-century documentation on the Dene of the Mackenzie River region offers an unusually extensive set of census data that permit derivations of rates of attributed female infanticide in a controlled historical context. Further, the census data allow one to determine the effect of introduced infectious diseases on the population level of these Dene and thereby to assess the validity of the depopulation theory that has been advanced in support of the argument for aboriginal unilocal-unilineal social organization among the Mackenzie Dene.

NINETEENTH-CENTURY OBSERVERS' STATEMENTS ON FEMALE INFANTICIDE

In 1858 Chief Factor James Anderson (1907 [1858]) of the Hudson's Bay Company, "previous to delivering up the charge of the Mackenzie's River District," submitted a report on the fur-trade posts of the district in which he provided a population count of the Indians trading into each "fort" or post. Excepting the Fort Resolution Dene population, the Indian populations resorting for trade to the posts of the "McKenzie's River District" showed a marked preponderance of males over females. For Forts Liard, Simpson (and its outpost, Big Island), Norman, Good Hope, and Rae, Anderson specifically attributed "the disparity in the sexes" to selective female infanticide. He stated, however, that through the (presumably hortatory) efforts of the company's officers the practice had all but ceased by 1858.

In an earlier period, other traders in the Mackenzie region had made note of female infanticide: Keith (1890:11) in 1812 in reference to the

"Long Arrowed Indians" (Hare), and Wentzel (1889:86) and Edward Smith (HBCA B.200/a/3/fol. 23) in reference to the Dene populations of the Upper Mackenzie and Liard regions, although both of the latter (writing in 1807 and 1823, respectively) believed the practice to be lessening.

Anderson (1907:115) commented, "I have not heard that female infanticide prevails among the Loucheux [Gwich'in]," but a few years later Kirkby (Kirby [Kirkby] 1865:418) and Hardisty (1867:312) did assign the practice to the Kutchin. More precisely, Jones (1867:327) stated that the fact that "Kutchin women do not kill their female infants [was] one of the changes introduced among them by the whites."

Anderson did not attribute female infanticide to the Dene population of Fort Resolution. The Chipewyans of Fort Resolution represent the westernmost postcontact extension of the Chipewyan nation, which ranged across the transitional boreal forest zone westward from Hudson Bay. The Chipewyans were involved in the fur trade considerably earlier and more regularly than were the Dene west and north of Great Slave Lake. Thompson (1916: 130) recorded female infanticide among the Chipewyans of the 1790–1800 period, but by the 1820s Franklin (1828:64) wrote, "I understand infanticide is now very rare amongst the Chipewyan tribes . . . which may be fairly attributed to the influence of the traders among them," in contrast to the female infanticide "frequently" practiced by the Dene of Great Bear Lake.

For the Yellowknives, I can find only Keith's (1890:107) equivocal statement of 1812: "The male sex appears to be predominant, and I presume that the female sex while in infancy are much neglected."

SOURCES OF POPULATION DATA, 1820S–1920S

By the time of Anderson's report in 1858, the Hudson's Bay Company had exercised a monopoly of the fur trade in the Mackenzie River region and adjacent lands for over thirty years. Soon after the coalition with the North West Company in 1821, the governor and council of the Northern Department of the reorganized Hudson's Bay Company charged each field officer "annually to furnish Registers of the number of Indians attached to their respective Districts and Posts" (Fleming 1940:126, see also 63). Under the conditions of full monopoly just established, all Indians now perforce had to resort to the company's posts for trade goods. By the end of the 1820s, the Dene population of the Mackenzie region (excepting, perhaps, a few Dogribs and some other stragglers) was accounted for and distinguished in terms of sex (except for some children, in some cases) and adult versus juvenile categories. After this initial decade of monopoly, the charge to provide full counts of all Indians (rather than just account book records of men and youths old enough to hunt and take fur) seems to have lapsed until Anderson's comprehensive report of 1858.

With the establishment of Anglican and Roman Catholic missions beginning in the 1860s, population data were recorded by the missionaries in the form of records of baptisms (including converted adults), marriages, and deaths. Missionary efforts no doubt quickly guaranteed the elimination of female infanticide as a statistically significant demographic factor. Through the years, as children were born to now-Christian parents, estimates of age gave way to more precise accounting. The mission-by-mission records, however, do not yield censuses per se.

The government of Canada tended to produce wildly inflated population estimates and/or repeat the same guess figures year after year until the signings of Treaty No. 8 in 1899–1900. The Department of Indian Affairs had then to begin its own record of the 852 Indians of the Northwest Territories and their descendants registered under that treaty. Not until after 1921–22, with the signings of Treaty No. 11, were government records established on the bulk of the Dene peoples of the Northwest Territories.

Alexander Mackenzie's descent in 1789 of Dehcho (the Mackenzie River) to the Arctic Ocean initiated direct contact between Europeans (as fur traders) and Indians in the Mackenzie River Valley. In the first thirty-odd years of contact, only a few of the reports from the often short lived trading forts of the North West Company are extant. But from the 1820s on, thanks mainly to the unified and centralized fur trade under the Hudson's Bay Company, the documentary record provides population counts of a high degree of reliability and completeness. Census data of such quality on a set of hunting peoples—beginning a generation after contact, spanning 150 years, and covering several thousand persons—are perhaps unparalleled in the ethnographic-historical record.

THE CENSUSES OF 1829, 1858, 1891, AND 1924: SEX RATIOS

In large populations worldwide, the sex ratio (SR), expressed in a figure signifying the number of males per 100 females, usually ranges between 99 and 104. Given the attribution of selective female infanticide in a population, a figure substantially in excess of these averages (say, 125) lends support to that attribution and gives some indication of the rate of female infanticide:

for example, SR 125 equals 20 percent fewer females than males in the population.

Four major censuses of the Mackenzie River region, twenty-nine to thirty-three years apart, represent two generations within the female infanticide era and two successive generations of the postinfanticide era. The sum sex ratios for the first two generations, represented in the Fort Simpson District Report of 1829 and the McKenzie's River District Report of 1858, are SR 142 and SR 129, respectively. Stated conversely, in 1829 there were 30 percent fewer females than males, and in 1858 there were 22 percent fewer females than males in the censused populations. That the disproportionate number of males to females in these two periods was the result of female infanticide is indirectly supported by the population counts of the two succeeding generations of 1891 and 1924. In these two latter generations, when putative female infanticide is one to two generations past, the sex ratios are essentially balanced: SR 103 and SR 98, respectively.

The details of the censuses of 1829, 1858, 1891, and 1924—matched by post and by traders' group designations—are presented in table 11.1. Particular features of table 11.1 call for comment. First of all, the total populations at each interval cannot be regarded as comparable counts from one generation to the next in that some of the censuses take in more posts, and therefore more peoples, than do others. The Dogribs are not distinguished in the 1829 census; in this record, as in more limited censuses of that decade, Dogribs were counted among the "McKenzie's River Indians" or identified in part as "Marten Lake Indians" (see the key to table 11.1). Other details regarding completeness and comparability vary from one census to the next.

An examination of table 11.1 according to the populations recorded fort by fort points up the inadvisability of inferring female infanticide on the basis of a male-skewed sex ratio of a single small population. Note, as an extreme case, that the 1924 Fort Wrigley Slave Indian population of 83 persons yields a sex ratio of 144, which exceeds the sum sex ratios of the regional censuses of both 1829 and 1858, periods of infanticide. As field ethnographers in such small communities are aware (see Kelly 1968:37–41), there may be a pronounced preponderance of one sex over the other at any particular slice of time. When the Wrigley Slaveys are placed in the immediate context of the two neighboring Slavey populations of Norman and Simpson (with whom some intermarriage occurs, hence the reordering by "tribe" in table 2), the combined population of 829 persons manifests a sex ratio of 103.

It is when larger populations manifest high (male-skewed) sex ratios—as in the total populations and sum sex ratios of 1829 and 1858—that one is assured that one or more sustained factors are operating to suppress the number of females. But by lumping sets of populations into a total figure, an aberrant low sex ratio in one or a few sectors—indicative of the absence of the more broadly experienced condition or practice—will be lost. The sex ratio of 86 for the 1858 Fort Resolution population of Chipewyans and Yellowknives is the salient case in point.

SEX RATIOS AND ADULT/JUVENILE DISTRIBUTIONS BY TRIBE, 1829 AND 1858

Table 11.1 presents four major censuses over a hundred-year period, with the breakdown by posts and groups "attached to" each post as originally recorded. In order to cover all bets, table 11.2 reworks the data from the two censuses of the infanticide era—1829 and 1858—to (1) distinguish sex ratios by the major extension of connubium, the "tribe" (see key to table 11.1 and column A of table 11.2); (2) distinguish adult sex ratios from juvenile sex ratios (column B, table 11.2); and (3) determine the percent of juveniles of each population (column C, table 11.2). These manipulations of the populations of 1829 and 1858 do not yield any consistent trend between juvenile and adult sex ratios; perhaps the reader can tease more significance out of these sortings than can I. One notes that Anderson's judgment—that by 1858 female infanticide had all but ceased—is not yet reflected in juvenile sex ratios at that date, except in the Dogrib population (line 2.4), where the juvenile sex ratio of 104 contrasts with the adult sex ratio of 136. That the 1858 population of Yellowknives and Chipewyans at Fort Resolution manifests a low total sex ratio has already been remarked upon; these two groups present complexities to which I shall attend in a later paragraph. In the tribal sectors identifiable in both the 1829 and the 1858 censuses (Slave, Hare, and Kutchin), adult versus juvenile ratios swing back and forth between higher and lower figures, by tribe and by census generation.

A generation later, in 1891, the essentially balanced adult and juvenile sex ratios for the total Mackenzie River District population (line 3.0, table 11.2) show that the demographic effect of the cessation of female infanticide had become manifest by this date. Summary data from the 1924 census and three more recent censuses provided at the bottom of table 11.2 (lines 5.0, 6.0, and 7.0) demonstrate the continuing though oscillating balance of the sexes in the postinfanticide era.

The percentage of juveniles in the populations does show a consistency from the 1829 generation on and is addressed in the next section. For the moment, it is necessary only to make clear that I have substantial confidence

TABLE 11.1 *Populations and Sex Ratios of the Mackenzie Dene, 1924, 1891, 1858, 1829*

Districts		NWT 1924			"Mackenzie River District" 1891		"MacKenzie's River District" 1858			"Fort Simpson District" 1829		
Contemporary "Tribal" Classification (1970)	Posts	Designation	Population	Sex Ratio	Population	Sex Ratio	Designation	Population	Sex Ratio	Designation	Population	Sex Ratio
Kutchin	"Youcon" (AK)				(no designations given)		L	842	129			
	Rampart Hse (YT)				164	86						
	LaPierre Hse (YT)				168	93	L	337	122			
	McPherson	L[a]	295	79	455	109				UL	68	100
	Arctic Red River	L	184	109			L, BdL	103	151	RL	93	124[b]
										BdL		128
										OH		187
Hare	Good Hope	H	370	100	547	90	H	364	160	RI	151	125
	(all groups)							(467)	(158)		(627)	(139)
							H	103	186	H	53	165
							N	43	143	Dh	101	135
							D	133	115			
Brl, Mt, S, H	Norman	H	370	98	324	121	S	84	140	MR	490	161
	(all groups)							(363)	(142)		(644)	(157)
	Wrigley	S	83	144	164	134						

Slave											
Simpson (all groups)	S	376	101	234	103						
						N	87	222	U	202	153[b]
						S,D,H	658	136	N	72	147[b]
							(745)	(144)	MR	620	151
									ML	115	113
										(1,009)	(145)
Providence	S	301	91	436	111						
Hay River	S	104	117								
Liard (all groups)	S	227	96	219	128						
						N	38	138	MR	350	116
						S	281	146			
							(319)	(145)			

continues

TABLE 11.1 *Continued*

Districts		NWT			"Mackenzie River District"		"MacKenzie's River District"			"Fort Simpson District"		
		1924			*1891*		*1858*			*1829*		
Contemporary "Tribal" Classification (1970)	Posts	Desig-nation	Population	Sex Ratio	Population	Sex Ratio	Designation	Population	Sex Ratio	Desig-nation	Population	Sex Ratio
Dogrib	By region:											
	Rae and north	D	712	110	711	94	D; a few S & Y	657	120			
	Yellowknife River	D	190	92								
	Great Slave Lake	D	95	111								
Chipewyan	Resolution	C	120	82			C & Y a few D	469	86			
	(all groups)	Y	176	86								
			(581)	(91)								
	Smith	C	179	88								
	Total Population:		3,782		3,422			4,199			2,630	
	Total SR:			99		103			129			142
	SR range:			79–144		86–134			86–186			100–191

(omitting "Youcon": P = 3,357, SR 129)

ᵃ For group designations, see the key.

ᵇ For these particular groups, the children were not identified by sex; they therefore do not figure in the sex ratio. The population figures *do* represent the total number of persons.

Sources: DIA–AR 1924: census; Russell 1898: 160; Anderson 1907: 139; HBCA B.200/e/9.

Key to Group Designations

BdL   Bâtard Loucheux. Mixed Kutchin and Hare (Anderson 1907: 140). In the 1829 and 1858 censuses this regional band of mixed Kutchin–Hare was classified under Loucheux (Kutchin). Petitot (1876: 27), however, classified them under Peaux de Lièvre (Hare), possibly because by his time their continued trading association with Fort Good Hope linked them ever more firmly into the Hare nexus (and connubium) rather than the Loucheux orbit, which in the Mackenzie region centered on Fort McPherson after its establishment in 1840.

Brl   Bearlake Indians. As "Satudene," the Bearlake Indians were presented in the ethnographic literature as a distinct group by Osgood (1932). As the group designations of 1829 and 1858 indicate, from its establishment at the beginning of the nineteenth-century, Fort Norman (and the intermittently occupied post at the Fort Franklin site) drew groups variously designated as Hare, Dahotinne, Nahanni, Mackenzie River Indians, Slave, and Dogrib. Based on their exploitative range in the mountains west of the Mackenzie River, the Dahotinne/Mountain Indians have kept a distinct identity. Through their continuing focus on the posts of Norman and Franklin, the other variously designated groups came to share a regional–societal identity. Latter-day attachments of Dogribs to Fort Franklin and Slaves to Fort Norman have continued to feed into the varied dialectic–"tribal" heritage of the Bearlake Indians. Government band rolls have subsumed the Bearlake population under "Hare"; recent ethnographic designation (Basso 1978) has subsumed them under "Slave." Take your choice.

C   Chipewyan.
Dh   Dahotinne. See Rocky Mountain Indians (RMI).
D   Dogrib.
H   Hare.
L   Loucheux. Kutchin.
Mt   Mountain Indians. See Rocky Mountain Indians (RMI).
ML   Marten Lake Indians. Regional group of Dogrib.
MR   "Mackenzie River Indians." Slave (some Dogrib included).
N   Nahanni. See Rocky Mountain Indians.
OH   Outer Hare. Regional group of Hare north of Great Bear Lake.
RI   Rapids Indians. Regional group of Hare along Mackenzie River.
RL   Rat Hunter Loucheux. Mackenzie Flats (Arctic Red River) Kutchin.
RMI   Rocky Mountain Indians. In the 1829 census the Dahotinne, Umbahotinne, and Nahanni are designated as three groups of Rocky Mountain Indians. (Their adjacent regional ranges are specified in HBCA B.200/e/8.) In subsequent "ethnic" classifications the so-called Nahannis became a mélange of ambiguous identities and cannot be treated as or assigned to a single societal-tribal entity. For this reason, in table 2 the 1858 population designated "Nahannis" is noted but not analyzed as a tribe. The Umbahotinne, trading into Fort Simpson, probably in part merged eventually with the Slave of that region. For the purposes of table 2, I have also merged the Dahotinne (trading into Fort Norman) with the Slave, though there is probably equal justification for placing them with the Hare — or lack of justification insofar as the latter-day Mountain Indians (Mt) who are attached to Fort Norman are descendants of the Dahotinne.

S   Slave.
U   Umbahotinne. See Rocky Mountain Indians (RMI).
UL   Upper Loucheux. Peel River Kutchin, attached to Fort McPherson.
Y   Yellowknives. In linguistic-cultural terms, the Yellowknives (or Copper Indians, Redknives) were a regional division of the Chipewyan nation, but in the 1820s, especially, they were in sociopolitical terms a distinctive people.

TABLE 11.2 *Populations and Sex Ratios by Tribe, Adults and Juveniles; Percent Juveniles*

Districts and Posts (subsumed)	Year	(A) Tribes: Population and Sex Ratios			(B) Adults versus Juveniles: Numbers and Sex Ratios				(C)
		Tribe	Total Population	Total Sex Ratio	Adult Population	Adult Sex Ratio	Juvenile Population	Juvenile Sex Ratio	Percent Juvenile
1.0 "Fort Simpson District" (total)	1829	see table 1	2,630	•142	1,451	•149	1179	•132[a]	45
1.1 Simpson, Liard, Norman		Slave (t), RMI, and Dogrib	1,878	•142	1,018	•154	895	•127[a]	46
1.2 Norman, Good Hope		Hare (t)	391	•138	229	•139	162	•138	41
1.3 Good Hope		Kutchin	289	•148	167	•135	112	•166[a]	42
2.0 "McKenzie's R. District" (total, excluding "Youcon")[b]	1858	see table 1	3,357	•129	1,940	•127	1,417	•131	42
2.1 Simpson, Liard, Norman		Slave (t)	1,023	•139	563	•144	460	•134	45
2.2 Norman, Good Hope		Hare (t)	467	•165	310	•146	157	•214	34
2.3 Peel R., LaPierre, Good Hope ("Youcon" omitted[b])		Kutchin	432	•129	267	•115	165	•154	38
2.4 Rae, Norman		Dogrib (t)	790	•119	446	•136	344	•104	44
2.5 Resolution		Chip; Yknife	469	86	247	• 66	222	116	47
		Nahani	176						

3.0 "Mackenzie R. District"	1891c	see table 1	3,422	102	1,875	99	1,821	106	50
4.0 NWT	1924	see table 1	3,782	98	2,258	93	1,524	107	40 (39d)
5.0 NWT	1941	all NWT	4,052	102	2,405	104	1,647	99	41
6.0 NWT	1954	all NWT	4,023	•108	2,357	•109	1,666	107	41 (39d)
7.0 NWT	1961	all NWT	5,256	99	2,946	105	2,310	93	44

a "Children of both sexes." See HBCA B.200/e/9 (1829) in key.

b The "Loucheux of six tribes" trading into "Youcon" are omitted as their full tribal affiliation is in doubt. See Anderson (1907 [1858]) in key.

c An inclusion of 300+ Eskimos in population figures is suspected. See Russell (1898) in key.

d Estimated adjustment of percent juveniles to under 15. See DIA-AR (1924, 1954) in key.

Key and sources

• = A one-sample χ_2 test indicates that, given an expected sex ratio of 100, the probability is less than .05 that the observed sex ratio (or one of greater divergence from 100) could occur by chance.

(t) = most of the tribe included.

1829 HBCA B.200/e/9. Juveniles specified only as "boys" and "girls," plus "children of both sexes." Juvenile SRs are calculated from only those population segments (T = 2263) in which all individuals are specified by sex.

1858 Anderson (1907 [1858]). Juveniles specified only as male or female "children." The "Loucheux of six tribes" trading into "Youcon" are omitted as their full tribal affiliation is in doubt. Including the "Youcon" Loucheux, the entries of 1858 are altered as follows: 2.0 "McKenzie's R. District," total: total population, 4,199; total sex ratio, 129; adult population, 2,427; adult sex ratio, 123; juvenile population, 1,772; juvenile sex ratio, 136; percent juvenile, 42. 2.3 Kutchin: total population, 1,274; total sex ratio, 129; adult population, 754; adult sex ratio, 112; juvenile population, 520; juvenile sex ratio, 157; percent juvenile, 41.

1891 Russell (1898: 160). Juveniles specified only as "boys" and "girls" (the juvenile age cut may be higher than in the 1829 and 1858 censuses). An inclusion of 300+ Eskimos in population figures is suspected.

1924 DIA-AR (1924: census). Juveniles = under 16. (Estimated adjustment of Percent Juveniles to under 15.)

1941 RCMAFS (1941). Juveniles = under 15.

1954 DIA-AR (1954: census). Juveniles = under 16. (Estimated adjustment of Percent Juveniles to under 15.)

1961 DIA-AR (1961: census). Juveniles = under 15.

in the reliability and comparability of "juvenile" age estimates for both sexes made by the fur traders in the 1829 and 1858 counts. Schrire and Steiger (1974) have questioned the ability of the average European observer to estimate ages of non-Europeans and especially to distinguish between girls who married young and are, therefore, classified as "women" and unmarried male youths of the same age who are, therefore, classified by the observer as "boys" or some other juvenile designation. In the instance of the early-nineteenth-century fur traders of the Hudson's Bay Company, the criterion of male "adult" or "man" was derived from the classification of "hunter." Male youths began to perform as hunters in their early teens, as soon as physical development permitted; at that point, they were counted in the adult (i.e., nonchild) ranks by the post manager in his account books or other records. The cut between "boys under twelve" and men of fourteen years and older is explicitly made in MacVicar's Fort Resolution District Report of 1825–27 (HBCA B.181/e/1). There is no reason to doubt that the same criterion of classification based on hunting capability obtained in the 1829 and 1858 censuses. The scattered ethnographic evidence, including memory culture, indicates that girls were indeed married very young when they were not, in fact, given in marriage before puberty (Keith 1890; Hardisty 1867; Osgood 1932; Slobodin 1962; Helm 1967). [See also "Helene Rabesca" in chapter 18.] Therefore, the reasonable conclusion is that, corresponding to those male youths who from about age fourteen on are classified as "men," their female age-mates are classified as "women" in the 1829 and 1858 censuses. (The 1891 age cut may be higher.)

Although I can offer no confident explanation to account for the disproportionate number of adult females over males (SR 66) recorded for the 1858 Fort Resolution Chipewyans-Yellowknives, the data do not contradict Franklin's comments a generation earlier that by then female infanticide had substantially ceased among the Chipewyans. There are census data taken in 1823 and 1826 for the Chipewyan and Yellowknife populations then resorting to Fort Resolution, but the internal confusion the copyists manifest in assigning adult versus juvenile status, the fact that the Chipewyan sector at Fort Resolution represents less than 10 percent of the Chipewyan peoples, and the complexity of conditions of the fur trade, Metis-Dene marriages, and intertribal relations affecting the Fort Resolution population in the interval between 1823 and 1826 have led me to adjudge detailed analysis of the Resolution data to be unwarranted. Suffice it to say that, for that small sector of the Chipewyan nation "attached to" Fort Resolution as recorded in 1823 and 1826, the total sex ratios of 134 and 136, respectively, suggest female infanticide; there was an accompanying drop in population from 362 to 289, as the consequence of out-migration in the intervening years (HBCA B.181/a/7). The Yellowknife count (which is kept distinct from the Chipewyan count in this decade but not in the 1858 census) does not permit this interpretation. The 1823 count of the 192 Yellowknives yields a sex ratio of 102. The fact that the sex ratio of this same small population jumped to SR 129 in 1826, while their number dropped to 158, was the result of the massacre by the Dogribs late in 1823 of, apparently, mainly Yellowknife women and girls (HBCA B.181/a/7). [Also see chapter 12.]

JUVENILE POPULATION PERCENTAGES

From 1829 to modern times, a consistent feature of Dene demography is the high proportion of juveniles—38 percent or more, with one exception (the Hare Indians of 1858)—in the populations under scrutiny (column C, table 11.2). Of the total populations of 1829 and 1858, juveniles make up 45 percent and 42 percent, respectively. (Note, however, that these high percentages are in part the function of a low number of adult females.) These Dene percentages are comparable to the 45 percent juveniles (under fifteen years, estimated) in a censused population of 2,622 Yanomamo where, it is calculated, "female infants are subjected to an initial 25 percent infanticide rate above what males experience" (Neel and Weiss 1975:28, 38; see figure on p. 206 for additional comparisons of Yanomamo and Dene). In percentages of population under (documented or estimated) fifteen years of age, the Dene generations fall within the ranges found today in Third World countries. However, unlike those populations and contemporary Yanomamo of Venezuela-Brazil, and despite its high percentage of juveniles through the first half of the twentieth century, the population of the Mackenzie Dene was almost static (see table 11.3 on p. 208), thus implying a puzzlingly short life expectancy for postjuveniles. The Dene population "took off" only in the 1950s, following the introduction of effective treatment for tuberculosis as well as other forms of medical care. (Compare total population figures for the years 1951, 1964, 1970, and 1977 in table 11.3, where the population almost doubles in twenty-six years.)

Despite the high percentages of juveniles in the populations of both the infanticide and postinfanticide eras, when the juvenile versus adult proportions of generational populations are combined with the male versus female proportions, as illustrated by bar graphs in the figure on p. 206, the profiles of the infanticide era are at striking variance with those of the postinfanticide era. In the Mackenzie River District of 1858, as the more fully documented

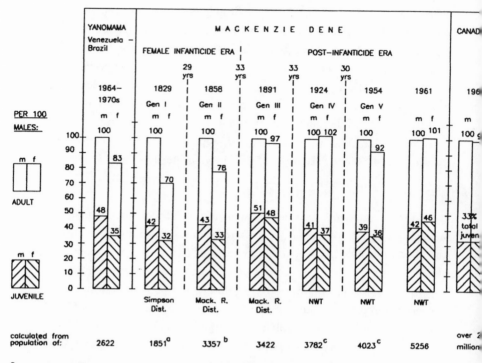

Number of females per 100 males: five generations of Mackenzie Dene.

case, 43 of every 100 males were juveniles; for every 100 males, there were 78 females (SR 129), of which 33 were juveniles. In terms of the breeding potential of the generations of the 1820s and the 1850s, the number and proportion of men and boys is of little consequence. Rather, it is the number and proportion of females in or about to enter the reproductive age that represents the breeding potential of those census generations. In the female infanticide era, the proportion of female children available to enter the reproductive period was no greater than that in the 1966 Canadian population: about 33 juvenile females for every 100 males. The chart also graphically demonstrates that only one full generation (33 years) into the postinfanticide era was sufficient to bring the number of female juveniles essentially up to parity with male juveniles, even as their mothers surviving into the post-infanticide era achieved near parity with the adult males. (See generation three [G3] in the chart on this page.)

The demonstrable increase in the postinfanticide era of the proportion of potential childbearers per 100 males has striking implications for the population history of the northern Dene in the face of the cultural and biological events of the contact era.

EUROPEAN DISEASES AND POPULATION LEVELS

In recent years, scholarly estimates of the size of protohistoric populations in the Americas have been dramatically revised upward, stemming in large part from revised estimates of drastically greater population loss due to the introduction of European diseases than had been reckoned by earlier investigators. These revised calculations aside, it has long been a truism that the spread of European diseases across North America, with or in advance of the Europeans, brought about the depopulation of the continent's natives. Certainly, the shocking descriptions and estimates in the historical record of native deaths from European-derived diseases encourage such a conclusion. In an earlier incarnation (MacNeish 1956a), I assumed that one such estimate of the 1780s regarding the southeasternmost Canadian Dene (the Chipewyans) might, if accurate, also be applicable to the Mackenzie Dene populations. Krech (1978) makes the assumption of depopulation stemming from European diseases his basis for arguing the loss of "matriorganization" among the Mackenzie Dene — excepting, of course, the Alaska-Yukon-derived Kutchin [Gwich'in] for whom the historical and ethnographic record from the beginning to present clearly documents a form of "matriorganization." Conversely, the same supposition of massive depopulation among the Northeastern Athapaskans has been posited by Service (1962) and Williams (1974) as the "reason" why the Mackenzie Dene peoples within the historic area presumably lost "patrilocal band" or "patrilocal-patrilineal" organization. [For this "problem" in social organization I refer the reader back to chapter 1.] These arguments have been advanced despite the lack of evidence in the historical and ethnographic record (Helm 1965a) of the existence of unilineal or unilocal organization of either persuasion.

I hope to make clear that the assumption from which these unilineal-unilocal arguments proceed—that of drastic depopulation—is without foundation for the Dene populations inhabiting the Mackenzie River region. The demographic data, in conjunction with what I believe are the most reasonable inferences to be drawn from them, demonstrate not only that population loss did not occur but offer an explanation for this nonevent.

TABLE 11.3 *Population of the Mackenzie Dene by Posts and Regions, 1829–1977*

Year	(A) Upper Mackenzie Posts									(B) Lower Mackenzie Posts				(C) A + B Total	(D) NWT Total
	Rae	Liard	Hay R.	Provi-dence	Simpson	Wrigley	Norman	Franklin	Total	G. Hope	McPherson LaPierre	Arctic Red R.	Aklavik		
1829	no	350	no	no	1,009	no	644	no	2,003	627	no	no	no	2,630	(3,077)
1858	657	319	no	no	745	no	363	no	2,084	467	337	no	no	2,888	3,357
1864–79	788	(250)	(100)	(415)	(300)	no	272		(2,125)	422	290	no	no	(2,837)	(3,414)
1881	615	216	no	456	500	no	254	no	2,041	583?	637?	no	no	3,261?	3,606?
1891	711	219	no	436	234	164	324	no	2,088	547?	623?	no	no	3,258?	(4,110?)
1924	712	227	104	301	376	83	370	no	2,173	370	295	184	no	3,022	3,782
1929	766	225	111	251	312	91	346	no	2,102	309	325	178	no	2,914	3,541
1934	774	237	119	272	341	109	371	no	2,223	342	368	178	no	3,111	3,854?
1941	686	202	147	376	378	77	200	174	2,240	337	308	331	no	3,216	4,090
1951	680	ª	470		668		305		2,123	257			673	3,053	3,838
1964	968	259	202	381	518	150	136	289	2,903	312	682	334	no	4,231	5,387
1970	1,202	321	239	473	623	169	164	360	3,551	355	610	410	no	4,926	6,285
1977	1,571	434	273	584	705	200	209	462	4,438	427	673	489	no	6,027	7,576

ª Liard is lumped with Simpson–Wrigley. See key.

( ) = estimate

no = post not open at that date

? = figures are questionable

Key and Sources

1829 HBCA B.200/e/9; HBCA B.181/a/7 (which records a Resolution population of 447 in 1826).

1858 Anderson (1907 [1858]).

1864–79 Petitot 1885:53.

1881 Russell (1898:160); Macfarlane (1881). ? = figures probably inflated by inclusion of Eskimos trading into McPherson, possibly Good Hope (Petitot 1865:53).

1891 Russell (1898:160); Canada (1966:25) (count of Resolution–Smith area, year 1899). ? = Same comment as under 1881. Also, high estimated total in D (4,110?) may in part be due to immigration of Chipewyans from Alberta to Smith: Smith pop. = 319 in 1899 (Canada 1966:25) versus 115 in 1889 (Macfarlane 1881).

1924 DIA–AR (1924:census). From NWT total, "500 nomads," with no post or tribe assignment have been excluded on the grounds they are probably fictional.

1929 DIA–AR (1929:census). From NWT total, "500 nomads," are excluded (see comment under 1924). Also excluded are "109 absentees" who may be part of the population that died in the 1928 influenza epidemic. These 1929 figures are suspect because they do not reflect the estimated 300 to 600 deaths in the 1928 epidemic (cf. 1924 figures).

1934 DIA–AR (1934:census). Again, figures are suspect. The Dogribs who traded into Fort Resolution (counted in D column) are recorded as 293. Many of the Resolution Dogribs died in the 1928 influenza epidemic; even the figure of 186 for Resolution Dogribs presented in the 1929 census is almost surely too high.

1941 Wherrett (1947:230).

1951 Canada (1957:22–3). Liard is lumped with Simpson–Wrigley. During the World War II years, a small number of Indian men "went off Treaty." As a result of becoming nonstatus Indians, they, their families, and their descendants disappear from government records as (Treaty) Indians.

1964 Canada (1964).

1970 Canada (1970).

1977 DIAND (1977).

[Here I augmented, sharpened, reworked, and rethought the nineteenth-century data on the populations that had been addressed in the seminar that yielded the last section of chapter 8.] The results, which include the Indian populations attached to all the Mackenzie River posts (and Fort Liard), are presented in table 3. These results require that I amend the statement [in chapter 7] that "the population level . . . evinces only a slightly declining, almost static quality" prior to the 1950s: "almost static," yes, but not even "slightly declining."

In table 11.3 the Mackenzie posts are divided into two sectors: the Upper Mackenzie posts, from the Great Bear River upstream (southeast), and the Lower Mackenzie posts, downstream (northwest) of Great Bear River. The populations trading into Lower Mackenzie posts are less "controllable" in terms of in- or out-migration from that set. Therefore, I have set the Lower Mackenzie posts apart from the posts of the Upper Mackenzie. The Upper Mackenzie posts are, by my best assessment of the historic record, a set in which no significant amount of migration "leakage"—say, less than 100 persons per census—occurred. Most of that leakage was at Fort Liard, into which populations from the southern Yukon and northern British Columbia may have been trading in earlier times, thereby somewhat inflating the 1829 and 1858 counts. Also, in the years between these two censuses, a few Hare may have shifted between Fort Norman (Upper Mackenzie) and Fort Good Hope (Lower Mackenzie).

The population counts in table 11.3, beginning in 1829, are presented as sets in terms of greater to lesser control over each set as a closed population: (A) Upper Mackenzie posts; (B) Lower Mackenzie posts; (C) Upper and Lower Mackenzie sets (A + B) combined; and (D) NWT total = A + B + the Fort Resolution and Fort Smith jurisdictions, where control over migration to and from the Northwest Territories and other aspects of the population history is least. At any level of inclusion, the population figures demonstrate that from 1829 to 1951 (after which date the population takeoff begins) there has been no overall drop through time in Dene population. In fact, deaths and suffering from alien diseases notwithstanding, the population of the Upper Mackenzie posts increased slightly over five generations (G): 2,003 persons counted in the year 1829 (G1), 2,084 in the year 1858 (G2), 2,088 in the year 1891 (G3), 2,173 in the year 1924 (G4), and 2,123 in the year 1951 (G5), for a total gain of 6 percent in 122 years or 2 percent in the 93 years between 1858 and 1951. Over the same 93 years, the combined Upper and Lower Mackenzie posts show a gain of 6 percent.

There remains the possibility of substantial population loss prior to 1829 due to introduced diseases. There is no account in the early historical records of infectious Old World diseases penetrating into the Mackenzie River region in the late eighteenth century, the period of protocontact and initial contact. Alexander Mackenzie (1970:76–77) and Samuel Hearne (1958: 115–16 n.), reporting information gained within a few years after the event, record that the smallpox epidemic of 1781–82 (Thompson 1916:109 and n.) spread through the Cree country and reached as far west as the Chipewyans of the Athabasca region, but neither they nor others suggest that the smallpox spread north to the Mackenzie Dene populations (counter to my speculations in MacNeish [1956a]). Wentzel (1889) cites "the death of many natives" as a factor in the low fur returns in the Upper Mackenzie region between the years 1800 and 1807. He gives no cause but in the same letter says that "no endemial diseases prevail among the natives." (His account of the winter of 1810–11 indicates a substantial number of deaths from starvation due to failure of hares, lack of large game, and severe weather. Periodic starvation induced by the instability of the subarctic subsistence base [Waisberg 1975] probably intermittently damped sectors of Mackenzie populations throughout the aboriginal era.) Except for Wentzel's equivocal statement regarding the years 1800–1807, I have been unable to find any mention in surviving accounts of the North West Company traders of existing or recent occurrences of severe disease in the Mackenzie-Liard region for the first two decades of the nineteenth century. In the decade 1820–29 Hudson's Bay Company traders' journals of the Upper Mackenzie do make mention of sickness and individual deaths from apparently infectious diseases, but no overall population drop is indicated. [Krech (1983:130) asserts that "depopulation occurred prior to the 1829 census" but provides no figures and no supporting citations.]

Negative evidence is never conclusive, but, in summary, it cannot be demonstrated or reliably inferred that substantial depopulation of the entire Mackenzie region occurred from the protocontact period to the time of the Fort Simpson District Report and census of 1829. In any case, after that date, and despite continuing accounts of periods of sickness, epidemics, and deaths from infectious diseases, the assumption of depopulation due to introduced diseases is falsified by the census data.

The assumption that, in the absence of modern medical service, permanent depopulation or continuing population decline is the inevitable consequence of epidemics of exogenous diseases is demographically naive (see, e.g., MacArthur 1967: esp. 346–49; Meister 1976). Immediately and specifically, what is overlooked by those who assume the historic depopulation of the Mackenzie Dene due to alien diseases is the significance of the probable reduction of female infanticide during the first half of the nineteenth century and its effectual elimination in the last half as a demographic counterbalance to mortality from exogenous diseases.

TOWARD POPULATION MODELS:
DISCUSSION AND DEFINITION OF TERMS

In developing demographic models of prehistoric hunter-gatherer populations, anthropologists have usually proceeded from an assumption of stationary population conditions—that, through time, vital rates and the relative age distribution remain constant, and the size of the population remains fixed, that is, zero population growth/loss (Weiss 1973). In a stationary population model, fertility and mortality rates may be posited high or low, but to hold to zero population growth/loss they must cancel one another. As noted in the introduction to this essay, to sustain a model of zero population growth in "primitive" societies some anthropologists have invoked the practice of female infanticide as a mortality damper on population, even in the absence of any direct evidence.

For model-building purposes, I here assume that in the precontact era the Mackenzie population as a sum set was stationary. (Both the reader and I recognize that, in actuality, there must have been indeterminate ups and downs in population as the generations succeeded one another.)

The vital rates for this aboriginal population are, of course, not recorded. There are, however, three quantifiable demographic dimensions of the Dene population recorded in the 1829 and 1858 censuses that offer a basis for creating models of protocontact and early contact populations: the number of individuals, their distribution by sex, and, as adults versus juveniles, their distribution by age. Notably, these demographic dimensions provide a basis for estimating rates of female infanticide as they affected the 1829 generation and the 1858 generation. By a further extension of inference, they suggest possible rates, or ranges thereof, for preceding protohistoric and prehistoric generations. The inferred rates of female infanticide suggest other demographic constructs to incorporate in the population models.

At this point, I specify an entity not ordinarily a feature of population models: the *census generation*. The two censuses of the infanticide era provide a count of those males and females alive at two slices of time, twenty-nine years apart, but these census populations reveal themselves only in gross generational chunks, divisible by age only into adult and juvenile. Analysis in terms of population pyramids and age cohorts and vital rates per year or per quinquennium, and so on, is precluded. Thus "generation" must replace the narrow age cohorts that are ordinarily employed in demographic formulations. A census generation (hereafter "generation") is defined as a population at one slice of time (census year) of the same genealogical rank or remove from the ancestral or descendant population that precedes or follows it. (The census years of the Dene data dictate intervals of twenty-nine to thirty-three years between the actual generations under study. This interval range exceeds the twenty-six or so years usually posited as a generational span in "primitive" societies.)

In the Dene census data, it is *per generation* that imputed female infanticide rates are manifested. For present purposes, therefore, the *female infanticide rate*, designated I_f, is defined as the percent of females, born of a generation (e.g., $G1$) of females, *who would have survived* other mortality factors to become part of the next generational cohort ($G2$) if they had not been deliberately eliminated at birth. In this study I_f—or a reasonable range for I_f—is inferred from the ratios of the number of females per 100 males (the converse of SR) per generation. The working assumption is that the female/male ratio of a generation would be at parity had not the special practice of female infanticide been carried out. (Subsumed is the further working assumption that the worldwide tendency for higher postnatal mortality of males cancels out, in a census generation containing all ages, the worldwide sex ratio at birth of circa 105.) The gross count of female infanticides—the actual number of females eliminated at birth—is not determinable, as we have no assured basis for estimating the numbers of individuals, female or male, who died from causes other than infanticide between one census generation and the next.

Several ballpark figures for female infanticide rates can be inferred from the census data of the infanticide era. The female/male ratio of adults in the 1829 census could serve as a basis for an estimated I_f of the juveniles of the initial contact generation. That is, assuming that the adults of 1829 are between fourteen and forty-four years of age, one would take their female/male ratio as a crude reflection of the generational infanticide rate for the interval (1785–1815) when these adults were being born, with 1800 as the mean "generational year." For the Upper Mackenzie posts, the adult population of 1829 yields a ratio of 65 women per 100 men (adult SR 155); the combined Upper and Lower Mackenzie posts yield close to the same proportion: 67 per 100. The 65–67 per 100 ratios thus suggest an I_f on the order of 35 percent ($100 - 65 = 35$).

The juvenile female/male ratios of 1829 are 78 per 100 (juvenile SR 128) for the Upper Mackenzie posts alone, and 76 per 100 for the combined Upper and Lower Mackenzie posts. The diminished rates for the juveniles might be taken to reflect a diminished I_f in some groups (brought about in the traders' opinion by their own efforts), at least during the early contact period, 1800–1829. Actually, in the adult female/male ratios of 1858 the women of the Upper Mackenzie population—if thought of as representing the female juveniles of 1829—retrogressed as a population to 69 per 100 (from the 1829 juvenile female/male ratio of 78 per 100); on the other hand, the women of the Lower Mackenzie posts did not (the combined sets of posts yield an adult female/male ratio of 72 per 100). This and other divagations in the overall progression toward the sex parity of the postinfanticide era reinforce the dictates of common sense that no one figure should be taken as an exact index of a female infanticide rate for any generation or population sector thereof. The figures do suggest that an I_f of 22 percent—derived from the 78 per 100 female/male ratios of children (SR 128) in the Upper Mackenzie posts in the year 1829 and the 78 per 100 female/male ratio (SR 129) for the Dene population of the 1858 census—is a reasonable overall rate to assign to the 1829–58 period. As a likely underestimation of the I_f rates affecting at least some prehistoric generations (which, based on the adults' 65–67 per 100 female/male ratio of 1829, might sometimes have approximated 35 percent), an I_f of 22 percent serves as a conservative rate to employ in the population models.

I have developed a set of four diagrammatic population models to explore the capacity of a population to sustain increased mortality through introduced exogenous diseases, generation by generation and without population decline, after it has abandoned female infanticide. These are presented in the figure on p. 215, Population Models. Unfortunately, the corpus of standard demographic theory and practice does not provide concepts, terms, and definitions exactly appropriate to the issue or applicable to the data of the present inquiry. I have, therefore, revised standard concepts and definitions and (so far as I can determine) invented some new ones. Definitions of *generation* and *female infanticide* rate, as they have been tailored specifically to the new data at hand, have already been presented. I now reiterate these and introduce other necessary concept-definitions:

> *Generation* (G1, G2, G3 . . . Gn). A population of the same genealogical rank or remove from the ancestral or descendant population which precedes or follows it.

> *Adjusted Maternity Performance* (AMP). Per female of one generation (e.g., G1), the mean number of offspring *who would survive* ordinary mortality fac-

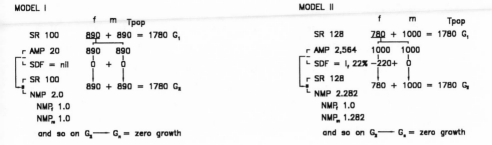

MODEL I

	f	m	Tpop
SR 100	890 + 890		= 1780 G₁

```
 ┌ AMP  20        890      890
 │ └ SDF = nil     0  +  0
 │ ┌ SR 100
 └ │            890  +  890  =  1780 G₂
   └ NMP 2.0
      NMP₁ 1.0
      NMP_m 1.0
```

and so on G₂ —— Gₙ = zero growth

MODEL II

	f	m	Tpop
SR 128	780 + 1000		= 1780 G₁

```
 ┌ AMP  2,564    1000     1000
 │ └ SDF = l, 22% −220+  0
 │ ┌ SR 128
 └ │            780  +  1000  =  1780 G₂
   └ NMP 2.282
      NMP₁ 1.0
      NMP_m 1.282
```

and so on G₂ —— Gₙ = zero growth

MODEL III

	f	m	Tpop
SR 128	780 + 1000		= 1780 G₁

```
 ┌ AMP  2,564    1000     1000
 │ └ SDF = nil     0  +  0
 │ ┌ SR 100
 └ │           1000  +  1000  =  2000 G₂
   └ NMP 2.564
      NMP₁ 1282
      NMP_m 1282
```

and so on G₂ —— Gₙ = 28.2% increase
per generation: 2564G₃, 3287 G₄,
4214 G₅, etc.

MODEL IV

	f	m	Tpop
SR 128	780 + 1000		= 1780 G₁

```
 ┌ AMP  2,,564    1000     1000
 │ └ SDF = D, 16.5%  −165  −165
 │ ┌ SR 128
 └ │            835  +  835  =  1670 G₂
   └ NMP 2.14
      NMP₁ 1.07
      NMP_m 1.07
```

AMP 2.564   1070.5 1070.5
SDF = Dl 6.5% −176.5 −176.5

```
 ┌ SR 100
 └ NMP 2.14     894  +  894  =  1788 G₃
```

and so on G₃ Gₙ = 7% increase per
generation: 1913 G₄, 2047Gₙ, etc.

---

f=female   m=male
Tpop = Total population
SR=Sex Ratio G=Generation
AMP= Adjusted Maternity Performance

SDF=Special Death Factors
l, =Female infanticide rate per generation
D, =Alien disease death rate per generatior
NMP=Net Maternity Performance

Population models.

tors to become the population of the next generation (G2) in the absence of
mortality due to the special death factors (SDFs) of female infanticide or introduced diseases. Among the Mackenzie Dene, death rates due to ordinary
mortality factors (e.g., endogenous infectious diseases, accidents, starvation,
childbearing, etc.) are not determinable from the data and are posited as
"given" constant rates by sex and age through the generations. (Gross maternity performance, left as an unestimated "given," would be a number of live
births per female per generation.)

Special Death Factor (SDF). For the purposes of the population model, SDFs are of two sorts, I_f and D_a, expressed in percentage rates and in number of persons derived from those rates:

FEMALE INFANTICIDE RATE PER GENERATION (I_f). Percent (e.g., I_f = 22 percent) of females, born of one generation of females, *who would have survived* other mortality factors to become part of the next generation if they had not been eliminated at birth.

ALIEN (INTRODUCED) DISEASE DEATH RATE PER GENERATION (D_a). Percent (e.g., D_a = 16.5 percent) of individuals, equally male and female assumed, born of one generation of females *who would have survived* ordinary mortality factors to become part of the population of the next generation if they had not died of alien (European–introduced) infectious diseases, usually contagious, or their secondary effects (e.g., death by starvation due to incapacitation). The D_a of 16.5 percent used in Population Model IV is a hypothetical construct for illustrative purposes and is not a known rate of death from alien diseases.

Net Maternity Performance (NMP). Per female of one generation (e.g., G1), mean number of offspring who survive both ordinary mortality factors and SDFs to become the population of the next generation (G2). I use net maternity performance in place of net reproductive rate to distinguish the net production of females (NMP_f) from the net production of males (NMP_m) under the practice of female infanticide. See Population Model II, where sum NMP is 2.282 but is divisible into NMP_f 1.0 and NMP_m 1.282.

FOUR POPULATION MODELS

POPULATION MODEL I. Population Model I on p. 215 offers a hypothetical stationary population in which *no* female infanticide is practiced (SR 100). In this stationary population model, whatever the number of live births to the females of one generation (G1), they are counterbalanced by postnatal mortalities. Thus, in the course of their collective reproductive life the women of each generation produce two children each, one male and one female, who survive as the following generation (G2) to replicate the sex ratio (SR 100) and population number (1,780) of their mothers' generation. In the absence of SDFs in this population model (that is, neither female infanticide nor alien diseases), the AMP (2.0) equals the NMP (2.0), split evenly, 1.0 to 1.0, between females and males surviving to G2. Population Model I does not correspond to the (reasonably inferred) demographic attributes of precontact or postcontact Mackenzie populations.

POPULATION MODEL II. This is another stationary population model. It is, however, designed as a hypothetical construct of demographic attributes of aboriginal (prehistoric) Mackenzie Dene. Therefore, the SDF of a female infanticide rate (I_f) of 22 percent is introduced into the model. The I_f of 22 percent produces in each generation the proportion of 780 females per 1,000 males (SR 128). To maintain, generation after generation, a population of 1,780 persons (zero growth / loss), the 780 females of each generation must, in the course of their reproductive lives, average an AMP of 2.564, producing 1,000 male children who will survive ordinary mortality factors to become the males of the next generation and 1,000 female children *who would have survived* in the absence of the SDF of female infanticide. However, of these 1,000 females, 220 (22 percent) are eliminated by infanticide from the population of the next generation. In this stationary population model, then, the AMP of 2.564 is reduced by female infanticide to an NMP of 2.282, in the proportions of one surviving female (NMP_f 1.0) to 1.282 surviving males (NMP_m 1.282).

POPULATION MODEL III. This is a geometric increase model designed to project the consequences of the "instant" elimination of female infanticide (I_f) on the hypothetical aboriginal population of Population Model II, in the absence of the introduction of another SDF: alien disease deaths (D_a). As Population Model III demonstrates for the first postinfanticide generation, G2, the sex ratio shifts from 128 to 100, and the population rises from 1,780 to 2,000 as 1,000 females replace the 780 females of G1, adding 220 potential breeders to the population. Between G4 and G5, about 100 years from G1, the population doubles. As with Population Model I, Population Model III does not correspond to the actualities of historic Dene demography (that is, prior to the 1950s).

POPULATION MODEL IV. This model is designed to reflect, in a highly simplified form, the extent to which the historic Mackenzie Dene could sustain mortalities from introduced diseases without a permanent drop in population. Population Model IV begins, in the G1 generation, with the hypothetical aboriginal stationary population of Population Model II: a population of 780 females per 1,000 males (SR 128) that was produced by an AMP of 2.564, counterbalanced by an I_f of 22 percent. For the

G2 generation, the I_f of 22 percent is eliminated as an SDF but is replaced by another—a D_a of 16.5 percent. This results in a population decline of 6 percent (110 persons, from 1,780 to 1,670) from G1 to G2. However, since the D_a rate is distributed between males (165) and females (165) equally, the G2 females have a population gain of 55, or 7 percent (NMP$_f$ 1.07), over their mothers' generation (which suffered an I_f of 22 percent), even while the males drop in number. The 835 females of G2, maintaining the AMP of 2.564, recoup their generation's population loss in the G3 generation in the face of a continuing D_a of 16.5 percent and an NMP of 2.14, split equally by sex. Holding to the same rates, the population will grow at the rate of 7 percent per generation.

If, in the same model, per-generation D_a is increased to 22 percent (i.e., equal to the prior I_f), the population drops from 1,780 to 1,560 through the 22 percent loss of males as well as females but then stabilizes at that figure. With an AMP of 2.564, the D_a must exceed 22 percent for the population to go into a continuing decline. If a hypothetical aboriginal stationary population is modeled on an I_f of 35 percent, counterbalanced by an AMP of 3.08, then, holding to AMP 3.08, the population can, with the elimination of female infanticide, sustain a D_a of 20 percent; after the G2 generation, it can begin to increase in numbers. A more complicated model of stepped reduction of I_f to zero over two generations, countered by a stepped rise of D_a, can be manipulated to approximate the census counts and sex ratios of 1829, 1858, and 1891. But whatever ratios and rates are posited, to accord with reality they must maintain the population level through the historic era.

CONCLUSION

Male-skewed sex ratios in the census generations of 1829 and 1858 support the statements of European observers that selective female infanticide was practiced in the first half of the nineteenth century by the Mackenzie Dene populations. There are no proportional data in the historical record to demonstrate that depopulation of the Mackenzie Dene from exogenous diseases occurred in the first forty years of direct contact, 1789–1829. In any case, from 1829 on, the census evidence firmly negates the supposition of depopulation in the historic era. The argument that depopulation due to European diseases brought about the "loss" of a hypothetical unilineal and/or unilocal social organization of Dogribs, Slaveys, and Hares is, by the evidence, invalid. The essential continuity of the population level from 1829 to the advent of effective medical care during the 1950s suggests the rate at which exogenous diseases replaced selective female infanticide as a mortality factor after 1860; in succeeding generations, proportionately more males died than before, but more females lived, resulting in a basically balanced sex ratio and a slight increment in population up to the mid–twentieth century.

from "Female Infanticide, European Diseases, and Population Levels among the Mackenzie Dene," 1980a

DOGRIB ORAL TRADITION AS HISTORY: WAR AND PEACE IN THE 1820s

In contrast to the prior chapter, which is based on Euro-Canadian records, this chapter comes from what the people tell of their history. It draws on the oral accounts of twelve Dogribs and the efforts of three ethnologists (June Helm, Beryl Gillespie, and Nancy Lurie) as receivers and recorders of native lore. Beryl Gillespie also retrieved the relevant documentary material from the Hudson's Bay Company's Archives. From these various contributions data were coordinated in several tables that are not presented here. So once again the researcher is advised to seek the original publication if fuller data are desired.

This study developed in the context of a substantial compilation of narratives about times past that had accrued in more than a decade of field research among the Dogribs. A number of testimonies by several middle-aged and elderly Dogribs delineated past circumstances, events, and persons that were congruent with the published historical record since the later part of the eighteenth century. This encouraged us to seek to identify persons and situations known to us only from the oral tradition through fuller search and interpretation of materials preserved in the archives of the Hudson's Bay Company. After preliminary attention to demonstrable or potential historicity of Dogrib oral tradition, we address the question of the historicity of one Dogrib legend as it can be validated from the documentary record.

DOGRIB ORAL TRADITION

In 1970 the Dogribs number about 1,700, approximately double their population of one hundred years before. Only with the young adult generation has a significant sector of the population become bilingual in Athapaskan and English and literate in the latter language. In terms of cultural idiom and perspective, only since the 1950s did the Dogribs as a people begin to move beyond oral tradition as the sole vehicle of their own perceived history.

The folk histories of peoples at the "band" or "hunter" level of sociocultural integration are generally dismissed as neither having a sense of linear time nor embodying historical realities. Yet as independently verified by the Euro-Canadian record since about 1770, in one class of narratives within their oral tradition Dogribs evince a firm comprehension of both historical actualities and their temporal succession. It seems evident that the sharp sense of "time's arrow" in this sector of Dogrib oral tradition is, in fact, based in the swiftly successive effects of the impinging European presence on Dogrib experience. Features of the evolving European-derived impact on Dogrib experience serve as time and sequence markers. We leave as an open question whether in truly aboriginal times generations experienced changes sufficiently fast paced and emergent one from the other to permit a developmental perspective in their folk history.

Dogribs recognize that some of the happenings recounted in their oral tradition occurred "thousands of years ago" or at least long before the advent of the Europeans. Some may truly be classed as myths. Others, although remote beyond temporal reckoning, treat of a world much as it is today. But neither sort seems to be consciously conceived as falling into a temporal succession; we therefore refer to that era as Floating Time. After the era of Floating Time, however, Dogrib oral tradition enters Linear Time.

Within Linear Time Dogrib tradition first recognizes a protocontact period wherein, from afar, the European fur trade affected the behavior of Indian groups that in turn affected the course of Dogrib experience. In Dogrib oral tradition the protocontact period corresponds to that time when enemies, sometimes identified as Enda (Cree) and sometimes as Tedzont'in, were, unlike the Dogribs, armed with guns. The European record provides the information that in the 1780s Dogribs and Yellowknives were in conflict (Hearne 1958 [1795]) and that from at least 1770 through 1790 Cree incursions occurred along the southern rim of Dogrib territory and along the Mackenzie River as well (Mackenzie 1970 [1889]; Fidler 1934).

Dogrib folk history distinguishes a subsequent stage, the early contact period. Dogribs recognize that in this period, which began in the last decade of the eighteenth century [see chapter 13], they obtained guns and other implements through direct contact with fur traders. A marked feature of the period for them was their harassment by the Yellowknife Indians, also known in the European record as Copper Indians and Red Knife Indians. As far as living Dogribs are concerned, the historic Yellowknives, who linguistically were a branch of the Athapaskan-speaking Chipewyans, and Chipewyans in general are encompassed under the single term Tedzont'in, consistently translated by English-speaking Dogribs as "Chipewyans." When speaking of the enemy Yellowknives of the early nineteenth century, Dogribs commonly refer to them as "Akaitcho's bunch" (*Ekeco weceke*, Akaitcho/his followers). The context of narrative or conversation makes it clear when Tedzont'in are the historic Yellowknives or a broader category of Chipewyans, particularly the present-day Indian population of Fort Resolution, into which the descendants of "Akaitcho's bunch" of Yellowknives eventually disappeared (Mason 1946; Gillespie 1975). From here on we shall refer to Tedzont'in who are "Akaitcho's bunch" as Yellowknives.

In the European chronology, the protocontact and early contact periods extend from about 1770 (possibly 1750) to the 1830s. Calculation of the sequence of events since then continues in Dogrib tradition to be marked in terms of kinds of effects from or relationships with Europeans—by the advent of the missionaries in the 1860s, for example, and the succession of "chief" types predicated on changing economic and political relationships with white institutions [see chapter 10].

Of the human figures that the Dogribs identify in their oral tradition covering the early contact period only Akaitcho is known to Canadian history. He was the prime Yellowknife leader who aided John Franklin's first expedition of 1819–22 [see the last section of this chapter]. Franklin's (1823, 1824) published account and the unpublished notations of traders of the period reveal Akaitcho and the Yellowknives in the years between 1812 and 1823 as plunderers, bullies, and sometimes assassins of Dogrib Indians. Franklin's record of his second expedition of 1825–27 provided the first of several published reports of the destruction by Dogribs in 1823 of a band of Yellowknives led by Long Legs. According to these accounts, that slaughter, reinforced by an influenza epidemic a decade later, broke the aggressive spirit of the Yellowknives (Franklin 1828; Back 1836; Simpson 1843; Richardson 1851).

With distinctive perspective and emphases, Dogrib oral tradition attests to a number of "facts" of the period of hostilities between the Yellowknives and the Dogribs that have been preserved in the European record of the 1820s. Dogrib folk history of this period, as recounted by several informants, recognizes that Akaitcho rescued starving white men (survivors of Franklin's first expedition) at Fort Enterprise and that Akaitcho and the Yellowknives traded into Old Fort Providence (abandoned in 1823 following the coalition of the Hudson's Bay Company with the North West Company). Both of these forts are designated in Dogrib by the term *mola konk'e* (white men house/place of), but Dogribs correctly identify the separate sites of the two installations.

That both are designated "*mola* house" emphasizes that Dogribs know that they were not manned by Hudson's Bay Company personnel (who were *kwet'in*, "stone [house] people," referring to the Hudson's Bay Company's stone fort at Churchill on Hudson Bay) but by North West Company personnel (as *mola*, coterminous with "Frenchmen") or, in the case of Fort Enterprise, by men provisioned from the North West Company post of Old Fort Providence.

One story in the oral tradition for this period tells of the magical enticement to slaughter of a band of Yellowknives by Dogribs. Possibly the story has its origin in the historical destruction of Long Legs's band of Yellowknives in 1823; however, the episodes in the tale do not correspond to the account given a few months after the event by the Dogrib Kanoobaw, who may have been a participant in the action (HBCA B.200/a/3 fol. 3). In any case, the tradition in no way emphasizes or glorifies Dogrib ferocity or fighting prowess, nor does it attribute the eventual peace between Dogribs and Yellowknives to the effects of the 1823 slaughter of Long Legs's band. (The loss, mostly of women and girls, reduced the Yellowknife tribe from 192 to 158 souls [HBCA B.181/a/7].) Rather, the thematic thread running through Dogrib folk history of this period (and Kanoobaw's account) is the unmerited mistreatment that the Dogribs endured at the hands of Akaitcho and his Yellowknives. Dogrib tradition stresses that the Dogribs were "friends to everyone," in contrast to Akaitcho and his "bunch," who traveled a circuit up the Yellowknife River, along the edge of the barrens toward the Coppermine River to Great Bear Lake and then south again through Dogrib country, pillaging and killing "Bear Lake Indians" as well as Dogribs. The personal ferocity of Akaitcho is almost equaled by that of another named figure in Dogrib tradition, the lustful Yellowknife T'asinghon. Only after T'asinghon had seized, abused, and killed several Dogrib women was he finally destroyed.

In the corpus of Dogrib oral tradition, perhaps second in popularity only to the story of "The Captive Woman" [see chapter 15] is the account of how the Dogrib leader Edzo (Edze, "Heart," in its antique form) confronted the Yellowknife leader Akaitcho, with the result that peace was established between the two peoples. The popularity of this story is manifested in the fact that the four major testimonies were volunteered, not elicited, in two cases when the ethnologists were in determined pursuit of other kinds of data.

The theme of the Edzo-Akaitcho legend is uniform; so essentially are the major components of the plot. Some episodes, however, are dropped or altered in one or another of the five major testimonies. Details and name identifications of secondary actors in the plot may vary, and in a few instances they conflict; inadequate translation and/or inadequate comprehension by the ethnologists may account for some of the discrepancies. Of course, these Dogrib testimonies are free texts, and individual variations in choice, elaboration, and emphasis of episodes and details are to be expected.

The testimony of Joseph Naedzo (1887–1973), the Bear Lake Prophet, is presented here (greatly abbreviated), primarily because one detail specific to Naedzo's version has been especially important in pursuing evidence in support of the historicity of components of the tradition.

NAEDZO'S TESTIMONY

In the time when the Dogribs and the Yellowknives were at war, they did not show themselves to one another. That is how it used to be.

Akaitcho wanted to kill Dogribs and he knew that Dogribs went [toward the barrens] in summer [August] to kill caribou for clothing. So Akaitcho and his band of Yellowknives camped on the Dogrib "road" in wait for Edzo and his band of Dogribs. With Akaitcho's band was Katehwi, a Kwelont'in, with his band of Kwelont'in. Although Katehwi was traveling with Akaitcho, he was a friend of Edzo, too.

Somehow learning that Akaitcho and his band were lying in wait, Edzo and his band slipped past them. But Edzo determined to return to "find out what Akaitcho has on his mind." His band, fearful, refused to accompany him. But Edzo persuaded four men to turn back with him. One was his brother, Satl'iweta [Sun Ray's Father]. The five Dogribs made a portage to Gots'unkati [Cloudberry Lake, on modern maps Mesa Lake] and followed the lake to its end. When they got to the portage on top of the hill they could see Akaitcho's camp.

After nightfall Edzo stole into Akaitcho's camp to the tent of Katehwi; only Katehwi's wife was there. Edzo told her to tell Katehwi to come see him. Edzo returned to where his men were waiting, and at midnight Katehwi arrived. Katehwi told Edzo, "It is no use, the way Akaitcho is barking. He says, 'If I see Dogribs I want to see blood on my hand!'" But Edzo persisted, saying, "If we run now, we will be running forever." Katehwi finally said, "It's up to you" and left.

The next day Edzo and his men saw a Kwelont'in and one of Akaitcho's men coming across a portage carrying their canoes. Soon the two started to paddle across the bay. As soon as the two men saw the five Dogribs sitting on the height of the portage, the Kwelont'in, Katehwi's man, paddled on across the bay, but Akaitcho's man, whose name was Tatsonke [Raven's Foot], turned back in terror, carrying word of the Dogribs to Akaitcho's camp.

When after an interval the Dogribs and their ally saw people coming in the distance, the Kwelont'in counseled the Dogribs to use what they knew of ink'on [medicine power]. Edzo called upon his brother Satl'iweta, and Satl'iweta began to sing, thrusting his forearms into the earth. He pulled out the head of a Yellowknife and from the head took out the man's spirit. He tore the spirit in half and sat on half of it. The other half he let go, but it did not go back. In this way he deprived Akaitcho's band of their spirits. Satl'iweta then said, "Right now they are coming wild, but once they reach here I do not think they will do any harm."

A great crowd was coming. Katehwi with his band was walking ahead. When they got close, Katehwi's men started to shoot, just with powder. That means peace. And Edzo and each of his men fired one shot in the air, like saying "hello." As soon as Akaitcho's bunch heard the shots they started to run. They were so many that it sounded like thunder. Katehwi sat down next to Edzo, with his men around him. Now that Akaitcho's men were getting close, Edzo sat down with his back turned to them. As Akaitcho's men arrived, they sat down, sat down, sat down. They were sweating; they were afraid there was going to be a war.

Akaitcho was the last to arrive. He said, "I came here to make peace. But you do not look like you are going to make peace, the way your guns are sticking up." Akaitcho carried a big knife [lahwin]. He said, "If you have nothing to fight me with . . . !" and he threw the knife toward Edzo, where it stuck in the ground. Edzo did not move.

Akaitcho made a long speech, but Edzo did not move or answer. Akaitcho then said to Edzo, "I thought you were a great talker even though you are young. But you must be too worried now. You cannot speak." Twice more Akaitcho made a long speech and twice more addressed Edzo, but Edzo neither moved nor spoke. Finally, Akaitcho spoke of his people that the Dogribs had killed, his son among them. After he finished, he said again to Edzo, "How come you don't answer?"

Then Edzo lifted his head and turned partway toward Akaitcho. "How come you talk so nice now?" he said [sarcastically]. "I think you have had a bellyful. I don't have a bellyful yet. How come you talk so nice? There are still lots of young girls, who is stopping you from stealing them?" And then Edzo turned toward the assembled enemies and said, "You talk nice. It sounds good. I'll talk the same as you now!" and his voice was so loud that the branches of two nearby trees leaped in the air. At that Akaitcho was so frightened he started to weep. After Akaitcho started to cry, they did not say any more words.

That is the way they made peace. So we are friendly with everyone now. Everywhere you go we are friends. If we had not made peace there would be fighting until now. Now everybody can get a decent sleep. That is good. That is the way it happened. [Translated from tape by Vital Thomas.]

Naedzo's account ended at this point. Other testimonies conclude in this vein: Edzo's band joined the others, and they all had a big feast and danced for two days and nights, and everyone was happy. The dance circle, trampled by so many feet, can still be seen at Gots'unkati.

HISTORICITY IN NAEDZO'S TESTIMONY

Akaitcho is an indisputable historical figure. Beyond this fact the question is whether verification of the historical reality of other components of the legend is embedded in the European documentary record. Specifically, is there independent evidence of the existence of other characters named in the tradition and for the climactic episode, the Dogrib-Yellowknife confrontation?

THE CHARACTERS

Naedzo's full testimony, and some of those of other Dogribs, introduces additional, minor Dogrib characters by name that we have not presented in this abbreviated version. The major characters in Naedzo's (and others') account are, apart from Akaitcho, the two Dogribs Edzo and Satl'iweta; the Yellowknife Tatsonke, follower of Akaitcho; and the alien Katehwi.

A major difficulty in the historical identification of Dogrib "players" in the legend lies in the fact that during the critical decade of the 1820s only some Dogribs were in trade contact and usually infrequently. Furthermore, for that decade and the next only the Fort Simpson records survive; records from Fort Norman, the other main point of trade for Dogribs, are lost. (Fort Rae, the first regular post actually in Dogrib country, was not founded until 1852.) Missionary records do not begin until 1859. Given such scattered and piecemeal documentation, the identification of Edzo and Satl'iweta with persons in the European record is less than assured.

Some Dogribs claim descent from Edzo. One was the late chief Jimmy Bruneau (1882–1975), who traced his descent from Edzo as a great-grandson in the male line. The conjunction of Bruneau's testimony with European records leads to a tentative identification of the legendary Edzo as a historically recorded Dogrib chief of 1850: "the Martin Lake Chief Tecon-nebetah [Tecon's Father]" (Richardson 1851). There are also references to "Takenbethaw"/"Tackabethaw" in a journal attributed to E. Smith (PAC MG 14 D6).

Even more tenuous but possible is the identification of Satl'iweta (Sun Ray/His Father) as the father of the Marten Lake Dogrib "Sa-kli, le Rayon de Soleil," whom the missionary Petitot (1891) first encountered as a family head in 1864. Under Dogrib rules of teknonymy, an individual becomes "Father of So-and-so" or "Mother of So-and-so" as soon as his or her first-born infant is named. If in fact the documented Sun Ray (Rayon de Soleil) of 1864 was the son of the legendary Satl'iweta, Sun Ray's Father, Sun Ray need only have been a small child at the time of the confrontation.

Since after 1823 all Yellowknives traded into the Hudson's Bay Company post of Fort Resolution, the search for Akaitcho's frightened follower, Tat-sonke (Raven's Foot), was easier. "Tatsan Kay," also called "Corbo" (Fr. *corbeau*, crow or raven), is identified in the post accounts of Fort Resolution (HBCA B.181/d/3b and B.181/e/1 fol. 11) as the second son of the second brother of Akaitcho. Estimated to be age fourteen in 1825/26, "Tatsan Kay" would have been about eighteen in 1829, a date whose significance is brought out later.

What about Katehwi? In Dogrib tradition this intermediary is identified as some sort of alien, neither Dogrib nor Yellowknife. In some testimonies he is said to speak Cree. Naedzo's testimony, however, specifies that Katehwi is a Kwelont'in and the leader of a band of Kwelont'in. The striking feature of the term Kwelont'in is that Dogrib recognition of such a people has not been uncovered in field research except as the group is immortalized in Naedzo's testimony. The same condition holds for the personage Katehwi; he figures by name in four of the five major testimonies and is named in more truncated accounts as well. Yet this person appears in no other aspect of Dogrib legend or folk history. It cannot then be argued that a character, real or fictitious, and a unique band/tribal identification have been trans-posed from another domain of Dogrib knowledge or lore into the tradition of the Edzo-Akaitcho confrontation.

We became strongly suspicious that Katehwi was a leader of a band of Chipewyans attached to Fort Resolution as fur hunters and sometime fort provisioners. Several such leaders repeatedly feature in entries in the Fort Resolution post journals of the 1820s. After reviewing published and archival sources, our suspicions focused on Le Camarade de Mandeville, who figures in explorers' accounts of 1833–34 as a leader "having an extensive knowledge of the country northward and eastward of Great Slave Lake" (Back 1836;

King 1836). The "country northward," especially, was Akaitcho's range and the region where Gots'unkati, seen on today's maps as Mesa Lake, is located.

The arrival of "Mandeville" at Fort Resolution is recorded in the Hudson's Bay Company journal entry of July 27, 1820: "two of Ft. Wedderburn [Hudson's Bay Company post at Lake Athabasca] Indians arrived as also 5 of Ft. Chipewyan's [North West Company post at Lake Athabasca] at the NW Fort [the North West Company fort locally in competition with Fort Resolution]—Mandeville the great chief of the NW at Athabasca Lake is the leader of these [Chipewyan] Indians—whom I gained over to our [Hudson's Bay Company's] interest" (HBCA B.181/a/3 fol. 5).

But whence the Dogrib name Katehwi? A passage in the Fort Resolution post journal of 1822–23 yields the critical cross-identification of his French name with his Athapaskan appellation: "In the evening [of August 30, 1822,] Catooelthel (commarade de Mandeville) and Band arrived" (HBCA B.181/a/4 fol. 13). The identification of Catooelthel as Le Camarade de Mandeville is repeated in the Fort Resolution account book of 1834–35 (HBCA B.181/d/4b fol. 10d). With many variant spellings (e.g., Cassetooelthil, Caetlooelthel, Catouelthele), this band leader's activities are repeatedly noted in the Fort Resolution journals of the 1820s and 1830s. For the Chipewyan name that the English speakers were struggling to transcribe, Katehwi is as likely a transposition into Dogrib phonology as one can expect; the meaning of the name Katehwi is unknown to Dogribs.

What about Naedzo's identification of Katehwi as a Kwelont'in? Transposed into Chipewyan, Kwelont'in should become *tthelon-hot'ine*. L. Menez, resident Oblate father at Fort Resolution, pointed out (personal communication) that to Chipewyans *tthelon* refers to the Thelon River region, especially the headwaters and Upper Thelon area that lie east of Great Slave Lake (the Thelon River eventually discharges through Chesterfield Inlet into Hudson Bay). A band, any of its members, or an individual inhabiting or exploiting the Thelon area would be designated in Chipewyan as *tthelon-hot'ine*. To McVicar, the trader at Fort Resolution writing in 1825–26, the Thelon River was the "Thulloo-dessy or Chipewyan River, known only from Indian report" (HBCA B.181/e/1 fol. 2). It is the Thelon (also the Thelew, and, as Thelew-ey-aze, Thlew-y-aze, and Thlewy-dezza, the Fish or Little Fish River) in the accounts of explorers Back (1836) and King (1836). For Back and King, Le Camarade de Mandeville described and mapped the portage route via the Upper Thelon to the Great Fish River (Thelewy-cho-dezza), today the Back River. And in March 1834 at the explorers' base, Fort Reliance, at the eastern extremity of Great Slave Lake,

"The Camarade de Mandeville made his appearance with two sledges of dried meat, which he and his son had dragged from their lodges, situated on the banks of the Fish [Thelon] River, distant about five days march" (King 1836). King's sketch map suggests that the site of Le Camarade's lodge was on the Hanbury River, a branch of the Thelon. Thus several strands of evidence tie Catooelthel/Le Camarade de Mandeville, the *tthelon-hot'ine*, to the legendary Katehwi, the Kwelont'in.

That for 140 years and in relation to one event only the names of Katehwi and Tatsonke should survive in Dogrib folk history may seem surprising. But consider the case of T'asinghon, mentioned earlier, another alien who also figures in only one story in Dogrib oral tradition. T'asinghon was the vicious Yellowknife who abused and murdered several Dogrib women before one cut his throat. When I first recorded the story of T'asinghon at Rae in 1962 (on the same day that Nancy Lurie recorded it at Lac la Martre!), I assumed that T'asinghon was a fictional character, a mythic creation symbolizing Yellowknife cruelty. But here is the testimony of the "Marten Lake" [Lac la Martre] Dogrib Kanoobaw, as recorded by the trader at Fort Simpson on April 7, 1824: "last spring a Red Knife (Tausigou) who had already pillaged us of 3 of our women and murdered them, tore a fourth from us, this last, while her Husband [i.e., "Tausigou"] was asleep put an end to his existence by cutting his throat!" (HBCA B.200/a/4 fol. 2). The only major discrepancy between Kanoobaw's account and four present-day testimonies of record is that the present-day versions credit a Dogrib man (identity varies) with finishing off T'asinghon after the woman had stabbed him in the throat.

Given that not only Akaitcho but also Katehwi, Tatsonke, and T'asinghon, aliens all, must by all evidence be recognized as historical persons, surely there is no less reality to the Dogrib Edzo.

THE CONFRONTATION

The demonstrable historicity of so much of Dogrib oral tradition led us (Helm and Gillespie) in an earlier draft of this paper to conclude that an encounter between Edzo and Akaitcho and their followers, probably mediated by Le Camarade de Mandeville, did occur in the caribou lands in the late summer of some year in the decade following 1825. At that writing we had no independent verification of the actuality of such an event, as archival research had been carried only up to the year 1826. Subsequent work in the Hudson's Bay Company Archives by Gillespie yielded the critical passage from the November 26, 1829, entry in the Fort Simpson post journal. Two youths sent to the fort by François Beaulieu, a Metis who operated as a some-time outpost trader at Lac la Martre, "brought news from the Marten Lake Slaves [Dogribs] have account of the S. [Slave] Lake Chipewyans being in that direction—with Ekycho Copper Indian Leader between whom and the Slaves some words were exchanged not of a very consiliating nature the Chipewyans present became mediation [sic] and they separated with mutual reproaches for the past—and strong languidge implying another attack" (HBCA B.200/a/11 fols. 13d, 14).

Despite its garbled syntax, the entry confirms that a tense encounter took place between Dogribs (who to the Fort Simpson trader were "Marten Lake Slaves") and Yellowknives under the leadership of Akaitcho and that a party of Chipewyans who traded into Fort Resolution ("S. Lake") mediated between the aggrieved parties. There is no mention of Edzo, Katehwi, or Tatsonke, who would have been eighteen in 1829. The locale of the encounter is not specified. That the report came to the Fort Simpson trader in November does not preclude a late summer confrontation, as specified in the legend, for in the records of the period there is frequently a considerable lag between an event in the bush and the time that someone arrives at the fort to report it to a trader. There is only one significant discrepancy between the brief "news" sent by Beaulieu and present-day Dogrib testimonies on the confrontation. According to Beaulieu, no degree of resolution of hostility occurred. In all the modern testimonies, however, the denouement is the resolution of hostilities, so "now everyone can get a decent sleep." In four of the five major testimonies (Naedzo's is the exception), the peace was sealed by the dancing together of the erstwhile enemies.

In Dogrib traditional understanding medicine power is mandatory to the full control of events, as demonstrated in Satl'iweta's magical capture of the Yellowknives' spirits. At the same time, for Dogribs great oratory has the power to dominate the public mind, as Edzo's performance attests. Certainly, the story line and aspects of the episodes in the legend may have been conventionalized in the transmission of the tradition to accord with these emphases in Dogrib culture. Exactly because these are fundamental comprehensions, however, we think it likely that in some fashion the Dogribs did muster their medicine powers against their enemies and that the protagonists Akaitcho and Edzo did exchange high-flown oratory.

To the present day feasting and dancing together have been the definitive affirmation of amity when bands of Dogribs or Dogribs and friendly aliens meet. From this enduring cultural conception an evolving Dogrib tradition may have created the final episode of the dancing "seal" upon the peace. In all testimonies the coda of the legend is finis forever to Dogrib-Yellowknife hostilities. One easily comprehends the catharsis that the Dogrib audience experiences at "peace forevermore!" In this respect, as gratifying to the ethnohistorian as Beaulieu's "news" may be as confirmation of the confrontation, it is aesthetically a disappointment. But Beaulieu's "news" of "strong languidge implying another attack" is not necessarily conclusive. After all, that account as received into the documentary record involved at least five links in a chain of testimonies: from (1) Dogribs who may or may not have been eyewitnesses to some of the events to Beaulieu; from (2) Beaulieu to the two youths who carried his message to Fort Simpson; from (3) those youths, who doubtless communicated through (4) an interpreter to the trader Edward Smith; and from (5) Edward Smith's written version to us. Whatever the actual events, each link in the chain of transmission of the "news" offered opportunity for interpretation, distortion, and omission. In fact, on April 3, 1830, some four months after receipt of Beaulieu's news at Fort Simpson, the trader at Fort Resolution noted what was probably the same news in a more positive tone: "arrived 2 Red Knives from their Chief (Akaitcho) . . . I am informed that Akaitcho has established a Peace with the Slaves of Mackensie's River District" (Provincial Archives of Alberta 74.1/128).

As corroboration of the legend's assertion that an overt resolution of hostility was achieved, Dogribs point to a circular area of distinctive vegetation on the shore of Mesa Lake as the remains of the circle beaten by the dancers who sealed the peace at Gots'unkati. [In September 1998, Dogrib schoolchildren visited the site to see that evidence from their people's history.]
from Helm and Gillespie, "Dogrib Oral Tradition as History," 1981

I recorded Naedzo's telling of the oral tradition of the confrontation between Edzo and Akaitcho at David Wetade's home in Rae on January 29, 1969. In November 1996, participants in the Dogrib Language Workshop, led by Leslie Saxon, transcribed and translated Naedzo's narrative word by word from the tape. A copy of the text and translation may be found at the Dogrib Regional Education Authority in Rae-Edzo.

AKAITCHO

The Yellowknife Indian leader Akaitcho stepped upon the stage of Canadian history in the afternoon of July 30, 1820, when he met Capt. John Franklin and affirmed his willingness to guide and provision Franklin's expedition of exploration "to the shores of the polar sea." A year later, almost to the day,

Akaitcho and his band delivered Franklin and his complement to a point on the Lower Coppermine River within five hours of the ocean. The drama of the succor of the starving survivors by Akaitcho and his followers the following November assured Akaitcho's place in history.

Known in Franklin's time as Copper Indians, the Yellowknives were the northwesternmost division of the widespread Chipewyan peoples. Speaking a somewhat distinctive dialect of Chipewyan, they were a small "tribe" of about 190 souls in 1820. Akaitcho, "Big Foot," was the paramount leader. His band included about forty men and boys. The Hook and Long Legs, who were also involved in the Franklin expedition, headed smaller groups.

Ranging broadly in the caribou lands from the east arm of Great Slave Lake to the Coppermine River, Akaitcho and the Yellowknives traded as meat provisioners into the North West Company post of Fort Providence on the North Arm of Great Slave Lake (not the present Fort Providence on the Mackenzie River). For at least a decade the Yellowknives had pillaged furs, stolen women, and occasionally killed Dogrib and Bearlake Indians, their neighbors to the west and northwest. Dogribs were forced to avoid parts of their traditional hunting range during Akaitcho's years of aggressive leadership.

[As the first part of this chapter documents,] Akaitcho's ferocity is featured in Dogrib lore to the present day. Franklin and his officers experienced Akaitcho's character in more diverse aspects. At their first meeting in 1820 at Fort Providence, Akaitcho was at pains to impress Franklin with his dignity and importance. Franklin was to discover that Akaitcho did not easily yield in matters regarding his own judgment or self-interest. After the expedition was under way, Akaitcho resolutely balked at attempting the journey to the arctic coast in one season, pointing out that when he had agreed to do so he had no idea of the "slow mode of traveling" of Franklin's party. In consequence, the expedition established winter quarters at Fort Enterprise on Winter Lake. The following spring Akaitcho had a try at demanding immediate distribution of promised trade goods before he would undertake the summer's expedition to the coast. When other Yellowknives did not support his allegations of bad faith, Akaitcho backed down, offering as justification that "as the leader of his party, he had to beg for them all."

When, after the terrible overland return from the arctic coast, the starving remnants of the Franklin expedition were rescued by Yellowknives, Akaitcho revealed another facet of his character. Treated with the "utmost tenderness" by their rescuers, Franklin and his party from Fort Enterprise were conveyed to the camp of "our chief and companion Akaitcho." There, in Franklin's words, Akaitcho "shewed us the most friendly hospitality and all sorts of personal attention, even to cooking for us with his own hands, an office he never performs for himself." To survivor George Back, Akaitcho was "generous and humane."

By 1825, when Franklin arrived at Fort Resolution to launch his second overland expedition, Akaitcho and the Yellowknives had suffered a change of fortune. In consequence of the merger of the North West Company and the Hudson's Bay Company in 1821, the post of Fort Providence had closed in 1823. Akaitcho and the Yellowknives now perforce had to direct their trade into Fort Resolution in company with Chipewyans already attached to that post. (Their intermarriage and absorption into that population resulted in the eventual disappearance of the Yellowknives as a distinct people.) Driven by vengeance or desperation over killings perpetrated by Yellowknives earlier in the year, in October 1823 Dogribs attacked the Yellowknife Long Legs and his band, who were encamped in the area between Hottah Lake and Great Bear Lake. Thirty-four Yellowknives perished—four men, thirteen women, and seventeen children. This was a bitter reversal. Akaitcho refused to join Franklin's expedition to Great Bear Lake, sending word that he and his hunters would not go into the lands where their kinsmen had died, "lest we should attempt to renew the war." The tense encounter recorded in Dogrib oral history apparently was the first since the destruction of Long Legs's band.

Akaitcho reemerged in the history of northern exploration in the winter of 1833–34 during an "appalling period of suffering and calamity" at Fort Reliance, the base George Back had established for the overland search for the explorer John Ross, believed lost in the polar region. Akaitcho's energy and resolve in the hunt and the example of psychological fortitude he set in that time of famine commanded Back's admiration. Yet later in his journal Back remarked that Akaitcho, who was then about fifty years of age and in poor health, had lost much of his authority over the Yellowknives.

In 1838 word came to the trader at Fort Resolution that Akaitcho had died that spring. One Dogrib account has it that Akaitcho was buried on an island in Yellowknife Bay.

from Helm and Gillespie, "Akaitcho," 1983

The two accounts in this chapter take us back in time to the eighteenth century. The first comes from the written record of a young Englishman, the other from a Dene telling of a first-time encounter between Indians and white men.

LIVING OFF THE LAND WITH THE CHIPEWYAN INDIANS IN 1791–1792

In 1821 the amalgamation of the Hudson's Bay Company and the North West Company marked the beginning of the long contact-traditional era. Fifty years before, in 1771, the first European traversed the land that became the Northwest Territories from the mouth of the Coppermine River to that of the Slave River when Samuel Hearne, taken by Matonabbee and his band of Chipewyans to the "copper mines" near the shores of the Arctic Ocean, was returning to Fort Churchill on Hudson Bay. Twenty years later, in 1791, Peter Fidler, another young employee of the Hudson's Bay Company, set out with Chipewyans for a winter's slow travel. At that time, scarcely two years had elapsed since Alexander Mackenzie had descended Dehcho, looking to open the land of the Dene to the fur trade. Between Mackenzie and Hearne, the giants of European exploration in early contact times, Peter Fidler is only a historical blip. But his daily account of eating and surviving with his Indian companions in the winter of 1791–92 provides an unparalleled record of what it was like for the human carnivores at the top of the food chain in the boreal forest.

"1791 September 4th Sunday. In the afternoon I embarked with 4 canoes of Jepewyans, in order to remain with them, & acquire the Language." So begins the journal that Peter Fidler maintained until April 10, 1792, when he returned to his point of departure on Lake Athabasca. [Throughout this chapter abbreviated month-plus-day notations follow the U.S. convention: April 10 becomes 4/10.]

Fidler was the last of a handful of young employees of the Hudson's Bay Company—William Stewart (1715–16), Richard Norton (1717–18), and Samuel Hearne (1770–72)—who in the eighteenth century traveled solely with Indians through the winter in Chipewyan lands west of Hudson Bay. None of these young men was "in command." As a lone white, each was dependent on Indian goodwill, knowledge, and skill. As Matonabbee did with Hearne, Thooh, "the man that has the Care of Me," was the Chipewyan who assumed responsibility for Fidler.

Much ethnographic information waits to be teased out of Fidler's (1934) succinct journal entries, but their truly unique contribution to the anthropological record lies in Fidler's dogged day-by-day notation of game taken and number of persons sharing it. In combination, these data allow the calculation of per-person consumption by people living entirely off the land for thirty weeks through the winter of 1791–92. I have found no evidence of a comparable record of sustained and exclusive exploitation and consumption of big game in North America.

In contrast to Hearne's (1958 [1795]) great trek with Matonabbee and his band of Chipewyans, Peter Fidler's travel with his "Jepewyan" companions was very circumscribed, as shown in the accompanying map. Through that winter they moved from Lake Athabasca to Great Slave Lake and back again along a corridor of travel some two hundred miles long by forty miles wide in a low, swampy (though frozen), wooded extension of the physiographic Interior Plains of North America. Its eastern side abuts the Canadian Shield. In place of the barren-ground caribou, prime prey of the Chipewyan peoples, the food animals were bison, moose, and beaver. Twenty years before, Hearne and Matonabbee entered this corridor in search of Cree who at that time had penetrated the Slave River area, displacing an apparently Dene population (Gillespie 1981). Certainly, the displaced Dene were not Chipewyan Dene. Some Chipewyans had been pushing west in advance of the European fur traders. Now Fidler's companions were beyond the habitat of the resource base of Chipewyan livelihood from time immemorial, the migratory caribou of the Shield.

Fidler's record, then, provides an aberrant story of Chipewyan subsistence, and it offers no account of aboriginal techniques of big game hunting. Peter took with him "1 Quart of Gunpowder, 50 Ball, & 4 lb of Shot, [and] 4 Flints," although it is not clear whether this supply was for trade purposes or was his own. In any case, Peter had a supply until near the end of his tour, when "[March] 5th Monday [1792] Gave Thooh the last of my

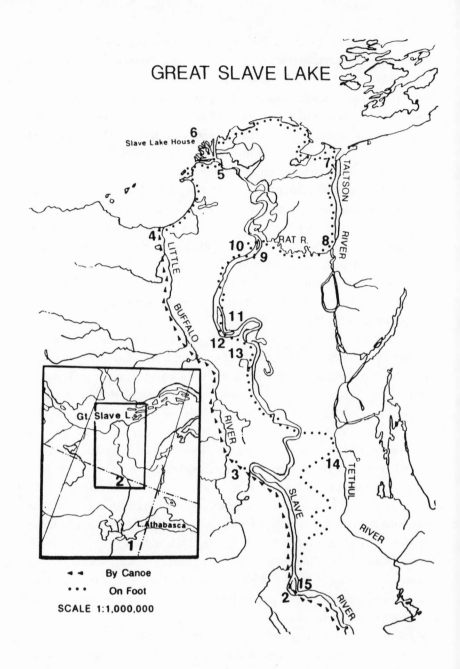

GREAT SLAVE LAKE

Slave Lake House

TALTSON RIVER

LITTLE BUFFALO RIVER

RAT R.

Gt. Slave L.

L. Athabasca

TETHUL RIVER

SLAVE RIVER

◄ ◄   By Canoe

• • •   On Foot

SCALE 1:1,000,000

Ammunition." The scattered evidence in the journal indicates that all bison and moose taken by Peter's companions were killed by firearms. Midway through the winter Fidler refers to a party of Chipewyans, whom we will meet again, as "nearly starving thro hungar & they have not even any Ammunition to kill any animals with."

The personnel of the group with Fidler was, excepting Thooh and his wife, chronically unstable. But the day-by-day spatial progress of the group was, after freezeup, when the canoes were abandoned, both literally and figuratively pedestrian: sometimes they moved camp every day, perhaps three to seven miles; other times the camp might sit for a very few days. The longest pause for Peter was for ten days (11/16−11/26) at a fishery at the mouth of the Rat River (Locus 8 on the map on p. 236).

To arrive at the best estimate of the pounds of food and the kilocalories consumed by these de facto carnivores, a few judicious calls on their behavior are required. All ethnographic evidence assures us that the Dene hunting camp is a commensal unit, and Fidler's comments bear this out. Those who join the camp overnight share in the commissary. Peter does not tell us if (or how much) food was carried away by those departing his camp. The assumption is that in the case of small parties it was an inconsequential amount. In one place in Peter's narrative, however, internal evidence points to a departing crew of about twenty-five persons carrying off substantial poundage of

---

Map of places and dates in the peregrinations of Peter Fidler and companions during the winter of 1791–92. 1. 8/4 Depart from Lake Athabasca for Slave River. 2. 9/11 At the end of several portages, meet and camp with a small party of Cree, "barberous rascals," returning from attacks on Dene beyond Great Slave Lake. 3. 9/14 Portage from Slave River into Little Buffalo River ("Eggid da zal la dezza"). 4. 10/6 Arrive at shore of Great Slave Lake at freezeup "so that we cannot proceed any farther with our Canoes." 5. 10/16 "Arrive at the Tents . . . [of] 10 Canoes here that were stopped by the Ice on the early setting in of Fall." 6. 10/28 Arrive at Slave Lake House of the North West Company. 7. 10/30 Arrive at the mouth of the Taltson River ("Tall chu dezza"). 8. 11/16 Arrive at the mouth of the Rat River ("Gin dezza or Muskrat River"). 9. 12/10 Reach the Slave River, opposite the upper end of McConnell Island. 10. 12/26 Cross the Slave River and put up on the west side in company of another tent of Chipewyans. 11. 1/7 Camp on Big Island in the Slave River. 12. 1/18 Joined by "2 Tents [whose occupants are all] in a wretched condition" (see text). 13. 2/5 Joined by another starving party (see text). 14. 3/1 By this date they were in the drainage of the Telthul River ("Thay thule dezza"). For the next four weeks they work their way southward. 15. 3/28 Now Peter's party is just below the rapids (at present Fort Smith) near where the Cree war party was encountered the previous autumn. From here Peter and his companions proceed severally to the post on Lake Athabasca. Our narrative stops here.

edible tissue. The amount of wastage of edible tissue (and potential bone grease) cannot be derived from Fidler's account. He does not indicate that there was wastage. In flush times, scrap edibles may have been left behind when the camp moved. When on the move the men would have had to choose between being able to hunt and transporting supplies by hand toboggan or tumpline, so it boiled down to what the women could drag or pack. Fidler sometimes mentions that the women were making drymeat; this would reduce the weight to about one fifth of fresh meat. We know from Peter's narrative that the women brought the meat from the kill sites (obviously, not far from that day's encampment); the camp did not move to kill sites. This could occasion wastage. We may surmise that the women were not meticulous when great quantities of meat were available. The cooking technique was roasting. Throughout the entire winter Peter lamented the lack of a kettle. Stoneboiling apparently was mainly and only occasionally used to render bone grease.

Other sorts of uncertainties must be addressed in the body of the essay. But the basic, indeed required, assumption is that on the whole the people involved ate almost all the edible tissues and fats that their prey afforded them.

FIDLER'S RECORD KEEPING

Peter Fidler's journal provides a day-by-day record of the game taken by his party. With few exceptions, Fidler entered the sex of each "buffalo" and moose killed and noted when the animal was "young." Several times he noted that a female was fat. Beaver followed bison and moose as a source of sustenance. Peter sized the beaver killed according to the Hudson's Bay Company's rating of beaver pelts: "beaver," "large beaver," or "old beaver" for the standard or full-sized pelt; "¾"; and "½," "half," or "young." The few other mammals—nine porcupines, two wolverines, and one hibernating bear—taken over the seven months add up to very little nourishment, indeed. Peter trapped a few marten for their pelts (10/12, 10/19, 2/29) but does not indicate that they were eaten. Only in the cases of the waterfowl that constituted the party's only food in the first week of travel and of the fish, mostly *inconnu* (misidentified by Peter as "jackfish"), that his camp group relied on for a few days in November does Peter fail to give us an exact count.

Peter is a paragon in his unfaltering enumeration of game taken. Obviously, living off the land through the winter in the subarctic forest concentrated the diarist's attention wonderfully—and his appreciation as well, as shown in his comment on a "Wolverin which we snapped up before it was well warmed thro —a delicious morsel!!! but what cannot hungar do" (11/ 28). He was not always so meticulous, however, in enumerating the human beings who made up the commensal unit of fluctuating size that fed off the animals killed. He always noted persons leaving (and returning to) his group. Also, he consistently noted the number and ethnicity ("Jepewyan," "Canadian," etc.) of the persons in small parties traveling the Slave River route between the North West Company post on Lake Athabasca and the outpost on Great Slave Lake who camped overnight with his party. Unfortunately, it was exactly when a group of significant size joined his party for a number of days that Fidler does not count noses for us. Rather, we are faced with such entries as "10 canoes [of people] here that were stopped by the Ice" (10/16); "Gabble & his Family arrived" (11/25); "the 2 Tents joined us that the man came from the 15th Inst" (1/18).

How many people were in Gabble's family, in "10 Canoes," in "2 Tents"? In some cases, later commentary in the journal allows us to establish the number in a party or arrive at a reasoned estimate. A "family," with no other information, is probably best reckoned as a man and wife with two or three subteen children. I have adopted the convention that, as estimated, two subteen children equal one adult and that three equal two adults, and they are so scored in the personnel counts. The small canoes employed by the Chipewyans in this era and area carried at best two or three persons (Gillespie 1976), and certain journal entries bear out our convention of assigning 2.5 persons per canoe.

Putting a number to the human contents of a tent is more vexing when the text suggests, as in the case of the aforementioned "2 Tents," that "tent" is not equivalent to a single family. Peter's remarks led to the guesstimate that the visitors' two tents contained the equivalent of thirteen adults. This unwelcome crew—"I am afraid they will remain with us, & eat what we should require for ourselves"—was with Peter's group for seventeen days (1/18– 2/3). This is the only interval where the count may be "off" by more than one or two persons for more than a day or two or so. If the calculation of the size of this crew is off by three persons, it alters the mean number of adult equivalents per day in the daily commensal unit by 0.2 or 0.3 (adult) persons during the entire span of the 207 days in which we follow Peter and his companions.

The entries throughout his journal indicate that the bulk of the personnel in Peter's commensal group as it expanded or shrank were men and hunting-age youths. Only the mature men had wives.

At this point, it is well to make clear that certain rules of evidence have been followed in assigning amounts, proportions, and nutritional values of animal tissues consumed by Fidler and his companions: (1) guesses by the author (myself) are not to be included in the calculations; (2) "estimated," undemonstrated, or undocumented assignments of weights, proportions, or values by others are to be rejected in favor of documentations of precise data sets; (3) from among sources offering precise data, the source with the greater number of specimens and the more highly quantified amounts and values is to be used; (4) the conservative side should be chosen in arriving at judgmental decisions. Adherence to rules 1, 2, and 3 promotes satisfying rule 4.

EDIBLE TISSUE ON BISON, MOOSE, AND BEAVER

Thanks to Peter's record keeping, we know the kinds and numbers of animals on which Peter and his companions preyed. But the average weight of each kill must be settled upon.

Modern ethnographic field data on the parts of moose and caribou eaten by Chipewyans (Jarvenpa and Brumbach 1983) and their Dene congeners, the Dogribs (Helm field notes: "We eat everything except the manure"), are echoed in Hearne's (1958 [1795]) account of the gustatory pleasures of the Chipewyans of his and Fidler's day. Fidler's Chipewyan companions, like Hearne's, would have eaten the intestines, "the parts of generation" of both sexes, the udder, and the fetus. These edibles are not considered in modern sources on bison (e.g., Koch, Crouse, and Seideman 1988; Halloran 1957). The tongue, lungs, liver, heart, kidneys, "sweetbread," "tripe," and "head [including brain?] and cheek meat" of beef cattle amount to 4.9 percent of live weight (Iowa State University n.d.). Rounding to 5 percent, this percentage is applied to bison. Thus these extracarcass tissues add approximately 50 pounds to the 410 pounds of edible tissue yielded by the dressed carcass of a 1,000-pound foraging bison. Altogether, then, these consumable tissues add up to 46 percent of the live weight of range bison.

Other products of bison and cattle that are edible are blood (4 percent of live weight, though only a portion would be recovered), hide (7 percent of live weight), and bone grease and marrow. Wheat (1972) arrived at 6 pounds as the bone grease and marrow fat yield per adult plains bison. Hearne (1958 [1795]) writes of Chipewyans recovering the blood of caribou and of Cree sucking the blood from the wounds on freshly killed buffalo and moose. Some 120 years later, Russell (1898) "frequently" saw Dogribs emptying the caribou stomach "to use it as a receptacle for containing the blood until frozen." Fidler's party consumed part of a bison hide (11/18) and at least two batches of bone grease (10/12, 12/4). Not included are estimates (see rule 1, above) of blood, hide(s), or bone grease in the calculations of pounds of edible animal products available to Fidler and his companions.

This establishes a percentage formula for calculating the pounds of consumable tissue yielded by a bison. But we must settle on the average weights of the seven "bulls," nine "cows," and seven "young buffalo" killed by Peter's party. Fidler and his party were preying on woods bison. The average weights of plains bison, *Bison bison bison*, cannot be taken as average weights of woods bison, *Bison bison athabascae*. From Hearne on, European observers of woods bison have judged that they were a larger variety of bison than plains bison. The woods bison were nearly exterminated by the beginning of this century. Unhappily for our purposes, from 1925 to 1928 plains buffalo (6,673 of them) were introduced into the one remaining population of woods bison (about 1,500). Thus, most of the bison in Canada's Woods Buffalo National Park, which abuts the area where Peter and his party wintered, "are assumed to be *athabascae* x *bison* hybrids," according to McDonald (1981). McDonald does not determine the overall body size of *B. b. athabascae*, but he does provide the allometry of the skull volume of *athabascae* relative to *B. b. bison*: 1.22. Lacking any better comparative data on relative size of *B. b. bison* and *athabascae*, I adopted the value of 1.2 as the ratio of live weight of woods bison to plains bison. Multiplying the average weights of four sample populations of plains bison (Park 1969; Halloran 1957) by the factor 1.2 produces a range of estimates of the live weights of male, female, and yearling woods bison. I selected two of the four sets of reconstructed woods bison weights as "high" versus "low" weight averages for the woods bison killed by Peter's party. From these hypothetical live weights, the pounds of consumable bison tissue are derived at the rate of 46 percent of live weight.

Peter's party killed nine male moose, three females, and one "young" moose. Schladweiler and Stevens (1973) calculate the approximate mean whole body weight (rounded) of adult male moose at 730 pounds, of adult females at 670 pounds, and of yearlings at 530 pounds. The average carcass yield of yearlings, cows, and bulls combined was 55 percent of whole body weight (comparable to the bison carcass/live weight ratio of 54 percent).

Gaida and Marchello (1987) record the "average yield [by weight] of *lean edible tissue*" (my emphasis) of the whole body of the moose to be 36.5 percent and that of the moose carcass to be 67 percent. There is no clue as to the average fat deposit on moose. If the dressed carcass of this cervid conforms to the lean-to-fat ratio (92 percent to 8 percent) that we arrived at for the bison carcass, then the average moose carcass would yield lean meat at the proportion of 36.5 percent of whole body weight plus fat deposits at approximately 3 percent of the whole body weight. I am more confident that it is reasonable to apply to moose the proportion of 5 percent extra-carcass edible tissues established for beef cattle. Granting these extrapolations, the proportion of consumable tissue on the whole moose adds up to approximately 44.5 percent (36.5 percent lean carcass meat plus 5 percent extra-carcass tissues plus, more arguable, 3 percent carcass fat). Among the modern Dene moose hunters of the Mackenzie Delta, Derek Smith (1967) estimated, rather obscurely, "a utilization of 45 percent live weight."

Thirty-seven large beaver, eighteen three-quarter beaver, and twenty-nine "half" or "young" beaver were eaten. Adult beaver range from about 30 to over 70 pounds, averaging about 44 pounds. I have set 44 pounds as the weight of Fidler's "old" or "large" beaver, 33 pounds as the weight of his three-quarter beaver, and 22 pounds as the weight of his "half" or "young" beaver.

The other mammals—nine porcupines, two wolverines, and one bear—that were eaten contributed so very little (perhaps 300 pounds) to the food supply of Peter's groups that they do not warrant fretting over average live weights or consumable proportions thereof.

HOW MUCH DID PETER FIDLER AND HIS COMPANIONS HAVE TO EAT?

I have been concerned to calculate the proportion of consumable tissue on the three significant food animals—woods bison, moose, and beaver—with which Peter and his companions sustained life and energy between September 4, 1791, and March 28, 1792. In the end, how much everyone or anyone had to eat depended both on the number and size of the animals killed and on the number of persons in the food-sharing assemblage.

Parties joined Peter's base group—however it may be distinguished—from overnight to, in a couple of cases, a fortnight or so. For example, the number of persons, that is, adult equivalents, in Peter's nightly camp ranged from as many as thirty-six between October 25 and October 29 to as few as three persons in the following four days. To match people with food units (pounds and kilocalories), I have converted gross counts of people into person-days. Person-days are reckoned by the number of persons per day in the commensal unit multiplied by a specific span of days. The number of persons in commensality during the 207 days adds up to 2,872 person-days. Thus the mean number of persons feeding off the commissary was 13.9 (adult) persons per day. [Tables 3, 4, 5, and 6 in the original paper (Helm

1993) present the data from which the conclusions—including high and low estimates—in this and the following three paragraphs are drawn.]

By live weight, about 20 tons of moose and bison (by the high estimate) were killed by Peter's party, plus close to 1.5 tons of beaver. These tonnages yielded about 7 tons of consumable bison tissue and about 2 tons of consumable moose tissue. Beaver (by the high estimate) provided almost 0.75 ton of edible tissue. The figures add up to 19,800 edible pounds. Reckoning with low estimates, about 17,670 pounds of edible tissue from these three species were available. Converting the total poundage of consumable tissue to mean pounds available to each person per day reveals that, by the high estimate, each adult equivalent had almost 7 pounds (6.89) per day. By the low estimate, each person had a little more than 6 pounds (6.14).

Even if one grants that the estimates of poundage of consumable tissue are on target, there remains a major problem in settling on an estimate of the food energy available. In the estimates and calculations leading to establishing pounds of edible tissue, there was continually the problem of assessing the proportion of fat deposits. This problem obtrudes in the conversion of available poundage into food energy, that is, kilocalories. For bison and moose, the available calculations of kilocalories per weight unit are explicitly based on the "lean meat" or "muscle" (or a terminological equivalent) of the animals. Only in case of the data on beaver is it likely that at least some of the fat deposits on the beaver were part of the tissue analyzed for caloric value. Raw beaver tissue (as reconstructed) was by weight comprised of about one part fat to two parts protein.

The bison and moose tissue specimens analyzed in the sources consulted were comprised specifically of lean tissue only, with the proportion of about one part fat to ten parts protein for bison and one to twenty for moose. Lard (rendered hog fat) contains 900 kilocalories per 100 grams. Beef kidney fat (suet) yields almost as much food energy, 854 kilocalories per 100 grams. "Separable fat" on retail cuts of beef is about 18–12 percent water and mostly ranges between 700 and 775 kilocalories per 100 grams (Watt and Merrill 1963). The separable fat range suggests 740 kilocalories per 100 grams as a conservative median food energy value of total raw bison and moose fat (including pelvic deposits). If one could establish what proportion of bison and moose tissue is usually comprised of fat, one could achieve a better estimate of the food energy yielded by the total amount of tissue ingested, in this reckoning, by Fidler and his companions.

I have calculated the mean kilocalories that would have been available from *lean* bison meat and moose meat for each person (adult equivalent) per day, according to high and low estimates of pounds of consumable tissue. The high versus low estimates produce, respectively, about 4,370 kilocalories per person per day versus 3,880 kilocalories. But these estimates are definitely below the food energy available, for they lack the caloric value of any proportion of fat deposits. When estimating consumable tissue on bison and moose carcasses, I posited the proportion of 92 percent lean meat to 8 percent fat deposit. There are 626 kilocalories per pound of 100 percent lean bison tissue; a pound of bison tissue at the proportion of 92 percent lean meat to 8 percent fatty tissue provides 845 kilocalories. When the comparable increase in kilocalories for lean-plus-fat moose tissues is added, while holding the calorie count for beaver steady (see discussion above), the mean caloric intake per person (adult equivalent) rises, at the high estimate, from 4,370 kilocalories per day to 5,780 (rounded to nearest 10 kilocalories). And bone grease and marrow are not included in the caloric calculations.

One recommended daily dietary allowance for boys age sixteen to nineteen engaged in moderate physical activity in a temperate climate is 3,600 calories per day (Church and Church 1963). This is the *maximum* caloric intake recommended by this authority for any sex or age group. Men age twenty-five should receive 3,200 kilocalories, women age twenty-five should receive 2,300 kilocalories per day. Obviously, Peter's companions were on the whole engaged in more than moderate physical activity (hunting, transporting and processing kills, moving camp, etc.) in, for most of the period, temperatures well below freezing. At the low poundage estimate (6.14 pounds) of 100 percent lean meat consumption, the daily mean food energy ration per person is 3,880 kilocalories; this ration barely exceeds the modern maximum recommended dietary allowance of 3,600 kilocalories. The high poundage estimate (6.89 pounds per person-day) of all-lean meat provides 4,370 kilocalories, which exceeds the modern recommended allowance by about 20 percent. But, as indicated, an all-lean assumption is insupportable. The high poundage estimate with 8 percent fatty tissue at 5,780 kilocalories exceeds the modern recommended maximum intake by 60 percent. Low poundage (6.14 pounds per person-day) at 8 percent fat yields 5,140 kilocalories per person.

"EITHER A FEAST OR A FAMINE"

At various intervals, people entered into and left the commensal body in which Peter Fidler participated. Only Peter and Thooh and his wife shared in the commissary for almost all 207 days. So only for these three may we suppose that for somewhat more than half a year they averaged, at a *low* estimate, a daily intake of about 6 pounds of animal tissue and 5,140 kilocalories.

In regard to two major groups who in midwinter joined Peter's group for a number of days, we can be sure that they had not been ingesting a daily average of 6 pounds of tissue, lean only or with fat, month after month. One, the "two tents" crew, were "all in a wretched condition not any thing to eat & their faces much frost bit" (1/18) when they arrived. The other group was dying, piecemeal, of starvation. A middle-aged man and a twelve-year-old boy died between January 31, when "2 good loads of meat" were dispatched to them, and February 5, when the survivors—two women (one "far advanced" in pregnancy), a man, a ten-year-old boy, and two small children—arrived at Peter's encampment at midmorning. "Their withered imaceated skelleton like look was enough to move even the hardest heart" (2/5).

In the ten days from January 22 to January 31, one moose and ten bison were killed by the hunters in Peter's camp group. At the low estimate, these kills yielded 6,000 pounds of edible tissue. On February 2 and February 3, within three days after relief was sent to the starving party, three "tents," equaling an estimated twenty-five persons, decamped. With the arrival of the starvation victims on February 5, Peter's campmates consisted of four men (including Peter and Thooh), three women, and three children. The departing "tents" evidently had carried off almost every scrap of provisions, for Peter's journal entry for February 7 says that "our allowance [is] only one handful of Beat meat [pounded meat] per day each person without any fatt which [the fat] was all used the day after they [the starvation victims] joined us." Then on February 8, "Fortune favours us got five ½ & 2 large Beaver." These kills must have yielded about 80–100 pounds of edible tissue for nine adult equivalents. By the eleventh, "This morning all our stock of provisions was shared out which was very soon done being only one Beaver Tail amongst 4 men, 3 women, & 3 children." In three days (February 8–10), nine adult equivalents ate at least 3 pounds (low estimate) or 2,500 kilocalories of beaver meat per person per day. This was as scarce a time as Peter had seen, excepting perhaps the day when "one partridge . . . was divided amongst 10 people" (9/12) or when eight dined on a piece of buffalo-hide mattress (11/18). Within forty-eight hours of consuming the beaver tail, the men killed three buck moose, "so that thank God we again began to set famine at defiance" (2/12).

Fidler describes the style of gormandizing when provisions permitted:

"Last night according to the Indians invariable custom when they have any thing we [nine persons] had [eight or nine] Beaver stuck on sticks all around the fire [so thick] that we could scarcely see it & kept eating at spells the greater part of the night" (12/14). The pleasures of indulgence aside, the Indians' intensive eating—"when they have anything they can never rest till all is consumed" (9/11)—lays up meat and fat on the consumer that, as a concentrated portable energy supply, improves on even "beat meat." Feast is provision for famine.

That Peter and his companions as a commensal body were consuming 6–7 pounds of animal tissue per person—at 4,370–5,780 kilocalories—may seem by modern urban standards beyond credible levels. But daily meat rations for male workers in the nineteenth-century fur trade, as surveyed by Wheat (1972), were in this range and, at 8 pounds, beyond.

From Peter's account, in this essay I have addressed only one side of a story of survival—the kind and amount of animal flesh that kept human beings alive in that environment through the winter of 1791–92. The other side of the picture of how to stay alive is only touched on. The mutual help and responsiveness to the needs of others, the web of communication over distance between groups who accepted one another as part of a sharing communal body are the other side. It is lodged in brief notations or, in many cases, between the lines of Peter's usually unelaborated narrative. That story waits to be revealed.

Let's let Peter have the last word: "[April] 10th Tuesday [1792] upon the whole this has been rather an agreeable winter than otherwise the principle difficulty we laboured under was the want of a Kettle & being at some few times reduced to very short allowance in provisions which is ever the case with any person that may accompany Indians."

from "'Always with Them Either a Feast or a Famine,'" 1993

WHEN THE FIRST PALE MEN CAME TO LAC LA MARTRE

In the summer of 1789, while Alexander Mackenzie descended Dehcho to the Arctic Ocean, Laurent Leroux went to Lac la Martre to open trade with the Dene of that area. Mackenzie and Leroux were the first whites to enter these respective regions. Vital Thomas tells a story of the first "Pale Men" at Lac la Martre, but the tale does not fit the visit by Leroux in 1789. By August 24 Leroux had pulled back to Yellowknife Bay, where he built a "house," Old Fort Providence, in which he wintered, whereas Vital's story specifies contact at Lac la Martre in winter. But apparently Leroux later did build a post on Lac la Martre "which was occupied intermittently until other posts on Mackenzie River were opened" (Cooke and Holland 1978; cf. Stein-bruck 1999:9). Here is Vital's account.

An old fellow told me this story. It must have happened about two hundred years ago. It is an old story about the first traders, before the priests came.

It was winter and there were no caribou. The Dogribs of Marten Lake were up at the far end of Marten Lake fishing to stay alive. It was hard work chopping through the ice with horn chisels to set their nets. Some Indians came through and told them that the Pale Men were at the other end of Marten Lake. The Marten Lake people had never seen a white man. So two or three men decided to go down there just for the visit. In those days there were enemies everywhere, strangers who might kill you. So they had to be careful.

When they arrived, the Pale Men came out of a beaver house. That's what it looked like to the Indians; a "mud house" they called it. [The shelters of the first traders were probably low walled, chinked with mud, and roofed with sod.] The Indians were a little afraid at first, but the Pale Men made good signs. They didn't have any interpreters in those days, so they made signs that said, "No guns." So the Indians went in their house, and there they saw all kinds of stuff. The Pale Men showed the Indians pelts and all by signs told them, "If you bring us pelts we will give you this stuff." One Indian was given an ice chisel, and to all the other Indians the Pale Men gave chewing tobacco.

That same day the Indians went back home. But they kept smelling that tobacco, and it stank. They said to each other, "That stink might scare the fish away," and they threw the tobacco away in the snow. When they got home the one man showed everybody his ice chisel. As soon as the Indians saw that, they all went crazy for fur. Everyone went out into the bush and began to set deadfalls. Indians had never hunted marten before, but the Pale Men wanted marten skins. Some Indians got twenty, thirty marten. In no time the bunch had over a hundred marten. The fellows who had visited the Pale Men had been shown how to dry the skins. So the Indians dried them and took them to the Pale Men's camp.

For their furs the Pale Men gave the Indians ice chisels and files. They showed the Indians how to use the files and how to sharpen them, all by signs. The Pale Men were short of files, so first they began breaking the files in two, then into four pieces, and they were still getting fur for it. For one pelt, an Indian got a piece of broken file.

Using a metal ice chisel, Rae, 1967. "As soon as the Indians saw that [metal ice chisel], they all went crazy for fur." Andrew Ts'etta on Marian Lake.

Gee whiz, the Indians sure were glad to have those things. Especially those ice chisels. They had always had to use horn to chisel through the ice before. But when they got home and tried out their ice chisels they found them so good that they said, "The ice chisel is the best thing in the world we could find! The ice is just like rotten wood now!"

from Helm and Thomas, "Tales from the Dogribs," 1966

From two historical overview chapters, part II has, chapter by chapter, moved back in time from the 1970s to the late eighteenth century, to earliest contacts between Dene and Europeans. This final chapter of part II returns to the mid–1970s, to the watershed in Dene-government relations that the Mackenzie Valley Pipeline Inquiry proved to be. The two parts of this chapter were written in response to evidence and actions emerging from the inquiry. (For my testimony as a consultant to the inquiry, see chapter 8.)

THE INDIAN BROTHERHOOD AND
THE MACKENZIE VALLEY PIPELINE INQUIRY

In the last ten years [1969–78] the indigenous peoples of the Northwest Territories have been caught up in a succession of momentous political events and pressures. For the Dene, an initial clue that massive changes were afoot in the federal government's vision of its relationship and responsibility to native peoples came in 1968 when at the annual treaty payments government representatives broached the topic of "talking about the land." At the same time, the administration of aspects of treaty relations between government and "Treaty Indians" was being transferred from the federal to the territorial government. Concurrent developments, perceived only piecemeal by natives on the land, were the energetic hydrocarbon explorations by multinational firms under government encouragement, financial and otherwise.

In 1969 came the Canadian white paper on Indian-government relations, essentially an enunciation of a "termination policy," U.S. style. [I have come to characterize this misbegotten scheme as the Canadian reinvention of the square wheel.] Vigorous protest by Indians across Canada blocked its implementation and, in the Northwest Territories, eventually checked the takeover by the territorial government of the administration of Treaty responsibilities to the Dene. Apparently as an effort to backpedal on the white paper

termination issue, the federal government began to fund native political organizations across Canada in order to develop political bodies with which
the government could negotiate future relationships between the federal state
and its indigenous peoples. One of these bodies, the Indian Brotherhood of
the Northwest Territories (IB-NWT), mustered the fourteen Dene chiefs
to file a caveat against further land use or development by nonnatives in the
Indian region (450,000 square miles) on the grounds that aboriginal rights to
the land remained, despite the Treaties of 1900 and 1921, which purported
to "extinguish" those rights.

With the results of the caveat effort still pending (supported in the territorial court, later rejected by higher courts on a technicality), Canadian Arctic Gas Pipeline Ltd. made application to construct a forty-eight-inch natural gas pipeline from the Alaska North Slope field across to the Mackenzie
Valley and thence down to Alberta. The recently formed native political organizations of the Northwest Territories—the IB-NWT, the Committee for
Original Peoples Entitlement (COPE), Inuit Tapirisat (ITC), and the NWT
Metis Association—responded with the position: no development without
native claims settlements.

This truncated account sketches some of the background that contributed
to the creation of the Berger Commission or, its formal title, the Mackenzie
Valley Pipeline Inquiry (MVPI), whose charge was to conduct an inquiry
into the social, environmental, and economic impact of the proposed Mackenzie Valley natural gas pipeline. The Berger Commission provided a public
forum for the native organizations to present their concerns and positions
regarding the pipeline "development" and, more broadly, on the rights and
relationship of the indigenous peoples vis-à-vis the intruding southern Canadian society and the nation-state. *Dene Nation: The Colony Within*, edited
by Mel Watkins (1977), presents largely but not exclusively materials that the
IB-NWT presented to Mr. Justice Berger in the course of the MVPI hearings, which ran from March 1975 to October 1976 (see Berger 1977).

Most of the twenty-one documents offered in *Dene Nation* are revised
and abridged from presentations to the formal hearings of the MVPI. At the
time of their testimonies, contributors to the formal hearings were (as classified by myself) *elected officers of IB-NWT*: Georges Erasmus (president),
George Barnaby (vice president); *regular staff of IB-NWT* (white "consultants"): Peter Puxley (involved in the IB-NWT since its formation), Wilf
Bean; *special full-time IB-NWT staff*, dealing with land claims and development issues: Phoebe Nahanni and Steve Kakfwi, Dene, and, as "outside"
consultants and researchers, Mel Watkins (whose national political promi-

nence cast him as the *éminence blanche* in the minds of some anti-Brotherhood whites) and Arvin D. Jelliss; *other elected native officials*: Gerry Cheezie (chief, Fitz-Smith Band), George Kurszewski (president, Fort Smith Metis Association), and Bob Overvold (executive director, NWT Metis Association); *expert witnesses for IB-NWT*: Peter H. Russell (political economist), Michael Asch and Scott Rushforth (anthropologists); *"ordinary" Dene citizen*: Charlie Snowshoe.

Hundreds of persons testified at the informal MVPI community hearings that were held at each of the settlements of the affected region; the transcripts ran to over 6,000 pages. From these, three statements by politically articulate natives—Phillip Blake, René Lamothe, and Frank T'Seleie—were selected for inclusion in *Dene Nation*.

Two papers in *Dene Nation*, "The Distribution of Economic Benefits from a Pipeline" by John F. Helliwell, outside consultant, and "Aboriginal Rights" by C. Gerald Sutton, legal counsel for the IB-NWT, were not part of the Berger hearings. Also, two position documents have been included: the "Dene Declaration," passed at the second Joint General Assembly of the Indian Brotherhood and Metis Association of the NWT on July 19, 1975, and the proposal of October 25, 1976, for an "Agreement in Principle between the Dene Nation and Her Majesty the Queen, in Right of Canada."

Dene Nation is not the "Voice of the People." No more than any other set of citizens, the Dene people as a totality do not comprehend all of the issues confronting them nor hold uniform opinions on all of them. Nor does the volume give a sense of the differing political stances and strategies of the Indian Brotherhood, the Metis Association, COPE, and ITC or of the disaccords that have arisen within each of these organizations. These observational asides in no way diminish the value of *Dene Nation* in providing cogent analyses and official IB-NWT position statements on the profound problems and great issues that shadow the future of the native peoples of the Northwest Territories.

Experiences, conditions, and issues arising from the economic, social, political, and cultural subordination of the Dene to institutions and forces of the "outside" world—national and international—form the theme of the presentations. (The following review is selective.) Charley Snowshoe's account of "A Trapper's Life" encapsulates one man's experience. As a teenager he returned to Fort McPherson from the Aklavik residential school and began to learn trapping from his dad. Finding summertime wage labor, he married in 1960, "but in 1970 I started thinking about wages." After going to an "upgrading school" he got an office job.

That's when they started coming in with these low-rental housing and welfare. The people, the native people of the North, were independent until you brought in that low-rental housing, and that's where we first got sucked into that business. They subsidized the oil, the gas, taking our own houses away from us, moving us from where we used to be, where we could cut wood for ourselves in town. We were working every day then, not like today. That's the start of spoiling people. I was one of them.

Charley Snowshoe was "kicked out of school . . . for saying 'Go to hell' to the supervisor." A young Metis, Bob Overvold, renders the same judgment on the Euro-Canadian school system in more encompassing terms:

By having "successfully" (I use the term with tongue in cheek) gone through the school system I have become almost totally conditioned to fit into southern society. On the other hand, what these many years have taken away from me has caused irrevocable damage to me as a Dene: it has caused a split between my parents and myself that may never be healed; it has caused me to lose my Dene language; and, most significantly, has left me in somewhat of a limbo—not quite fitting into Dene society and not quite fitting into white society.

As young native officeholders, George Barnaby, George Kurszewski, and Gerry Cheezie document the frustration of their efforts to affect territorial and local levels of government. Wilf Bean, a former government employee, explains why local electorates have no voice in or control over the political and economic affairs of their communities: the much-vaunted Local Government Program that began in 1968–69 is structured simply and singly to extend the administration control of the territorial government over the local units.

The anguished and sometimes angry testimonies to the subordination of the Dene to the forces and imperatives of the greater system deal with immediate and urgent issues. Michael Asch's article provides a historical dimension. His analysis concentrates on the economic relationships between the Dene and the greater world. He succinctly documents his thesis that "the genesis of many problems for Native people was the fact that, unbeknownst to them, the relationship with the fur trade in the period after 1870 created an exchange in which they received immediate material well-being in return for economic dependency on outside agents: a dependency which became reality after the collapse of the fur trade and which has been maintained through post-war government intervention." He also warns of the illusory nature of the "benefits" stemming from a short-term boom in wage labor offered by pipeline construction.

A fine piece of research is Scott Rushforth's analysis of the economic significance of "country food" in the local community. Reckoning its "replacement value" (i.e., the cost of equivalent meat at local store prices), Rushforth demonstrates that from June 1974 to May 1975 $186,000 to $200,000 worth of game and fish from the land fed the 350 Indians of Fort Franklin and their working dogs. Unfortunately, though obviously known to him, Rushforth bypasses the opportunity to drive home the significance of "replacement value" in light of the assessment by Gemini North for its employer, Canadian Arctic Gas Pipeline, of the economic viability of the Fort Franklin community. In Gemini's report, the *value in kind* [my emphasis] of game resources from Fort Franklin for the 1970/71 season was estimated at about $3,238" (Gemini North Ltd., 1974, 2:222). Since Gemini North does not provide a figure on the pounds of game taken, it is difficult to comprehend the base for the dollar figure arrived at. Taking Rushforth's 1974–75 estimate of 34,700 pounds of edible moose and caribou taken by the Fort Franklin people, the "value in kind" offered by Gemini North comes out to approximately 10¢ per pound. This kind of reckoning makes it easy to adjudge many of the small native-dominant communities of the North to be economically unviable.

Arvin D. Jelliss addresses the other end of the economic spectrum in his inquiry into where the economic rents accruing to natural resources in the Northwest Territories have gone. The figures on the natural gas enterprise at Pointed Mountain in the southwestern Northwest Territories speak for themselves: up to 1976 (and at that year's values) the rents from the Pointed Mountain project amounted to $66.3 million. Of these, "United States consumers received . . . 76.5 percent in the form of undervalued gas prices, Canadian entities in British Columbia received . . . 22.5 percent in the form of excess transmission charges, and the federal government received $0.6 million or 0.8 percent from royalties." Compared with total construction phase outlays of approximately $15 million, local Indian income from wage labor on the project added up to somewhere between $96,000 and $125,000, most of which immediately returned, through purchases, to the "outside."

Political predilections aside, it is small wonder that the word "colonialism" recurs in these writings. Mel Watkins's analysis of Canada's history as an underdeveloped region providing staple exports to serve the needs of more advanced industrial areas places the Northwest Territories situation in broader perspective. The thrust of his paper is an argument in support of the official IB–NWT position of "alternative development"—the call for a "two-sector economy" with a nonrenewable resource sector under white ownership but subject to Dene control and a renewable resource sector under Dene ownership and control. Such a goal can be effected only by having in native hands the power to protect their own land.

C. Gerald Sutton argues that the treaties made with Indian peoples of the North American continent "are not treaties of cession of sovereignty but treaties ceding rights to land in sense of property rights only." His argument buttresses the IB–NWT position that not only have native rights in the full sense not been extinguished but are unextinguishable. In Peter H. Russell's analysis, there is nothing in the British North America Act that precludes legislative recognition of collective Dene title to the land and "devolution of governmental responsibility" to Dene institutions, these being "the two basic instruments" that the IB–NWT proposes to secure the survival of the Dene as a distinct people of a nation within the Canadian state. These are the political issues that the two final selections in the volume address. Georges Erasmus, president of the IB–NWT, calls for "'Dene government' within confederation"; this requires setting up "our own system with political juris-diction over a defined land base." The issues informing this proposition are set forth formally in the "Agreement in Principle between the Dene Nation and Her Majesty the Queen, in Right of Canada," the proposal presented to the government and people of Canada on October 25, 1976.

The recommendations of Mr. Justice Berger and especially the National Energy Board against the construction of the Mackenzie Valley pipeline shifted the whole issue of environmental and social impact from the North-west Territories and swung hydrocarbon interests and the government to promote an Alaska Highway–Yukon route. A skeptic may suspect that this is a move of simple expediency in that the fewer natives and other groups fear-ful of despoliation of land and lifeways in the Yukon Territory are seen as too weak to muster the resistance that the groups concerned with the Northwest Territories did. However, it must be recognized that the native associations of the Northwest Territories were not against the pipeline or development per se. Their strategy was to use that immediate economic and energy issue as a lever to achieve their basic claims.

[Writing this review in the late 1970s, I ended with a query:] The ques-tion remains whether or to what extent the Canadian government will re-spond to the call from native groups, and echoed in the Berger report, to

negotiate in good faith a new and unique kind of recognition and implementation of the rights of indigenous peoples in their homeland.

from [Review of] **Dene Nation: The Colony Within,**
edited by Mel Watkins, 1978

*The government did respond to the call. See Update 2000 at the end of the chapter on
the progress toward the implementation of indigenous rights.*

DENE DEPENDENCY AND DENE SELF-DETERMINATION

*The material reviewed so far came mainly from the presentations by the IB-NWT at the
formal hearings of the MVPI. That which follows draws on the community hearings.
E. R. Weick, an economist in the Department of Indian Affairs, was attached to the
Berger Commission for the entire span of its activities. Ed Weick's gift to me of his complete set of the community hearings transcripts enabled me to write the following study.*

THE DENE TESTIFY

From March 1975 to October 1976 Mr. Justice Berger, as commissioner of
the MVPI, took testimony relating to the potential environmental, economic, and social impact of the construction and operation of a pipeline and
energy corridor through the Northwest Territories. (See Gamble [1978] for
a summary of the inquiry process.) Formal hearings involved sworn testimony and submissions from the applicant pipeline companies, an environmental organization, white business and other special interest groups, and the
several native organizations of the Northwest Territories. Of special interest,
however, are the informal community hearings, which were held in almost
every community in the western Northwest Territories and at which all local persons were invited to speak. This record runs to over 6,000 pages of
transcript.

The community hearings provided a forum for the enunciation of Dene
experiences, values, concerns, and fears by the Dene themselves. Beyond specific questions about and positions on the proposed pipeline, the Dene spoke
to several broader themes: personal, cultural, and regional histories; accounts
of life on the land and love of the land; anxieties over and evidence of damage
to the renewable resources of the land by "development" activities; knowledge of, experiences with, and attitudes toward white culture and society in
general and government in particular; economic worries; present and anticipated social problems such as alcohol abuse; circumstances and understandings at the signings of Treaty; inherent rights as human beings; Indian ab-

original rights; and affirmation of the IB-NWT position: no development without settlement of Indian land claims. Many of the testimonies richly reveal Dene perceptions of the erosion of the self-sufficient structure of action of their community-societies.

"The Olden Days"   Pat Bugghins, a Treaty Indian in his midfifties, testifies, through an interpreter, at the community hearing held at the small Indian enclave in the town of Hay River:

> [The people] used to make their living off the land. . . . When they wanted to go some place or they want to go in the bush, they never used to wait for somebody to help them. . . .
>
> In them days there used to be about 20 or 25 families get together, those married people used to get together and they used to take their family out in the bush and that's where they used to make their living, right off the bush.
>
> In those bunch there used to be about four or five good hunters and those five good hunters used to be a good Welfare to [their] own people. He [the hunter] used to be a good Welfare because he's keeping everybody well-fed because they're doing the hunting for them. (MVPI-CH, 6:499)

Hay River is now [1976] a town of over 3,000 persons, 90 percent of them "others." Ted Bugghins, a kinsman of the first speaker, describes what it was like before World War II, before Hay River became the terminus of the gravel "all-weather highway" from the South.

> There's a priest and there's Hudson's Bay manager, that's all the white man used to be in Hay River. You never heard no people complaining about being broke all summer. Right from springtime till in the fall, people used to have money all the time and the people, they used to live real good. Not like today.
>
> They never used to have Welfare in them days. If you were going to take your family in the bush, you used to go to Hudson's Bay Store and that's where you'd get all your supplies from.
>
> I look at it today now. If anybody wanted to go in the bush, well he's got to go across and see the Welfare and they got to look around so somebody

can pay for their charter plane. The only way the people can take their family in the bush these days is somebody's got to pay for their charter plane, the plane's got to make two trips out in the bush before they can move.

If you want to know what done that to the people, I'll let you know right now. White man done that to the people. White man made the people more poor than what they used to be in the olden days. (MVPI-CH, 6: 491–92, through interpreter)

Fred Andrew, a well-known "old-timer" of Fort Norman, says:

I was brought up real pitiful, real poor. I am a Mountain Indian. My dad must have really loved me because he hunted for me, he went out and got rabbits for me, and fish for me. That is how he brought me up.

. . . My dad used to tell me when I was young, watch other people, how they work. And if they work good, follow them. Do as I tell you now and you will live to have a grey hair. Now I think about my dad, and I am proud of him for talking to me like that when now I know my hair is all grey. And many times I think about how my dad used to talk to me.

. . . Now the kids are going to school. They're growing up a different life from what I grew up. Even if an older person went to talk to them, they would not take that, they would not listen. (MVPI-CH, 10:887–89, through interpreter)

Whiteman Education and the Culture Gap   A grandmother, Martha Rabiska of Fort Good Hope, says:

I teached all my children how to live in the bush. They know how to make snowshoes, how to make their living in the bush. They [the people] are talking about their childrens going to school today. It's true. When a parent raised a child, this child respected his mother. Today, the childrens that are going to school outside the community, when they come back they have no respect for their mother or their dad; they have no respect for nothing. (MVPI-CH, 19:1905, through interpreter)

Elizabeth Yakaleya, another grandmother from Fort Norman, issues a poignant appeal:

[W]hen I heard . . . my grandchild, talking, and when he said "I don't know anything of their way of life in the bush," it brought tears to my eyes, but in a way it is our fault. When they go to school and come back [for] two months [in the summer], we could take them out in the bush and live out there with them and teach them our way of life, but we never do that.

. . . I am speaking to you people that's in here, the Native people, the father and mother of your childrens. Speak to your children in your old tongue, teach them the way of life at home, it is good to speak English and do the things that whitemen do, but it is good to be our own self in our own language and live the way we used to in the land. (MVPI-CH, 10:941–43, through interpreter)

Youths who have gone through the schooling system of the 1960s and 1970s frequently express resentment and anger. James Caesar of Good Hope says:

Until I was eight years old I have lived with my parents out in the bush. During those early few years of my life I have inherited my language and culture, thus I inherited the Dene way of life. . . .

Then in the summer of 1962 I was persuaded by teachers to attend school. My sister and brother and myself boarded a plane to attend the Sir Alexander Mackenzie School and was a resident at Grollier Hall, a Roman Catholic hostel at Inuvik. At that time I did not know any words in English or other foreign languages. Most of the punishments, discomforts and frustrations imposed upon me were because of my language and culture. I think partly because of the colour of my skin. I was too stubborn to stop being a Dene.

I attended school there for two years during which time I learned very little of value. I then decided to remain home for the '64–'65 school year to get away from the whiteman's system. Even then I learned that my decision was not to go on undebated because my parents were threatened by teachers and local government people, that if I stayed, they would forfeit any more Government aid. (MVPI-CH, 18:1820)

Between these youth and the older Dene, the generation gap becomes a culture gap. Roy Fabien documents this change from his own life:

I'm a young native Indian [born in 1951]. I've got an education, I've got a job with the government, and there is one thing that people, like O.K., most of the native people say, "O.K, we got to grow up our children so that we can use them when they grow up and they can fight for us."

I grew up here in Hay River. I went to school until I was about 16, and then I quit, then about three years later I went back to Fort Smith for the Adult Education program and I got my Grade 11 . . . and I worked in Smith for one year.

But since I was about 16–17 years old I been travelling around trying to figure out, you know, where I'm at, what I can do for my people; and so I thought like if I got this education then I would be able to do something for them.

But—and then so I come back to Hay River, I came back here last year after spending about five years out of Hay River and thinking that, "Here are my people and I'm going to try and help them through education."

So I come back and I find that people don't accept me as I am. They expected me to come back as the way I was five years ago, not the way—they really can't accept me as I am because they either can't accept the changes I went through or it's something else. I can't understand what it is.

So I'm not really accepted back into the culture, maybe because I lost the knowledge of it. So now I'm sort of—and then I can't really get into the white society because I'm the wrong color. Like, there's very very few white people that will be friends with native people. Any of these white people that are friends with native people, it's, you know, it's like a pearl in a pile of gravel.

For myself, I find it very hard to identify with anybody because I have nobody to turn to. My people don't accept me any more because I got an education, and the white people won't accept me because I'm not the right color. So like, a lot of people keep saying, "O.K., we've got to educate these native—these young native people so that they can become something." But what good is it if the person has no identity? (MVPI-CH, 6: 557–58)

A Package of Dependency   The personal history of Mary Rose Drybone, a woman in her midthirties, encapsulates experiences common to her generation. She, like a number of the Dene testifying, offers analysis and indictment of the package of dependency delivered to the northern natives.

The school was built here [Fort Good Hope] in 1952. That year I was nine years old. I never spoke nor understood no English at all. When I started going to school I didn't like going to school at all because it was a great change compared to living in the bush with my parents. One reason I didn't like the school was because I couldn't speak English.

When you are in the bush like a family everybody takes part in doing the everyday chores. My dad would go to visit his traplines by dog team. There was no such things as skidoos [snowmobiles], and then my mother would be busy tanning hides and us children would cut wood or haul some clean snow for cooking and drinking water. There was no danger of pollution in those days.

[Tuberculosis] got the best of my father and I am proud at this moment to say that my father is a real—or was a real Dene. Because he made his living off the land for us. There was no Welfare at that time. He died in 1953 but left a memory for me and my brother to be a true Dene and we are still and we'd like to keep it that way.

. . . [The witness, her mother, and her brother had also contracted TB.] So after a year in the hospital I went to the mission school as mother and brother had to go to the [Charles Camsell] hospital in Edmonton for better medical treatment in order to survive the deadly sickness.

I went to school in Aklavik for three years and four years here [Fort Good Hope]. All that time I never saw . . . my mother and brother for five years. I was very lonely but [back at Good Hope] I was still happy because I was still living in the bush, a life on the Dene land with my uncle and aunt, they took care of me.

I went to the bush and the fish camp. Those days everybody was out in the bush where they belonged. Very few people stayed in town. Then in 1958 the Government program slowly crept into this community. Like the hostels, whiteman's education, low rental houses, and, the worst of them all, alcohol and Welfare.

You think the Dene beg on their knees for those programs? No way. The so-called Government threw it at us and we accepted their trick.

. . . Mr. Berger, I am the social worker for this community. I started to work on March the 19th, 1974. . . . After I worked a year, let me tell you I have never seen anything like it. This program was made up in the whiteman's way. We Dene people have no say in it. Everything about social development is policy here, policy there, and the boss, the so-called whiteman or Government in Inuvik whom I am working for, I think expect they could give me orders. I ignore them because I am a Dene and I know the Dene problems. I have no intentions to hurt and destroy my people. They have been hurt too many times in the past and the present by the Government. I tell them, you are in Inuvik, you do your own thing, and I'll do mine. (MVPI-CH, 20:1939–43)

Subordination Paul Andrew, the young chief of the Fort Norman Band, points out that the recent innovation of "local government" undermines the Indian band council system and is illusory besides:

I was . . . one of the very few fortunate native people [in that] I was able to secure a job with the Territorial Government . . . [as] Settlement Secretary. One of the terms of reference of that particular job was to work for the Territorial Government. Pardon me, I mean work for the Settlement Council but get paid by the Territorial Government. That by itself indicates the type of struggle [confusion] that can exist in a position such as this.

It was quite obvious also that this whole Settlement Council system has never worked and never will work because it is a form of tokenism to the Territorial Government. And an Advisory Board, whose advice [is] not usually taken. . . .

[I]t seems like one of the aims of the Territorial Government was to create a conflict among the native communities that already had an existing governing body, such as Band Councils, by introducing the Settlement Council. . . .

The frustrations that I found [in] the position was that I was told that I was working for the people. But I was continuously getting orders from the Regional Office. They were the ones that finally decided what would happen and what would not happen. (MVPI-CH, 10:875–76)

The proliferation of installations for the transient white bureaucratic elite in what were once fur post and mission stations renders visible the subordination of the Indian community to the national system and its agents. Phillip Blake says:

I am a Treaty Indian from Fort McPherson. I have worked as a social worker here in Fort McPherson here for the past five and a half years. . . .

I am not an old man, but I have seen many changes in my life. Fifteen years ago, most of what you see as Fort McPherson did not exist. Take a look around the community now. And you will start to get an idea of what has happened to the Indian people here over the past few years.

Look at the housing where transient Government staff live. And look at the housing where the Indian people live. Look at which houses are connected to the utilidor. Look at how the school and hostel, the R.C.M.P. and government staff houses are right in the center of town. Dividing the Indian people into two sides.

Look at where the Bay [Hudson's Bay Company] store is, right on top of the highest point of land.

Mr. Berger, do you think that this is the way the Indian people chose to have this community? Do you think the people here had any voice in planning this community? (MVPI-CH, 12:1078)

Scores of testimonies bear witness to the erosion of societal self-sufficiency and self-determination. This final selection from the testimony of Robert Clement, a young Treaty Indian of Fort Norman, captures the range of issues.

There are so many pressures on the people nowadays, and everything has to be done right away. The pipeline, the gas line, the [proposed Great Bear

River hydroelectric] dam. The government wants the people to get snowed under.

If we did have enough time on our own, we could work it out together on our own feet. If we had as much time now as the government has, to try to brainwash us, we could work it out and get ourselves back together.

Now the government tells us that they want the pipeline right now. Right this day Arctic Gas is out drilling along the proposed route. The Government must still think we are brainwashed because they think we still agree with the pipeline.

There is no way.

I remember a few years ago, people lived in their homes, they got their own wood and hauled their own water. People were happier then. When they didn't have to depend on the government all of the time. We were happier then and we could do it again.

But look what has happened. Now the government gives the people everything, pays for the water and the fuel and the houses, the education. It gives the people everything, everything but one thing. The right to live their own lives.

And that is the only thing that we really want, is to control our lives, our own land. (MVPI-CH, 10:897)

Some of the concern expressed in these testimonies over the loss of a self-sufficient system of action takes the form of a seemingly too rosy retrospective view of living off the land. But the Dene are aware that the actualities of the hunting-trapping life involve many hardships and preclude many comforts. Alfred Lennie of Fort Norman asks: "Why should our kids get educated and go sit on the lake and set a fish net and freeze their fingers when they have got education? Why should they do it? . . . Nobody's going to . . . put on a pair of snowshoes and tramp snow down and set traps in forty or fifty below weather when he has got education" (MVPI-CH, 10:963). The point is, of course, not that most Dene reject the comforts and entertainments of monetized urbanism per se (for they are like most of the world in this respect) but that many have come to recognize that, to date, the price has been loss of decision about and control over their own lives. Life on the land symbolizes a more autonomous, less harassed existence. In the judgment of Chief Gerry Cheezie of Fort Smith, "I think the feeling of the people you [Mr. Berger] have talked to throughout these communities say that they want some kind of development but a controlled development; not something that is imposed by somebody else. . . . They're saying that for once . . . we've got to have a chance to decide what we want for ourselves" (MVPI-CH, 33:3229).

STRUGGLE AND PARADOX

As the Dene look to the future, self-determination—economic, cultural, political—is the core issue. On October 25, 1976, the IB-NWT submitted to the federal government a position paper in the form of an "Agreement in Principle between the Dene Nation and Her Majesty the Queen, in Right of Canada." In the scope and inclusiveness of the formulations in this statement, the Dene bypassed the constraints of the existent Canadian political structure, rejected "the tradition in Canada that [native] rights must be extinguished," and drove to the heart of the economic, social, and cultural issues they deem vital to their continuation as "a People."

In the name of "the Dene Nation," the IB-NWT called upon the Government of Canada to negotiate with the Dene according to principles set forth in the agreement. These principles include the right to recognition, self-determination, and self-definition as Dene; the right to practice and preserve their languages, traditions, and values; the right to develop their own institutions and enjoy their rights as a people in the framework of their own institutions; the right to retain ownership of so much of their traditional lands; and, under such terms, the right to insure social and economic independence and self-reliance. To these ends the agreement calls for, "within [the] Confederation [of Canada], a Dene government with jurisdiction over a geographical area and over subject matters now within the jurisdiction of either the Government of Canada or the Government of the Northwest Territories."

In essence, the preferred "Agreement in Principle" proposes for the Dene people collectively an extent of self-governance over their land, lives, and fortunes unparalleled in the history of Indian "claim settlements" in North America. The mode, means, and procedures by which this self-governance would be realized are not specified. If attained (in whatever specific form), the paradox remains, however, that Dene self-determination will necessarily be phrased within the context of the nation-state in which the Dene are embedded. Dene government will have to be structured as a countervailing system, not as a free choice of polity. The formation and structure of the IB-NWT itself reflects the working of these forces. Created in response to the pressures and demands of the national system, the IB-NWT's organization and programs have been developed in reaction to that system and in some ways constrained by it as well. As one consequence, a "class" of IB-NWT officers and activists, mostly young and with advanced schooling, emerged from the Dene populace. In time, within that group disaccord regarding strategy and procedures developed and culminated in a rupture over leadership.

The Dene Nation is itself an emergent polity construct conceived as a counterpoise to the forces of the national system. In the internal affairs of traditional life, there was no overarching Dene polity or tribal polities in the sense of coordinated political authority within the several major linguistic-territorial sectors. In critical contrast to the present day, few issues of consequence had to be faced or decided upon by a group as a whole.

The testimonies at the community hearings have documented the extent to which [since 1950] decisions critically affecting Indian life have been made and implemented by an alien society. Now, with recent changes in the national political climate, the Dene are called upon—as a single, total entity—to organize and represent themselves as an interest group in the face of the interlocked imperatives of the government, the "energy crisis," and multinational corporations. In creating a Dene polity, they are required to make decisions regarding internal structure, strategy, and goals so they can be pressed further to respond to the demands of the greater systems external to them and yet in which they are enmeshed.

How shall all those decisions be made? Who shall set policy and make decisions? What shall be the mode, means, and procedures of self-governance if some kind or degree of a "Dene government" comes into being? What will be the economic support base for such a "government," and how will that base be structured and administered? (IB-NWT leaders are aware that the Alaska Native Claims Settlement Act of 1971—the best "claims settlement" so far—came "down clearly on the side of money, not land" and that the economic and administrative structure of village and regional corporations with shareholders and an emerging managerial class "was designed to bring the natives into the mainstream of American capitalism" [Forrest 1976:18].)

Indians active in the IB-NWT or attentive to problems of the present-day and future political scene are aware of the paradox that achievement of a substantial degree of Indian economic and political self-determination threatens the sociopolitical autonomy, self-sufficiency, and consensuality in Dene life that traditionally were lodged in the local group and local community. The IB-NWT espouses the principle of full participation and agreement by all Dene in the formulation of policy. Yet in the general assemblies held by the IB-NWT, decisions are reached by the majority vote of a few score delegates drawn primarily from the elected leaders of the government-defined "Indian bands," that is, "band chiefs" and "band councillors."

In seeking strength through unification, can the ancient social values and principles based in the small-scale, intimate society be sustained, or at least satisfactorily transmuted, rather than obliterated? George Barnaby, a young Dene who resigned from the Northwest Territories Legislative Assembly in frustration with the Euro-Canadian governmental system with its imposed time tables, political hierarchy, and parliamentary rule, has pinpointed the issue:

> See the way people make decisions when a group goes hunting. They sit around in the evening and drink tea and talk about everything. They talk about the weather, they talk about where the moose might be, they talk about times they've hunted in the past. Everybody talks, everybody listens to everybody else.

> You never tell anybody that they're "out of order." It's like a group of people who live in the bush. People realize what they need and everybody talks about it. It comes out through conversation. There's no formal decisions. Nobody makes any motions. People just talk until there's a general agreement, nobody gives orders to anybody else.

> It should be the same with all Dene decisions. People should be allowed to get together to decide what they want, not everybody wants the same thing; that's fine. A true Government would be people themselves deciding what they want and then helping each other get what they want.

> . . . If we go through a whole Dene movement and we end up with native people just giving orders to their own people, we're not better off than now, when white people order us around. (*Native Press*, October 22, 1975, 12)

> *from "Indian Dependency and Self-Determination," 1980b*

Update 2000   The Dene Nation that emerged from the IB–NWT of 1975 remained the sole negotiating organization of the Indians of the Northwest Territories until 1989, when the Gwich'in regional group pursued an independent course, settling its claims with the federal and territorial governments in 1992. The Sahtu Dene and Metis of the Great Bear Lake area followed in 1993. Three other Dene regional organizations, the Deh Cho First Nations of the South Mackenzie and Liard River areas, the Dogrib Treaty 11 Council, and the Treaty 8 First Nations of Great Slave Lake and Slave River are in various stages of the process of negotiating issues around land claims, aboriginal rights, and self-governance.

From Fort Liard on January 31, 2000, Northern News Services reported: "Aboriginal leaders from around the NWT are ready to talk about a Mackenzie Valley pipeline, but they want it to be built on their terms. . . . Fort Liard Chief Harry Deneron, who initiated the meeting, was named chair of a working group that will include a delegate from each region of the NWT. . . . Future meetings will involve representatives of industry and government. . . . The challenge will be to keep the aboriginal peoples' agenda from being secondary to that of industry and government, Deneron acknowledged."

Part III | BEING DENE

As this volume developed, it fell into four parts. Chapter 1 is set apart as an introduction to emphasize what I learned through the years as an ethnologist, especially as I weighed what I learned against anthropological formulations about the social organization of hunter-gatherer peoples of the world, past and present. The chapters in part I are mainly flat-footed descriptions of kinds of community, daily life, and livelihood among the Mackenzie Dene of about half a century ago. The topics addressed in part II required more range of research, assessment, and judgment in pulling together strands of documentary and oral historical evidence— with much needed evidence missing—in order to arrive at the best, that is, most justifiable, conclusions about the course of events, actions, and circumstances throughout the contact era. The chapters in this final section, part III, attend more directly to ingredients of old-fashioned anthropological "culture" that E. B. Tylor, a father of anthropology, enunciated some 130 years ago: "knowledge, belief, art, morals, law, [and] custom." The final chapter considers two persons as they lived out their lives as Dene.

TRADITIONAL KNOWLEDGE
AND BELIEF

The title of this chapter is a gross exaggeration. The chapter barely touches on what Dene culture holds and once held as measures of meaning and understanding. Here I attend only to "three understandings" and "four legends." I selected them because they are salient features of Dene cultural holdings and because I have had occasion to think about them. Of the three understandings, "power" is by far the most deeply embedded in the traditional Dene worldview. It has implications for the understandings about blood and femaleness and about nakan and suffuses three of the four legends.

THREE UNDERSTANDINGS

POWER

Only late in my research on the Dene of the North did I explicitly concern myself with the concept of what in English is usually called "medicine" but what is better expressed as "power." The root term in Slavey and Dogrib is ink'on; Chipewyan adds a di-minutive, ink'onaze. The months at Jean Marie River, my first field site, were not evocative of material on medicine power. In part this was due to my lack of grounding in the topic, in part the shared incapacity of those who could not well handle one another's language to exchange understandings, and in part because, as Louis Nor-wegian indicated, there was not much said about power at Jean Marie River. One can often pick up on the concept of power through legends, magical stories, narrations of personal experiences, and other kinds of talk. Little of this went on at Jean Marie River, at least with the two ethnologists. Since I had no good grasp of what one might learn, when I came to explicate my field notes I fell back on the terminology of the anthropology of that period, "guardian spirit" and "shaman." These terms I came to eschew.

I now find that my efforts to comprehend what was known at Jean Marie River are not at variance with those fuller understandings that later I reached with Dogrib

friends. In fact, however, I did not attend to ink'on *in the material that Dogribs provided through the years until I took up the topic of the three prophets who arose among the Dogribs at the end of the 1960s. To understand the prophets and their understandings, I had to attend to the meanings and manifestations of* ink'on, *"power." The concept was entwined with the people's comprehension of the qualities of the three prophets (see my* Prophecy and Power among the Dogrib Indians *[1994]).*

Franz Boas (1910:336) characterized "the fundamental concept bearing on the religious life of the individual" in aboriginal North America as "the belief in the existence of magic power, which may influence the life of man, and which in turn may be influenced by human activity. In this sense magic power must be understood as the wonderful qualities which are believed to exist in objects, animals, men, spirits, or deities, and which are superior to the natural qualities of man." Before the coming of the missionaries, the Dene had no institution of church, congregation, or priest. But the people shared understandings about power. The affirmation of that knowledge for the individual comes through personal experience: one's dreams (as Louis describes below) are evidence, as well as the experience of persons cured by power and game taken through power. (Goulet [1994] and Rushforth [1992] provide rich discussions of the relationship of personal experience to knowledge among the Dene.)

This section starts at Jean Marie River (Helm 1961), where I was to gain some understanding of ink'on *from Louis Norwegian.*

In several conversations, Louis Norwegian, who at that time (1951–52) was forty-five years old, provided these understandings of power: in the old days, everybody, men and sometimes women, had medicine. It was good for curing, just like a white doctor's medicine. It was good for the hunt, too. With medicine you just think about the kind of animal you want to kill. It's pretty easy then to do so.

A man would dream that someone came and told him where to find medicine, what kind of plant was good medicine. When the man awoke, he would see an animal going away from him. That animal was the person who had talked to him in the dream. That person would come back at other times, too—like when a man was using his medicine for curing—and tell the man what to do. The animal that was seen going away was not eaten by the man. It would come in dreams and talk to the man. A man would never hunt or eat that animal. [During a brew party, Gabriel Sanguez pointed out to me with a jolly laugh that "nobody ever has moose or brew!"]

The teens were a good age to have these dreams. Sometimes a man was older than that when he dreamed the first time. A good way to get dreams was to go into the bush. Sometimes the dream visitor would give the dreamer a piece of fur or maybe a piece of moccasin. The person would keep that gift with him and sleep with it.

When a "medicine man," *dene ink'on helin*, was called on to cure, he was given payment, such as a pair of mitts or moccasins, before the curing was performed. Singing was an important part of the event, which is today called in English a "medicine sing."

As for magical tricks, Louis recalled that he saw "one old medicine sing guy" take a bullet in the palm of his hand, pull the cartridge away, and melt the lead right in his hand. When he threw the lead in the fire, it burned just as if he had thrown grease into it. He also used to take a file or any other piece of iron and work it with both hands so that it bent and then went back to its real shape without being softened.

Except for the reference to "plant(s)" as a source of power/medicine, Louis's comprehension of how power is gained is congruent with that which Vital Thomas and other Dogribs expressed to me twenty years later. Jimmy of Jean Marie River provided a view of "medicine" very different from that of Louis. I later came to the conclusion that the "medicine" that Jimmy described was Cree-style "medicine." Vital made the distinction: "The Crees handle root. They are different from Indians [that is, Dogribs, Dene]. They use roots. We don't call that *ink'on*, we call it root—*nahdi*, like a serpent or something." Dogrib Vital Thomas described an encounter with a Cree-Metis "medicine man" in his youth: "He takes a sackful of little roots and he says, 'Suppose you hunt moose, you find the tracks and can't keep up with it. Just crumble a little piece on the track and the moose will turn back, you don't have to hunt for him. Same way with fur too, just one little crumb will help you trap a thousand dollars' worth.'"

Vital's characterization of Cree-style medicine neatly fits Jimmy's descriptions: medicine is taken out of the ground. The person takes sticks, leaves, roots, stuff like that and makes them into a little bundle, maybe about a cupful. The Cree make really good medicine. A person will pay two or three hundred dollars for just a little bit. Some people around here have medicine of their own making [Dene-style?]. Old men have medicine of that kind. Medicine is good for hunting and trapping. If you are hunting a moose and use medicine, the medicine will make the moose go crazy and run right toward you, or lie down and let you come up and shoot him easily. It is not good to carry medicine when drunk because if you get mad and wish that somebody will die, then it will happen. Medicine works for whatever you want it to work for—you think about what you want, and it happens. It can be used to get a woman, but it is not good to do that, to use medicine to make a woman go crazy.

From the Dogribs, I grasped that a Dene medicine man (or woman) gets power in the way that Louis understood, that is, through a dream in which an other-than-human being comes as *ink'on* bestower, and "whether an animal comes in its own form or in human guise [in the way Louis described] it is an actual being that is there and speaking; no incorporeal essence or metaphysical entity, generic or individualized is involved" (Helm 1994:77). That being is *ink'on* and can be summoned with a song. And what one "has in his mind," what one "knows," is *ink'on*. (Vital Thomas told of another way one might gain *ink'on*. A child might encounter people in the bush and learn from them, then later find no one there, just some ptarmigans or wolves. These were the animal form of the *ink'on* bestowers.)

I recorded close to forty Dogrib stories and anecdotes about *ink'on* powers. For one thing, a person with great *ink'on* might magically transform him- or herself into an animal or manipulate physical objects. For example, the Bear Lake Chief, who died in 1913, was known as "a great medicine man, so everybody was scared of him." One time the Bear Lake Chief and companions came to an Eskimo (Inuit) camp. (Dogribs occasionally encountered Copper Eskimos in the barrens.) The others did not want to approach, but the Bear Lake Chief said that he knew (through his *ink'on*) that he could not be killed, and they went in the camp. One Eskimo started to shoot the Bear Lake Chief with a bow and arrow but found that he could not string his bow. So he threw away his bow and seized a muzzle-loader. The Bear Lake Chief cried out, "Shoot!" but the Eskimo could not, and his gun started to melt. "So you know how strong that medicine the Chief had," concluded Vital.

One great endowment of *ink'on* was the capacity to control food animals; the other was to cure. In 1962 Jimmy Fish of Rae told about a curing at which he was present. The person with curing *ink'on* was Toby Bearlake, the son of the Bear Lake Chief. Jimmy's friend Joe fell sick. Joe asked Toby Bearlake to help him, offering Toby a white fox pelt as pay. The old man began to sing and told Joe that he was sick "because of one of the girls." Joe did not want to say what he had done because, Jimmy explained, there are many people in the tent at a curing, and a person may not want to tell the truth in front of them. Jimmy had been with Joe when he had "done something wrong." Joe had had illicit sex with a girl. "The old man knew it," Jim said. "That's what he was singing." As the old man pressed Joe to confess, the girl told Joe to tell the truth. Joe then confessed, "and that old man cured him right away."

Some men have *ink'on* for hunting. (See chapter 10 about the overarching *ink'on* for the hunt possessed by the legendary *wedzitxa*.) A man who has *ink'on* for caribou may be told by his *ink'on* that a particular part of the caribou should not be eaten. "There's one man here in Rae," said Vital Thomas, "anytime he kills a caribou, no one, especially women, is going to touch the head, the heart, or the throat bones. Even that man *himself* cannot eat the throat bones. That's one thing you shouldn't laugh about. People don't like to talk about it."

From the Dogrib accounts and stories about *ink'on*, I arrived with some confidence at a formulation of traditional conceptualizations of *ink'on* that seem to have been broadly shared among the Mackenzie Dene:

> *Ink'on* is not free-floating. It is lodged in, comes from, is exercised by some being (or possibly a natural phenomenon). In this sense, in order to delimit it as an instance or an attribute, it is better in English to think of *ink'on* as "*a* power" or "*a* powerfulness" rather than as "power" unqualified by an article.
>
> From experiences with other-than-human beings of the non-Christian world—experiences that until years are gained usually must remain secret or at least veiled—*ink'on* adepts come to know something that *empowers* them to *compel* change in human beings or in circumstances that affect human beings. Although the *ink'on* adept may compel circumstance for the welfare of the individual (restoration of health) or the group (control of game animals), the potency of *ink'on* itself is not intrinsically either moral and good or maleficent. Bringing what he "knows" to bear on his own intent, the *ink'on*-endowed aims to succeed in the hunt, cure, win over an opponent in the hand game, call up the wind, trace missing travelers, combat another's *ink'on*, inflict misfortune on or kill another with *ink'on*. With one exception, the *ink'on*-endowed imposes his effects on events and conditions apart from the exercise of volition on the part of other human beings. That exception is the curing of sickness that results from breach of moral norms. In order for health to be restored, the afflicted person or another person knowledgeable of the "wrong" behavior must choose to reveal the act that the curer-adept had divined. (Helm 1994:77, 69)

BLOOD AND FEMALENESS

Early European observers judged the treatment of women among the Dene to be harsh in (unstated) comparison to that of privileged or idealized European women of their time. White men seldom missed picking up on the strictures placed on menstruating women, especially the requirement that they walk apart on snowshoes off the beaten trail when people were on the move. The restrictions added to the stock of "evidence" of the belief held in the world's cultures about the "impure" or "polluting" nature of women during their menses; this was a recurring topic in the emerging discipline of anthropology.

I had no theoretical commitments or preconceived explanations for Dene concerns about women's menstrual state or about blood in general. Making a conceptual connection between the two was no theoretical leap; it was merely that I learned that blood is dangerous as I was learning about life at Jean Marie River in the early 1950s. The same understandings were held by Dogribs and probably other tradition-minded Dene at midcentury.

The reader will not find the word "femaleness" in the dictionary. But it is femaleness that is the concern once a girl reaches the menarche. It is not gender or womanliness or femininity. What is at issue is the biological femaleness of that half of the human race at sexual maturity.

Certain beliefs and practices [in 1951–52 at Jean Marie River, "Lynx Point"] have a common underlying theme, the danger of blood and the concomitant need to handle it carefully. This anxiety regarding blood is manifested in the alacrity with which any blood from slain animals or from accidents to human beings is wiped up from the floor of the cabin. Children are thoroughly aware of the necessity of observing this practice. "Clean it up, it's not good to leave blood on the floor!" a twelve-year-old girl counseled when a scuffle between two boys in our cabin resulted in a nosebleed. One person explained that if children should urinate on blood left on the floor, "bad luck" would follow. Another stated that a woman or child would die if they stepped in the blood of an animal that had been taken through the use of "medicine."

The idea of the danger of blood must enforce in the mind the restrictions on women at the menstrual period and after parturition. All the women at Lynx Point observe the menstrual tabus. In the instance of the one woman from an acculturated trading-post family who married into the community, social pressures, especially from the matriarchs of the community, forced her conformity to this tradition.

A menstruating woman is a threat to the well-being of a male and thus sexually tabu. During her period the woman may not cross the threshold of the cabin. At Lynx Point two reasons are given for this injunction: to ignore it would bring tuberculosis to her husband and children and (apparently the more common explanation) would bring bad luck to her husband in his trapping, snaring, and hunting. In recognition of this proscription, houses are built with either a low large window or a "little door," an opening in the wall about three feet high, through which women leave the house to attend to elimination needs during their period. They either go into a brush shelter built directly around the small exit or go into the bush. They must not use the outhouse lest their blood contaminate the family. The menstrual bandages are either thrown into the fire or deposited at some distance in the bush.

During her period a woman "sits down" in one corner of the house, usually next to the special exit. She does not walk around the house, nor does she indulge in even common household tasks such as washing and cooking. Her activities are restricted to such small immobile pursuits as needlework. If a couple has no children of a helpful age, the entire burden of woman's work such as preparing dog food, fetching water, washing clothes, and cooking devolves upon the husband. [One husband, scrubbing diapers while his wife embroidered, exclaimed to me, "Mary sit down. By gosh, too much work!"] On her first menses, the adolescent girl moves into a tent. In the present day her stay is limited to the number of days of her period. A female relative may stay with her if the tent is any distance in the bush. [In Rae in the 1960s some Dogrib mothers attempted to meet the rule of isolation of daughters at menarche by bringing the girls to the hospital.]

Again, during and after childbirth the discharge of blood imposes restrictions on a woman and her husband. Some Lynx Point women still retire to a separate tent, even in midwinter, for parturition and the recuperation period. After childbirth, as during her menses, a woman "sits down," remaining in one corner of the dwelling for as long as any bleeding continues. Sexual abstinence by husband and wife is observed during this period.

Two other interdictions on women, not directly involving blood but concerned with the idea of the threat of femaleness, are actively observed. These are tabus against a woman stepping on or over a man's rifle or his cap. The rationale again is that these actions will bring him bad luck in hunting. In reference to these tabus it may be worth noting that the rifle is not only an objectively important possession for hunting but is commonly employed as a phallic symbol in joking conversations. Although no such clear-cut analogic expression was observed in regard to the man's cap, certain behavior and attitudes suggest that the cap is a more or less covert symbol of masculinity and manhood.

from MacNeish, "Contemporary Folk Beliefs of a Slave Indian Band," 1954

Ethnographic reports on Northern Athapaskans usually have references in English to "bushmen," "bad Indians," or, as at Jean Marie River, "spies." (See Basso [1978] for a compilation of the literature.) Among the Mackenzie Dene the common designation in their own languages, as recorded by English or French reporters, is nak'ane, nakani, nahgan, naqane, nakan, *or other variant. Here I have employed* nakan.

Of all the extant aboriginal folklore [in 1951–52] at Lynx Point [Jean Marie River], the belief in *nakan* [Dogrib *nàhgan*] was one of the liveliest in terms of the amount of attention directed toward it. The *nakan* are mysterious people who are believed to roam the bush in the summer. When speaking of them in English, people at Lynx Point generally use the word "spy." Indeed, both Indian and white "spies" are believed to exist. The latter are in some instances identified as actual foreign agents or soldiers such as Russians. In general discussion, however, no distinction is made between the behavior of Indian *nakan* and white "spies." The description of behavior appears to apply to both varieties, Indian and white. At Lynx Point some Dogrib Indians are identified as being *nakan*. Similarly, a group of Indian *nakan* live near Fort Nelson in British Columbia, but they are said to have roamed as far north as Fort Wrigley.

Nakan are to be feared only in the summer. During the winter months they live underground "like bears," subsisting on the meat they dried the previous summer. They also lay in a wood supply for the winter, kept, with their meat, inside their subterranean dwellings. The only external evidence of these lairs is the smoke from their fires, which issues from a small hole in the ground. *Nakan* stay underground all winter; thus no tracks belonging to them are ever seen in the snow. One old man of the community once came upon the sign of a *nakan* dwelling in winter: he saw smoke coming out of a hole in the ground. He departed immediately but did not mention his experience until spring.

With the advent of spring, when the growth of foliage renders visibility in the bush very poor, *nakan* emerge from their winter lairs. Sometimes they travel alone, but usually they are in groups of six or seven. There are no women *nakan*, only men who prowl through the bush and, hidden by dense foliage, spy on villages, seeking to capture women and children. In response to a question, one man surmised that they must all be young men because "they try to find the girl, I don't think old men do that." Although they desire women for sexual purposes, this aim apparently does not extend to the children they abduct. They merely want children because the *nakan* are "not married."

Informants had never "heard" of *nakan* killing a man, although in former days men would occasionally kill a *nakan*. Indeed, men today may pursue *nakan* to frighten them away from the village. One man stated that sometimes, when men trail a *nakan*, they find the tracks leading to an underground dwelling where the *nakan* has fled. If one man remains at the *nakan* lair after the other men depart, "sometimes *nakan* coming up again." At this point in the narration, there was nervous laughter and a reference to being "shy." It seems likely that the *nakan* would attack the man sexually, but the speaker was too embarrassed to say so directly.

Nakan sometimes make their presence known in the bush by whistling, especially to women. Men often identify a *nakan's* presence by coming across strange boot or shoe tracks in the bush. Unlike ordinary Indians, *nakan* seem always to wear hard-soled footgear rather than moccasins. And unlike Indians, they do not keep dogs.

Forest fires are sometimes attributed to *nakan*. These forest fires develop from the signal fires that a *nakan* lights to communicate with a "partner" who then answers him with another smoke signal. Certain recent forest fires have been thus attributed to this activity of *nakan*, because boot tracks were found in the vicinity of the fire.

It seems that *nakan* are credited with no real supernatural powers, yet certain of their attributes and activities set them apart from ordinary people. Indeed, some of the attributes puzzle people. Where do *nakan* get their rifles, boots, clothing, and other equipment? How do they manage to survive the mosquitoes as they roam the bush in the summer? One man surmised that they must have some sort of insect repellent.

That the fear of *nakan* is lively in most women and children is evidenced by the fact that, though intrepid in entering the bush alone in winter, they are timorous of it in summer. [Nancy Lurie was on a berrying expedition with Dogrib women at Wha Ti when one sighted a *nakan* and came stampeding out of the bush.] Children generally do not go into the bush in the warm months unless accompanied by adults, nor do the women enter it alone. On several occasions, Teresa and I were requested by a child or an adult woman to accompany that person on some task that required entering the bush. [In the summer of 1952, when Teresa and I were preparing to camp out overnight in the bush at a small distance from the settlement of Jean

Marie River, I jokingly asked Louis Norwegian if he thought *nakan* might get us. Louis replied, with some seriousness, I think, "I don't think *nakan* want white woman." So much for our usefulness in Louis's view! But Irene Sabourin, Jimmy Sanguez's mother-in-law, came unasked to lend us her .22.]

People report experiences that they or others of their acquaintance have had with *nakan*. Marcel told of encountering a *nakan* in his youth while he was tracking moose. The *nakan* was sitting on a log with his back to the hunter. He "looked awful, like a Cree half-breed. He had a beard and a scarf tied around his head." Marcel quietly departed, though he hid in a tree later when he heard sounds that he thought might be those of the *nakan*.

The disappearance of a twelve-year-old boy from a neighboring Slavey settlement about four years ago is generally attributed to abduction by *nakan*. The child was camping with an adult relative in the bush in the spring. The man left the camp for a while, and when he returned the boy was gone. Men from both communities aided in the search and followed the boy's trail for some distance. The trail eventually disappeared, and, after that point, it is surmised, *nakan* captured him. Subsequent reports filtered back to the relatives that the boy was seen in the vicinity of Fort Nelson.

One Lynx Point member was attacked by a *nakan* when he wandered, intoxicated, into the bush. He returned home bruised and battered, and the next day the men found the scene of the struggle where the bush was trampled and torn up and the tracks of the *nakan* were discovered. The wife of the assaulted man has several times reported hearing *nakan* in the bush or espied them peering through the window. A fruitless pursuit on the part of the men usually follows such a report.

In the summer of 1952 news came down the Mackenzie River via the riverboats that a group of white "spies," wearing uniforms, had been seen by an Indian tending his rabbit snares. The local Slaveys there organized a search posse, but, after considering the possibility that the "spies" might put up a fight, they thought better of their project and returned home. Among the recipients of the rumor there were speculations that the "spies" might be Russians.

The belief in *nakan* has a well-documented history among the interior Athapaskans. In earlier days, could it have had grounding in reality, in surreptitious wife-stealing and raiding practices? One long-time white settler, Poole Field (n.d.), recorded the actual killing of a *nakan* by a band of Mountain Indians with whom he was traveling near the headwaters of the Nahanni River around the year 1905. After several days of being trailed by *nakan*, a member of the Mountain Indian party shot one of the *nakan*. His bloody trail was followed some distance, and it was evident that the other *nakan* were carrying the wounded individual. Later a married woman of the band confessed that the "Liard Chief's son" was her lover and that it was probably his party that were the *nakan*. Field subsequently verified her supposition—it was her lover who had been wounded, and he died a few months later.

from MacNeish, "Contemporary Folk Beliefs of a Slave Indian Band," 1954

FOUR LEGENDS

From my records I have chosen these four examples from oral tradition because they probably have been the most widespread throughout Denendeh and are best known to people individually. The first presentation is three episodes in the myth cycle of "Always Walking," who changed landscape features and animals into their present aspects. The Copper Woman, the second legend, is again a mythic explanation (of the "copper mines" Hearne sought) and perhaps a lesson in human relationships. The third, the tradition of the girl who mated with a dog, is found in other Dene people's story inventories, but as narrated here it tells of the origin of the Dogrib tribe. The fourth legend, "The Captive Woman," is based on documented events of 1714 and 1715 and treats of the coming of the white man and the fur trade to the Dene.

A possible candidate for inclusion was the story cycle laid in early contact times that stars Ehts'ontsia, a magically empowered hero who defends his people and attacks Cree enemies. Gabriel Sabourin (Slavey) and Vital Thomas (Dogrib) told me parts of the Ehts'ontsia saga. Many stories in the cycle, told by Madeleine Mouse, Charlie Cholo, Julian Hardisty, and Ginger Villeneuve, were collected by Robert G. Williamson (1956) at Fort Simpson in 1952.

ALWAYS WALKING

The Dene divisions share the episodic saga of the Two Brothers who moved through Denendeh creating features of the land and changing the relationships between people and animals. (Petitot's compilation [1888] of Dene traditions offers Gwich'in, Hare, Dogrib, and Chipewyan legends about the Two Brothers.) The mythic stories emphasize one of the brothers, the one called Yampa Deja by Slaveys, Yamonzhah by Dogribs, and Yamoria by Sahtu Dene (Sahtuot'ine/Bearlake Dene).

In English, these names have been variously translated as "Always Walking," "Always Moving," "Around the World," and "Walks around the World." George Blondin (1990, 1996) and, drawing on lore known to old Madeleine Mouse, Robert Williamson (1955) are major sources for episodes in the exploits of Always Walking. Christopher Hanks (1997) relates archaeological and physiographic features of the land to the Yamoria cycle of the Sahtu Dene, as do Thomas Andrews, John Zoe, and

Aaron Herter (1998) for Yamonzhah of Dogrib legend. Here is a sampler of stories about Always Walking.

Old Gath-lia's Tale of Yampa Deja   *When I met Angus Sherwood in Norman Wells in the early 1950s he was probably in his late sixties. I am sorry to say I know very little about his life. As a trapper-trader, he and his wife had lived for many years in the northern bush of British Columbia before settling in the Northwest Territories about 1924. Angus Sherwood's letter introduces Always Walking through an account of Gath-lia, a Slavey "medicine man." Angus writes:*

During the winter of 1925 I had Joe Hope and Methe, an old Mountain Indian, fishing at Fish Lake about 60 miles from Fort Simpson. John Hope and I made several trips by dog team to bring fish home. Old Gath-lia and his wife were living there at the lake. They were living in a pole and brush lodge, dressed in the old rabbitskin clothing. Joe and I would visit with the old couple but could not stay long. The weather was cold and their small fire would not keep us warm. When Gath-lia came to our tent which had a stove, he could not stand the heat and would sit outside and have his head through the flap. He would tell us of the old days and of "Yampa Deja" which Joe Hope translated as "Always Walking."

Gath-lia was reputed to be a very strong medicine man and had done some wonderful things. He was old and feeble when I knew him and loved the old ways. I knew, as he did, that it was his last winter. I offered to bring him and the old wife into the fort for care but he said no. He wanted to die in the way of his fathers. He died by the camp fire as the spring thaw came. We buried him there. The old wife wanted to stay there alone but we brought her to the settlement where she died shortly after. They were about the last of the old primitives who did things the old way and lived in the bush the year around. They were fine people and I doubt if there was any evil in Gath-lia's medicine. He and "Old Francis" of Fort Liard were really a good influence among their people, as much so as a good Christian clergyman is with his flock.

On a clear night Gath-lia pointed to the Big Dipper and showed us one of the stars in the Dipper's handle that has a smaller star showing to one side. He said that the Indians had long lines of caribou snares, set in gaps of a brush fence like the Slave Indians do for rabbits. An evil spirit in the form of a big raven robbed the snares and the people were starving. "Always Walking" heard of their troubles and came to help. He dressed in caribou skins and waited in a snare. The raven flew over low to look at the caribou and "Always Walking" shot an arrow into his tail. This threw the raven out of balance and he could only fly in an upward spiral. The raven reached the Big Dipper and that is the double star we see today.

Gath-lia said that is why Indian children catch bulldog flies alive each summer and push small straws into their tails and release them. They always spiral upwards and go to the stars as did the raven.

from a letter from Angus Sherwood, February 21, 1956

Gath-lia was the father-in-law of Louis Norwegian's uncle. He performed a medicine sing over one of Louis's sisters when she was a little girl. Louis recalled one curing performance by old Gath-lia in which he sucked out some blood and spat it in his hand. There was something all twisted like a hair or a worm in the blood. It was alive and moved in his hand.

Louis Norwegian's Recall of Yampa Deja   *As a boy, Louis Norwegian heard stories about Yampa Deja from Old Sanguez of Jean Marie River, but he had not heard stories for many years. In 1952 Louis recalled this from Old Sanguez's lore.*

In the old days the animals used to eat people. That was before the two brothers made a trip from Great Slave Lake to the Arctic Ocean. These brothers started out from Great Slave Lake when they were young men and followed the Mackenzie River downstream. One went along one side of the river, and the other went along the other side. They did not see each other until they reached the ocean. By the time they had finished the trip they were both old men, so old that they leaned on sticks as they walked. As they made their journey they "fixed" the animals so they would not eat men; they fixed the fish too. In Louis's account:

The moose used to eat people. One of the brothers [Yampa Deja] went to talk to the moose. He gave the moose some willow. He asked the moose, "How did that taste?" The moose said, "Pretty nice." He told the moose, "You better eat willow after this." The moose never ate people after that. Also, there was a bird, an eagle, that used to eat people. The brother climbed up into the nest. There were two baby birds there. He threw one baby out of the nest. Then a storm came, lots of thunder and lightning. The baby bird said, "That's my father coming." ("Father comes," say Indians when a big storm comes up.) After the storm, the father bird came. Then there was another storm, with thunder and lightning. "That's my mother coming." The mother bird came. The brother gave the birds fish, saying, "You better try eating that." The eagles ate the fish. "How did that taste?" The eagles said, "Tastes pretty good." He said, "You better eat fish now, don't eat people anymore." After that, those birds just ate fish.

During the lifelong trip of the brothers down the opposite sides of the Mackenzie, several new features of topography were formed. Near Wrigley Harbor, in the region where Great Slave Lake drains into the Mackenzie, Yampa Deja hunted a giant beaver. The spot was formerly known to Indians for this reason as Beaver Point. All the islands around Wrigley Harbor were originally "beaver food"—caches of poplar piled up for winter fodder. One of the nearby hills is flat on top, as if it had been cut off. Here the hunter sat, watching for the beaver. He did not get that beaver, however. One time that beaver smacked its tail against the water where Mills Lake is now. The blow from the tail enlarged Mills Lake to its present size, and the water that was splashed out formed the smaller lakes around Mills Lake.

The hunter continued to hunt beaver along the length of the Mackenzie. Mustard Lake [at the headwaters of the Horn River, which drains into the Mackenzie from the east] was one place where he stalked a beaver. Here again he was unsuccessful. Finally, he did kill two beavers, a "small" one and a "medium." [This rating is derived from the fur buyers' classification of beaver pelts.] Near Fort Wrigley on the Mackenzie River there is a big reddish rock that stands up high and has willows growing around it. "They say" that is where the brother killed and cooked a beaver; the fire is still burning. [Here Louis's story—or my record of it—conflates this site with the site of the burning seam of lignite on the Mackenzie River that was noted by Alexander Mackenzie in 1789 and is still burning today.]

In Great Bear River there is a big arrow sticking out. That is where he shot at an owl. During the last war [World War II], when the Army tried to take boats up the Great Bear River, they could not get through because of this big arrow sticking up, blocking the passage of the boats. [The "arrow" is probably a huge, oblong rock rising at an angle from the water at the south end of the twelve-mile set of rapids of the Great Bear River. The statement about the difficulty of passing the arrow with boats probably refers to the fast, shallow rapids. In the 1940s an attempt was made to deepen the channel there, but it was unsuccessful, and large vessels still, as of 1955, cannot pass through the rapids.]

from MacNeish, "Contemporary Folk Beliefs of a Slave Indian Band," 1954

Yamonzhah and His Beaver Wife *Yampa Deja of the Slaveys is the Dogribs'*
Yamonzhah, and his brother is Sahzha (Little Bear). In their childhood, so the Dene
stories go, together the Two Brothers played many superhuman but cruel tricks on their
fellows. In the part of the Yamonzhah saga told by Vital Thomas, the beaver hunted
by Yampa Deja in Louis's story starts out as a human female.

Yamonzhah found a girl. She was all by herself; her family had been killed.
Yamonzhah said to her, "We might as well stay together." But he told her,
"I never stop for anything, I just keep going. If you want to follow me, all
right." So the girl followed, followed. But she told Yamonzhah, "Don't ever
step in grassy water or over a little creek. Just keep on the dry places. Don't
ever go across a wet spot. If you do, you'll be sorry." For a while Yamonzhah
did as she told him, but one day he came to a tiny creek, a little wet place
with not more than an inch of water. "I don't think she'll care about this,
there's hardly any water." So Yamonzhah crossed it and kept going. But finally he stopped and began to wonder, "Where did that girl go?" He waited
and waited and at last turned back. Where he had crossed that little grassy
swamp there was a big lake, and right in the middle of the lake it was all
pushed into a big beaver house. When Yamonzhah saw the beaver he said,
"Who are you?" And the beaver said, "It's too bad. I can't follow you anymore. I used to be your wife, but I've turned into a beaver now." And
Yamonzhah answered, "If I ever catch you, you'll turn into a woman again."
So he started to chase the beaver.

When they came to Marian River, he lost her. [Yamonzhah is in Dogrib
Country as Yampa Deja is in Slavey country.] He looked for her everywhere,
digging into the bush. And around Shotti Lake today there are all kinds of
little creeks, made when Yamonzhah dug in the earth. But he couldn't find
her. When he got to Marian Lake he was so tired he sat down on Shiagu.
That's a mountain on Murphy's Point. Way up on the top of it you will see
a flat rock. Yamonzhah made that when he sat to listen to which way the
beaver had gone. He heard a big noise of a beaver chewing down toward Old
Fort. Old Fort is on a long, long point. That point is the dam the beaver was
trying to make there, across to the other side. Just before Yamonzhah got
there the beaver saw her husband, so she dived and hid. Yamonzhah followed
her around the south shore of Great Slave Lake right around to the west side.
Finally he came to the end of a point where he heard the beaver again. That
point is called *tsa kon*, "beaver house." There the beaver had made a house,
and there she had a baby.

Yamonzhah dug into the top of the beaver house. You can see the hill where he dug his hole. He took the young one out of the house and killed it. The mother fled down the Mackenzie River, and Yamonzhah followed her, carrying the body of the young one.

There is a burning place down the Mackenzie. You can see smoke there once in awhile today, winter and summer. That's where Yamonzhah cooked the little one. As he was cooking the young one, the grease melted down and started to burn, and Yamonzhah said, "This will last forever, this smoke." And that's what has been burning there until now.

from Helm and Thomas, "Tales from the Dogribs," 1966

THE COPPER WOMAN

In 1820 at Fort Chipewyan, Rabbit's Head, an old Chipewyan, told John Franklin (1824) the tradition of "The Copper Woman." Sixty years later at Fort Liard, Petitot (1888) recorded "La femme aux métaux" as told in Chipewyan by Alexis Ennaaze, a mixed Cree-Chipewyan. Ninety years later at Rae, Joseph Naedzo from Great Bear Lake told the legend with many of the story elements of both Ennaaze's and Rabbit's Head's versions.

There was a Chipewyan woman, and Eskimos stole her. They took her to an island off the coast and gave her to a young man. The island was full of copper, nothing but copper. The woman had a little knife made of copper and a dress out of copper. It was shining and went *dling! dling!* Everything was of copper.

After she had had two children, she decided she must see her people "before I die." She made a packsack big enough for two babies and her bedding and all. And she left her husband, packing two babies.

She went the length of the island, and when she reached the other end of it she didn't know what to do. She had no canoe, nothing. Then a wolf came up and asked, "What's on your mind?" The woman replied, "I want to find my relatives, but I don't know how. This is an island." The wolf said, "Put your babies back in the bag and I'll show you the road to the mainland. Follow me." And the wolf walked just that deep [halfway up his forelegs] in the ocean. The woman packed her babies and followed him. There was deep water on both sides, it was so blue. But where they were crossing, it was just like following a road. She was just about worn out because she couldn't rest while she was in the water. Twice she leaned on a staff to rest, like this [posture illustrated]. And when she rested the third time on the staff, only then she saw land ahead.

Finally she got to the mainland. She sat down to cool off and took the babies out of the pack. The wolf asked, "Where are your relatives?" The woman said, "I don't know, it's been so long." The wolf said, "Wait for me. I'll look for them. Stay here till I come back."

Long after the wolf left, she saw something way off in the water. It looked like lots of canoes. She thought it was Eskimos, and she didn't know what to do. She hid her babies in a little cave in the rocks. But when the canoes got close, they turned out to be a herd of caribou crossing. She hid behind a rock where the caribou were passing. She had her little copper knife, and for every caribou that passed alongside her, she gave one poke [illustrated with gestures, poke, poke, poke]. Finally, there was a big pile of caribou that she had killed with one poke of her knife. Thousands and thousands of caribou were crossing. It was just like she had brought the caribou. It had been too far for the caribou to swim across. Now they were following the woman's road. That's how all the caribou moved to the mainland. They followed the woman.

She skinned the caribou she had killed and saved all the hides. She made a floor and walls, and then she built a fire and roasted caribou. As each was cooked, she put it in the cave. Finally, she filled the cave. The ones that were not cooked she piled alongside the cave, hundreds of them. She told her children that anytime they were hungry, "Here are caribou already cooked, and if you eat all this, there's a big pile out there." When she had finished the wolf came back.

The woman asked, "Where did you find my relatives?" The wolf said, "They are a long way away. Go straight south where the sun is up now. At the left you'll see a big mountain. Head for it. On the left side of the mountain keep going straight." The woman went to her two babies in the cave. "I'm leaving you here. Don't be scared, there's plenty to eat. Look after yourselves till I come back." So she left, going straight for the mountain on the left side of the sun. Walking, walking, walking. Each day when the sun came up she started again, straight south.

After many nights she saw a bunch of men, hunters. They were ready to grab her—they'd been away so long without seeing a woman. She was so pretty and her dress was so nice, all of copper, and shining. They all wanted her. But the woman says, "Don't touch me till we get close to your country. Don't touch me before that because I'm bringing good news. You won't be sorry."

Every night someone tried to get her, but every night she said the same words. So they left her alone. One of the leaders was a cruel man. Finally, halfway to their country, he sat alongside the woman. The woman repeated, as she had said over and over, "I won't stop you, but let me get close to your country." But the man said, "We've heard enough! Now!" And he threw her down and raped her. Then they all took turns, every one of them.

After all of them had raped her, the woman sat up on her knees, like, not moving [illustrated with rigid back and each hand resting on a thigh]. She began sinking down into the earth. The men asked her to come with them. "No! Nobody is going to move me now. It's too late. You should have listened to my words. I'm sorry for you. I would have brought good luck to your country. Now I am going to be here forever."

The men tried to move her, but she was like a stone. They begged her, but she couldn't move. The earth was as far as her knees now. The woman said, "Go, you'll never move me now." Needing food, they left her, but they soon killed plenty of caribou to eat, so they turned back to fetch the woman. The earth was up to here now [midthigh]. She was sinking in the earth. The men again tried to move her, but it was no use.

She said to them, "I'm going to tell you something. A person that eats drymeat with fat and comes to visit me is going to find rocks mixed [shot through] with copper. The man that eats nothing but liver and visits me, he is going to find a big chunk of copper, not mixed, pure. And the man who visits me and eats a chunk of meat without bone is going to find copper that is all split so it is easy to make axes and knives out of it." And she said, "From now on, call this place Sat in the Same Place Mountain."

Later, the men again returned to the woman. Now only her head was out. Again she gave them her last words about the copper. And a year or two later, the men again went to see her. Now she was completely covered with earth. The man who ate drymeat with fat found pieces of mixed copper and stone. The one who ate liver found a big chunk of copper. The one who ate meat without bones found copper all split.

[Naedzo concluded,] She was right. They have been doing that for so many years. That's as far as the story goes.

This story was retrieved in part from Vital's recall of a telling by Naedzo and in part from a tape I made of Naedzo that Vital translated. Neither effort was on one of Vital's good days. Fortunately, Alphonse Eronchi dropped in while I was trying to sort out two garbled denouements about pieces of copper. Alphonse made it clear that the third kind of copper was lamellar, "split" into a form that could easily be shaped into knives or other implements. In Alphonse's version of old-timers' lore, it was the man who did not eat fat who would find the flakes of copper.

[Naedzo went on to say,] Whenever the Chipewyans [Tedzont'in, Naht'in] hunted people, they used arrow points only of copper and knives only of copper, and if you killed a Chipewyan you would find that his axe was copper. They got it all from Sat in the Same Place. When I was [a young man] hunting, they showed me that hill. If I weren't blind, I could find it.

The woman never went back for her children. When they grew up, they married each other and raised children. They made their own language. That's why when you hear Eskimos talk they don't have long words, just short ones, like "tuk tuk tuk tuk."

from field notes of January 5, 6, and 7, 1970, Rae

THE ORIGIN OF THE DOGRIBS

In 1866 Phillippe Yettanetel, a Dogrib at Great Bear Lake, told Petitot (1888) the story of the origin of the Dogrib people. Almost one hundred years later, Vital Thomas recounted essentially the same tradition to me.

At the start there were no Dogribs. There was some kind of war, maybe between the Slaveys and the Chipewyans or Eskimos. We don't know where the woman came from. Anyway, there was a war and everyone killed except one girl who hid herself. Afterward, as she went around the deserted camps to pick up drymeat, she found a black dog still alive. She started to move, looking for rabbit tracks, some place where she could make a living. And she took the black dog with her. Finally, she made a camp with a tipi of spruce boughs, and she put out rabbit snares. She lived by herself there with the black dog.

She lived in that camp so long that finally she was in the family way, although she didn't know where it came from. But when the baby was born, it wasn't a baby—it was five pups. At first she was ashamed of herself and just threw the pups away, but finally she made a kennel for the little pups and fed them every day.

Each day she went out to the snares. But she began to notice when she came back that there were tracks of little kids in the ashes of her camp. "But," she asked herself, "how come? There is nothing here but the pups playing." So one day she decided to try to catch them. She pretended to go to the snares, but she slipped back. She peeked through a hole in her tipi, and inside she saw five little children playing. There were three boys and two girls.

When the mother saw those little kids playing, gee whiz, she wanted to grab them, and she ran right inside the tent. But she only caught hold of two boys and one girl. The boy and girl that she didn't catch turned back into dogs. Those two pups she killed. But the ones she had grabbed never turned into pups again. And that's how the Dogrib people started. Those two boys that she raised were the finest hunters and the bravest fighters and the best medicine men that ever lived.

from Helm and Thomas, "Tales from the Dogribs," 1966

THE CAPTIVE WOMAN

This oral tradition derives from documented events in the earliest days of the Dene fur trade, as recorded in the York Fort post journals of the Hudson's Bay Company of 1715–17. J. G. E. Smith (1996) provides succinct accounts of both the recorded facts and the story about the woman that Chipewyan elders of the Northlands Band of Manitoba told him. In the post journals, the woman (apparently only in her teens) was the Slave Woman, who escaped from the Cree. In 1714 she encountered English goose hunters out of York Fort and was taken to the fort. The next year, "serving as guide and interpreter she led employees of the Hudson's Bay Company [from their bayside post] to their first meeting with the Chipewyan in the Indians' home territory. As well, she was instrumental in establishing peace between the Cree and their traditional enemies, the Chipewyan, an absolute requisite before the Chipewyan could be brought into trade with the Company" (Smith 1996:96).

I call the girl the Captive Woman rather than the Slave Woman to avoid confusion over her tribal affiliation; she was Chipewyan. She appears with a Chipewyan name in recorded legend tellings by Chipewyans: to Petitot she was Shanaretther, which he translated "La martre que saute" or Leaping Marten, and Jim Smith presents her name as Thanadelther. ("Tha" signifies "marten.") The only personal name in the Hudson Bay's Company's documents was recorded in English as "marten shake." Can this be an effort to render "shaking," à la Petitot's "Leaping"?

The young woman fell ill at York Fort and died in February 1717.

Along with Chipewyans, Slaveys and Dogribs claim this woman as the heroine who first brought word of the Pale Men to them, as her own people, so that they too might trade furs for guns with which to defend themselves against their enemies. The Chipewyans' enemies were Cree. To the Slaveys and Dogribs, enemies might be either Cree or Chipewyans. The Slaveys' stories usually opt for Cree. (Mackenzie writes of the fear of Cree attacks by Indians "who have no arms" living along Dehcho as far down the river as present Fort Wrigley.) As a Dogrib, Vital Thomas firmly designates in English the enemy as Chipewyans. (These are "Tedzont'in," like "Akaitcho's bunch" in chapter 12. Dogrib Louis Whane also specified "Tedzont'in" in telling the legend to John B. Zoe in 1996.) Here is Vital's version of the legend.

The Chipewyans were the worst people of all. They didn't have a friend anyplace. Fight, fight, fight. They killed everybody—Slaveys, Dogribs, Loucheux, Eskimos. The Chipewyans never gave others a chance to fight back. At daylight a hundred and fifty or two hundred Chipewyans would move up to a camp and jump right on top of the poor Indians or Eskimos caught sleeping. They would kill them all with clubs and spears. Then they would take the scalps and carry them all the way down to Calgary or someplace and sell them to the Hudson's Bay Company. Sometimes the traders would say, "What kind of fur person is this? This looks human." But the Chipewyans would answer, "No, it's not human. It's a kind of animal that lives in the water." [The Slavey legend has this same story element.] And the traders never knew they were human scalps.

One time the Chipewyans killed so many Indians they were overloaded. They couldn't carry all the scalps by themselves. So they said, "We'll keep one woman alive to help with the packing and sewing and to make moccasins and cook." So they took that woman with them on their trip outside. But when they came to the traders' place they told her to hide, because of course they didn't want her to show herself.

The woman watched them packing a bale of scalps into a mud house. Since she had never seen a white man's house before she thought it was a mud house like the beavers make. She knew that the Chipewyans would kill her later, so she said to herself, "I can die here or die on the road. What's the difference?" She slipped up to the kitchen door after the men had gone in the other door, and she made signs to a white man there to hide her.

When the Chipewyans finished their trading they went out to look for the woman, but she was gone. They went back to the store, but the white men said they had not seen her. The Chipewyans wanted to fight for that woman. The traders didn't like the way they were acting, so before the Chipewyans could make trouble they took them to the warehouse, locked the door, and set it on fire, and they roasted all those fellows to death. [I have not encountered this ferocious embellishment in other versions of the story.]

Then they asked the woman to tell her story. She told them what had been going on for years and years, how she had been brought by the Chipewyans to the white men's country and how through the years the Chipewyans had "killed hundreds and hundreds of my people."

The woman stayed with the Pale Men all through the winter. They taught her to shoot with a muzzle-loader. When March came the Pale Men asked the woman, "Can you make it to your country?" And she said, "Yes, I think

I can make it." So the traders sent two guides to go with her. They took her to some place around Slave Lake. Then the two men said, "We'll let you go now if you think you can make it." And she said, "Yes, I know where I am now." So they left her, and she kept on going. She was packing snowshoes, a rifle, and food.

She found an old track of snowshoes and started to follow it. Two young men were on top of a hill looking for caribou. In the distance they saw a guy with a gun walking. When they saw that they got scared, because only the Cree and the Chipewyans had guns. One of the boys said, "Let's follow him. If he is looking for trouble we will kill him." So they began to trail him. Looking at the track, finally one boy said, "This can't be a man, because the step is too short. Let's follow her, she can't do much to two of us." The other fellow was scared, so the first one led. They followed her until she crossed out of the bush onto a lake. And the one fellow told the other, "Have your bow and arrow ready." Then he whistled to her. As soon as she heard the whistle, she turned her head and then just dropped, because she was so glad and so scared at the same time.

She told her story to them. "To the south [actually, east] there are lots of Pale Men who live in mud houses. They are the men who buy the scalps of our people, because the Chipewyans tell them they are animal furs. Those Pale Men taught me how to load and shoot a gun. Next year they are coming to this country, and they will bring guns like this for us."

So that's the way the Dogrib people found out for the first time about the Pale Men and where the scalps of their people were going. And that woman married the brave man who had followed her and whistled to her.

from Helm and Thomas, "Tales from the Dogribs," 1966

By the modest expectations of the Queen's Printer, Canada's government printer, The
Dogrib Hand Game *became a runaway best-seller when it was issued in 1966: "long
before Christmas it went Poof to the extent of 800 copies." Almost all ethnographers
who have worked with Canadian Dene give some sort of an account of the rules of
play of a hand game, but none of them is in-depth. The account in* The Dogrib
Hand Game *is, but only because Jimmy Fish put his incisive mind to work with me,
using flashlight batteries for players and kitchen matches for tally sticks, over and over
until I grasped every rule, hand signal, and possible move in the play of the game.*
Mahsi cho *again, Jimmy.*

The Dogrib hand game is a fast-tempo, astute guessing game played to the
accompaniment of vigorous drumbeats and chanting. The game is strictly a
man's game. Women watch; they do not play or bet. The game sessions observed in 1962 at Rae were part of the festive and sociable season around
Treaty. [See chapter 17.] This sketch is drawn from those occasions of play.

For a game session a tent is erected and a tarpaulin laid upon the ground
under the tent. There are two teams. The players of each team arrange themselves in a single line along one side of the tent to face the opponents on the
other side. Throughout the game session, players of both teams maintain the
characteristic kneeling-seated posture of the Indian man: buttocks resting
on calves and ankles and against the feet, which are folded alongside or un-
derneath the buttocks. Behind a team currently in action are ranged its
drummer-chanters. The sides, flaps, and back of the tent are rolled up, and
in a complete circle, several bodies deep, are crowded spectators. A bucket
of water or a kettle of tea and a tin cup or two are usually somewhere in
the center space for the refreshment of the players. These are provided by a
nearby household.

One team at a time operates as the active playing team. Each playing
member of that team hides a token in one of his two fists. By means of a

hand signal, a single member of the opposing team guesses simultaneously against each of all the opposing men as to which hand of each man holds his token. It is the objective of the guesser—whom I shall also call the captain—to "kill" in each guess as many men as possible by correctly guessing the disposition of the concealed tokens. Once all opposing players are killed, the right to be the playing (hiding) team then passes to the other side.

It is the playing team that scores. For every man that is missed on each guess, the playing team receives one tally stick. If the playing team can accumulate all the tally sticks twice in succession, the men of this team have won a game and will be paid individually by opposing bettors on the opposite team. The function of the guesser of the nonplaying team is to eliminate as quickly as possible all the players of the active team so that the right to be the active hiding team, and therefore scoring team, may again return to his side. Only by being in action as the playing team can a team hope to win games.

The style and impact of a hand game in action elude precise description. The tempo of play is fast and hard, with the deafening clamor of drums and the shouted chant of the drummers accompanying the play. The intensity of the syncopated beat that goes from loud to louder as climaxes in the game occur imparts a driving quality to the play. In response to the throb of the drums (or on some occasions to their own voices chanting without drums) the players of the hiding team move in rhythm. From their hips up, the kneeling men bob, weave, and sway. One part of the play involves a crouching position to reshuffle the concealed token and then the raising of the torso and the offering of the arms folded or outstretched to the guess of the opposing captain. The captain's guess may be delayed for many seconds or even for a few minutes as he calculates the disposition of tokens against him. The men's arms are now in action to augment the rhythmic movements of their torsos. After the guess, the rhythmic movements continue as the members of the playing team open their fists to reveal the tokens and after a few seconds again go into the reshuffling crouch. The rhythm of the bodies tends to be strong and with jerking movement in accent to the beat of the drums. Men have their individual styles of responding to the rhythm. Some are more emphatic and dramatic than others, but all are in movement. Players may close their eyes or roll them heavenward, producing on some faces a trance-like effect. The two-syllable unit of chanting cry made by the drummers is delivered with wide-open mouth, head thrown back, with strained features by some and at full voice by all.

The members of the opposing team sit quietly watching the action. The guesser for their team is also in bodily repose, although his visual attention to the actions of the playing team is pronounced. Most spectators stand, but a few old men looking on maintain either the male kneeling-seated position or the cross-legged tailor pose for hours on end.

COMPOSITION OF THE GAME

ITEMS IN THE GAME

There are three kinds of necessary objects in the game.

Idzi. Each player while in action holds in one of his two hands a concealed token, called *idzi.* It may be a button, a coin, a wad of tin foil—any object small enough to be completely concealed within the closed fist. Some men ensure the concealment of *idzi* by tucking their thumbs inside the closed fingers of the fist.

Detsin. The Dogrib word *detsin* (*decin*) is usually translated "sticks." We shall refer to *detsin* in English as stick(s), tally (tallies), or tally stick(s). There must be as many tally sticks as there are players on a single team, plus one or two extra tally sticks. In the present day, when the maximum number of players allowed on each team is fifteen, there is always only one additional tally stick, making a total of sixteen tallies in use in the game. The tally sticks are not of any special design or manufacture. They are made on the spur of the moment when a game is in the offing and are simply peeled sapling (willow or poplar) sticks about a foot long, tapered by axe to a point at one end.

Saikwi. Saikwi is sometimes referred to as "peg(s)" by English-speaking informants. At least two *saikwi* are provided at the beginning of the game, since this is the minimum number required to complete a single game. More *saikwi* may be made and used as needed. Visually, most of the *saikwi* used in the games were distinguishable from tally sticks only in that they were unpeeled.

One of the secondary items ordinarily used in the games at the fort is the typical Athapaskan tambourine drum. Usually there are as many of these employed in the course of the game as there are drums available and willing drummer-chanters to perform on them.

Some players may use a jacket, a cap, a piece of blanket, or any other cloth-like item under which to hide their hands while shifting *idzi* from one fist to the other. Each player provides his own hiding blanket (or shares his neighbor's) or not, as he wishes; it is not a required item. Those not using a blanket place their fists between their thighs as they shift *idzi.*

Two sides play in opposition to one another. We will refer to each opposing side as a team, although there is no coordination of play among its members. In former days, each team was composed of members of a regional group. The attempt is made to maintain this practice in spite of the fact that present-day fort living has somewhat broken down these distinctions. The teams observed in 1962 were, by designation of Chief Bruneau, to be composed of members of the two major demographic divisions of Rae, respectively, the Island men and the Point men. It was hoped that the Lac la Martre men would arrive at the fort in a body so that they could form a team in one of the sessions. This, however, did not come about.

In former days, we were told, the game might be played with up to twenty men on each side. Nowadays, the game is never played with more than fifteen men on each team. We could not elicit a rationale for this cutoff number. The game may be played, however, with any number less than fifteen. At the commencement of the game session for the day there may be only four or five men on each team. Other men up to a total of fifteen join in later. Some may drop out, however, for the space of a few plays or for the day. In either case, other men, up to a total of fifteen on each team, may take their places.

The teams must always have the same number of men. If one team adds a man, so must the other. If a man from one side wishes to drop out, a member of the opposing team must also do so to even the weight of the teams. In the latter case, one man explained, teammates will urge the poorest player (that is, the one most often "killed") to drop out. As each side adds a man to increase the equal complement of each team, a tally stick is added to the total set. No tallies are removed from play, however, should team complements be reduced later by men dropping out of the game.

At any moment of play only one team is operating as the playing team, or *idzi* men, the men attempting, by the concealment of their *idzi* in one or the other hand, to outwit the guesser of the opposing team. Except for the captain (i.e., the man who is doing the guessing), the members of the opposing team are inactive.

Each side has its own drummers. These drummers need not be players on the team, but some players when not in the playing line may serve as drummers. A man whose drumming-chanting is admired may be asked to accompany a team. Drums only accompany the team that is in action as *idzi* men, that is, the playing team as opposed to the guessing team. When the guessing team wins the right to become the *idzi* men or playing team, the "drums cross over," that is, the same drums are thrown across the center space to the drummers for the new playing team. As an alternative to drum accompaniment, the *idzi* men may provide their own rhythm with the gambling chant.

In the sessions we observed at Rae, drums were the order of the day, and this appears to be the customary accompaniment for games at the fort, where drums already made and available can easily be rounded up for the game. The gambling chant unaccompanied by drums was performed briefly, partly, it appeared, for our benefit and our tape recorder and partly to give the drummer–chanters a needed rest. In the hand game sessions of the Hare Indians of Fort Good Hope that I saw in 1957, the unaccompanied gambling chant, sung by the men in the playing line, always began each round of play. Only after some minutes did the drummers with their distinctive chanting cry move in at full voice.

CAPTAIN OR GUESSER

The active antagonist of the playing team is the captain or guesser of the opposing team. He is the only player in action on the guessing team. He attempts to kill as many of the *idzi* men in as few plays as possible in order to eliminate all of them with few or no tallies taken on their part. This allows the drums to cross to his side so that his team may again become the playing team and have a chance to score. The term *captain* is not used in English among the Dogribs; I have borrowed the term from Johnny McPherson of Fort Simpson.

Each guess by the captain is given in the form of a resounding clap followed by a stylized hand signal. On each guess the captain guesses simultaneously against every man in the active playing line opposing him. That is, if there are eight men active in the opposing line, his signal will indicate his guess as to which hand of each man holds an *idzi*.

The guesser is selected on his teammates' consensus that he is the one most likely to kill the most men of the opposing team. If he loses too many of his guesses, he feels pressure to retire as captain. At a critical moment of the game when the guesser has been unsuccessful in his last few efforts to eliminate one or a very few remaining men opposing him, he may choose to relinquish his role to another man who may be more successful, or he may temporarily yield his role as guesser to a teammate for the next couple of plays only. Such a substitute, temporary guesser does not receive all the tallies under the control of the regular captain. The substitute continues in his role until he uses up (loses) all the tallies the captain allotted him.

The captain also signals to the opposing players on those occasions when the game calls for inactive men on their team to move up into the playing line. These signals are given in the form of stylized hand signals indicating the number of men required.

Tallies   At the inception of the first game of the day, one tally goes to the team that wins the right to start as *idzi* men. Throughout the entire playing for the day, every time each man on the playing team is missed in the guessing, one tally is received by his (the playing) team. The one exception to this rule is on a final play before *naidah* (the play to try to "raise the dead," to restore those killed to the playing line), when there may be more survivors on a playing team than there are tallies left to the opposing captain. In this case, all remaining tallies go to the *idzi* team, but there is no carryover of the debt of tallies owing to that team. The extra tallies owed are canceled out by the following *naidah* play. (*Naidah* is explained in Rules of Play, below.)

Each time the total number of tallies is won by a playing team, that team gets one *saikwi*.

Saikwi   One *saikwi* represents the winning of all tallies by a playing team. When a team wins a *saikwi*, this peg is thrust upright in the ground on that team's side of the tent. That team then begins another round of play, attempting to win a second *saikwi*, a third, and so on, before it is stopped by having all its men killed.

A team may have one or more *saikwi* standing at the time it loses its right to be the *idzi* team by having all its men killed. The rules of payoff intervene to account for and eliminate all pairs of standing *saikwi* that the team may have won (see the following section). But a single, unpaired *saikwi* remaining to a team that has lost the right to be the *idzi* team is vulnerable to attack by the opposing team, which is now the *idzi*, or playing, team. This is because the new *idzi* team is now in a position to win a *saikwi*, and whenever one team gains an upright *saikwi*, the upright *saikwi* (if there be one) of the opposition is eliminated, taken down. In other words, the winning of a *saikwi* by one team cancels out an upright *saikwi* of the opposing team.

Payoff   Bets are paid when at least two upright *saikwi* are possessed by a team *and* all its men have been killed. As long as a team can keep some *idzi* men alive, it goes on to try to win yet another *saikwi*, then another, and so on. Payoff is made on two *saikwi* or any multiple of two. A team paid off on two *saikwi* has won a single game. Payoff that does not occur until four *saikwi* are upright by the side of a team terminates a double game and doubles the payoff rate. At the end of a triple game (i.e., involving six *saikwi*), the payoff is tripled. Whenever payoff occurs, all *saikwi* involved (i.e., the maximum multiple of two) are put down.

Whenever a team at the time of payoff holds an odd number of *saikwi* (such as three, five), that last odd *saikwi* is not involved in the payoff and therefore remains standing. To reiterate a point made above, that one odd *saikwi* will be lost (taken down) should the opposing, now the playing, team win a *saikwi* before all its men are killed. This rule holds equally should a team lose its right to be the playing team after winning only a single *saikwi*.

Game Session: Game, Round, and Set   It seems convenient here to introduce terms I coined to define the total day's play of the hand game and certain cycles within it. No directly comparable native terminological distinctions were elicited from consultants. The terms now introduced may be best defined in terms of completed events.

Game Session. The total course of play through the day.

Game. A game is completed at the time of payoff of bets. It may be a single, a double, or a triple game.

Round. Each time a *saikwi* is won by the playing team, a round is over.

Set. Each time the drums cross over, a set is completed. "Drums cross over" signifies that the playing team has had all its men killed and thereby has lost its right to play. The opposing team therefore receives the drums and becomes the *idzi*, or playing, team at this time. As stated before, a game cannot be won until at least two consecutive rounds have been completed by the playing team (i.e., until that team has won two *saikwi* in a row) before all *idzi* men have been killed.

A set may be over for a team without that team having achieved completion of a round; that is, in a game employing the stated maximum number of men, a team may not have won all sixteen tallies before all fifteen of its men are eliminated. Drums cross over on each occasion when all fifteen men are killed. On the other hand, a set may include the winning of zero, one, two, three, and so on rounds, indicated by the number of *saikwi*. As stated above, if a set upon completion includes two completed rounds (two *saikwi* won) or more, payoff occurs at that time. If at the completion of a set the team which has just lost the play holds an odd number of *saikwi* (has consecutively won an odd number of rounds), it maintains the one odd *saikwi* upright in the ground. That is, the team still holds a credit for winning that last set, until and unless the opposing team is able to win the next round as players. In other words, a team may lose the drums, that is, terminate its set, but still have the credit of a leg-on game, so to speak, in the form of one *saikwi* still upright (whether or not a game was completed). If the men can regain the drums by preventing the opposing team from winning a round, they then have a chance to make game, that is, to try for another round to complete their pair of *saikwi* and be eligible for payoff.

Penalties   Should an *idzi* man deliberately cheat (such as switching his *idzi* after the captain's guess), his whole team "loses right away and pays off." If an *idzi* man should make the honest error of continuing in play after he has been killed (by misreading the guessing signal, for example), then the drums go to the other team. If the captain pays the wrong number of tallies for the men he missed on his clap, then that guess "doesn't count"; the captain makes a fresh guess.

Should a mistaken count be made by the playing team of the number of its men surviving a successful *naidah* play, the error is merely pointed out and rectified, with no penalty attached.

Betting   Wagers are placed individually by each man with one or more members of the opposing team. No man may participate in the game without having at least one person on the opposing team with whom he bets on the outcome of each game. He may, if he wishes, ask two or three or more men on the opposing team to take his bet that his own side will win. Only players bet; no side bets are made by spectators. Drummers who are not also participating in the game as players need not bet. The betting of one individual against another of the opposing group, rather than group against group as units, is apparently characteristic of Indian gambling games throughout North America.

Bets are paid when at least two upright *saikwi* are possessed by a team and when all its men have been killed. The amount of wager is standardized; [as of 1962] a single game is "worth" one dollar. In other words, every time a team wins a single game, each member of that team receives one dollar from each of his betting partners on the opposing team. If a double game is won, members of the winning team receive two dollars from each of their betting partners.

THE INITIAL PLAYOFF

The game session for the day begins with an initial playoff to determine which team will start as *idzi* men. One man from each team operates as a starter. Each starter holds his *idzi* in one hand, and each guesses against the other. If in the first round of guessing both guess wrong or both guess right, they must then try again until one outguesses the other. For example, if the first man guesses wrong, that is, misses his opponent, his opponent gets a tally stick. But if the opponent then in turn also guesses wrong, the stick is thrown back in the middle, and the men try again. When finally one man "misses" the other man (that is, he guesses incorrectly) and his opponent guesses correctly, the winning man, he who was missed, retains one tally for his side, which gets to start the game session as the playing team. The other tallies then go in the center between the two teams.

A game session can start (and be played through) with only a few men on each team. Whenever there are more than eight players per team, however, only eight men of the playing team form the initial playing line. From now on, let us assume for simplicity's sake that each team has the maximum complement of men (fifteen) and of tallies (sixteen).

THE LINEUP

At the inception of the first round of the day and at the beginning of every subsequent round, the playing team puts only eight of its fifteen men into the active playing line. Seven remain in reserve. As long as a man is missed by the captain, he remains in the line. As soon as he is guessed against correctly by the captain, he ceases to play; he is "dead." The reserves may move into the line, and the dead men may come alive under circumstances specified below.

THE COURSE OF PLAY

At the beginning of a round, the captain of the guessing team faces an active line of eight *idzi* men of the opposing team. He will attempt to kill as many men as possible on each guess. We will often use the word "clap" to indicate the signaling of his guess. Any time after the crouching *idzi* men have straightened up, indicating that each has his *idzi* in the hand he wishes, the captain may clap against them. After the clap, each man opens the hand indicated for him by the captain, displaying either that it is empty or that it holds the *idzi*. In the latter instance that man is then dead, and he drops out of action. The survivors then go into the crouching position, reshuffle their *idzi*, and straighten up again to wait for the second clap.

After each clap and revealing of *idzi* the captain takes as many tallies from the pile in the center as there are men that he missed, and he throws these tallies across the intervening space to the playing team. The captain continues to clap against the initial line of eight men until those men are all eliminated before they have won sixteen tallies or until sixteen tallies are won by those members of the first line who still survive.

If all the first eight players are eliminated before sixteen tallies are won, the seven reserves then move into the line as a total body of replacement. These men will now try to win all the remaining tallies before all are killed.

If all fifteen players, that is, both first line and reserves, are killed before they win the sixteen tallies, the drums cross over to the members of the opposing team, who now become the players of the new set. However, the team that has just lost the drums retains those tallies which it has won. This team, now represented by its captain, also has the use of the tallies remaining in the center to pay off wrong guesses against the now-playing team until the center tallies are exhausted. Should this occur before the first playing team can gain control of the drums and become the playing team again, the captain must then draw upon the tallies at his team's side to pay off wrong guesses. It may be, however, that he will be successful in eliminating all fifteen opposing players before he has to draw upon his reserve tallies. In this case, his team commences again as the playing team with the advantage of holding a certain number of tallies at the beginning of this new set.

Whenever sixteen tallies have been won, the playing team gains one *saikwi*. Furthermore, they win the right to try on the next play to "make *naidah*," that is, to bring alive those men killed in previous plays of the set. The right to make the play for *naidah* may be won by those men surviving from the original lineup, by the survivors of the second line (made up of the seven original reserves), or, if this is a second or subsequent *naidah* play, by a mixed crew of surviving first liners and reserves and survivors of men "raised from the dead" in the prior *naidah* play(s).

A general rule in the Dogrib hand game is that, except for the original eight-man lineup at the commencement of a round, there may be no more than seven men in subsequent lines of the set. This rule is overridden, however, at the time of play for *naidah*. This is the occasion when more than eight men may be in the line at one time. In the *naidah* play, all men alive who are not already in the fighting line join that line to participate.

Thus, for example, if the sixteen tallies are won by one or several members of the first line who still survive, all seven reserves join these survivors to try for *naidah*.

Naidah is "raising the dead men." When all alive men have joined the line and are ready for play, the captain claps. *Naidah* is made if the captain misses one or more of the men in the line. *Naidah* fails if all men are killed by that clap. If *naidah* fails (all players now being dead), then the drums cross over to the captain's side, his team now becomes the playing team, and a new set commences. If *naidah* is made, then all men except those killed in making *naidah* come alive again. If, as is usually the case, the survivors of the *naidah* play number fewer than eight, then the number of resurrected men necessary to total eight joins the new fighting line.

If *naidah* fails, all sixteen tallies go to the center. The team that has just lost the drums still gets a *saikwi* for the sixteen tallies, however. If *naidah* is made, the playing team retains as many sticks as there were survivors of the *naidah* play. The remaining sticks are thrown to the center to buy back the dead men. All these sticks in the center are now for the use of the captain once again.

TERMINATION OF THE DAY'S SESSION AND RETURN MATCHES

There is no predetermined number of games, sets, or rounds to be completed in order to finish a day's session. A game session simply runs until everyone is pretty well exhausted, usually a matter of eight to ten hours of play. If the teams are evenly matched, the session may end in a draw, each side having won an equal number of games. In this case, the teams agree to play three more games; that team winning two out of three is the winner for the day.

It is the prerogative of the losing team to request a return match. The winning team may not propose a new game to the defeated. In former times, however, when several regional bands would gather, the winners of an initial game session would, after two or three days, be challenged to play against another regional team that had not yet played. The winning team of that session would then be challenged by yet another "bunch," and so on. In 1962 the hoped-for arrival of the Lac la Martre men en masse would have allowed this principle to be carried out. They would have performed as a new challenging team to the Point men, whose team had won the first game session of the season. [At this point in our monograph, *The Dogrib Hand Game* (1966), there is a hypothetical play-through of the hand game that livens up the barebones rules set forth here.]

The hand game is seen as one of intellectual skill and judgment tempered by luck [or medicine power, *ink'on*]. The ethics of the game are that "you've got to play honest"; there is no sleight-of-hand in the game, only the skillful outwitting of opponents. This quality is embodied in the social logics of the game: if one man cheats, his side will have bad luck and lose for the whole game session.

The contest of wits is between each *idzi* man and the captain. The essence of being a successful *idzi* man is to scramble one's pattern of shifting *idzi* so that the captain is unable to detect and plan for any regularity, thus allowing at least a fifty-fifty chance of being missed. A player who allows himself an idiosyncrasy in *idzi* handling that can be discerned by the captain or who follows a repeated pattern of shifting will get killed quickly each time he comes into play. Such was the case with one old gentleman in the observed sessions who was eventually urged by his teammates to drop out of play. In another case, a young player started as an *idzi* man, but as he was killed about five times in succession as he came into the line, he gave up and for the rest of the session drummed only. However, he still maintained his betting arrangements with the men on the other team.

A skillful *idzi* man becomes cognizant of the capacities of various captains who may oppose him. For this reason, when one of the opponents of the playing team takes over from another as captain during a round, he claps repeatedly to draw the attention of the *idzi* men so that each player can judge the new psychology with which he must now deal. As the *idzi* man is at this juncture often doubled over to shift his *idzi*, a nonplaying teammate may also nudge him to draw his attention to the new guesser.

It is in the role of captain or guesser that a man has the greatest opportunity to exploit successfully his memory, judgment, and skillful observation of opponents. The ideal guesser is one who from the first game catches and remembers cues about *idzi* handling and patterns of shifting in each of his *idzi*-hiding opponents.

Certain immediate tactics employed in the game build team and individual esprit. The chanting or backing of a playing team by drummers is certainly such a device. In the crescendo of the drums that builds around a surviving *idzi* man "to make him smart," even the uninformed spectator is made aware of the heightened suspense and team support. The good-sport attitude of killed players is expressed in hearty laughter as they reveal *idzi*. There are at times, however, excited exchanges between teams that suggest roughly good-natured slanging. Jimmy Fish says that in the old days the play-ers "sure used to talk mean to each other," yelling, for example, "You're a no-good player!" This behavior suggests the jocular insult verging on offense that is familiar in some Western competitive play and that, in the same seem-ingly paradoxical fashion, also accompanies expectations of good-sport be-havior at specified moments. All of these expected patterns of behavior op-erate to sustain the excited, almost frenetic quality of play that makes for a properly thrilling game.

The hand game, in the eyes both of the Dogribs and of the uninvolved observer, presents none of the social problems of gambling with cards. The hand game is but part of a festive week when the whole community looks forward to a period of group entertainment and pleasure and a break in rou-tine. At this time, by community expectation, most work other than daily chores is in abeyance and in fact is not seasonally appropriate. The pleasure and value of the game do not lie in monetary gains. The financial loss is slight for all participants. Since teams probably never go through more than twenty games in a session and are often evenly matched, it is unlikely that more than five dollars would be lost by any man in the course of a day's play.

The hand game has two qualities which distinguish it from other forms of gaming play among the Dogribs: it is a community and group festive event, and it serves as and is recognized to be an expression of intergroup competi-tion, reinforcing intragroup identification. The hand game is played at those times and seasons of the year when group assemblage and interaction are stressed.

The identification of opposing teams with regional bands finds its reflec-tion in the fact that neither Jimmy Fish nor Vital Thomas could provide a native word to designate the generic concept of a team. Both stated that one simply designates the teams involved by the regional group name. The theme of the hand game competition as one between regional groups carries over to the intertribal level as well, as a tale of a game played against Chipewyans attests.

There are two seasons or seasonal activities at present that regularly call forth the game. One is midsummer at the time of gathering for Treaty, when some of those Dogribs who spend much of their year in bush settlements come into the town to join the fort dwellers. The fall caribou hunt is the other occasion of the year in which the hand game is commonly played to-day. While in the hunting grounds, on many nights the crew may play the hand game until midnight or later. Jimmy Fish stressed the playing of the hand game on the return journey, implying that the playing of the game is an expression of the euphoria of the successful hunters. In the hand game played on the fall hunt, drums are not usually used; rather, the characteristic humming-chanting melody is employed. By their own chanting the *idzi* men provide the rhythm for their movements. The common item for betting on these occasions is the drymeat taken on the hunt. Some men, we were informed laughingly, returned from the hunt with only a little "parcel" of drymeat to show for their month's efforts; they had lost the rest gambling.

Dogribs comment that the hand games of the present day are no longer so long lasting or so well played as in former decades. The Slaveys of Fort Simpson ceased the play of the hand game after 1928, as a mourning tribute to the many dead in the great influenza epidemic of that year. The younger generation had not seen the game until visiting Liard Slaveys reintroduced it in 1955.

from Helm and Lurie, The Dogrib Hand Game, *1966*

The enjoyment and exhilaration shown in the vigorous hand games played by the Hares of Good Hope that I saw in 1957 and by the Dogribs at Rae in 1962 led me to speak, on the last page of The Dogrib Hand Game, *of a strong cultural investment in the hand game. But I asked whether this investment can survive the attrition of acculturation, especially the breakdown of old regional affiliations and the alienation from traditional cultural interests and values.*

For a summary description of the Dogrib hand game along with other Dene's versions and Dene games in general, see Traditional Dene Games: A Resource Book *(published by NWT Municipal and Community Affairs, no date of publication).*

In all cases and on all occasions, the guessing signal indicates that the *idzi* hand is the one that currently is being held on *that side of the body* which the signal designates. For simplicity's sake, the diagrams of pairs of hands presented below the photographs assume that right hands are being held on the right side of the body and left hands on the left. They are seen from the captain's position. The hand that the captain signals as the *idzi* hand is darkened. Only a few of the signals are presented.

Men of the playing line, each shuffling his idzi *under his jacket. The drummer on the far left of the photo is Jimmy Fish, who explained the game to me.*

One manner of presenting concealed idzi. *Three upright* saikwi *are in the foreground.*

A crossed-arm style of presenting concealed idzi. *The captain's signal always indicates the side of the body where* idzi *is, not the hand. If in this photo both men have* idzi *in the right hand, then to kill both of the men the captain's signal must indicate "left."*

Drums cross over (a set is completed), and the captain-to-be, Joseph Whane, is pulling together the tally sticks held by his team.

Members of one team signaling "six" to their opponents, indicating the number of idzi men who should move into the playing line.

Chief Jimmy Bruneau as captain, making the signal diagrammed below.

Captain Joseph Whane making the signal diagrammed below. The man of the playing team displaying his idzi in the left foreground appears to be the end man of the line. If so, he has succeeded in being missed, as he holds idzi in his left hand, and the captain's thumb indicates that his guess is that this end player had idzi in his right hand.

A "dead man," John Beaulieu, holds the tallies of his team while his teammates try to make naidah.

Captain Joseph Whane making the signal diagrammed below.

This chapter describes some of the kinds of events and times to which people looked forward before there were cars, radio, television, and easy access to urban entertainments. The hand game (chapter 16) is a truly indigenous creation. Treaty time and New Year are observances that were introduced and set by the whiteman calendar and then further shaped by the native people. The brew party was the third major secular institution adapted from Euro-Canadian "offerings." Accounts of other less structured kinds of pleasures in Dene life begin and conclude the chapter.

FUN AND DEPORTMENT

Two stories told by Dogrib Vital Thomas convey not only the enjoyment of group dancing but Dene emotional styles as well. The first story, about the boy who did not shame himself, reveals a major value in social deportment, equanimity.

THE BOY WHO DID NOT SHAME HIMSELF BEFORE STRANGERS

A young man got married. His father and mother told the boy and girl how to behave themselves among strangers so that nobody would laugh at them. Even now, some old fellows teach a boy and girl the same thing when they get married: "You should keep your eyes down. Don't watch your husband, don't watch your wife when you are among strangers. Or those strangers may say, 'That boy is looking at his wife. He must be jealous.'"

The boy and girl got married in the spring. That fall, after freezeup, there were no caribou on the lakes or in the barrens. Finally, word came that there were caribou past Lac la Martre. The Dogribs, the Slaveys, and the Mountain Dene from across the Mackenzie all joined together that winter to hunt the caribou. When the snow began to melt in the spring, all the different Indians started back to their own countries for hunting.

By this time the young couple had a baby boy named Baptiste, and the young fellow had found a friend, a Mountain Indian boy. When all the

peoples began to separate, the Dogrib boy was sad because the Mountain Indian boy was leaving. So he asked his parents if he could spend that spring with his friend and come back to his folks in the fall. His father and mother didn't want it, and the girl's father and mother didn't want it. But the boy kept begging, "He is so good to me. I have lost all my brothers and I am just alone with my parents. It's like I found a brother." So finally the parents said, "Okay, if you come back next fall."

So the young man and his wife spent the spring in the mountains with his friend. After the spring hunt, they all went to a big meeting place. The trading chief of the Mountain Dene got all kinds of stuff from the trader, and he made a feast. In those days, all the trading chiefs got feasts from the Hudson's Bay. The Bay still gives our chief stuff for a feast. Then the people began to dance. When there was a full crowd, the Dogrib boy started to dance, because strangers might say he was jealous if he stayed out of the dance. We would say the same thing now.

So the Dogrib boy and his wife jumped into the dance circle. You know how it is, when someone wants to get into the dance he separates two other people and gets in between them. So as the people kept coming into the ring, the boy's wife got moved way across the circle, from him. And the people were dancing, dancing all night, all the next day, and when night came again, that young man was so hungry and so weak. His wife was way across the circle, and he didn't want to yell to her, "I'm hungry! Cook something for me!" And he didn't want to leave the dance to talk to his wife because people might say he was jealous.

At last the songs were getting pretty low. Everybody was pretty near all in; they were waiting for someone to make a song. They were all tired, but they were waiting for another song. And the boy didn't know what to do, he was so hungry and tired. Pretty soon the sun started to rise again. So he said to himself, "I better figure some way to tell my wife that I want her to cook something for me." So he started to sing, "Mbadzi Wemon, lidi warewo," "Baptiste's Mother, I feel like having a drink of tea." It was a new song, a pretty good one. When the band heard that song they all started going again. And all those people danced for two more days without stopping.

The young man didn't want to come out and say anything to his wife, because he was a Dogrib and everyone else were strangers. His father and mother had told him how to behave before strangers so he wouldn't shame himself. In the old days I heard that song once.

from Helm and Thomas, "Tales from the Dogribs," 1966

Part of a tea dance circle of Slaveys and Dogribs, Fort Providence, 1967. In the tea dance the only musical instrument is the singing of the dancers.

THE ETHOS OF THE ET'AT'IN

The Et'at'in, whose modern settlement is at Gamiti (Rae Lakes), are the Dogrib regional band whom we first met in Petitot's account of the caribou kill in 1864 (chapter 4). One time, Vital Thomas said:

The happiest fellows are the Et'at'in. [Why's that?] Because there's more life in them. Even in the olden days, there was always fun. If you meet some of them in the old days, maybe two miles from here, it don't matter if they are in a canoe, with dog teams, or are hunting, they are always singing. Always happy. They like to gamble and dance. Everything is fun.

There's a story about that, Johnny Black's story. It was in the time when they [Black and his Et'at'in companions in the story] had never seen the fort. [This was Old Fort Rae, where trading ceased in the first decade of the twentieth century.] There were five boys. And they had to go get groceries [supplies].

"So [as Johnny Black tells it] we passed Faber Lake, five or six of us young fellows, none of us married. We were breaking trail, with one man running ahead of the dogs. We got to Old Fort and there we saw a fiddle dance for the first time. And someone was playing a mouth organ. That was the first time we ever saw a mouth organ. So one of the boys bought a mouth organ.

"We left the fort and came back as far as Faber Lake. We will get to our home camp the next day. At Faber Lake there were houses, but nobody was home. So we stopped there for the night, we'll be home the next day. So we unhitch and feed the dogs and have a lunch. And one fellow says, 'Let's have a dance.'"

You know, the night is long around the end of December, just before Christmas. The nights are about two days long! [Vital laughs.] It gets dark about five, and day comes about eight in the morning. So the fellows eat and then they start to play the mouth organ and dance and are dancing. It didn't seem long because they were having all kinds of fun. And then it was just breaking daylight, and one of the fellows went outside and said, "Gee whiz, it's breaking daylight. The night didn't seem to be long!"

And the mouth organ player was bleeding from both sides of his mouth! [Vital laughs and gestures in the back-and-forth movement of a mouth organ.] So they got no sleep. They hitched the dogs and started out again.

from the field notes of August 14, 1962

BREWING

Coming "out" from Lac la Martre in December 1959 after seven months of residence, Nancy Lurie and I learned that the law prohibiting the purchase or consumption of alcoholic beverages by the Treaty Indians of the Northwest Territories had recently been rescinded. Hard liquor and beer were now legally and easily available to Indians in the large white-oriented settlements, and orders for alcohol to be flown into outlying Indian settlements were soon booming. An early result was a heavy expenditure of money on manufactured alcoholic beverages. The making of home brew essentially disappeared from the North.

The personal and social problems coming in the wake of now-legal alcohol consumption were soon manifest. The Dogribs of Rae were the first Indian group to attempt to control alcohol consumption. In 1976 a referendum at Rae resulted in the prohibition of possession or consumption of alcohol within thirty miles of the settlement. Outlying Dogrib bush hamlets followed suit, as did a number of other native settlements in the Northwest Territories. In following years, native communities have gone dry and wet again. Alcohol abuse has become a serious threat to the well-being of Dene and Inuit peoples of the North.

During our first summer (1951) at Jean Marie River, "Lynx Point" Slavey friends showed growing trust in us by offering brew to Teresa Carterette and me. (Our own first effort at brewing, featuring canned tomatoes, was godawful.) In the fifteen months that Teresa spent with the people of "Lynx Point," she had full opportunity to learn the protocol and progress of the brew party. Brewing became the focus of her ethnographic attention as it interwove with the rest of life in that small community. The following account is from a manuscript completed by Teresa Carterette in 1953.

Everyone at Lynx Point [Jean Marie River] will declare that brewing is the means to a good time. Aboriginally, the northern Dene, like all North American Indians, had no knowledge of alcoholic beverages. Rum was introduced by the fur traders, and, according to the Lynx Point people, it was the fur traders who began to manufacture fermented beverages from flour and baking powder and from some of the plants found in the area. Like the rifle, the steel trap, the outboard motor, and other technological equipment, alcoholic stimulants are associated with the white man's technological superiority, and their quality is assessed by several of the criteria applied to commercially produced beverages such as clarity, strength, and color. Since the law prohibits [as of 1951–52] Treaty Indians from purchasing and consuming alcoholic beverages, they take recourse to surreptitious production in the home.

The principal alcoholic beverage produced at Lynx Point is brew. Some people occasionally manufacture beer from malt and hops sold to them illegally by a trader, but the price makes this a luxury. The men used to make moonshine from dried apricots. Marcel and Karl explain that the old people were afraid that moonshine would do permanent harm to the stomach and asked the men to stop making it. Although they talk appreciatively of its strength and clarity and still have the copper coil equipment, no moonshine has been produced for many years because of the old people's request. Except for a very rare drink given to them by a white man or a non-Treaty native, the only time that Lynx Point men drink commercially produced alcoholic beverages is when they are at Hay River during the spring buoy setting on the Mackenzie River between Hay River and Fort Simpson. The men, along with the community-owned powerboat and barge, are hired annually for the job by the government. Two things stand out in every reference to the buoy-setting job: the good pay received for the job and the good time associated with the opportunity to drink beer at Hay River.

Brew is made in four- to six-gallon enamel pots and allowed to ferment for a minimum of forty-eight hours. Every household owns one of these pots, and old bottles and jars are saved to store brew. It was becoming fash-

Having some brew, Jean Marie River, 1952. Teresa Carterette, Charles Gargan, and Louis Norwegian on the powerboat, brew pots in the foreground. From 1951 to 1952 the powerboat's name was changed from **Merry Jane** *to* **McGill Lake** *because Johnny was caught with brew on the boat by the police. "That's what we do when there's bad luck."*

ionable to own a strainer to remove the currants from the surface when the pot's contents were ready for drinking, and both Marcel and Karl had invested in a set of plastic glasses for drinking parties. The ingredients used to make brew are all food staples: molasses, sugar, raisins or dried currants, water, and fast yeast. It costs approximately $2.25 [as of 1951–52] to make four gallons of brew. Light table molasses produces an amber color, is less bitter, and is considered better than dark molasses, but several persons use dark molasses because it is cheaper. Daniel commented with pride that one of the traders had remarked, "Only you fellows buy the light molasses— everybody else gets the dark stuff." Canned fruit such as tomatoes, apricots, peaches, and dried prunes may be substituted for the raisins or currants. Karl told of an occasion at Fort Providence when nothing else was on hand, and a friend had used raspberry jam to make "pretty good stuff." Ozzie, who usually found it difficult to allow his brew to ferment long enough, would add a tin of beets to "make it work faster." To "work," brew must be kept warmish regardless of how cold the weather may be; the cabin or tent must be kept above freezing temperature.

The proportions of ingredients, particularly the amount of sugar, varied to some extent among different brewers. It was generally agreed that brew should be strained, bottled, sweetened a second time, capped, and kept for a month to make it really good. Brew made in this fashion was described as clear and strong, "just like beer." Zachary was the only one who approximated these standards of production. Henri approximated these standards only because he no sooner finished one pot than he began another. Everyone else tended to keep his brew only long enough to allow it to ferment and lose its sweetness. Only a small part of a pot is put aside in old jars or rum bottles for drinking the following day or to be saved for some individual who is not likely to be present during the early part of the drinking party.

Men, adolescent boys, and women all make brew often, but it is generally for the consumption of the men, who frequently ask their wives or sons to prepare brew for them. The pot of brew is considered the property of the person who owned the ingredients, and no one else, except possibly the person who prepares it, may take some of the brew without the owner's permission or instruction.

Brew drinking always occurs in a group; there is no solitary drinking. Marcel once recounted as a matter of extraordinary interest how his wife had gotten drunk alone the previous evening because everyone had been sleeping the brew off when she had decided to start drinking. He had stayed sober to make certain she did not wander out to the outhouse and fall asleep in the subzero weather.

Men hold drinking parties considerably more frequently than do women or adolescents, for it is rarely that a group of men returns from the trapline or from Fort Simpson that there is not a brew party. Although New Year is celebrated with drinking, and Sunday is spoken of as a day of rest and brew drinking, a brew party may occur any day of the week when men return from any extended work period. Children talk of how their fathers will drink brew on their return from the trapline or from Fort Simpson.

The brew party begins in the house of the person who owns the brew. Those who have been invited begin the drinking, but once drinking is under way an uninvited adolescent or adult may drop in and stand around until offered a cup. The owner of the pot fills a pitcher and sits at the kitchen table with his male guests, who sit on benches and trunks facing the table. The women sit in a separate group near the bed, which is usually on the opposite side of the room. At first, people wait for the host to refill cups and tumblers. Drinking is casual but very steady, and the host refills cups as soon as they are emptied. From time to time he serves his wife and other women guests, but they receive considerably less than do the men.

Each time the host fills the cups he apologizes for the poor quality of the brew, usually remarking that it is too sweet and not strong enough, and explains that he has only a small amount of brew on hand, usually half a pail left from the last time. He makes this last statement despite the fact that everyone is quite aware that it is in all probability untrue. Brew making, while it is a simple operation, takes a couple of hours, and with the children of the community continually visiting and exchanging information it is impossible for a person to keep brew making a secret. While no reply is made to the declaration that there is little brew on hand, every deprecating remark by the host about the quality of the drink is met with reassurances that the brew is excellent and strong. The guest thanks the host profusely, and on every refill he counters the apology with praise and emphatic thanks. Often there is a slight smacking of the lips and the appreciative exclamation, "Strong!"

The men begin by conversing in low tones and behaving in the usual constrained manner. Those who have returned from town or the trapline report all they have heard, seen, and done, the number and kinds of tracks in the bush, the presence of strangers in or near the area they have visited, changes in the physical features, arrivals in Fort Simpson, prices of furs and commodities, game law gossip, purchases, and events occurring at other settlements. A man who has shot a moose recounts the details of tracking, the weather, the terrain, and the kill.

Gradually, there is a relaxation of mood. Conversation becomes louder and more animated. Where formerly the entire group of men formed the conversational group, one man at a time commanding the attention of all the others, the group now begins to break up into small conversational units. Ozzie, Arnie, and sometimes Karl are by this time playing the fiddle and guitar and singing. Marcel occasionally joins in the singing, and Henri starts to dance about. The barriers between male and female are removed, and a man will make joking, flirtatious remarks to any single or widowed woman in the room.

The married women, who have had little to drink, frequently leave the principal scene of drinking and go to visit another woman who may have some brew. For the most part, married women do not drink as much as the men or the widowed women. There are occasions, however, when brew drinking is unusually heavy and prolonged, and some of the women get drunk enough to require assistance in walking. A couple of women had a reputation for wanting to fight when drunk, something which usually did not occur until a person had drunk a considerable amount.

When the host's visible supply of brew has been exhausted, as he has been predicting since the beginning of the party, one of the guests issues invitations to people to come to his house for a drink. Most of the guests make it to the next house, but one or two may wander home to sleep or decide to visit some other house. If the men decide that a particular member is already drunk enough to cause trouble by becoming aggressive, they try to avoid inviting him to the next house. If they succeed in dodging him or in persuading him to go home to sleep, and he should arrive later, everyone will hide his cup as he enters. This is rarely effective, since the person simply remains until the others are forced to offer him a cup or forgo any more drink themselves. Drinking continues as long as anyone is willing to volunteer his brew or as long as someone is successful in wheedling another cup. Some of the men will wander off to visit or go home to sleep; others will fall asleep on the floor and remain undisturbed until they awaken. Frequently, a man is so drunk that he has to be taken home. If an argument and fighting begin, people usually manage to get one of the combatants home. Throughout these activities the children and adolescents go from house to house collecting and disseminating information about the proceedings.

Most brew parties stretch over a period of two days. Unless a new group returns from the trapline, the second day's drinking is usually moderate, and activities are quiet. People who served brew the previous day have usually managed to save a couple of quarts, and the men will sit about for a few hours drinking and conversing in a quiet, leisurely fashion. Those who have pressing chores perform them.

The limitations set on brewing are defined by three major considerations: economic values, familial values, and the reputation of the community. Drinking takes place only after a man has fulfilled his economic role, and an individual observes a number of precautions to protect himself and his family from danger to health and survival. Sobriety is the major condition that provides for social controls during a brew party. Irrespective of age and sex, the role of the sober individual is to prevent conflict and to protect the intoxicated from harm. While the children may tease an intoxicated adult, they are often called upon to help the man or woman home. As disseminators of news, the children are often responsible for preventing serious fights from developing. The sober humor the drunk and watch over him. They hide weapons in the event of a fight, seeing to it that intoxicated individuals neither inflict nor receive physical harm. So when a fight is about to start the sober intercede to separate and pacify the combatants. The adult male will separate the quarreling men, the adult female will persuade her husband to go home, the child will appeal tearfully to his parent, and the old lady will cackle and scold and tug at her son.

In the host's house the baby from his hammock looks on at all the activities. If a guest mother leaves the scene of the drinking, she is likely to take her baby with her. It is actually a rare occasion when the women all repair to the safety of a house away from the drinking activities. The two instances when this occurred during my year at Lynx Point were both occasions when there were Fort Simpson men present whose behavior proved that the people's apprehensions were well founded, since one proceeded to destroy property, and both sought a fight. Generally, however, the mother absents herself only briefly from the house where the drinking party is in progress. She sometimes leaves the baby in the father's care. Especially if a toddler, the baby will find the way to father's lap during the drinking. Accustomed as the little one is to handling all objects in sight and imitating others' gestures, the toddler frequently picks up the brew cup and tries to take a sip. If the cup does not contain much brew, the baby is often allowed to drain it. David, for example, would sip, smack his lips, and shake his head, smiling appreciatively, much in the manner of his mother when she downed a cup. His mother and the other children would laugh and encourage David to repeat his actions.

From later childhood into their early teens, neither boys nor girls are given brew. For the child this parallels the change from demand to scheduled feeding. Children are very rarely offered brew by adults. When an adult does give a child a cup, it is after he has become intoxicated himself. At this stage, brew, like other foods, is stolen by the child.

There is little doubt that for the young child the contrast between the reticence of the adult when sober and the chaos of the brew party sometimes results in frightening experiences. The children may be somewhat apprehensive about their parents' behavior: one thirteen-year-old girl would scold her mother for becoming garrulous. A younger girl (in the Emotional Response Test) said that she was afraid when people drank and that the worst thing that could happen would be that her mother would drink. Karl told of having been frightened as a small boy when people fought. On the other hand, the mood of the children when they anticipate a brew party is one of pleasurable excitement. They look on the interval of drinking as a time when adults behave in unaccustomed and interesting ways which the children discuss long afterward among themselves; and they realize that the control adults exercise over them is considerably modified by the adults' divided attention and relaxed behavior. The children, moreover, are inveterate mimics, fascinated by any individual's physical oddity or atypical behavior, and the brew party provides them with much material for this sort of entertainment. They mimic the men's convivial singing, Henri's abortive attempts to jig, the expression on Karl's lips when he sits talking drunkenly. The girls on several occasions reenacted one particular instance of sexual behavior which they had found especially entertaining because it had occurred in an upright position.

From the very beginning of the brew party there is always a small cluster of visiting children in the shadows intently watching every move the adults make. Once in awhile a few of them will scamper off to report on the proceedings. The women, particularly, rely on the children as sources of information, and many a woman shows up just in time to fetch her quarrelsome husband home because the children warned her that he was about to get into a fight. When someone has to be helped home, the women and the older girls, especially, are the ones who perform this duty. One of the more amusing incidents occurred one evening when from our window we saw Marcel reeling toward our cabin. As he passed his own house, three of his youngsters ran out, surrounded him, and swiftly swept him homeward. In their role as messengers, children frequently carry invitations to brew parties.

Adolescent males begin to make an occasional pot of brew when they are in their midteens. By this time they have already experienced intoxication. For the adolescent, participation in brewing activities parallels his acquisition of appropriate drinking behavior in which physical aggression is somewhat controlled and sexual flirting takes the form of verbal teasing and such joking as puns and double entendres. Where the adult man stylizes his sexual overtones into verbal teasing or joking, the adolescent may resort to force. Although the adult may become argumentative and get into a fight, he very often exercises control when faced with a less sober drinking partner and even goes so far as to interfere, something which children and adolescents never do, when another man seems to be losing control. Fighting among the adult men occurs only when they are intoxicated, and the men themselves make attempts to avert it. Fighting within the nuclear family appeared to be especially deplored. Not only was it rare, but when it did happen it usually involved an adolescent male. It seems that self-control is learned as the adolescent suffers scoldings, temporary alienation from the person he offends, and a reputation that has the effect of prolonging his exclusion from adult drinking activities.

Women drink less frequently than men and in smaller quantities, but they do manufacture brew for themselves, hold brew parties, and occasionally approximate the degree of intoxication common among the men. Women who approximate the men's standards of drinking behavior suffer no apparent sanctions. The men speak of the women's drinking without embarrassment. The principal consideration tempering a women's drinking was her responsibility in caring for her baby. People expressed wonder at having seen women with small babies on their backs staggering and stumbling about at Fort Providence drinking parties. The principal change in drinking behavior that comes with old age occurs for the women, who by this stage are freed from the responsibility of caring for very young children. Karl's mother-in-law's behavior resembled more closely that of the men. She talked loudly and laughed a great deal, engaging in a great deal of physical contact. At the New Year dance it was she who sang the first two chants and led the first dance, directing a long oration to the men who sat in a semicircle against the wall.

In brewing the most caution is observed toward all whites and government personnel. The Indian agent, the game warden, and the police are most feared, and people will abstain from drinking if a visit from them is anticipated. Occasionally, the Lynx Point people are caught unaware by a government agent, and there are hurried attempts to cover up if the men are not too drunk. One spring, several of the men had been drinking when the police's outboard motor was heard approaching from downstream. Immediately, the people hid the brew and sprayed the tent with fly tox to cover up its smell. When the police stopped in, Indians and police exchanged a few words on the prevalence of flies that spring.

Whether legal sanctions are imposed by government agencies depends not only on the ingenuity of the Lynx Point men in disguising their activities but on the disposition of government agents to overlook the illegal activities. Among government personnel there is frequently the feeling that the law depriving the Indian of the right to drink alcoholic beverages is an unjust one. For example, in arresting Ozzie, the police (Mounties) explained that they did not care if a man got drunk so long as he was not brought to their attention. In this instance, Ozzie had been reported by someone who would in turn report the police to higher authorities if they did not make an arrest. Marcel recounted several times that the police had told him they did not care how much the Indians drank in the bush as long as they did not find out. Similarly, when the chief game warden stopped in one summer Sunday afternoon to find most of the men intoxicated, he was considerably annoyed but did no more than issue a reprimand and warning.

Non–Lynx Point, nongovernment individuals are judged primarily on their relation to some member of Lynx Point and the people's knowledge of their attitudes and drinking behavior. Some Metis are invited to participate on those occasions when they happen to be at Lynx Point. Some Slaveys, even relatives, who are disliked and distrusted are excluded even when they arrive in the midst of festivities. The principal fear is that they will gossip about Lynx Point.

Except for brew drinking, there is at Lynx Point no other form of group activity to occupy leisure time. The extent to which the people's time is taken up with religion is small. Religion comes to the bush rarely, and ceremonials, except when the priest says Mass, are nonexistent at other times than New Year. The men average perhaps one church service a month at Fort Simpson; the women and children rarely get to church. Such diversions as music, drawing, games, toys, swimming, skating, and ball playing are exclusively the diversions of the nonadult. Even visiting is rare among adults, especially males, and never while sober does it take the form of group visiting as it does in childhood.

From childhood, the individual associates pleasure with brewing, and as an adult he sees it as the avenue to pleasurable experience—the recapturing of nonadult camaraderie and freedom from responsibility. He may have feared the aggressive behavior associated with the drinking party, but he has learned that it is only a temporary condition and that his fellows protect him from and forgive aggression as long as it occurs only when he is intoxicated. At such times he is not fully responsible; he is enjoying the recreation which he has earned by fulfilling his economic and familial roles and by behaving in a manner which makes him an acceptable participant in drinking activities.

from "The Relationship of Drinking to Other Behavior in a Slave Indian Society," unpublished manuscript by Teresa S. Carterette

NEW YEAR AT "LYNX POINT"

Looking back on the good old days (chapter 9), in 1971 Naedzo lamented, "Now, New Year day is just like any other day." The following account draws on Teresa Carterette's notes on her participation in the New Year celebration at Jean Marie River on January 1, 1952.

New Year observances have a strong tradition in the North and are derived from the old Scottish celebration continued in the North by the Scottish factors and clerks of the Hudson's Bay Company. A transcription from company records at Fort Simpson reads:

> 1883, January 1. The morning was ushered in by a salute fired by our people at the windows and doors, after which they came to wish us a Happy New Year—and in return, in conformity to the custom of the country they were treated, the men to half a glass of brandy each, and the women with a kiss, and the whole of them with as many cakes as they chose to take and some raisins. One of our gentlemen who had a bottle of shrub treated them to a glass, and after some chit-chat conversation they retired, firing a salute on going out. In the evening they played at Blindman's-bluff, concluding the fête by a supper at the hall. I also gave each of the men a fathom of twist tobacco and a clay pipe. (Cameron 1912: 193)

Some activities of a similar nature—in which the Indians, saluting with rifle shots, formally pay a visit to the trading establishments and receive small gifts—are carried out [as of 1952] in the present-day Forts Simpson and Providence. In earlier years, according to Marcel, the New Year at Fort Simpson was a major event, and Indians from as far away as Head-of-the-Line, Liard, and Wrigley would come to Simpson for the festivities, which included dancing jigs and reels. As far as Marcel knows, other bush Indian settlements do not hold their own New Year observance as do the Lynx Point people. The Lynx Point celebration was instituted by Old Mink [Old Sanguez] in the early days of the community. Most of the activities are patterned on the traditional celebrations at the forts, although, as will be noted, at least one aboriginal element has been incorporated.

At Lynx Point, people begin to plan for the celebration days in advance. It is hoped that there will be plenty of "meat" (i.e., something more than small-game flesh) for the feast. If the hunters are fortunate in securing plenty of moose in the weeks before the New Year, some of the best pieces are put aside for that day. In the year of the fieldwork, it was decided to change the locale of the feast from Karl's house (Old Mink's former house) to Daniel's, because in former years people had become "too drunk" at Karl's place. Marcel feels that excessive drinking is not in the proper spirit of the occasion, and he probably was the major force behind the change. (His stratagem, however, was in vain.) Men must start the brew for the occasion at least two days in advance. Each family decides on its food contribution to the party. Much of the preparation of the food, which is cooked the day before, is carried out by the men, suggesting the ritual importance of the act. Arrangements are made for sufficient tables and chairs to be brought to the house where the feast is to be held. On New Year Eve, some of the men are apt to call in a friend or two to help them sample their brew to "see if it is ready," in which case they are not likely to stop until the pot is emptied. Toward midnight on New Year Eve, a few rounds of ammunition are fired in anticipatory celebration. On New Year morning, several men or boys may gather at the host's house to aid in last-minute preparations.

The formal observances on New Year Day may be considered to have three parts: the procession, the feast, and the postprandial singing and drumming. The formal events begin when the members of the household selected to commence the procession leave their dwelling and start for the next house. Upon arrival, a salute is fired over the roof by the men. Then the visitors enter the dwelling and shake hands with the resident adults, first the men and then the women. Each household in the community is approached in this fashion, the throng growing as each family visited joins the procession to the next house. Teresa Carterette's notes of January 1, 1952, record the events of the day.

> From my window I see the group approaching Marcel's house. The men, led by Henri and all hatless [a most unique occurrence, emphasizing the solemnity of the occasion], precede the women who are accompanied by the children. They move in single file, and there is a space of a few yards between the men and women. After shooting one round over the roof of the house, the men set down their rifles and go in, followed by the women.
> In about five minutes the men begin to come out and move in a single file toward my house. At the right side of the house, which is the one in their path, they shoot their rifles over the roof and then come in—Henri is the first—and shake hands with me. "Happy New Year!"
> At the feast, Henri sits at the centre of the long side of the table, facing the room. Marcel sits on his left, then Lem Yukon. On Henri's right are Isadore Loche, Bill Yukon, and Old David. On the left, Zachary, Daniel, and Ozzie stand facing the men who are sitting. Karl sits at one end of the big table. This end has no place setting.
> At the women's end of the room the younger kids play, talking fairly loudly. Henri rises and delivers what I later learn is a prayer. One of the men calls to the kids to keep quiet. Karl asks someone about the salt. As he finishes talking, Henri walks around to the cookstove with a plate of food

which he throws into the fire. He then returns to the table, and everyone sits down. A grace is said, and the sign of the cross is made before the serving begins. For the most part, things are passed as requested, and it is the men who take the initiative.

As soon as grace was said, the spirit of the gathering changed to one of laughing and joking. (Most of the men were somewhat high.) But Marcel, who was directly opposite me, remained very sober and quiet, keeping his head lowered most of the time and at times almost visibly wincing at Henri's remarks.

The meal ended with the grace being said again, and as the sign of the cross was completed, everyone yelled "Happy New Year!" and two plates of cigarettes were brought out and passed around. After the men had thus finished, they reset the table, and the rest of the women and the children ate, but without any of the ceremonial being enacted.

We see that certain explicitly solemn and religious usages are attached to the feast: an initial prayer, a food offering, and a grace before the meal, followed by a repetition of the grace and the sign of the cross after eating. Marcel states that the food offering and presumably also the initial prayer of which the offering is the culmination are observances instituted by Old Mink and are not practiced at New Year feasts at Fort Simpson. The prayer is the same each year and is a request that everyone here today, especially the old people, will be here next year also. The person who makes the prayer also makes the food offering. The purpose of throwing the food into the fire at the conclusion of the prayer is, according to Marcel, to bring "good luck."

When Old Mink was alive (i.e., before 1928), he sang Indian songs after the banquet, accompanying himself on the drum. There was no dancing. Today, Nelly May's mother sings songs after the feast. One of the old woman's most common songs was composed by her first husband, who died at Fort Providence in the great influenza epidemic of 1928. The song is about "a creek this side of Providence." (The first husband of the old woman was evidently a virtuoso, for Marcel has heard that "he make up lots of songs. Jesus Christ, nice songs. At Providence, everybody else play the drum, and he sings. Don't dance, just drums with song.")

According to Marcel, there should be a session of drumming and chanting, with dancing tea-dance style. There might also be square dancing, with violin and guitar accompaniment. On New Year of 1952, however, everyone got "too drunk" to dance. Many of the men managed to maintain their high state from the night before by having several cups of brew before the dinner. After eating, the brew party began again in earnest at Henri's house and elsewhere. It was evident, from Marcel's behavior at the time and from later comments, that Marcel has a sense of solemnity and tradition in regard to the New Year observance, and he feels that intoxication before and during the feast vitiates the dignity of the occasion. "Nice if you don't drink before dinner. In Old Mink's time, didn't drink before."

from **The Lynx Point People, 1961**

FESTIVITIES OF TREATY TIME IN RAE

The official events of Treaty for the Dene of the Northwest Territories include a public meeting of representatives of Indian Affairs and other branches of the Canadian government with the chief and councillors of the government-recognized "bands" in front of an Indian audience. After what are often mutually unsatisfactory exchanges regarding government regulations and Dene needs and complaints, treaty is paid. Each man, woman, and child registered on the band roll receives $5. The chief receives $25, and the councillors get $15 each. After treaty payment most of the Indians line up for the TB X-ray. Inoculations are also given to children at this time. After transactions between Treaty Indians and government are over, Indian-organized festivities follow.

The festivities at Rae following the formal treaty sessions in 1962 were to have begun July 4, but because of delays in obtaining enough firewood to cook the feast food they were put over until July 5. All during July 4 canoeloads of wood were brought from across the lake to the village, and there was constant activity as men came down to the shore, unloaded lengths of dry wood, and trotted off to the various houses with them.

As is customary, food or money was donated by the Indian Affairs Department, the Hudson's Bay Company, the Oblate mission, and individuals in the community. A Dogrib acquaintance commented that public announcements make selfish persons who could donate uncomfortable, since everyone notices whose name is not mentioned. Under the direction of Johnny Simpson, Chief Bruneau's *k'awo*, on July 5 all the food was brought to a designated point and distributed among the various households. All day various women cooked at their homes, and at six o'clock the food was ready to be brought to the feasting place. That year the feast was held beside the *k'awo*'s house, but the location may vary from year to year.

Inclement weather threatened the festivities, and all day the people anxiously watched the skies and speculated whether the light, intermittent rain would prevent the feast from taking place as scheduled. Indian Affairs had donated frozen buffalo meat, and if this were cooked it would keep for a day along with other food, but concern was expressed that canned goods might spoil in a day once they were opened. We were told by Johnny Baze that the signal for feasting would be the firing of a gun, probably around six o'clock. The hour passed, and we were sure the feast had been postponed until the next day, but at 8:30 the shot sounded. A few minutes later our friend, beaming, appeared at our door, saying that he himself had fired the gun and that we should get ready to go to the feast.

In accordance with custom, we [Nancy and June] gathered up plates, cups, spoons, and knives in knotted tea towels to take to the feast and prepared to carry these bundles along with our ethnographic gear. Our house was in the part of the village located on the Island, and the feasting place was some distance away on the Point, the mainland jutting into the lake. As we were about to set out on foot, a young man called from the shore and asked if we would like a ride in his canoe. We happily accepted and squeezed ourselves and our gear into an already well filled canoe. All around us other motor-driven canoes full of people, reminding us of tourists on a picnic excursion, headed across the water to the landing near Johnny Simpson's house. By the time we arrived, a multitude had already gathered, and many children were running about.

The feasting area consisted of a line of six tents, end to end, with the sides rolled up. On canvas that had been laid on the ground, the people sat in parallel rows, each two facing each other and back to back to the next set of rows. There were six such double rows, everyone crowded close to his or her neighbor. The men tended to sit along one side of the line of tents and the women along the other, but there was some mingling of the sexes. Most children present were not included in the feast; they stood just beyond the tents, watching. The chief and councillors sat in a line at right angles to the long rows. Another tent, forming an L at one end to the main set of tents, served as a distribution and briefing area for the men who would serve the food. It is typical of Dogrib gatherings that involve communal eating that the women cook the food and the men serve it. Generally, young unmarried men do the serving. Johnny Baze said he had been asked to take charge of the serving crew, some thirty men.

Presently, Johnny went down the rows grabbing up rolls of oilcloth which

At the Treaty feast, Rae, 1967.

various people had brought and laid them out like a tablecloth between the lines of people facing each other. Again, this is typical in that even when stopping for tea on the trail plates of food are placed on a strip of oilcloth. People got out their plates and knives and spoons, carefully turning their cups upside down so that they would not be filled with food. When everybody was assembled, the men proceeded with the serving. In the course of his work in directing the serving crew, Johnny had taken careful count and later told us that exactly 250 people were served, not counting children who were given feast food brought home by their parents. It was quite clear that many people came with the intention of carrying food to their homes; one old lady with a fair-sized plastic wash basin in lieu of a dish or bowl had it generously filled by the servers.

Because we were all so crowded together, it was necessary for the serving men to walk on the oilcloth. First, the servers came around with a kettle of mildly sweetened and very runny rice and raisins. A dollop or two, depending upon the diner's inclination, was deposited in each dish. This was followed by a generous helping of pork and beans deposited in the middle of the rice and raisins. Then men came around with cardboard boxes filled with hunks of bannock and store bread, to be followed by another man with a cardboard box filled with butter, which he ladled out by means of a table knife, slapping a pat of sorts on each hunk of bread. Into the middle of the rice and raisins and pork and beans another server emptied a large spoonful of canned fruit, and then another came around with a kettle of fruit jam, using each person's own spoon to ladle a good-sized helping into the middle of the rice and raisins, pork and beans, and canned fruit. A chunk of boiled buffalo meat was then dropped into the by-then colorful accumulation in each dish. Finally, men came around with boxes of store-bought cookies, oranges, and hard-boiled eggs still in the shell. At last, tea, already sugared and boiled with canned milk, was poured into the cups.

After all the food was served, everyone sat quietly chatting. Then Chief Jimmy Bruneau got up to speak. The chief spoke about the custom of Treaty feasts and said that on this day, as for many Treaty times, the people gathered to eat together. As always, the food had been given by the Hudson's Bay Company, the Indian agent, and others who were named. The chief looked forward to feasting next year and hoped that after he died the custom would continue as it always had. He ended his remarks with a prayer admonishing the people to think of the Virgin and to pray that they would have the same things again, year after year. He said that in the old times the chief used to distribute many things for everyone to eat. Although no fish was served at this feast, it is a mainstay of the Dogrib diet, and the chief commented with satisfaction that the people have fish and so cannot say they have no money. The fish gives them their sustenance, and thus they will continue to live.

The group then recited a prayer together, and after the amen they set to eating. The actual consumption of the meal went very quickly, taking about twenty minutes. At this point Councilman Alexis Charlot spoke, saying that he had been asked to do so but could add little to what the chief had said. He did, however, repeat some of the matters which had been brought up at the formal treaty talks the day before, particularly the liquor problem and the planned curfew and siren, "the bells on sticks." He spoke of the need to look out for little children and to bring them up properly and religiously. Passing reference was made to the prevalence of white intervention in Indian affairs. His remarks closed on the hope that they would have good gambling and good dancing and no drunkenness. This was followed by a prayer and finally a loud shout from all, "Mahsi!" (Thanks!). Tobacco and cigarettes were passed after the final prayer, and the dishes and food were then gathered up and in some cases given to children to take home. A few people sat around smoking and chatting. The actual feasting had begun a little after 9:30, and by 11:15, when the tents were struck, the people began forming a circle for dancing. A Mountie appeared in the dress uniform he had worn at the formal treaty discussions and danced a few rounds beside the chief.

At Rae the days are still long in early July. Although the dancing began close to midnight and lasted about five hours, it was never darker than twilight. Dancing during the evening of the Treaty feast was all of the type known as the tea dance. The tea dance has no accompaniment except the human voice, the dancers gathering into an ever-widening circle, moving with mincing steps clockwise, crowding tightly, shoulder to shoulder, and facing into the center of the circle.

As far as we could tell, only the men sing (though Vital Thomas says women also sing). The people's voices rise and fall in melodies and cadences of a compelling beauty once the alien ears become attuned to them. [Our tape recordings are in the Northwest Territories Archives.] A man would start a song; the rest would then pick it up and continue along. (Johnny Base estimated that there are probably twenty-five or more separate songs sung at the tea dances.) As soon as one song was finished, a new one was begun. Children ran about playing and shouting to one another, adults who did not join the dancing gossiped and chatted, and a general festive hubbub formed a background to the clear notes of the singing. There was no dance leader, and people joined the dancing circle wherever they chose to elbow their way between two dancers, often joking as they did so. One middle-aged woman who spoke a little English waited for the circle to move along until two old men appeared in front of her. Forcing her way between them, she laughed over her shoulder, "I like to dance between these old men."

After Treaty time, when we tried to learn more about the dancing, we were told that in the old days it was better. Persons said that they now lack good singing leaders. Years ago the dancing circle sometimes became so large that it was almost impossible to hear across it [see the story that starts this chapter], so it was necessary to have a good leader to start a song in order that the whole group could sing and dance in unison. The leadership of singing seemed to be spontaneous, the man with the loudest and clearest voice beginning a song and sometimes drowning out alternative choices that someone else might start. The words of the songs were simple and repetitive, but the breathy, repetitive sounds that formed a chorus in many of the songs were distinctive. [See Gertrude Kurath's chapter 3 in *The Dogrib Hand Game* for musical notations and analysis.]

On the afternoon of the next day, July 6, the hand game began. A poker game had been in progress near Johnny Simpson's house for a good part of the day, but a little after three o'clock it broke up to commence the hand game. The men were gathered under several tents, set up as they had been for the feasting, and an outside stove burned brightly so that the men could

Card game, Lac la Martre, 1960. Card games are apt to spring up at any time of leisure. Isador (Fish) Zoe facing the camera and his mother Rosalie Fish behind him.

heat and thereby tighten the drumheads at regular intervals to preserve the proper tone.

The game continued until 10:30, about seven continuous hours of play in all. Individual players would go into Simpson's house to eat or retire temporarily from the game, but the game went on, and the spectators knelt or stood around the players to watch. Although women do not play, they followed the action with interest and apparent understanding. Children played a boisterous game of tag, dodging and yelling among the spectators and throwing a string-wrapped rag ball at each other. They were careful not to intrude on the adult game, and so no one paid any attention to them or scolded. It was a happy time for all. Later, during the second hand game session, card games were played by little groups gathered near the hand game proceedings.

At the first session the hand game players had wanted to start another game, but the chief's wife scolded them to stop gambling and begin dancing. The dancing, which followed the hand game and continued again well into the night, began with drum dancing. The drum dance is also done in circular form, but the dancers dance tight up against one another front to back in a sort of shuffle. It is almost impossible to maintain any semblance of a dance step and even to keep the beat because the dancers are so crowded together. The drum dancing was obviously not as popular as the tea dancing, and after only four or five songs the drums were put away, and the group finished with tea dances. At times, well over a hundred people joined in the tea dancing, but the drum dancing attracted only fifty or sixty people into the circle. Generally, the tea-dance circles were maintained more symmetrically than the drum-dance circles. The drummers in the drum dance stand to one side of the circle, decide on the songs, and lead the singing, but the male dancers may join in the singing. Both men and women dance the drum dance as well as the tea dance, and the observer cannot help but be struck by the lack of any salacious overtones in either style of dance, although both involve close bodily contact between the sexes squeezed together in the circle.

Petitot provides an account of dancing by the Et'at'in almost a hundred years before:

> *On May 26, [1864,] my good neophytes came to ask my permission to have a grand dance of farewell. Their families are soon going to separate until the following fall. They go frolicking off, shoveling the snow on the rock to form a vast ring, lighting a great fire in the middle, and beginning their performance at five o'clock in the afternoon. They danced all night, a night without darkness, crying out, "Eh! Ah! Eh!" fit to make the rocks tremble.*
>
> *The dances of the Dene offer no kind of danger to morals. They do not touch each other. Each is covered with a fur robe or a covering of wool; the old men and women take part as well as the children. They go in little leaps and a circular promenade from left to right, then from right to left [these reversals of direction are not in modern dance, which is always clockwise], accompanied by savage vociferations and clamors but in good cadence. (1891 : 241–242, my translation, abridged)*

The next day at Rae was overcast, and there was talk of another hand game, but none was held. Several people said they were waiting for the Lac la Martre men to challenge the winners; it finally developed that the Lac la Martre men did not come. Eventually, a return match was held between the original groups on Sunday afternoon, July 8, and continued for ten hours. It was followed by another dance, beginning with a few drum dances and finishing up with tea dancing that went on until six o'clock in the morning. Some fascinating acoustical effects were produced at the second tea dance by the many dogs tethered close by the dancing area that added their enthusiastic ululation to the songs.

The combination of chanting at the hand games and all-night singing finally took its toll. Several of the men were so hoarse they could barely speak above a whisper by the time the treaty celebrations were over.

from Helm and Lurie, **The Dogrib Hand Game, 1966**

WOMEN'S WORK, WOMEN'S ART

This is an excerpt from a short essay in a volume featuring a handicraft collection at Haffenreffer Museum of Brown University that demonstrates the artistry of the native women of subarctic America from the mid-nineteenth century to the present. The collection reveals the reworking of European-derived motifs in the evolving native aesthetic traditions and displays as well the variety of trade materials that women incorporated into their decorative art: glass beads, silk floss, horsehair, wool yarn, stroud, velvet, braid, and silk ribbon. In the following passages I suggest the pleasure and pride that northern native women find in beautifully executed "women's work."

Except for a few scraps of evidence that may be recovered by archaeologists, a visible record of subarctic Indian women's handiwork in prehistoric times is lost to us. But as the historic era dawned successively from east to northwest through the North, accounts of the earliest European observers tell of the embellishment that Indian women, using only indigenous materials, lavished upon clothing, footgear, and accoutrements. On his downstream journey on Dehcho in 1789, Alexander Mackenzie encountered an encampment of Slavey and Dogrib Indians clad in decorated leggings and fringed garments of "well dressed" caribou and moose skin. Some tunics were "embroider[ed] very neatly with Porcupines Quills & the Hair of the Moos Deer painted [colored] Red, Black, Yellow & White." Belts and garters of porcupine quills woven with sinew were, Mackenzie recorded in his journal, "the neatest thing of the kind that ever I saw" (Lamb 1970:184).

A hundred years later in most parts of the Mackenzie region cloth apparel had essentially replaced the Dene's basic clothing of dressed skins. Whatever this shift to manufactured materials may have lacked in the way of exoticism to the eye of the foreign traveler, it brought a substantial reduction in women's labor on hide preparation. When a family was clad entirely in dressed skins, furred or sueded, the demand on women's time and energy must have been great indeed. [See Helene Rabesca's account in chapter 18.] Hides of moose and caribou did continue in constant use for mittens and moccasins through the mid–twentieth century. For bush activities through the long winters, nothing could equal native hand- and footgear. It was a woman's responsibility to keep her family shod year-round in moccasins. One moose hide is barely sufficient to meet the moccasin needs of two adults for a year. About ten pairs of moccasins can be made from one moose hide: a woman needs three or four pairs and her husband at least four pairs per year (Helm and Lurie 1961). Before the introduction of moccasin rubbers to protect the moccasin from destructive dampness in the warmer months, many more pairs per year were needed.

A woman's aesthetic standards and pride in her handiwork do not start with the decorative elements with which, past and present, she has embellished items of hide apparel. The hide itself is subject to aesthetic appraisal. To gain approval, the dressed hide must be supple, smoothly and evenly scraped, and smoked an even, rich, golden brown. An elegant pair of moccasins must not only display attractive designs and colors executed in fine floss work or well-stitched beading, but the hide must also be handsome.

Aesthetic judgments attach to many aspects of native crafts, as illustrated by an incident at Rae some years ago. The anthropology division of the National Museums of Canada had arranged for the construction of a birchbark canoe in the aboriginal form, which had been supplanted by canvas canoes in the early 1920s. That successful "sale," followed by another the next year, stimulated an elderly widower to repair to an island near Rae, where he spent the summer alone, crafting yet another birchbark canoe. When it was finished, the canoe was brought to Rae, where it evoked a lively interest among the Dogribs. But the older men and women arrived at a collective judgment: "He should have had a woman do the sewing." Although "seaworthy," the canoe's stitching of spruce root that pieced the sections of birchbark together was uneven. Spruce-root stitching, on birchbark baskets or birchbark canoes, is women's work and should be executed handsomely.

To the earlier amateur and museum collectors, only a woman's handiwork, not the woman, was of consequence. Those past artisans are nameless and unknown to us. In the native world, however, the creator of every piece of woman's craft was known. For many of the finest creations of a bush Indian wife, her husband served as a kind of traveling art gallery. When men went by dog team to the trading fort, particularly at Christmastime and Eastertime, to trade their furs, their wives usually stayed behind. But the embroidered or beaded yoke of her husband's parka and his decorated moccasins, newly made for him to wear at the fort, advertised a woman's handiwork.

From afar in space and time, we admire the skill and artistry of the anonymous women whose accomplishments are revealed in museum collections to

"Dress" ankle-wrap moccasins for Easter, Rae, 1971. Joseph Naedzo (center) and Chief Jimmy Bruneau (right) await the serving of the Easter feast at the chief's house, wearing new, richly embroidered moccasins. Beryl Gillespie Collection, Northwest Territories Archives.

be found throughout North America and Europe. One would like to think that these women, and those many more whose work has been lost to us, received in their lifetime the appreciation of their handiwork that young Slavey women knew in the early years of the nineteenth century, when, we are told, "[the trader] Mr. Wentzel has often known the young married men to bring specimens of their wives' needlework to the forts and exhibit them with much pride" (Franklin 1824:81).

from "Women's Work, Women's Art," 1989

NINHTS'I NETSÀ

Sometimes Nature brings unexpected fun for the children. From the field notes:

After five days of heat here at Rae, with the lake in glassy torpor, big wind come! It rained a bit earlier in the day, bringing some relief, but not enough after the buildup of heat and apathy. Then out of the north comes the wind, sucking a black cloud in its wake. The first gusts call the people out of the

Ninhts'i netsà! Moving the pups, Rae, 1962.

tents. Dotted about the lake are canoes, quickly turned and running before the wind. Those with kickers and loaded with firewood are soon straight to shore, but the lone paddlers bob and toss. They seem not to be spared a glance by those on shore. The men are running to pull beached canoes higher on the rocks and to get them braced and overturned before the wind pitches them about. The precious kicker is carried to the bucking and billowing tent. The women grab axes and begin beating the tent stakes tighter into the earth. In the urgency there is also exhilaration in the approaching storm. Those children too young to be useful are in delight—leaning into the wind, arms extended, hair tossing, shirts and skirts flying. Two little girls grab pieces of cardboard carton for sails and shields. All are laughing. The dogs, the barometers of the camp, respond to the flurry and action by leaping against their chains and voicing their high, strangulated yelp of excitement. The two clown-faced pups, staked at the water's edge, alternate between leaping frenzy as the children run between them and huddled misery beneath the spray of the waves. Two small boys decide first to move the pups farther up on the shore, then to erect a hopeless windbreak of cardboard. Finally, they fall back on the first plan, and the pups now circle outside my window, restless at their new anchorage.

The rain has come now, and the camp is in unaccustomed silence. Doors and tent flaps secured, each family is in its refuge. It is eerie to hear no dogs, no children, only wind and waves.

from the field notes of July 21, 1962, Rae

I hope that these accounts of two Dene lives, Helene Rabesca, a Bear Laker, and Louis Norwegian, a Slavey, help to personalize some of the broader ethnographic and historical views in this book. I regret that I recorded almost no consistent life history materials. They would surely have enriched the source material of future ethnohistorians.

This volume is dedicated to Teresa and Nancy, my two American field companions, and to Louis and Vital, two of my Dene friends/teachers. Vital Thomas has a brief biography in Prophecy and Power among the Dogrib Indians *(1994). This chapter offers a study, rather than a biography, of Louis Norwegian. Of a very different genre is the first part of the chapter: a remembering by Helene Rabesca (née Yambi) of what life was like at the start of the twentieth century.*

HELENE RABESCA, 1897–1996

At Lac la Martre, Nancy Lurie had two interview sessions with Helene Rabesca in August 1962, when Mrs. Rabesca was sixty-five years old. Two young Dogribs served as interpreters, Mary Adele Jeremik'ea (later Mrs. Charles Bishop) for the first interview and Alexis Nitsiza for the second session. Mrs. Rabesca shifted back and forth on topics. The presentation here does not follow the zigzag sequence of her narrative, and I have rephrased, rearranged, and dropped some of her account as it was received by Nancy in translation.

The time frame of Helene Rabesca's account is the first quarter of the twentieth century. Her story impinges on Naedzo's remembrance in chapter 9. Naedzo was eleven years older than Helene, who was born in November 1897. Naedzo followed the Bear Lake Chief; Helene was the youngest child of the Bear Lake Chief. Naedzo's memories are of group esprit and hunters rallying to the leader's call, of the days when "every one goes like we are one." Helene's personal memories are those of a lonely, unhappy, abused child-wife. In place of the great days of Naedzo's remembrance, Helene details minutiae of the struggle to be warm, clothed, and fed and of

women's toil. In his old age Naedzo laments, "Nowadays, it is not as good as before, because no one listens or cares for one another." Helene sees people's loss of strength and health since white men came but remembers that in the old days people suffered exhausting exertion and came close to starving: "Since the white man came, things have improved."

Nancy's comments on the sessions with Helene are illuminating; they follow.

The first interview with Mrs. Bruneau Rabesca was a near fiasco. I had asked Mary Adele Jeremik'ea (serving as interpreter) to find out if Mrs. Rabesca could talk to me now. I wanted to set out to Mrs. R's house, but Mary Adele sent Sonny Fish. Sonny told Mrs. R that she was supposed to come to my house to tell stories, so she arrived hot and a bit annoyed just as I was zipping up my case to trundle over in the event that she was available. I got Mary Adele to apologize to her as much as possible. Mrs. Rabesca sat down by the tape machine and asked if she'd get paid. I said, of course, that old Mrs. Beaverhook had asked me to order dress goods as payment to her, but I could get Mrs. R whatever she liked. She brightened at that considerably and asked for five yards of dress material, a nice print. Also there was a can of peaches which she realized I'd brought out as a gift for her, and good feelings were restored all around.

At one point she commented, "I thought maybe because you are a white woman you don't want to come and sit in my house." I'm sure she knows I visit around. My peremptory order, as she misunderstood Sonny's version of my message, bore out her worst suspicions. The fact is, I haven't gotten to know the Rabescas before this. She's a proud woman and has not come to visit as other women have, and her husband, Bruneau, visited only when I saw him outside and invited him in. I was relieved, however, that she admitted to her feelings and could laugh about them once the rhubarb was straightened out.

The interview went on with little prompting by me. Mrs. Rabesca grasped what I wanted and simply took off like a bird in flight, responding to my enthusiastic smiles whenever I caught on to the gist of her narrative through her expression and an occasional word, with Mary Adele cueing me in now and then.

Like other women, Mrs. Rabesca's gestures are part of the story, small movements and detailed, using her fingers to show how things are pointed or smoothed or scraped. Her expression was serious, and, unlike Adele Pig (Mary Adele's grandmother), who laughed uproariously at her own funnies, Mrs. Rabesca would wait to see if Alexis (the translator for the second interview) got the point of amusing things. Then she smiled quickly, her mouth almost shut, her eyes almost closed. I found hilarious the scowls and expressions of wonder that accompanied her account of the white naturalists whom her father guided. They were among the first whites she had ever seen, and it led to some funny impressions.

Of special interest is that Helene Rabesca is really a Bear Laker; the Bear Lake people apparently remained bushier than others until more recent times. [In Helene's youth there was no trading post on Great Bear Lake. Fort Norman on the Mackenzie and Fort Rae on the North Arm of the Great Slave Lake (later on Marian Lake) were the nearest posts for the Bear Lake people.] Until her marriage to Bruneau Rabesca, Helene's recollections are really a Bear Lake story. Her narrative begins with the first two sentences below.

BEING A YOUNG WIFE (1912–1925)

I got married when I had not yet had my first menstrual period. [According to Rae mission records, Helene was married in 1912 at the age of fourteen.] Three years after I got married I had my first period, and two years after I had my first period I started to have children. [Giving a girl in marriage before her menses occurred in the old days. Sexual intercourse was not to be initiated until menses. Vital Thomas tells a Dogrib humorous story, purportedly true, of a man staking a claim to an unborn girl by doing bride service, hunting, and attending to camp tasks for the parents for months. But when the child was born, it was a baby boy!]

When I had my first child, a baby boy, I didn't know how to look after children because I was just a young girl. My mother never taught me how to look after children. In the winter when I was caring for my children, I made them clothes. I used caribou hide to make my little boy a snowsuit. [NL: This is Mary Adele's term for a garment in which the shirt and pants are sewn together.] In the wintertime, even though it was cold we women would look for moss and chop out a block and take it to the tent and put it on the poles above the fire for drying. After the moss was dried we used it for baby diapers. [This was still a common practice in the 1950s.] That's how I took care of my children. [Mary Adele gives a literal and convoluted description of a moss bag of caribou hide with moss inside as a diaper and a fur bag to keep the baby's feet warm.]

In wintertime we used only caribou hide for dresses. When we had to go out for wood or work outside, we wore dresses of caribou hide with the hair on and wore the hair side against our bodies. I used to have those kind of dresses for wintertime. [Of the early 1890s in "the Hudson's Bay Company's territory," Russell (1898:169) says, "The women wear light print dresses which are a poor substitute for the warm skin clothing of former times. A few gowns of dressed leather are still worn by the Dog Rib women, and both sexes wear capotes of caribou skin in the hair while traveling in winter."]

When a woman had lots of children, she made clothes for the children in the summer, because the animals' hair is not too long in the summer. [The hunt for caribou hides for winter clothing occurs in August and September when the new pelage is short and sleek.] So children's clothes for winter are made in the summer. For summer clothing, they used thin [unfurred] hide. They also used hide for men's pants and tops. For summer clothing they used thin hides, and for winter they left the hair on. Women were working hard making clothes.

In the wintertime nearly every day we had to change the spruce boughs [that serve as the floor] inside the tipi. When the needles got dry, the boughs were thrown away. In the wintertime we did not get enough sleep because it was so cold inside the tipi. That was before the white men came, so we had only caribou hides for blankets. Especially for the baby it was very cold.

After I had my first baby boy I learned how to do woman's work. When we traveled, we women had to pack our babies on our backs, and we used only caribou hide for blankets [to bind the baby to the mother's back]. When we stopped, I used to put up the tipi by myself. My husband went hunting because there was nothing to eat. My husband wouldn't make a fire before he went hunting because he would say he was too hungry. So I put up the tent myself and made a little fire for my baby. After I put up the tipi, it was very smoky and cold, and my baby would cry.

I had my first canoe after I married. I took my baby with me and went with my husband everywhere he went. Even when there was a big river, I'd still have to paddle on it. When we crossed portages, I carried my baby on my back with the caribou hide. I used two straps for the baby (one across the shoulders and one on the waist), and I carried the canoe across the portage. After we took the canoes across the portage we had to go back for our things we left on the other side of the portage, and we put them in the canoes and took off again. When we had to go from one place to another in the wintertime we used the sled. Even in the summertime we always traveled. [Throughout her narrative, Helene emphasizes *summer* travel by canoe, although winter travel by foot must have occupied as much of the year. Pad-

Elise Nitsiza laying a spruce-bough floor, Lac la Martre, 1959.

dling must have seemed more arduous to her in terms of the many miles
of canoe-and-portage travel between the hunting grounds of the Bear Lake
Band, over the height of land, and the point-of-trade at Fort Rae.]

[Nancy asks about childbirth.] Nowadays, when women have babies it's
just like they can't work, but before, we weren't like that. Since the nurses

and doctors came, when something is wrong the women always ask the doctors, What's the matter? What should we do? We didn't do that. In the old days, we didn't know what "to catch cold" means. We used to eat fish, caribou, moose, anything that we could catch, and sometimes we used to drink the blood. It goes inside us and our blood is dark and we feel always warm. We used to be younglike. Even the girls worked like men, but nowadays young girls are like old ladies and can hardly work. When my baby was born I stayed in bed for only one day. There was nothing to eat so we started to travel, and I packed my baby on my back. That's what I did when I had my baby.

To feed a baby when the mother didn't have much milk, you cooked blood and fed it to the baby, and sometimes you cooked fish eggs and made them something like milk. That's what you fed the baby even though it was a small baby. [Dogribs and Slaveys say rabbit brains also served as a substitute for mother's milk.]

Today when a woman is expecting a baby the doctor says not to work and they obey him and now the women don't work. Before, the old-time women used to have lots of work, they used to have to do moose hides and they had to fix caribou hides for blankets. When we traveled by canoe we used to travel even if it was windy. When it's windy, even if the baby is crying we have to paddle fast. We nursed the baby and then we had to paddle fast. We had to travel because we had nothing to eat. That's what I did until I had three children and my [first] husband died [in 1925]. Since I have been staying with Bruneau [b. 1897] I haven't had to do much work. [Helene and Bruneau Rabesca married in 1929; she was about thirty-one years old at the time.]

I was scared of my [first] husband because I got beaten every day. I was scared of him. That is why when he told me to eat something I ate anything. That is why my hair is white. My parents had told me not to eat certain things, but I was scared of my husband so I ate everything that he told me to eat and that is why my hair is turning white. It is no good to stay with a man when you get beaten every day so that you always have to cry. He stayed with us [Helene's adoptive family] for two years because he wanted to marry me. After I married him I got beaten nearly every day, and every day I cried. I had two children, and after the third child came he stopped doing that, but before I had my third child I got beaten nearly every day. I didn't visit around to see what people were doing. I never looked at people with my own eyes because I was scared of my husband.

My parents were from Bear Lake, but I didn't stay with my father and mother. I was adopted by someone from Bear Lake. I didn't know anything about Rae. After I was married, my husband and I stayed [traded] at [the present] Rae but we always went out traveling. We never stayed at the Old Fort Rae. After my husband died I stayed at Rae and I got married to Bruneau. The first time I came to Lac la Martre was when Bruneau brought me here. [Bruneau Rabesca was a widower whose first wife, Marie Nitsiza, was from a Lac la Martre family.]

They called my father Kotchilea Weta, Kotchilea's Father. [Kotchilea or Gots'ia is also known as Toby Bearlake.] My dad was like a big shot for the Hudson's Bay Company. The person who adopted me was like a father to me, but my real father was much higher than he was. My real father was called Ek'awi [Trader]. Nearly all over the North I think they heard of my dad. [Her father was the Bear Lake Chief, also known as Gots'ia Weta, K'aawidaa, and so on, of whom Naedzo spoke in chapter 9.]

I was the last one [the youngest] of our family. Only three of us are living [in 1962]. [One is Gots'ia or Kotchilea, b. 1896.] Adele Zoe [b. 1891, Mrs. Andre Zoe of Lac la Martre] isn't of my family. There was a woman who got a baby, they said, by my father and that's how come I call her my sister.

At Fort Rae when the white men made my father like a Hudson's Bay manager they gave him things and he gave them to the people. [See chapter 10 on trading chiefs.] That's how the people got a little bit richer [came to have more goods].

I grew up at Great Bear Lake. Not exactly grew up, when I was small my parents came here [Dogrib country generally]. At Bear Lake there were no white men. I first saw white men when we went down to Old Fort Rae [Ninhsi Kon]. My father was an old-style leader, he "worked" at Old Fort. My father gave me away when we stayed down at Old Fort.

In 1993 Thomas Andrews, with John B. Zoe translating, interviewed the very aged Mrs. Rabesca at Lac la Martre and got this account: Helene's family, the Bear Lake Chief with his wife and three young children, was on their way to Old Fort Rae, traveling the Indàà trail, the canoe-and-portage route linking Great Bear and Great Slave Lakes. It was spring, the ice was still on the lakes, but the snow had melted from the land when Helene's mother died. [This was in 1906, as deduced from church records.] Two weeks later the Bear Lake Chief and the children reached Gameti (Rae

Helene Rabesca at age ninety-five, Lac la Martre, 1993. Photo by T. D. Andrews.

Lakes). *Here they waited until the ice was gone and then continued on. When they arrived at the present location of Rae, there were five tents. [A free trader had a post there.] They set a net and left for Old Fort Rae the next day. The children were baptized at Old Fort.*

In July of the same year as the death of his wife, the Bear Lake Chief was forced to marry another woman. She said she was carrying his child and accused him of this "on the steps of the church" at Old Fort Rae, but after they got married he found out she was not pregnant. Helene says that her father had no intention of marrying again after Helene's mother died. Helene was adopted out at this point, as the woman the Bear Lake Chief married did not want to raise his children. Helene never saw her father again.

TRAVELING WITH WHITE MEN, 1903

In 1903, three years before Helene's mother died and when Helene was six years old, Edward A. Preble of the Bureau of Biological Survey of the U.S. Department of Agriculture employed two Indians to take him and his companion, James MacKinlay, on the canoe-and-portage route from Old Fort Rae to Great Bear Lake. In his report Preble (1908) does not give the names of these two Indian men, and he makes no mention of other persons going with them, but Helene's story of traveling to Bear Lake with her father and her mother in the company of two white men must be an account of Preble and MacKinlay's journey. The Indian whom Preble refers to as "the guide" would be K'aawidaa, the Bear Lake Chief.

We saw a government white man at Old Fort. That white man asked my father to go with him. When we were at Old Fort there were my father and my mother and me, three of us, and another [Indian] man, four of us, and two white men. [Older siblings are missing in this account.] We were using [old-style birchbark] pointed canoes, and the white men had a [modern canvas] canoe, and we were on our way to Great Bear Lake. I don't exactly know what the white men were trying to do, but I think they were trying to measure the land.

We were traveling on Marian Lake and we stopped [apparently near Xàeliìn, Marian Lake Village] and discussed about continuing with the white men, where they were going. They [the adult Indians] made up their mind, and we went with the white men. I was too small so they didn't let me paddle. My mother used a birch canoe and my father used a birch canoe too. The white men used a canoe like the ones of today. There were three of them in one canoe. [Evidently, the other Indian was in the white men's canoe as a third paddler.] We were following those white men and we were much behind. There were too many portages. My father worked hard, but we were too slow and we couldn't keep up with them. We packed their stuff over the portages. We went over lots of portages, and we stopped at a place called *de gozi* [cave?]. It was a long time ago but I still remember. We then traveled to a place named [probably] Ints'in Dii [a big island in Hottah Lake], and there we stopped and spent a holy day [Assumption Day, August 15?]. After we spent the holy day we traveled on the river called Ints'eeti [the river flowing from Hottah Lake, that is, Camsell River] and then went on toward Bear Lake. We stopped at a place and my mother quit paddling. It was hard and she said she quit. When my mother stopped paddling, the white men said they wanted to keep on. My mother said "no." We had traveled with them all the way from Old Fort, but that's the way the white men are, stubborn. [Preble says, "On August 22, our guide declined to conduct us farther, apparently not having personal knowledge of the route."]

To me, those men didn't look like other white men. These were the first white men I had seen, and other white men [apparently those at Old Fort and new Fort Rae] didn't look like them. They said they were taking pictures [Preble's report features a number of good photographs] and measuring the land. He [Preble] wasn't doing anything, my father had to do things for him. He was collecting things of our land. He was collecting mice, fish, and other things. He put them in a suitcase which was about this [two feet, gestures] high, and it had like five little floors [compartments]. He collected lots of things and put them in that case. [Preble records collecting small mammals, including muskrat, red squirrel, mouse, three species of rats, and two species of shrew.] He said that he was going to take them to his land. When we stopped at a place for camping, all the white man does is collect things. When we spend the night, he just sets traps for mice. And when we were on the portages and carrying things, he carried just a gun and equipment for the gun. He carries it across the portage and then he doesn't come back to get anything else. When we cross the portages my father has to do all the work.

When we separated from them, we went on our way back to where we saw all the people. We hadn't seen the Indian people in the bush for a long time.

LIVING

Before we had canvas tents, we made tipis out of caribou hides. In the wintertime it was cold with a very small fire in the middle of the tipi. Drafts came in through the smoke hole and along the edges on the ground. We could hardly sit inside the tipi because it was so cold. In those days we didn't have any mosquito net. In the summer, to keep the mosquitoes out of the tipi, we built a fire in the middle of it and let all the smoke escape from the hole at the top and the mosquitoes didn't come in. You see how mosquitoes fly around today. In those days we didn't have any mosquito net, but we used our tipi with the fire as a mosquito net.

After I was married my husband made a canoe for me, a little canoe out of birchbark. To make a canoe, my husband got the wood [for the gunwales and ribs], and I got the birchbark and sewed the pieces together with spruce root. When my husband finished the frame, we put the birchbark on it. Then we got a lot of spruce gum and boiled it and spread it where the birchbark was sewn. After we put the gum on it, we would put the canoe in the water. If water leaked in, we would take the canoe up again and put more gum on it. Finally, if there was no leak, we could use it. [In the second interview, Helene went into a much more extensive and precise description of how a birchbark canoe is constructed. In that account she presents the picture of a group of men and women working together on gender-assigned tasks, not a single man-and-woman team. Canoe construction is ordinarily described as a group enterprise. Helene's references to life with her first husband give a sense of a highly aberrant isolation from group life.] Whatever I have told you about the canoe, I should know because I did the work on it, half the work on it myself. [NL: Such precision! She did the *woman's* half.]

In the old days, we didn't have any tea or tobacco or anything like that. If people wanted something to drink besides water, they took the inner bark of the spruce tree and boiled it. We boiled the fish we caught and drank that water. To cook, we put a pole up and hung the food from a line with a wooden hook. In those days we didn't have any tea kettles or pails to get water, so we used birchbark to make dishes. In the summertime we collected birchbark to make pails for water, and we put gum on where we sewed the pail. In winter we took snow in the pail inside the tipi to melt it. I'm just telling about things that I did myself. I can't tell some of the stories because I don't remember them all. [Nancy asks about stoneboiling.] I didn't do it myself, but I have seen it done. They take a birchbark bucket so high [gestures a big one, twenty inches in height at least] and they seal it with spruce gum. They put water and whatever they are going to cook in the bucket and then they put in at least four or five red-hot stones, about the size of that [one-pound] butter tin, taking the ashes off first. They don't want what's cooking to stick to the bottom so they shake the bucket every once in awhile. When a rock is cool they take it out and put new hot ones in.

In the old days, when the people didn't have plates, they made their own of wood, about so [gestures ten to twelve inches] long. They used a crooked knife to make them. Only those men who were good at it made those plates. And they used to make a big spoon to serve things, like boiled fish. When the white men came it was better. Before that, people were very, very poor. [The translators used the English word "poor" here and throughout Mrs. Rabesca's narrative. Older English speakers often use "pitiful," in the sense of a condition exciting pity and compassion. The Dogrib word *etee't'in*, glossed as "pitiful," "poor," and "miserable" in the new Dogrib dictionary, is undoubtedly the word Mrs. Rabesca was using.]

For fishhooks we would kill a muskrat, take out its two upper teeth, and split them in two. That's what we used for a fishhook. For line we took willow bark and twisted it as if we were making sinew and tied that to the end of a long pole. If we didn't want to use a pole, we just tied the line to the rat's teeth. For bait, we sewed fish around the hook. Sometimes we'd take a pole with a line on the end with the rat tooth and tie a rock to the pole and leave it in the water. We would leave it like that for a day and then check to see if the pole was moving; that meant we caught a fish. If we don't catch any fish then we don't have anything to eat. Often my husband went out getting fish like that.

Some people were better off and other people were worse off in living. We didn't even have a stove. [It is not clear if Helene is speaking of herself and her first husband or of her people generally.] We didn't have time to make everything we want, especially in winter. The only thing we needed badly was to catch some kind of animal to feed ourselves, so we would get muskrat teeth and make hooks and get willows and peel the bark and braid it and make a cord and tie that to the hook and set it in the lake under the ice. That's how we got some fish. That's how the people made their living.

It sounds like there was nothing good in the old days, but in summertime berries were growing. And some men made bows and arrows. They used to make lots of arrows and fill a container as big around as that tobacco tin there [no identifiable word for "quiver"] to carry them. At the end of the arrows is bone. They carried their arrows on their backs. Sometimes there are about five arrows without heads [bunts?]. When they are hunting with bows and arrows, even at a long distance, they shoot, and down goes the animal. They hunted ducks from canoes, but only those who were good with bows and arrows could get lots of ducks. They could hit ducks with arrows from here to the school [100 feet]. In wintertime we could hardly use bow and arrows because it is cold and we couldn't use guns because we had no ammunition.

In the summertime, when we had no shot and my husband could not get us anything to eat, we would take a long pole and make a spear point out of stone and bind it to that pole. [Is the point really of stone? Or is it bone?] When we see a fish under the water, we throw the spear at it. Also, we used a spear if there was a caribou or moose out on the lake. Many men would go out with my husband [in canoes] to surround the caribou or moose. They all took their spears and tried to kill it. If it goes to an island or on land and they go fast and catch it, they all use their spears and kill it. Then we have something to eat.

When the first guns came, people used balls in the winter and the other kind [shot] in the summer for things like ducks. We don't get many balls [in trade], just a few. We used those to kill caribou. After a caribou is dead, they cut it open to see if there are balls inside, and they take the balls out because we don't get enough balls. Sometimes we get around fifteen or ten, so we save those balls to shoot again. We try to use a ball three times, but when it gets too small we can't use it.

When they see an animal, the men have to do so much work—put powder in the gun, tear a piece of rag and poke it in the gun, and put a bullet in there, and a rag again, and then they're ready to fire. Only those who move fast have much luck with the gun. The one who doesn't move fast in loading his gun when he sees an animal doesn't have much chance to kill it. By the time he finishes loading the gun, the animal will be far away. In the wintertime, loading a gun was a cold business.

[Traveling with Dogribs in 1893, Russell (1893–94:34) wrote: "The supply of shot was now running low, the small stock of ball was cut up into cubes and rolled into a rough shot in a frying pan. . . . Their guns were of the pattern known as trade guns in the country. They are of small bore, long barrelled muzzle-loaders, and of very light weight. In using shot, twelve or fifteen pellets of BB shot are used to each load. They will carry balls with tolerable accuracy up to a hundred yards. The balls weigh twenty eight to the pound."]

At first I didn't know how to use a gun. When my husband went out and left the gun, if I saw anything like a ptarmigan I used the gun to kill the ptarmigan. We got only fifteen or ten of those balls for one year, so if we used all of them we killed squirrels and ptarmigans with sticks. [Mary Adele is impressed. "They ate squirrels!"] And that's how we ate. When I was first married there were two kinds of guns, shotguns and rifles[?]. We used shotguns to kill rats but later found out that muskrat is no good with holes in the fur like that. After my husband died we got .22s.

In the old days the people didn't have matches. They took a rock and those black things [burls (Kari 1987:188)] from the birch and struck them together [gestures with frequent strikes and blowing] until they get a little spark on some moss. Then they blow and blow to make a fire to cook things. In the wintertime when it was cold they used gunpowder and spruce needles. They put the spruce needles in one place [gestures a little pile] and put gunpowder in a gun and fire closely at the needles and a fire starts. Sometimes they had some matches, but not many. They counted matches out carefully.

In the old days when there were no rubbers, people used only moccasins for rubbers. To go anyplace when it rained they used moccasins. The moccasins were never dry, always wet. At the same time they didn't know anything about catching cold. There was no such thing. We walked in water about a foot deep [gestures] and it makes a noise like ka^np, ka^np, ka^np. We keep walking and walking. When we stop for a night or so, we try to dry our moccasins by the fire, but when we used those same moccasins the next day they got all wet again. We keep on like that. We keep on drying them, but they get wet again [a phrase dii hanì, dii hanì, dii hanì, "like this," repeated]. The wet moccasins tear, and when we stop at a place for camping we sew them up and keep on like that. We've been doing that until we first got rubbers. The people were very poor [see comment above on "poor"] and in very bad shape because of having to use these moccasins. Take a look today! We cannot take even two steps without our rubbers on. In the old days we had no rubbers at all. People were very poor in those days.

[Immediately following her point on the wonders of rubbers, Mrs. Rabesca switched her point of view.] Since we got all kinds of white man's food that go in our bodies and doctors' medicines that go in our bodies, people catch cold easily. In the old days we knew no such thing as catching cold. The people ate well, they ate meat and soup. After they had boiled their meat, they drank the soup. There was nothing wrong with them. They didn't catch cold easily like today. [Does "catching cold" encompass the two deadly respiratory sicknesses of tuberculosis and influenza?] There was no tea and tobacco in the old days, we just drank soup. We ate fish, meat, fish eggs, and meat of all kinds of animals. Our blood was strong, that's why we didn't catch any cold. [But in the next sentence Mrs. Rabesca says:] The people were very, very poor when the white men came.

We [that is, her own people] started to get white men's clothes when there were just a few houses at [the present] Rae. Before that, people used only hide to make clothes for women and men. People in the old days were used to wearing hide clothes. They never thought of white man's clothes.

It wasn't a long time ago when they started to make moccasins like the ones you see today. We got them from white men, the few white men at Fort Rae. [Mrs. Rabesca is probably including Metis in the "whitemen" category.] We saw those moccasins and started to make them in the same style. Before the white men came we had moccasins, but they didn't look like moccasins of today, they were pointed. The [round-toed] moccasins of today look like Cree (Enda) moccasins. Not long ago women started putting designs on the parka too; they got that idea from white men, too. White men brought the new styles to Fort Rae, and that's when I saw those new styles with the [embroidered or beaded] flowers on the parka. And they [the women] start to make that kind of parka, too. Before the white man came, the people had just hide clothes and jackets, and these were just bare, no decoration. Just hide, that's all. If they want to make something [ornamented], they used porcupine quills with sinew to sew them down. They put that on moccasins. It is not long since they [women] have had needles and thread, the ordinary thread of today, and they started making things, and it is much better.

[Mrs. Rabesca reflects on the old ladies of Lac la Martre whose thoughts Nancy had recorded:] The other ladies who put their voices in . . . [gestures at the machine], I guess they don't have the same feelings that I do. Those old days were hard for the people. Since the white man came things have

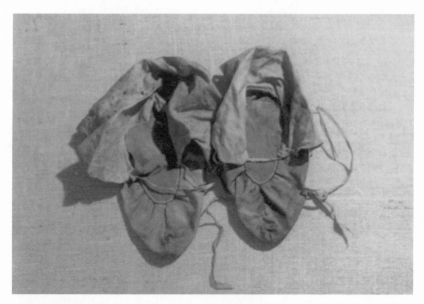

Old-style Dogrib moccasins, Rae, 1894. Frank Russell Collection, University of Iowa Museum of Natural History.

improved. Today if you have only one cent you're sure to get something for it, like matches.

Instead of talking about things of today, those women should have a feeling of the old days, how people were very, very poor. It seems to me they were talking like they were happy, and they weren't thinking about how they lived in the old days. When I hear them talking, I think they think they were very happy and have forgotten about the old days, how they had to work to make a living. [NL: As a matter of fact, Adele Zoe and Adele Pig are more jovial, but Madeline Beaverhook, the oldest woman here, has the same refrain as Mrs. Rabesca.] I, myself, am talking about the old days, how the people nearly starved and all like that, about the little things, how people made their living. I talk about how the people were very, very poor, I don't think other people talk like that. Like myself, I didn't grow up with new rubbers on my feet even though my father was a kind of leader. As I say, all the time life was hard. The people were very, very poor.

from Nancy O. Lurie's field notes of August 2 and 3, 1962, Lac la Martre

LOUIS NORWEGIAN, 1907–1977

Louis Norwegian was a Slavey, as were the other members of the kin-community of Jean Marie River. Except for his first year, perhaps, Louis spent his entire life at Jean

Marie River. In the discussion here I have reverted to the real names of people and places. Jean Marie River is the community represented as "Lynx Point" elsewhere in this volume, and Louis Norwegian is the person whom I called "Marcel Renard" in The Lynx Point People *(1961)*.

This presentation of Louis Norwegian is in a very different mode from the preceding one about Helene Rabesca. Mrs. Rabesca is met in translation from her own words by the translators' words that neither Nancy Lurie nor I embellished. This essay on Louis Norwegian, written in the mid-1950s, is an analysis of Louis as I and Teresa Carter-ette knew him for months (over a year in Teresa's case) when we lived with the Jean Marie River people. Except when he was away from the hamlet, we talked to Louis or saw him in action almost daily, and our field notes are filled with observations of or about him.

As I said in the introduction to the chapter on traditional leadership (chapter 10), I was led to that study by the need to understand Louis Norwegian as the leader among his male community companions in the cultural and historical setting. Although Louis discussed some of his own interests and predilections with us, this account derives from all dimensions of observation and interaction, including projective psychological tests. The emphasis here on personality analysis is very contrastive to the presentation of Helene Rabesca.

Louis Norwegian was the driving force in the set of acquisitions and enterprises by the community at Jean Marie River that I pseudonymously termed the "Lynx Point Venture." (The details of the Venture may be found in chapter 4 of The Lynx Point People.) It was, in fact, the Jean Marie River Venture. In scope and coordination, the Jean Marie River men's undertakings were unique for Dene of that time anywhere in the Northwest Territories.

According to Louis, his original desire was that, by joint expenditure and effort, the Jean Marie River men would be able to establish a sawmill similar to the one in Fort Simpson in which he and other Jean Marie River men had occasionally worked during the summer. (By 1972 they had a sawmill and other major acquisitions; see chapter 6.) In fact, the Venture was launched with the acquisition of a powerboat and barge by Louis and his closest kinsmen at Jean Marie River in the last years of the Second World War; high fur prices during the war allowed the men to make the first major investment in equipment. In the less than ten years between the middle of the war and 1951 (when Teresa and I entered the community) the people had acquired the major capital goods of the "outfit," which included an aging forty-foot powerboat, a sixty-foot barge designed by Louis with its construction overseen by him (as was later a new powerboat hull) as well as also tools, replacements parts, and several hundred dollars of fishing nets, and a couple of horses and attendant equipment. It added up to an approximate total investment of $5,600 in 1945–50 dollars. With this equipment *they took on several kinds of profit-making enterprises: buoy setting and beaching for the government, fishing in Great Slave Lake for sale to the mission and the Hudson's Bay Company at Simpson (in chapter 3, see the letter from Louis on the fall fishery), cutting and transporting cordwood, and various hauling jobs on the Mackenzie. Louis was pivotal in all the decisions and enterprises of the Venture. This sketchy background on the Venture enhances, I hope, understanding of Louis Norwegian. In my analysis of the Venture, the following characterization of Louis was presented as the final factor in the Venture, "The Personal Equation."*

Louis does not stint himself in the face of the challenge of the bush. And those same traits that make him a more successful hunter we see even more clearly in Louis's response to the demands of the Venture.

In an unstructured society such as that of the Slavey, where any special status is attained through achievement, the particular character of the individual is the keystone. A major key to Louis Norwegian as a person and as the leader of the Jean Marie River community is his approach to the physical world. In his excellence in the hunt and in bushcraft, Louis has fulfilled the prime prerequisite of leadership. It is in his nature to excel. Louis is a craftsman. He finds challenge in the physical world, and he delights in developing and applying his skills so as to master the technical and mechanical problems of the physical environment. The enjoyment and pride that he experiences in bushcraft seem even greater in application to the technical and mechanical challenges that the greater world has allowed him. Louis does not commit himself to the outcome of any venture, but he is intrigued and seems quietly confident when faced with a technical challenge. His characteristic response to a question regarding his potential ability to master a technical problem or attain a new skill is "Try, anyway."

Louis's ingenuity, patience, and careful craftsmanship are illustrated in the following incident. The long bushing of the propeller shaft of the powerboat became worn, causing the propeller to rotate off-center and to vibrate dangerously. He had diagnosed the trouble in its early stages and had ordered a new bushing from outside, but when it arrived it was the wrong size. To wait more weeks for a proper bushing to arrive would have meant inconvenience and financial loss to the group, so he undertook to manufacture a temporary bushing from the scanty materials at hand at Jean Marie River. The propeller shaft and its outer casing were removed from the powerboat. Louis, with Jimmy Sanguez assisting, melted soldering lead, by eye carefully centered the shaft in the casing, and poured the lead around it to form a new bushing. Then they whittled a pole to the size of the shaft and, after doing some rough

The powerboat and the barge, Jean Marie River, 1952. Louis Norwegian is leading Mac with Jimmy and Johnny Sanguez standing by.

filing of the pole, rammed it, wrapped in sandpaper, through the hole of the bushing until the bore was smooth enough to act as an adequate surface against which the shaft could turn. This improvised bushing served for several weeks until a proper brass one arrived.

Louis states that he usually does not like motion pictures, which could be seen Saturday nights in Fort Simpson. He doesn't like all that "sweetheart stuff," but he does like movies about boats and the war, and he described movies he enjoyed on sheep shearing in Australia and the locating and hunting of submarines by ASDIC.

Louis examined an angle measure on the back of our ruler. He explained to us how it can be used in building. He states that this is something that he has figured out for himself. Louis says he would like to know all about electricity. He says that he likes to work with lumber in the sawmill and in house building.

Louis frequently tinkers with clocks, radios, motors, any mechanical contrivance. He is pleased if asked to repair something. He studies and handles the object deliberately but delicately before starting to work. He verbalizes his admiration for a good tool or a good piece of work. His face really seems to light up as he talks of these matters. On the other hand, viewing a shoddy piece of workmanship, as, for example, the shelf made for us by Johnny, Louis is apt to shake his head and mutter, "Jesus Christ!" In this particular instance, he silently departed from our cabin, returned with his tools, and rebuilt the shelf properly. We once suggested to Louis that it was a pity he had never had the opportunity for any technical training. His response (paraphrased) was, "Well, things often look hard, but if you try to do them, sometimes you find out it's not so hard after all."

Louis was in his young adulthood when a white trader and trapper named McNeill lived at Jean Marie River, and for two years Louis was his trapping partner. This evidently was a period of opportunity for Louis to acquire technical knowledge (as well as to learn broken English), and he made the most of this association. McNeill had an outboard motor. This was Louis's first opportunity to learn the mechanics of a gasoline engine. Soon Louis owned his own kicker, the first Indian on the river, he mentioned to us several times with quiet pride, to own an outboard motor. In succeeding years, Louis has constantly sought opportunities for more experience and knowledge in mechanical matters and technical devices, using such social and business contacts with river pilots, traders, and government officials as have come his way to examine and, if possible, operate different devices, such as sawmill equipment, tractors, and diesel engines.

The kind of selection Louis has exercised in the acculturation situation is indicative of his character. It is the utilitarian advances of whiteman culture that have actively attracted him. The appeals and desires engendered in Louis in the contact situation have been limited almost completely to technological advantages. He shows no inclination to enter into the white Canadian social system and no real emotional investment in the system of manners, morals, and religion. He is a bush Indian whose dedication to the utilitarian cast of the native ethos has led him to select only those pertinent offerings or benefits from the culture contact situation.

The overall assessment of Louis's intellectual nature gained from observation of and interaction with him is that he is clever, and his cleverness, the ability to assess and evaluate in a practical way, which he shows in relation to the physical world, has, it seems, its counterpart in shrewdness in the realm of interpersonal relations. He is pragmatic and concrete-minded. He is primarily interested in those natural and social phenomena in which he can see immediate application or significance in his own life. The obverse of these

Louis Norwegian at age forty-five, Jean Marie River, 1952.

traits is that he does not appear to have any intellectual gift for or attraction to abstract thinking, broad ideation, or philosophizing. Now here, of course, there is a question that the kinds of opportunities and norms in Louis's cultural experience and the problem of linguistic communication between the ethnologists and him may have in the first instance inhibited and in the second obscured a potential abstract, nonutilitarian intellectual drive within him. But the psychological projective material on Louis leads the analyst George A. DeVos to support my observational assessment of a literal-minded practicality.

The second major aspect of Louis's personality pertinent to his role as leader is his approach to interpersonal relationships. One characteristic in this respect, perhaps the most salient, is his interest in male friendships. He has a talent for camaraderie and enjoys a friendship on this level. His friendships, however, are controlled; that is, he occupies a position of equality or of superordination in relation to others. He does not yield his personality to the domination of another, as we have seen Jimmy do in regard to Louis. With Teresa and me, Louis was willing to establish a friendship of the same order that he holds with Indian men. It was essentially a relationship of camaraderie, although Louis enjoyed exercising over us as well a protective role, that of a mentor quietly rescuing us from our follies in bushcraft. Louis's responses in the projective testing, especially in the TAT projective test, indicate that he does, in fact, feel more at ease in male-to-male camaraderie than in the man–woman relationship.

Louis can go beyond his bush community in his friendships and interests in other people; witness, for example, his friendship with McNeill, with the Metis river pilot Albert Loutit, and with the ethnologists, especially when these persons offered him a somewhat broader view of the world than he could obtain from his community kinsmen. His main area of identity and interest, however, is in the kin-community of Jean Marie River. But again, this identification is under control. That is, Louis does not sacrifice himself for the community. Rather, he uses the community both to its advantage and to his own advantage. That which honors Jean Marie River honors Louis, because he sees himself as a major figure in the community. He feels, in common with Jimmy and Gabriel Sanguez, an allegiance and sense of pride as a Jean Marie River man, but it is my feeling that this is because he has in large part created the good reputation that Jean Marie River enjoys.

Louis's kinship relations are another area in which we may look for a sense of affiliation and involvement. This sense does exist here, but again, as in his relation to the community as a whole, Louis uses his kinship relations to his own advantage. Though he probably finds satisfaction in having those relationships, he is not subordinated to them. He is not a Sanguez, even though he regards the Sanguez brothers [his parallel cousins through his mother] as his closest kinsmen. A statement by his teenaged daughter is suggestive. She commented that it makes her father "mad" to be called Louis Sanguez, as some unknowing whites at the fort have called him, because "he is not a Sanguez, he is Louis Norwegian."

I have suggested, from the observational material, that Louis enjoys the role of mentor—in other words, that of the "father." Analyst George DeVos feels this is very strongly manifested in Louis's TAT responses. Louis shows considerable concern over injury to the father figure, a concern which DeVos characterizes as ambivalent but a positive attitude on the conscious "surface." On one card Louis sees a dead man returning. "But," DeVos points out, "rather than stressing fear of the ghost Louis sees the spectre as trying to show something to his children. Here there is expressed a sense of continuity and heritage knowledge between the generations." Surely this spectre is to Louis's subconscious the wise and benevolent figure of Old Sanguez and perhaps a projection of Louis's desired role as well. Looking at Louis's family history, his ambivalence and yet attraction to the father figure becomes clearer. In a sense, he had no real father but, rather, three quasi fathers. First, there was his biological father, Old Norwegian, who is still living [as of 1952]. [As I recall after all these years, my guess was that Louis's mother was Norwegian's number-two wife and, under priestly pressure against bigamy, he abandoned her when Louis was an infant.] Louis maintains only a minimal relationship with this man, whom he seldom sees. Second, there is the man who was his mother's husband for all of Louis's knowledgeable life, Charles Sanguez [son of Old Sanguez by his first wife]. Though the relationship between Old Charles and Louis at present seems fairly amicable, one can discern in observation no particular warmth between the two men. Third, as a quasi father to Louis, there was Old Sanguez, the founder of the Jean Marie River settlement. It was this man who, in transmission of lore and standards, approximated most strongly the father role for Louis, and Louis's respect for Old Sanguez is evident to this day.

The overt manner of Louis's social behavior is, of course, immediately significant in his exercise of leadership. But further, I think, we can perceive in that behavior certain motivations and calculations that are never expressed verbally by Louis. In the work situation specifically, as it is seen in the execution of projects of the Venture, Louis's control and direction of any situation are held to a minimum of orders or of bossing the operation in general. Now this is the Slavey way of social or work behavior. There are some individuals, however, where ego demands for esteem and recognition break through the acceptable pattern, resulting in bossiness and leading to resentment on the part of others. To Louis the deed or result is more important than the name. For example, he was willing to relinquish the verbal title of "boss for the powerboat" to Gabriel. The important thing to Louis was that the powerboat continued to operate effectively, regardless of who had the titular control. The actual control in terms of organization and planning for the powerboat remained under Louis's direction. Louis wants things done in what he conceives to be the proper way, but in attaining this end he is well aware of the requirements of Dene ethos, and, accordingly, he threatens the autonomy of others as little as possible in the execution of group projects. Although Louis has never verbalized this outlook to me, I feel that he is well aware of the need to underplay his position of dominance as much as possible in order not to arouse resentment and anxiety in others.

Louis's drinking behavior, in contrast to his Sanguez "brothers" and indeed to all other men in the community except his brother-in-law William, is significant. At the stage of heavy drunkenness Louis frequently withdraws into himself. He may sit and croon old songs or just sit without overt activity. Irritability also occasionally emerges when he is drunk. The only time we saw him spank one of his children was when under the influence of alcohol. These traits can be seen occasionally under conditions of drunkenness in other men as well. But where Louis stands out is in the lack of childish behavior—the continual demand for cigarettes, the persistent calling attention of another to oneself in general, the desire to impose oneself as the central and pampered figure in the situation—that seems to be the mode for the heavily drunken male. Even in the extreme stages of drunkenness Louis either does not feel these needs or, if he does, at least he maintains control over himself to the extent that he does not give way.

Louis's behavior under intoxication reflects his general approach to human relationships. His overall orientation to others I would characterize as calculating and cautious. In the field our assessment of Louis underwent some evolution. Our first impression was of a quiet but confident personality. Louis, by bush Slavey standards, evinced a high degree of social ease and ability to interact, and he talked seemingly spontaneously. But we came to feel that behind this surface smoothness there was a cautiousness and constraint, a weighing of the situation. It was clear that he was conscious of himself as a figure of importance and as community leader. While others, especially in the earlier months, were quite openly cautious, reserved, and even anxious in their relationships with Teresa and me, Louis presented an assured facade. But he was careful to hide from us activities such as brewing which he thought might reflect negatively upon himself or upon the community in general.

As time went on, Louis openly gave us a few clues to certain underlying insecurities. On one occasion he spoke of the extreme shyness from which he suffered as a young man, in contrast to his cousin Gabriel Sanguez, who, he said, had never been shy. Louis said that as a youth he hated to go to the fort and walked with his head down all the time because of his extreme self-consciousness, and he was so shy he did not think he would ever get married. In conversation he also on several occasions revealed to us his fear of physical decline and decay. Thus we eventually came to see Louis not as a person relatively free of social unease and deeper levels of anxiety but as one who, despite these constrictive components of personality, has forced himself to approach new situations, to attempt to cope with them, and to attain a surface assurance of manner.

An important point already demonstrated about Louis's social behavior is that in the work situation he does more than his share. Excelling in the realm of physical effort and productivity is a requirement of the Dene leader. But in terms of idiosyncratic motivation, in Louis's case we may view it as a manifestation of the need to gain and maintain the esteem of others and also to prove himself to himself. A man who has these drives is in a psychic stance conducive to the attainment of leadership. The need to feel a sense of pride, self-esteem, and accomplishment seems to be a vital component of Louis's personality. But to reconcile this need with his caution and defensiveness and to make it palatable to the Dene ethos, he underplays its expression. For example, he will speak of his success in hunting by attributing it to good luck, thus achieving recognition of his accomplishment but not laying himself open to the charge of boastfulness. His self-view can be seen as operative in many interpersonal and social situations. It would seem to be an aspect of his ready assumption of mentorship and of his rejection of infantile behavior while drinking. His good name is important to him. He feels the need for respect. As part of this, he has a sense of his own dignity and of the dignity of the occasion, as in his disapproval of community drinking during the New Year celebration.

In this sketch of Louis's personality, the emphasis has been on those traits which apparently have been the effective factors in establishing his position of influence and leadership. Two main points may be made. First, it seems that the quality of control and calculation in Louis—the inhibition of spontaneous or ingenuous reaction and, as part of this, the calculation of the effect of his actions upon others—is a prime element in his position as leader. He has the problem, which on the whole he appears to have met successfully, of not threatening or antagonizing the individuals under his leadership upon whom he must rely for labor and cooperation. As a boss, he accedes to the Dene norm by holding directions, orders, and demands on others to a minimum. Seen from the viewpoint of the other persons involved, Louis's exercise of his role is relatively nonthreatening, that is, other men's view of their own autonomy is not shaken. Louis does not permit himself the childish gratification of gratuitous bossiness. The theme of personal autonomy in the Dene ethos is echoed in the ego-defensive propensities in his individual makeup. We may infer that his emotional cognizance of these forces leads him both to appreciate the autonomy anxieties of others and, by offering as little threat to them as possible consonant with his achievement goals, to protect his own vulnerable ego from hostility.

The second major trait manifested by Louis is, of course, that of achievement. He demonstrates superior industry, ability, and results in both the bush and the technical realm. From the point of view of others, this is a trait which makes him respectworthy, and being respectworthy is the first step toward effective influence and leadership. In earlier passages, satisfactions felt by Louis in his role in Jean Marie River have been suggested. In summation of these, we may say, first, that he finds satisfaction in having a good reputation, being seen as a man of reliability, ability, and accomplishment. Another satisfaction found by Louis in his role in Jean Marie River is that of pride of possession, specifically, of such large and expensive items as the powerboat and barge. Like his good reputation, this adds to his feeling of being a man of substance and respect. A third aspect of his satisfactions comes from his influence over others in his present role at Lynx Point. Again, this is part of his sense of being a person of substance and probably stems from a drive to play the role of "father"-provider. Finally, we arrive again at that more personal and idiosyncratic satisfaction that his position allows him to pursue more fully—the sense of mastery of the physical world for its own sake.

from **The Lynx Point People,** *1961*

THE DEATH OF LOUIS NORWEGIAN

While he was traveling back home from Fort Simpson to Jean Marie River, on another brand-new scow he had just built, Louis Norwegian died accidentally on the great river [the Mackenzie] on which he had sailed and worked all his life. He was seventy years old. This happened on Friday afternoon, August 26, 1977.

For unknown reasons (Louis was alone on the scow) his boat hit a barge which was tied to the shore at the foot of the Green Island rapids. Jimmy Sanguez and his wife, Marie Louise, who were sailing ahead of Louis, turned back to look for him and soon found his body floating and drifting along with the wrecked scow.

from "Remembering Louis Norwegian" by Henri Posset O.M.I., 1977

AFTERWORD

Early in October 1967, Nancy Lurie and I arrived in Yellowknife in order to go on to Rae and from there to Snare Lake. Snare Lake (today Wekweti) was a small community of Dogribs who came to Rae for the summer and each autumn returned to their settlement. We planned to assemble supplies at Rae for ourselves and the people at Snare Lake and hire a bush plane from Yellowknife to fly us and the supplies to the settlement. We waited in Rae for a month. Due to exceptionally warm weather, Great Slave Lake had not frozen at Yellowknife. The lakes near the barrens, including the one where the community was situated, were frozen. There was no landing strip at Snare Lake. So we were caught with planes on floats at Yellowknife that could not land at Snare Lake, where the lake ice required a ski plane. In November we gave up and went back to the States.

In 1967 the community at Snare Lake lacked any means of communication with "the outside world" except for a daily radio schedule. Thirty-one years later I received a letter from my Dogrib friend John B. Zoe. The first passages of his letter brought home the overwhelming impact of today's world on what was once an isolated all-Indian community:

> I just got back from Snare Lake today. The community there is having its struggles, mainly due to fast-paced development of the community. . . . It wasn't very long ago that they had no phones, radio, satellite, TV, modern houses, electricity, schools, offices, etc. It was a time when everyone knew what was going on, because information [came and] was seen when someone came to visit. Today there is an administration building with Fax machines, a boardroom table of solid wood, leather chairs, and a state-of-the-art recording system with microphones fully for every councilor equipped with a translation booth, capped off with a name tag. [The total population of the Snare Lake community is approximately 130.] Information is more filtered as to the goings-on, because it is so much. I think I'll leave the rest to your imagination.

from a letter from John B. Zoe, May 2, 1998

Actually, I do not think my imagination is up to it. Or perhaps I simply do not want to try to conjure up the kinds of changes, problems, and complexities that may be coming to Snare Lake and the people of Denendeh in the twenty-first century.

I hope that in some small way this book can add to the people's appreciation of their past as they prepare for their future.

A NOTE ABOUT
THE CONTRIBUTORS

When carrying out an archaeological survey along the Mackenzie River in 1950, R. S. ("Scotty") MacNeish learned from the Jean Marie River people that they wanted their children to learn English without sending them away to mission school. Learning of this quasi invitation, I invited Teresa Carterette, also a graduate student in anthropology at the University of Chicago, to join me in becoming a "schoolteacher" at Jean Marie River in the summer of 1951. After a year at Jean Marie River, Teresa S. Carterette took a Ph.D. in psychology at Indiana University. She is now professor emerita of psychology at Simmons College (Boston).

Nancy O. Lurie (Ph.D. in anthropology, Northwestern University) went to Dogrib country with me in 1959 and returned with me in 1962 and 1967. Nancy Lurie retired from the Milwaukee Public Museum as curator of anthropology.

Beryl C. Gillespie (M.A. in anthropology, University of Iowa) worked with Dene consultants in Dettah, Rae, Fort Franklin, and Fort Norman between 1968 and 1981, as well as carrying out archival research. She lives in Iowa City, Iowa.

Between 1951 and 1979 I (Ph.D. in anthropology, University of Chicago) carried out ethnological research at Jean Marie River, Camsell Hospital in Edmonton, Fort Good Hope, Wha Ti (Lac la Martre), and Rae. I am professor emerita of anthropology at the University of Iowa.

John B. Zoe and Thomas D. Andrews have contributed clarification, knowledge, and encouragement beyond what can be acknowledged here.

REFERENCES CITED

Unless otherwise indicated in the credit line that accompanies a chapter or subsection of a chapter, June Helm is the author of the material; the work from which it is taken is cited here under Helm.

A date of publication in italics indicates that the work cited is the source of a chapter or chapter subsection.

ADAMS, JOHN W., AND ALICE BEE KASAKOFF

1975   Factors Underlying Endogamous Group Size. In *Population and Social Organization*. Ed. Moni Nag. Pp. 147–74. The Hague: Mouton.

ADNEY, E. T., AND H. I. CHAPELLE

1964   *The Bark Canoes and Skin Boats of North America*. U.S. National Museum Bulletin 230. Washington, D.C.

AMSDEN, CHARLES W.

1979   Hard Times: A Case Study from Northern Alaska and Implications for Arctic Prehistory. In *Thule Eskimo Culture: An Anthropological Perspective*. Ed. Allen P. McCartney. Pp. 395–410. Archaeological Survey of Canada Paper No. 88. Ottawa: National Museum of Man Mercury Series.

ANDERSON, H. D., AND W. C. EELLS

1935   *Alaska Natives: A Survey of Their Sociological Educational Status*. Stanford: Stanford University Press.

ANDERSON, JAMES

1907   [1858] McKenzies River District Report. Copyist's manuscript of a report dated at Fort Simpson, May 19, 1858. In MS group MG 19/A29. Pp. 104–40. Ottawa: Public Archives of Canada.

ANDREWS, THOMAS D.

1990   Yamoria's Arrows: Stories, Place-Names and the Land in Dene Oral Tradition. MS on file, National Historic Parks and Sites, Northern Initiatives. Parks Canada. Yellowknife.

ANDREWS, THOMAS D., JOHN B. ZOE, AND AARON HERTER

1998   On Yamozhah's Trail: Dogrib Sacred Sites and the Anthropology of Travel. In *Sacred Lands: Aboriginal World Views, Claims and Conflicts*. Ed. Jill Oakes and Rick Riewe. Pp. 305–20. Edmonton: Canadian Circumpolar Institute.

ASCH, MICHAEL, THOMAS D. ANDREWS, AND SHIRLEEN SMITH

1986   The Dene Mapping Project on Land Use and Occupancy: An Introduction. In *Anthropology in Praxis*. Ed. Philip Spaulding. Pp. 36–43. Calgary: University of Calgary Press.

BACK, GEORGE

1836   *Narrative of the Arctic Land Expedition to the Mouth of the Great Fish River, and Along the Shores of the Arctic Ocean, in the Years 1833, 1834 and 1835.* London: John Murray.

BANCROFT, H. H.

1886   *History of Alaska, 1730–1855.* San Francisco: A. L. Bancroft & Co.

BASSO, ELLEN B.

1978   The Enemy of Every Tribe: "Bushman" Images in Northern Athapaskan Narratives. *American Ethnologist* 5:690–709.

BERGER, THOMAS R.

1977   *Northern Frontier, Northern Homeland: The Report of the Mackenzie Valley Pipeline Inquiry.* 2 vols. Ottawa: Minister of Supply and Services Canada.

BIRDSELL, JOSEPH

1968   Some Predictions for the Pleistocene Based on Equilibrium Systems among Recent Hunter-Gatherers. In *Man the Hunter.* Ed. Richard B. Lee and Irven DeVore. Pp. 229–49. Chicago: Aldine.

BIRKET-SMITH, KAI

1930   *Contributions to Chipewyan Ethnology.* Report of the Fifth Thule Expedition 1921–24. Vol. 6, no. 3. Copenhagen: Gyldenalske Boghandel.

BIRKET-SMITH, KAI, AND FREDERICA DE LAGUNA

1938   *Eyak Indians of the Copper River Delta, Alaska.* Copenhagen: Levin and Munksgaard.

BLONDIN, GEORGE

1990   *When the World Was New: Stories of the Sahtú Dene.* Yellowknife: Outcrop.

1996   *Medicine Power.* Hay River: Dene Cultural Center.

BLUNDELL, VALDA

1980   Hunter-Gatherer Territoriality: Ideology and Behavior in Northwest Australia. *Ethnohistory* 27(2):103–17.

BOAS, FRANZ

1904   Some Traits of Primitive Culture. *Journal of American Folklore* 17:243–54.

1910   Religion. In *Handbook of American Indians North of Mexico.* Bureau of American Ethnology Bulletin No. 30, vol. 2. Ed. Frederick Webb Hodge. Pp. 365–71. Washington, D.C.: Smithsonian Institution Press.

1974   [1889] On Alternating Sounds. In *A Franz Boas Reader: The Shaping of American Anthropology, 1883–1911.* Ed. George W. Stocking, Jr. Pp. 72–77. Chicago: University of Chicago Press.

BROWN, A. R.

1913   Three Tribes of Western Australia. *Journal of the Royal Anthropological Institute of Great Britain and Ireland* 43:143–94.

1918   Notes on the Social Organization of Australian Tribes. *Journal of the Royal Anthropological Institute of Great Britain and Ireland* 48:222–53.

BURCH, ERNEST S.

1980   Traditional Eskimo Societies in Northwest Alaska. In *Alaska Native Culture and History.* Ed. Yoshinobu Kotani and William B. Workman. Senri Ethnological Studies 4:253–304.

CAMERON, AGNES DEANS

1912   *The New North.* New York: D. Appleton.

CANADA

1957   *Peoples of the Northwest Territories.* Ottawa: Department of Northern Affairs and Natural Resources.

1964   *Traditional Linguistic and Cultural Affiliations of Canadian Indian Bands.* Ottawa: Department of Citizenship and Immigration, Indian Affairs Branch.

1966   [1899] *Treaty No. 8 Made June 21, 1899 and Adhesions, Reports, etc.* Reprint. Ottawa: Roger Duhamel.

1970   *Linguistic and Cultural Affiliations of Canadian Indian Bands.* Ottawa: Department of Indian Affairs and Northern Development, Indian Affairs Branch.

CARLO, POLDINE

1978   *Nulato: An Indian Life on the Yukon.* For sale by the author, 211 Southern Street, Fairbanks, AL 99701.

CHRISTIAN, JANE, AND PETER M. GARDNER

1977   *The Individual in Northern Dene Thought and Communication: A Study in Sharing and Diversity.* Canadian Ethnology Service Paper No. 35. Ottawa: National Museum of Man Mercury Series.

CHURCH, CHARLES F., AND HELEN N. CHURCH

1963   *Food Values of Portions Commonly Used.* 9th ed. Philadelphia: J. B. Lippincott Co.

CLARK, A. MCFADYEN, ED.

1975   *Proceedings: Northern Athapaskan Conference, 1971.* 2 vols. Canadian Ethnology Service Paper No. 27. Ottawa: National Museum of Man Mercury Series.

CONSTANTINE, CHARLES

1903   Report by Superintendent Charles Constantine, "G" Division, Fort Saskatchewan, Alberta, September 6, 1903. In *Annual Report, Royal North-West Mounted Police.*

COOKE, ALAN, AND CLIVE HOLLAND

1978   *The Exploration of Northern Canada.* Toronto: The Arctic History Press.

DARWIN, CHARLES

1952   [1871] *The Descent of Man and Selection in Relation to Sex.* New York: Modern Library.

DAVIS, RICHARD C.

1995   *Sir John Franklin's Journals and Correspondence: The First Arctic Land Expedition, 1819–1822.* Toronto: Champlain Society.

DAWSON, G. M.

1888   Notes on the Indian Tribes of the Yukon District and Adjacent Northern Portion of British Columbia. *Annual Reports of the Canadian Geological Survey* 3(1): 1b–277B.

DIA–AR (DEPARTMENT OF INDIAN AFFAIRS)

1924   *Annual Report of the Department of Indian Affairs for the Year Ended March 31, 1924.* Ottawa.

1929   *Annual Report of the Department of Indian Affairs for the Year Ended March 31, 1929.* Ottawa.

1934   *Annual Report of the Department of Indian Affairs for the Year Ended March 31, 1934.* Ottawa.

1954   *Annual Report of the Department of Indian Affairs for the Year Ended March 31, 1954.* Ottawa.

1961   *Annual Report of the Department of Indian Affairs for the Year Ended March 31, 1961.* Ottawa.

DIAND (DEPARTMENT OF INDIAN AFFAIRS AND NORTHERN DEVELOPMENT)

1977   Treaty List of December 1977. Yellowknife: Department of Indian Affairs and Northern Development. Mimeograph.

DRIVER, HAROLD E., ET AL.

1953   Indian Tribes of North America (map). Indiana University Publication in Anthropology and Linguistics Memoir 9.

DUCHAUSSOIS, PIERRE

1928   *Aux glaces polaires: Indiens et Esquimaux.* 2nd ed. Paris: Editions SPES.

ELLIOTT, H. W.

1887   *Our Arctic Province: Alaska and the Seal Islands.* New York: Scribner.

EMMONS, G. T.

1911   The Tahltan Indians. *Pennsylvania University Museum Anthropological Publications* 4:1–120.

FARAUD, H.

1866   *Dix-huit ans chez les sauvages.* Paris: R. Ruffet.

FERNEA, ROBERT A.

1995   Ethnography: Caveat Emptor. *Anthropology Today* 11(2):1–2.

FIDLER, PETER

1934   Journal of a Journey with the Chipewyans or Northern Indians to the Slave Lake and to the East and West of the Slave River, 1791–92. In *Journals of Hearne and Turnor.* Ed. J. B. Tyrell. Pp. 493–555. Toronto: Champlain Society.

FIELD, POOLE

n.d.   Unpublished letters, National Museum of Canada, Ottawa.

FLEMING, HARVEY R., ED.

1940   *Minutes of Council, Northern Department of Rupert Land, 1821–31.* Toronto: Champlain Society.

FORREST, ANN

1976   Development and Land Rights: The Case of Alaska. Dene Rights, Supporting Research and Documents: Vol. VII, Comparative Experience: 1–18. Indian Brotherhood of the Northwest Territories.

FOX, ROBIN

1980   *The Red Lamp of Incest.* New York: E. P. Dutton.

FRANKLIN, JOHN

1823   *Narrative of a Journey to the Shores of the Polar Sea in the Years 1819, 20, 21, 22.* 1st ed. London: John Murray.

1824   *Narrative of a Journey to the Shores of the Polar Sea in the Years 1819–20–21–22.* 2nd ed. London: John Murray.

1828   *Narrative of a Second Expedition to the Shores of the Polar Sea in the Years 1825, :826, and 1827.* London: John Murray.

FRIED, JACOB

1963   White-Dominant Settlements in the Canadian Northwest Territories. *Anthropologica* n.s. 5(1): 57–66.

FUMOLEAU, RENÉ

1975   *As Long As This Land Shall Last: A History of Treaty 8 and Treaty 11, 1870–1939.* Toronto: McClelland and Stewart.

GAIDA, URBAN, AND MARTIN MARCHELLO

1987   *Going Wild.* Sartell, Minn.: Watab Marketing.

GAMBLE, D. J.

1978   The Berger Inquiry: An Impact Assessment Process. *Science* 199:946–52.

1986   Crushing of Cultures: Western Applied Science in Northern Societies. *Arctic* 39(1): 20–23.

GARRIOCH, A. C.

1929   *A Hatchet Mark in Duplicate.* Toronto: Ryerson Press.

GEMINI NORTH, LTD.

1974   Social and Economic Impact of Proposed Arctic Gas Pipeline in Northern Canada. 7 vols. Yellowknife and Vancouver. Mimeograph.

GIBSON, NANCY

1988   Northern Medicine in Transition. In *Health Care Issues in the Canadian North.* Ed. David E. Young. Boreal Institute for Northern Studies, Occasional Publication No. 27. Edmonton: University of Alberta.

GILLESPIE, BERYL C.

1971   Ethnological Field Notes, Fort Norman and Fort Franklin. MS files of the author. Iowa City.

1975   Territorial Expansion of the Chipewyan in the 18th Century. In *Proceedings: Northern Athapaskan Conference, 1971.* Vol. 2. Ed. A. M. Clark. Pp. 350–88. Canadian Ethnology Service Paper No. 27. Ottawa: National Museum of Man Mercury Series.

1976   Changes in Territory and Technology of the Chipewyan. *Arctic Anthropology* 13(1):6–11.

1981   Bearlake. In *Subarctic.* Ed. June Helm. Pp. 301–13. Vol. 6 of *Handbook of North American Indians.* William C. Sturtevant, gen. ed. Washington, D.C.: Smithsonian Institution Press.

GODSELL, P. H.

1934   *Arctic Trader.* New York: Putnam's.

GOLDMAN, IRVING

1940   The Alkatcho Carrier of British Columbia. In *Acculturation in Seven Indian Tribes.* Ed. R. Linton. Pp. 333–89. New York: Appleton-Century.

GOULET, JEAN-GUY A.

1994   Ways of Knowing: Towards a Narrative Ethnography of Experiences among the Dene Tha. *Journal of Anthropological Research* 50: 113–39.

GREAT MACKENZIE BASIN

1888   *Report of the Select Committee of the Senate Appointed to Enquire into the Resources of the Great Mackenzie Basin, Session 1888.* Ottawa: Brown Chamberlin, Queen's Printer.

HALDEMAN, JACK C.

1951   Problems of Alaskan Eskimo, Indians, Aleuts. *Public Health Reports* 66(2):
        912–17.

HALLORAN, ARTHUR F.

1957   Live and Dressed Weights of American Bison. *Journal of Mammalogy* 38(1):139.

HANKS, CHRISTOPHER C.

1997   Ancient Knowledge of Ancient Sites: Tracing Dene Identity from the Late
        Pleistocene and Holocene. In *At a Crossroads: Archaeology and First Peoples in
        Canada.* Ed. George P. Nicholas and Thomas D. Andrews. Pp. 178–89. Ar-
        chaeology Press Publication No. 24. Burnaby, B.C.: Department of Archaeol-
        ogy, Simon Fraser University.

HARA, HIROKO SUE

1980   *The Hare Indians and Their World.* Canadian Ethnology Service Paper No. 63.
        Ottawa: National Museum of Man Mercury Series.

HARDISTY, WILLIAM L.

1867   The Loucheux Indians. In *Annual Report of the Board of Regents of the Smithsonian
        Institution.* Pp. 311–20. Washington, D.C.: Smithsonian Institution Press.

HARMON, DANIEL WILLIAM

1911   [1778–1845] *A Journal of Voyages and Travels in the Interior of North America.* To-
        ronto: Courier Press.

HBCA (HUDSON'S BAY COMPANY ARCHIVES), WINNIPEG, CANADA

        B.181/a/3 Fort Resolution Post Journal, 1820–21.

        B.181/a/4 Fort Resolution Post Journal, 1822–23.

        B.181/a/7 Fort Resolution Post Journal, 1826–27.

        B.181/d/3b Fort Resolution Accounts, "Chipewyan Balance Spring 1828."

        B.200/a/3 Fort Simpson Post Journal, 1823–24.

        B.200/a/4 Fort Simpson Post Journal, March 22–October 2, 1824.

        B.200/e/4 Mackenzie River District Report, 1823–24.

        B.200/e/6 Mackenzie River District Report, 1823–27 (signed in 1826).

        B.200/e/8 Mackenzie River District Report, 1826–28.

        B.200/e/9 Mackenzie River District Report, 1829–30.

HEARNE, SAMUEL

1911   *A Journey from Prince of Wales's Fort in Hudson's Bay to the Northern Ocean in the
        Years 1769, 1770, 1771, and 1772.* Ed. J. B. Tyrrell. Toronto: Champlain Society.

1958   [1795] *A Journey from Prince of Wales's Fort in Hudson's Bay to the Northern Ocean
        1769–1770–1771–1772.* Ed. Richard Glover. Toronto: Macmillan.

HELM, JUNE

1961   *The Lynx Point People: The Dynamics of a Northern Athapaskan Band.* National
        Museum of Canada Bulletin No. 176.

1965a   Bilaterality in the Socio-Territorial Organization of the Arctic Drainage Dene.
        Ethnology 4:361–85.

1965b   Patterns of Allocation among the Arctic Drainage Dene. In *Essays in Economic
        Anthropology.* Ed. June Helm, Paul Bohannan, and Marshall Sahlins. Pp. 33–45.
        Proceedings of the 1965 Annual Spring Meeting of the American Ethnological Society.
        Seattle: University of Washington Press.

1966   Changes in Indian Communities. In *People of Light and Dark*. Ed. M. van Steensel. Pp. 106–9. Ottawa: Queen's Printer.

1967   Ethnographic Field Notes, Dogrib Indians, Rae, N.W.T. MS files of the author. Iowa City: University of Iowa, Anthropology Department.

1968   The Nature of Dogrib Socio-Territorial Groups. In *Man the Hunter*. Ed. Richard B. Lee and Irven DeVore. Pp. 118–25. Chicago: Aldine.

1969a   Remarks on the Methodology of Band Composition Analysis. In *Contributions to Anthropology: Band Societies*. Ed. David Damas. Pp. 218–39. National Museum of Canada Bulletin No. 228.

1969b   Unpublished field notes on the records at St. Michael's Mission, Rae.

1972   The Dogrib Indians. In *Hunters and Gatherers Today*. Ed. Marco Bicchieri. Pp. 51–89. New York: Holt, Rinehart and Winston.

1978   [Review of] *Dene Nation: The Colony Within*. Ed. Mel Watkins. *Western Canadian Journal of Anthropology* 8(1):67–72.

1979   Long-Term Research among the Dogrib and Other Dene. In *Long Term Field Research in Social Anthropology*. Ed. G. Foster, T. Scudder, E. Colson, and R. Kemper. Pp. 145–63. New York: Academic Press.

1980a   Female Infanticide, European Diseases, and Population Levels among the Mackenzie Dene. *American Ethnologist* 7(1):259–85.

1980b   Indian Dependency and Self-Determination: Problems and Paradoxes in Canada's Northwest Territories. In *Political Organization of Native North Americans*. Ed. Ernest L. Schusky. Pp. 215–42. Washington, D.C.: University Press of America.

1981a   Dogrib Folk History and the Photographs of John Alden Mason: Indian Occupation and Status in the Fur Trade, 1900–1925. *Arctic Anthropology* 18 (2): 39–53.

1987   Horde, Band, and Tribe: Northern Approaches. Third Annual Presidential Lecture. University of Iowa, Iowa City.

1989   Women's Work, Women's Art. In *Out of the North*. Ed. Barbara A. Hail and Kate C. Duncan. Pp. 120–22. Bristol, R.I.: Haffenreffer Museum of Anthropology, Brown University.

1993   "Always with Them Either a Feast or a Famine": Living off the Land with Chipewyan Indians, 1791–1792. *Arctic Anthropology* 30(2):46–60.

1994   *Prophecy and Power among the Dogrib Indians*. Lincoln: University of Nebraska Press.

HELM, JUNE, ED.

1981b   *Subarctic. Handbook of North American Indians*, Vol. 6. Washington, D.C.: Smithsonian Institution Press.

HELM, JUNE, TERRY ALLIBAND, TERRY BIRK, VIRGINIA LAWSON, SUZANNE REISNER, CRAIG STURDEVANT, AND STANLEY WITKOWSKI

1975   The Contact History of the Subarctic Athapaskans: An Overview. In *Proceedings: Northern Athapaskan Conference, 1971*. Vol. 1. Ed. A. M. Clark. Pp. 302–49. Ethnology Service Paper No. 27. Ottawa: National Museum of Man Mercury Series.

HELM, JUNE, AND DAVID DAMAS

1963   The Contact-Traditional All-Native Community of the Canadian North: The
        Upper Mackenzie "Bush" Athapaskans and the Igluligmiut. *Anthropologica* n.s.
        5(1):9–22.

HELM, JUNE, AND BERYL C. GILLESPIE

1981   Dogrib Oral Tradition as History: War and Peace in the 1820s. *Journal of An-
        thropological Research* 37:8–27.

1983   Akaitcho. *Arctic* 36(2):208–9.

HELM, JUNE, AND ELEANOR B. LEACOCK

1971   Hunting Tribes of Subarctic Canada. In *The North American Indian in Historical
        Perspective.* Ed. E. B. Leacock and N. O. Lurie. Pp. 343–74. New York: Ran-
        dom House.

HELM, JUNE, AND NANCY O. LURIE

1961   *The Subsistence Economy of the Dogrib Indians of Lac la Martre.* Northern Coordi-
        nation and Research Centre NCRC-16-3. Ottawa: Department of Northern
        Affairs and National Resources.

1966   *The Dogrib Hand Game.* National Museum of Canada Bulletin No. 205. Ottawa.

HELM, JUNE, AND VITAL THOMAS

1966   Tales from the Dogribs. *Beaver,* part 1 (Autumn 1966): 16–20; part 2 (Winter
        1996): 52–54. Winnipeg.

HIATT, L. R.

1968   Ownership and Use of Land among the Australian Aborigines. In *Man the Hun-
        ter.* Ed. Richard B. Lee and Irven DeVore. Pp. 99–102. Aldine: Chicago.

HILL, JANE H.

1978   Language Contact Systems and Human Adaptations. *Journal of Anthropological
        Research* 34(1):1–26.

HONIGMANN, JOHN J.

1946   *Ethnography and Acculturation of the Fort Nelson Slave.* Yale University Publica-
        tions in Anthropology No. 33. New Haven: Yale University Press.

1954   *The Kaska Indians: An Ethnographic Reconstruction.* Yale University Publications
        in Anthropology No. 51. New Haven: Yale University Press.

HOSLEY, EDWARD H.

1968   The Kolchan: Delineation of a New Northern Athapaskan Group. *Arctic*
        21:6–11.

HOWITT, A. W.

1967   [1880] Appendix D: The Distribution of Food. In *Kamilaroi and Kurnai: Group-
        Marriage and Relationship, and Marriage by Elopement.* By Lorimer Fison and A. W.
        Howitt. Pp. 261–67. Oosterhout, Netherlands: Anthropological Publications.

HOWITT, A. W., AND LORIMER FISON

1885   [1880] On the Dene and the Horde. *Journal of the Anthropological Institute of Great
        Britain and Ireland* 14:142–69.

HYMES, DELL H.

1968   Linguistic Problems in Defining the Concept of "Tribe." In *Essays on the Prob-
        lem of Tribe.* Ed. June Helm. Pp. 23–48. *1968 Proceedings of the American Ethno-
        logical Society.* Seattle: University of Washington Press.

IOWA STATE UNIVERSITY OF SCIENCE AND TECHNOLOGY

n.d. Typical Yields of Products and By-products. Cooperative Extension Service. Ames: Iowa State University. Mimeograph.

JARVENPA, ROBERT, AND HETTY JO BRUMBACH

1983 Ethnoarchaeological Perspectives on an Athapaskan Moose Kill. *Arctic* 36(2): 174–84.

JENNESS, DIAMOND

1937 *The Sekani Indians of British Columbia.* National Museum of Canada Bulletin No. 84. Ottawa.

1943 The Carrier Indians of the Bulkley River: Their Social and Religious Life. Anthropological Papers of the Bureau of American Ethnology. *Bulletin* 133(25): 469–586.

JONES, STRACHAN

1867 The Kutchin Tribes. In *Annual Report of the Board of Regents of the Smithsonian Institution for 1867.* Pp. 320–27. Washington, D.C.: Smithsonian Institution Press.

KARI, PRISCILLA R.

1987 *Tanaina Plantlore.* National Park Service, Alaska Region.

KEITH, GEORGE

1890 Letters to Mr. Roderic McKenzie. In *Les Bourgeois de la Compagnie du Nord-Ouest.* Série II. Ed. L. F. R. Masson. Pp. 75–153. Quebec: A. Côté et Cie.

KELLY, RAYMOND C.

1968 Demographic Pressures and Descent Group Structure in the New Guinea Highlands. *Oceania* 39:36–63.

KELLY, ROBERT L.

1982 Hunter-Gatherer Linguistics and Long-Term Adaptation. *Haliksái* 1:45–53.

KELSALL, J. P.

1968 *The Caribou.* Department of Indian Affairs and Northern Development. Ottawa: Canadian Wildlife Service.

KING, A. RICHARD

1967 *The School at Mopass: A Problem of Identity.* New York: Holt, Rinehart and Winston.

KING, RICHARD

1836 *Narrative of a Journey to the Shores of the Arctic Ocean in 1833, 1834 and 1835.* 2 vols. London.

KIRBY [SIC, KIRKBY], W. W.

1865 A Journey to the Youcan, Russian America. In *Annual Report of the Board of Regents of the Smithsonian Institution for 1864.* Pp. 416–20. Washington, D.C.: Smithsonian Institution Press.

KOCH, ROBERT M., JOHN D. CROUSE, AND STEVEN C. SEIDEMAN

1988 Bison, Hereford, and Brahman Growth and Carcass Characteristics. In *Beef Research Progress Report* No. 3. Ed. Roman L. Hruska. U.S. Meat Animal Research Center in Cooperation with University of Nebraska College of Agriculture, Agriculture Experiment Station. U.S. Department of Agriculture ARS-71.

KRAUSE, AUREL

1956   *The Tlingit Indians: Results of a Trip to the Northwest Coast of America and the Bering Straits.* Trans. by Erna Gunther. Seattle: University of Washington Press.

KRAUSS, MICHAEL

1997   The Indigenous Languages of the North: A Report on Their Present State. In *Northern Minority Languages: Problems of Survival.* Ed. H. Shoji and J. Hjanhunen. Senri Ethnological Studies 44: 1–34.

KRAUSS, MICHAEL E., AND VICTOR K. GOLLA

1981   Northern Athapaskan Languages. In *Subarctic.* Ed. June Helm. Pp. 67–85. *Handbook of North American Indians,* Vol. 6. William C. Sturtevant, gen. ed. Washington, D.C.: Smithsonian Institution Press.

KRECH, SHEPARD III

1978   Disease, Starvation, and Northern Athapaskan Social Organization. *American Ethnologist* 5: 710–32.

1983   The Influence of Disease and the Fur Trade on Arctic Drainage Lowlands Dene, 1800–1850. *Journal of Anthropological Research* 39(2): 123–46.

LAMB, KAYE W., ED.

1970   *The Journals and Letters of Sir Alexander Mackenzie.* Hakluyt Society Extra Series Vol. 41. Cambridge: Hakluyt Society.

LEAF, MURRAY J.

1979   *Man, Mind, and Science: A History of Anthropology.* New York: Columbia University Press.

LEE, RICHARD B.

1976   !Kung Spatial Organization: An Ecological and Historical Perspective. In *Kalihari Hunter-Gatherers.* Ed. Richard B. Lee and Irven DeVore. Pp. 73–97. Cambridge, Mass.: Harvard University Press.

LEGAT, ALLICE, JOAN RYAN, SALLY ANN ZOE, MARIE ADELE RABESCA, AND MADELEINE CHOCOLATE

1997   *The Trees All Changed to Wood.* Dogrib Renewable Resources Committee. Dogrib Treaty 11 Council for the Arctic Environmental Strategy. Department of Indian Affairs and Northern Development.

LI, F. K.

1933   A List of Chipewyan Stems. *International Journal of American Linguistics* 7: 122–51.

LOWELL, ANTHONY M., ET AL.

1969   *Tuberculosis.* Cambridge, Mass.: Harvard University Press.

MACARTHUR, NORMA

1967   *Island Populations of the Pacific.* Canberra: Australian National University Press.

MACDONELL, JOHN

n.d.   MS among the Masson Papers, McGill University, Montreal, ca. 1800. From excerpts in typescript, National Museum of Canada.

MACFARLANE, RODERICK

1881   Population of the Hudson Bay District of Athabaska, 1881. McFarlane [*sic*] Papers. Record Group RC 10, BS, File 241209. Copyist's MS. Pp. 80–81. Ottawa: Public Archives of Canada.

MACKENZIE, ALEXANDER

1970   [1889] *The Journals and Letters of Sir Alexander Mackenzie*. Ed. W. Kaye Lamb. Hakluyt Society Extra Series Vol. 41. Cambridge: Hakluyt Society.

MACKENZIE, RODERIC

1795   An Account of the Athabasca Indians, by a Partner in the North West Company. In *Some Account of the North West Company Containing Analogy of Nations Ancient and Modern*. Vol. 3. Athabasca. Typewritten copy in National Museum of Canada from MS in Dominion Archives, Ottawa.

1960   [1889–90] Reminiscences, Being Chiefly a Synopsis of Letters from Sir Alexander Mackenzie. In *Les Bourgeois de la Compagnie du Nord-Ouest*, première série. Ed. L. F. R. Masson. New York: Antiquarian Press.

MACNEISH, JUNE HELM

1954   Contemporary Folk Beliefs of a Slave Indian Band. *Journal of American Folklore* 67:185–98.

1956a   Leadership among the Northeastern Athabascans. *Anthropologica* 2:131–63.

1956b   *Problems of Acculturation and Livelihood in a Northern Indian Band*. Contributions à l'Etude des Sciences de l'Homme No. 3. Pp. 169–81. Montreal.

MARTIN, JOHN F., AND DONALD G. STEWART

1982   A Demographic Basis for Patrilineal Hordes. *American Anthropologist* 84(1): 79–96.

MASON, JOHN ALDEN

1914   *On Work among Northern Athabaskan Tribes, 1913*. Geological Summary Report, Sessional Paper No. 26. Pp. 375–76. Canada.

1946   *Notes on the Indians of the Great Slave Lake Area*. Yale University Publications in Anthropology No. 34. New Haven: Yale University Press.

MCCARTHY, MARTHA

1995   *From the Great River to the Ends of the Earth: Oblate Missions to the Dene 1847–1921*. Edmonton: University of Alberta and Western Canadian Publishers.

MCCLELLAN, CATHARINE

1953   The Inland Tlingit. *Society of American Archaeology Memoir* 9:47–51.

1964   Culture Contacts in the Early Historic Period in Northwestern North America. *Arctic Anthropology* 2:3–15.

MCDONALD, JERRY N.

1981   *North American Bison, Their Classification and Evolution*. Berkeley and Los Angeles: University of California Press.

MCKENNAN, ROBERT A.

1959   *The Upper Tanana Indians*. Yale University Publications in Anthropology No. 55. New Haven: Yale University Press.

1969   Athapaskan Groupings and Social Organization in Central Alaska. In *Contributions to Anthropology: Band Societies*. Ed. David Damas. Pp. 93–114. National Museums of Canada Bulletin No. 228.

MCLEAN, JOHN

1932   *Notes of a Twenty-five Years' Service in the Hudson's Bay Territory*. Ed. W. S. Wallace. Toronto: Champlain Society.

MEISTER, CARY A.

1976   Demographic Consequences of Euro-American Contact on Selected American Indian Populations and Their Relationship to the Demographic Transition. *Ethnohistory* 23 : 161–72.

MORICE, A. G.

1905   *The History of the Northern Interior of British Columbia (1660–1880).* Toronto: William Briggs.

MURDOCK, GEORGE PETER

1949   *Social Structure.* New York: Macmillan.

NAHANNI, PHOEBE

1977   The Mapping Project. In *Dene Nation: The Colony Within.* Ed. Mel Watkins. Pp. 21–27. Toronto: University of Toronto Press.

NEEL, JAMES V., AND KENNETH M. WEISS

1975   The Genetic Structure of a Tribal Population, the Yanomama Indians. *American Journal of Physical Anthropology* 42 : 25–52.

NOBLE, WILLIAM

1981   Prehistory of the Great Slave Lake and Great Bear Lake Region. In *Subarctic.* Ed. June Helm. Pp. 97–106. *Handbook of North American Indians,* Vol. 6. William C. Sturtevant, gen. ed. Washington, D.C.: Smithsonian Institution Press.

OSGOOD, CORNELIUS

1932   The Ethnography of the Great Bear Lake Indians. In *Annual Report for 1931.* Pp. 31–97. National Museum of Canada Bulletin No. 70. Ottawa.

1934   Kutchin Tribal Distribution and Synonymy. *American Anthropologist* 36 : 168–79.

1936   *Distribution of the Northern Athapaskan Indians.* Yale University Publications in Anthropology No. 7. New Haven: Yale University Press.

PAC (PUBLIC ARCHIVES OF CANADA)

MG 14 D6 Fort Smith [*sic*] Post Jounal, 1826–27. ["Fort Smith" is an archive error; from internal evidence it is clear that this is the Fort Simpson Post Journal 1826–27.]

PARK, ED

1969   *The World of Bison.* New York and Philadelphia: J. B. Lippincott Co.

PETERSON, NICOLAS

1979   Territorial Adaptations among Desert Hunter-Gatherers: The !Kung and Australians Compared. In *Social and Ecological Systems,* Ed. P. C. Burnham and R. F. Ellen. Pp. 111–29. New York: Academic Press.

PETITOT, EMILE

1865   Comparative Vocabulary of Four Athapascan Tribes . . . Fort Good Hope, McKenzie River, Summer 1865. National Anthropological Archives Manuscript No. 151. Smithsonian Institution.

1876   *Monographie des Dènè-Dindjié.* Paris: Ernest Leroux.

1888   *Traditions indiennes du Canada nord-ouest. Textes originaux & traduction litterale.* Actes de la Société Philologique 16–17 : 169–614.

1891   *Autour du Grand Lac des Esclaves.* Nouvelle Librairie Parisienne. Paris: Albert Savine.

PHILLIPS, R. A.

1967   *Canada's North.* Toronto: Macmillan of Canada.

POSSET, HENRI

1977   Remembering Louis Norwegian. *Native Press,* September 2, 1977. Yellowknife.

PREBLE, EDWARD A.

1908   A Biological Investigation of the Athabaska-Mackenzie Region. In *North American Fauna* No. 27. Ed. Dr. C. Hart Merriam. Washington, D.C.: Government Printing Office, U.S. Department of Agriculture.

RADCLIFFE-BROWN, A. R.

1952   [1935] *Structure and Function in Primitive Society.* Glencoe, Ill.: Free Press.

1956   On Australian Local Organization. *American Anthropologist* 58(2) : 363 – 67.

RCMAFS (ROMAN CATHOLIC MISSION ARCHIVES AT FORT SMITH),
N.W.T., CANADA

1916 – 46 File tuberculose. Mimeograph.

REA, K. J.

1968   *The Political Economy of the Canadian North.* Toronto: University of Toronto Press.

RICHARDSON, SIR JOHN

1851   *Arctic Searching Expedition: A Journal of a Boat Voyage Through Rupert's Land and the Arctic Sea in Search of the Discovery Ships under Command of Sir John Franklin.* Vol. 2. London: Brown, Green and Longmans.

ROBINSON, M. J., AND J. L. ROBINSON

1946   Exploration and Settlement of Mackenzie District, N.W.T. Part 1. *Canadian Geographic Journal* 32(6) : 246 – 55.

ROWE, J. S.

1972   *Forest Regions of Canada.* Department of the Environment, Canadian Forestry Service. Publication No. 1300.

RUSHFORTH, SCOTT

1992   The Legitimation of Beliefs in a Hunter-Gatherer Society: Bearlake Athapaskan Knowledge and Authority. *American Ethnologist* 19(3) : 483 – 500.

RUSSELL, FRANK

1898   *Explorations in the Far North.* Iowa City: University of Iowa.

1893 – 94 Journal of Frank Russell, Bureau of American Ethnology. MS Vault No. 1274. National Anthropological Archives. Washington, D.C.: Smithsonian Institution.

SAVISHINSKY, JOEL S., AND HIROKO SUE HARA

1981   Hare. In *Subarctic.* Ed. June Helm. Pp. 314 – 25. *Handbook of North American Indians,* Vol. 6. William C. Sturtevant, gen. ed. Washington, D.C.: Smithsonian Institution Press.

SCHLADWEILER, PHILIP, AND DAVID R. STEVENS

1973   Weights of Moose in Montana. *Journal of Mammalogy* 54(3) : 772 – 75.

SCHRIRE, CARMEL, AND WILLIAM LEE STEIGER

1974   A Matter of Life and Death: An Investigation into the Practice of Female Infanticide in the Arctic. *Man* n.s. 9 : 161 – 84.

SERVICE, ELMAN

1962   *Primitive Social Organization: An Evolutionary Perspective.* New York: Random House.

SIMPSON, THOMAS

1843   *Narrative of the Discoveries on the North Coast of America Effected by the Officers of the Hudson's Bay Company During the Years 1836–9.* London: Richard Bentley.

SLOBODIN, RICHARD

1962   *Band Organization of the Peel River Kutchin.* National Museum of Canada Bulletin No. 179.

1963   The Dawson Boys—Peel River Indians and the Klondike Gold Rush. *Polar Notes* 5:24–36.

1966   *Metis of the Mackenzie District.* Canadian Research Centre for Anthropology. Ottawa: Saint Paul University.

1981   Subarctic Metis. In *Subarctic.* Ed. June Helm. Pp. 361–71. *Handbook of North American Indians,* Vol. 6. William C. Sturtevant, gen. ed. Washington, D.C.: Smithsonian Institution Press.

SMITH, DEREK G.

1967   *Natives and Outsiders: Pluralism in the Mackenzie River Delta, Northwest Territories.* Ottawa: Department of Indian Affairs and Northern Development.

SMITH, J. G. E.

1996   Thanadelther. In *Lobsticks and Cairns.* Ed. Richard C. Davis. Pp. 96–98. Calgary: University of Calgary Press.

SPENCER, HERBERT

1916   [1876] *The Principles of Sociology.* Vol. 1. New York and London: D. Appleton and Co.

STEARN, E. W., AND A. E. STEARN

1943   Smallpox Immunization of the Amerindian. *Bulletin of the History of Medicine* 13:601–9.

STEINBRUCK, JEAN

1999   *The Yellowknife Journal.* Winnipeg: Nuage Editions.

STEWARD, JULIAN

1955   *Theory of Culture Change: The Methodology of Multilinear Evolution.* Urbana: University of Illinois Press.

STEWART, E. G.

1955   Fort McPherson and the Peel River Area. M.A. thesis. Kingston: Queen's University.

STEWART, ELIHU

1908   *Down the Mackenzie and Up the Yukon.* London and New York: John Lane Co.

STUCK, HUDSON

1917   *Voyages on the Yukon and Its Tributaries: A Narrative of Summer Travel in the Interior of Alaska.* New York: Scribner's.

THOMAS, P. A.

1970   Kindly Despatch Miss Gadsby. *North* 17(1):6–19.

THOMPSON, DAVID

1916   *David Thompson's Narrative of His Explorations in Western America (1784–1812).*
        Ed. J. B. Tyrrell. Toronto: Champlain Society.

TOWNSEND, JOAN B.

1970   Tanaina Ethnohistory: An Example of a Method for the Study of Cultural
        Change. In *Ethnohistory in Southwestern Alaska and the Southern Yukon.* Ed. Margaret Lantis. Pp. 71–102. Lexington: University Press of Kentucky.

USHER, PETER J.

1971   *Fur Trade Posts of the Northwest Territories 1870–1970.* NSRG 71–4. Ottawa:
        Northern Science Research Group, Department of Indian Affairs and Northern
        Development.

VOORHIS, ERNEST, COMP.

1930   *Historic Forts and Trading Posts of the French Regime and of the English Fur Trading
        Companies.* Ottawa: Department of the Interior. Mimeograph.

WAISBERG, LEO G.

1975   Boreal Forest Subsistence and the Windigo: Fluctuation of Populations. *Anthropologica* 17:169–85.

WATKINS, MEL, ED.

1977   *Dene Nation: The Colony Within.* Toronto and Buffalo: University of Toronto
        Press.

WATT, BERNICE K., AND ANNABEL L. MERRILL

1963   *Composition of Foods.* Agriculture Handbook No. 8. Revised. Washington, D.C.:
        U.S. Department of Agriculture.

WEISS, KENNETH M.

1973   *Demographic Models for Anthropology.* Memoirs of the Society for American Archaeology No. 27. Washington, D.C.: American Anthropological Association.

WENTZEL, W. F.

1821   Account of Mackenzie River. MS MG 19–A20. Public Archives of Canada.
        Ottawa.

1889   Letters to the Hon. Roderic MacKenzie. In *Les Bourgeois de la Compagnie du
        Nord-Ouest*, première série. Ed. L. F. R. Masson. Pp. 85–105. Quebec: A. Côté
        et Cie.

WHEAT, JOE BEN

1972   *The Olsen-Chubbuck Site: A Paleo-Indian Bison Kill.* Memoirs of the Society for
        American Archaeology No. 26. Washington, D.C.: American Anthropological
        Association.

WHERRETT, G. J.

1947   Health Conditions and Services in the North-West. In *The New Northwest.* Ed.
        C. A. Dawson. Pp. 229–42. Toronto: University of Toronto Press.

WILLIAMS, B. J.

1974   *A Model of Band Society.* Memoirs of the Society for American Archaeology
        No. 29. Washington, D.C.: American Anthropological Association.

WILLIAMSON, ROBERT G.

1955   Slave Indian Legends. *Anthropologica*, no. 1:119–43.

1956   Slave Indian Legends. *Anthropologica*, no. 2:61–93.

YENGOYAN, ARAM A.

1970   Demographic Factors in Pitjandjara Social Organization. In *Australian Aborigi-nal Anthropology: Modern Studies in Social Anthropology of the Australian Aborigines.* Ed. Ronald M. Berndt. Pp. 70–91. Nedlands: University of Western Australia.

ZAGOSKIN, L. A.

1967   Lieutenant Zagoskin's Travels in Russian America, 1842–1844. In *Arctic Institute of North America: Translations from Russian Sources* No. 7. Ed. H. N. Michael. Toronto: University of Toronto Press.

ZASLOW, MORRIS

1971   *The Opening of the Canadian North 1887–1914.* Toronto: McClelland and Stewart.

INDEX